Badal Sircar

NATARANG PRATISHTHAN SERIES ON MODERN INDIAN THEATRE

BADAL SIRCAR

SEARCH FOR A LANGUAGE OF THEATRE

Edited by

KIRTI JAIN

for

Natarang Pratishthan

NIYOGI
BOOKS

NATARANG PRATISHTHAN SERIES ON MODERN INDIAN THEATRE

51, Bharti Artists Colony
Vikas Marg, Delhi-110 092
Tel: 91-120-4284132
email: natarangpratishthan@yahoo.co.in
website: www.natarang.org

Published by
NIYOGI BOOKS
D-78, Okhla Industrial Area, Phase-I
New Delhi-110 020, INDIA
Tel: 91-11-26816301, 49327000
Fax: 91-11-26810483, 26813830
email: niyogibooks@gmail.com
website: www.niyogibooksindia.com

Edited by Kirti Jain

Design: Shashi Bhushan Prasad

ISBN: 978-93-83098-96-5
Publication: 2016

Printed at: Niyogi Offset Pvt. Ltd., New Delhi, India

Dedicated to the memory of Babu and Bhabhi (my parents—Nemichandra Jain and Rekha Jain) from whom I learnt to question and also to dream

CONTENTS

THE THIRD THEATRE

LEGACY

FOREWORD

Natarang Pratishthan was set up as a contemporary theatre archive and resource centre by the eminent writer and theatre critic, the late Shri Nemichandra Jain with his personal collection of material on theatre and literature. Now in its 27th year of existence, the Pratishthan has a rich and well documented collection of books, journals, photographs, posters, brochures, play scripts, clippings and audio-video recordings relating to the practice of theatre in India, particularly North India. It is attempting to preserve for posterity this information on productions, actors, directors, writers and organisations, which presents an amazing plurality of visions. The Hindi theatre journal *Natarang,* continuously appearing since 1965, is published by the Pratishthan. It also organises public events including theatre festivals, seminars, exhibitions, lectures, dialogues, etc. Through these multifaceted activities, the Pratishthan attempts to initiate new areas of interdisciplinary debate and focus critical attention to the interface between the theory and practice of modern Indian theatre.

Natarang Pratishthan started a project of documenting important theatre directors of our time, covering their visions and style, working methods and productions. The focus during this project was on the work processes of directors in order to get an insight into the creative impetus of these practitioners. The directors shortlisted for this project were a mix of the pioneers of modern Indian theatre and a few promising new ones who are still evolving their methodology and styles, so as to get a sense of continuity of the creative expression in post-Independence theatre. The materials so collected are vast and complex.

To make this material accessible to a larger body of scholars and practitioners, Natarang Pratishthan is publishing a series of books, each devoted to a single director, which would use the archival material and documentation from the Pratishthan and from other diverse sources to give a comprehensive picture of the methods, development and contribution of the director in question. To begin with we have chosen Satyadev Dubey, Kavalam Narayan Panikkar and Badal Sircar. Much of the material used in these books has never been looked at before. The editors, Shanta Gokhale, Udayan Vajpeyi and Kirti Jain, have also commissioned new material on areas not covered by the archival collections. In some cases, fresh interviews have been included to get a picture of the present vision of the director. These are likely to be the most comprehensive books brought out on these directors.

What makes this series special is that the editors of these books are eminent creative people in their own right, and senior scholars who have had firsthand experience of the work of the directors they are working on and are therefore in a position to contextualise the contribution of the directors apart from analysing the collated material. The first book was on Satyadev Dubey, a stalwart of Indian theatre at a time when modern urban theatre was in the process of establishing itself. The second book in this series was on Kavalam Narayan Panikkar, a major figure in modern Indian theatre who being deeply rooted in the soils of Kerala has not only inherited the classical concepts and practices of Indian theatre but has also reinvented and revitalised them.

The third book in this series is on Badal Sircar, a major figure of West Bengal who became a national icon in theatre. He started as a playwright and, in the sixties of the past century, was widely acknowledged as a major playwright along with the Marathi playwright Vijay Tendulkar, the Kannada playwright Girish Karnad and the Hindi playwright Mohan Rakesh. The four brought a new energy in playwriting and created plays which were translated in many Indian languages and performed by major directors and groups of that period. The quartet brought forth a new theatre which was exploratory, interrogative and experimental. It was put together by these playwrights and it offered new challenges to actors and directors, not to speak of the new audiences they helped create and sustain. Badal Sircar's early plays constituted a significant part of this new repertoire.

Unlike other playwrights, Badal Sircar soon moved further to acting and direction. He was the only one amongst the four masters who involved himself actively and dynamically in theatre production. Exposing himself to the new trends in theatre that were emerging globally, he grew increasingly impatient with proscenium space and searched for greater freedom both in terms of physical space and emotional-experiential dimensions. He drew upon traditions of urban and folk theatre and brought together a new theatre into being called 'The Third Theatre'. Badal Sircar worked rigorously to evolve a new methodology of acting, direction, space arrangement etc. He not only practised it but became its most eloquent theoretician. Amongst the moderns in Indian theatre, he is perhaps the only one who through experiments and various exposures to different styles-visions-responses etc succeeded eventually to develop a comprehensive theory and practice of theatre which are both unique and bear the deep imprint of his personality and vision. From a wizard of words in his early playwriting Badal Sircar moved to creating a distinct theatre using minimal expression. From maximum words to minimum language. This book tries to trace the life, theatre, struggles and vision of an unusual master from a variety of viewpoints to bring together and analyse the wealth of his imagination, the significance of his experiments and the vigour and vitality as also failures of his theatrical vision.

Kirti Jain is a noted theatre person who has spent a large part of her life and career in directing and teaching theatre. Apart from being a Professor in the National School of Drama, New Delhi, she has been its Director for many years. In her theatre practice she has tried to explore with deep intensity and rare passion a theatre of wide social concerns and moral dilemmas. She has successfully experimented with texts other than playscripts, drawn from blogs, interviews etc, for creating vibrant and interrogative theatre. She brings her rich theatre experience and critical sensibility to bear up the work and achievement of Badal Sircar. Apart from writing a detailed introduction, she has collected some significant and rare material on the master.

We express our gratitude to Late Badal Sircar and Satabdi members for their constant help and cooperation, Natya Shodh Sansthan for providing some rare material on him, National School of Drama, Sangeet Natak Akademi, Delhi and UP Sangeet Natak Akademi for allowing us to use material in their journals, and thank all the contributors for their articles. Natarang Pratishthan is thankful to the JRD Tata Trust for supporting this project and publication. Thanks are also due to the Pratishthan staff whose hard work under the guidance of its director Rashmi Vajpeyi and archive chief S.N. Khanna made the documentation work possible.

We would also like to thank Niyogi Books for publishing the first three books in this series and editors Nandita Jaishankar and Mohua Mitra for their valuable inputs.

We hope that the books would be useful for discerning scholars and help them understand better the contribution of some of the directors whose struggles and anxieties, creativity and courage have made modern Indian theatre such a rich site of imagination and human exploration.

Ashok Vajpeyi
Series Editor

PREFACE

My first meeting with Badal Sircar was way back in 1972, when I was invited by All India Radio to interview Badal Sircar. I could not believe my luck—interview *the* Badal Sircar! After all he was one of the big four of modern Indian playwriting, and I would meet him in person! I had just finished my course at the National School of Drama (NSD), had studied Badal-da's plays, had been completely awestruck by *Ebong Indrajit* which I felt I hadn't fully understood. I remember the two sleepless nights I spent trying to prepare the questions for the interview. And answers, in case he quizzed me about his plays. He seemed quite formidable but was very friendly and encouraging during the interview. I also remember sitting for a long time in the lawns of All India Radio drinking tea and talking to Badal-da about his plays, his theatre and his politics. We also struck a friendship of sorts which continued for several years through letters, meetings, arguments and discussions. His passion and intensity fascinated me. Part of my idealism relating to the role of theatre in social change, I think, also came from him, the other part from my parents with their stint in Indian People's Theatre Association (IPTA).

With this personal contact I naturally followed his trajectory as a playwright and theatre person with greater involvement and interest. Therefore when Natarang Pratishthan asked me to edit a book on Badal Sircar I decided that this is my opportunity to pay tribute to a theatre person who stuck to his beliefs against all odds and at a great personal and professional cost; to a theatre person who followed a very unusual trajectory from the mainstream to the marginalised because he felt committed to the cause; a theatre person who became a legend and a trail blazer for the entire amateur theatre fraternity of the country but strangely was marginalised in his own state of West Bengal!

This book on Badal Sircar is part of a series of three books that Natarang Pratishthan had undertaken to publish on three Indian theatre directors. The task was given to me in 2009 and I was quite sure that I would be able to put it together in a year's time. Badal-da was still very much on the scene and when I told him that I was taking on this book on him he had seemed happy, probably because almost nothing had been published on him till then, in the form of a book. I met him at his residence in 2009-10 and gave him an idea of the kind of pieces I would be using in the book and he had given a few suggestions as to who I should speak to regarding the follow-up on his theatre work. I was very sure that I would be able to show him the final version of the book and get him to write a preface, but that was not to happen. I regret to this day the delay on my part in putting the material together, because we lost him and with it the chance to get him to see the book. The last I was in touch with him was in January 2011, over the telephone, when he was in Kerala to receive a Lifetime Achievement Award from the Kerala government. He sounded very happy and excited and expressed surprise at the sudden spate of awards and an Honorary Doctorate conferred on him by Jadavpur University, Kolkata. He also mentioned that he had been invited overseas to conduct some workshops and he insisted that he felt absolutely fit to undertake the tour. I was still wondering if I should try to meet him and clarify a few doubts before he left, when I heard that he was unwell and was in hospital. And then I could not reach him at all till he passed away in May 2011.

The task in putting this book together was to locate articles already written on him from the Natarang Pratisthan archives and other such collections and wherever absolutely necessary to get some new pieces written to fill in the gaps. While I was going through the material I noticed that there were many essays and reviews available of his work of the earlier phase when he was recognised primarily as a playwright and his plays were being staged all over India in different language translations. His writing – which was very witty, very specifically located in urban India, and addressing the middle class – generated a lot of excitement because people could immediately connect with it. One could see his immense facility with the craft of playwriting because each of his plays was cast in a different structure and posed different theatrical challenges. This was the phase, when, though he too was engaged in the practice of theatre, his identity was that of a playwright, and a very versatile modern playwright at that.

While I would like to see this phase as that of Badal Sircar as a playwright and would like to name this segment such, I know that he himself would be very unhappy with such a nomenclature and it could also be slightly misleading, as Badal-da was very active doing theatre and evolving his methodology along with writing plays. The articles in this section have been placed under the heading 'The Beginnings'. This also includes some excerpts from his 'Memoirs' as they provide a backdrop against which he was responding to the Indian realities. The excerpts selected also give an idea of his personality and social concerns, the influences that he was imbibing from society and theatre outside India, and sometimes the process of writing the plays. The article by Sumanta Bannerjee which was actually an exhaustive article on the entire career of Badal Sircar, has been cut into two parts for purposes of clarity: the first part that deals with his early playwriting has been included in the first section of this book and the second half dealing with his Third Theatre practice, in the second section of the book. Some interesting material which I found from the Natya Shodh Sansthan archives were discussions among contemporary directors and playwrights about Badal Sircar's work. Also, what gives a rare insight into contemporary responses are the notes written by directors and translators of his works. While there was huge amount of material on this phase of Badal Sircar, selection has been made so that the maximum number of plays get included for discussion and analysis and repetition is avoided as much as possible.

The second section of this book centres largely on his evolving the theory of the Third Theatre, its practice with his group and the journey Badal Sircar as playwright, director, actor and theoretician took to evolve the Theatre of Synthesis. The first article is therefore his own where he talks about evolving a new language of theatre and his concerns at this period of time. This was a phase where Badal Sircar was extensively interviewed regarding his evolving practice, the choice of texts, structures, spaces and the new relationship with his audience. Therefore some of those interviews are included in this section, each with a different focus. Despite intensive editing at several levels, some of these interviews and write-ups tend to be repetitive and the readers might find that a bit tedious. This was also a phase when he was travelling and conducting workshops all over the country to facilitate understanding of his Third Theatre practice. There has been considerable mystery surrounding the methodology of these workshops among those who have not been part of these workshops. I tried to locate material which would give us an idea of this methodology and we found an extensive interview by Sharad Nagar done for UP Sangeet Natak Akademi when Badal Sircar had conducted a workshop with theatre workers in Lucknow. I also arranged to talk to two visual artists, Suvobrata Roy Chowdhury and Sanchayan Ghosh who had attended his workshop while they were studying at Santiniketan. They gave a new perspective to the impact of his workshops and how it helped them in their visual arts practice. In a sense this is the substantive section where his social, political and aesthetic theory and practice has been discussed and to some extent analysed.

Badal Sircar, it is repeatedly pointed out, did not have as much impact in his own state as he did in the rest of the country. He certainly has been one of the most staged and celebrated playwrights in the country and has definitely also left an impact on the theatre practice in his own region. In the third section I have tried to look at the impact of his work in different parts of the country. For this I had to largely request theatre practitioners and scholars to write fresh pieces, some of which give us valuable insight on the nature of his work and the various directions in which his thoughts and practice have impacted theatre in India and its neighbouring region. I must say at the outset that this study of his impact is not comprehensive as I could not access scholars in all regions of the country to talk about it. In some cases there is more than one piece from a particular region but from different perspectives. The gaps are not deliberate or an oversight but resulting from the difficulty of finding the people who are willing to write on the subject and those who actually and finally meet the deadline.

One major problem that the reader might encounter is the varying focus of time in the articles compiled. The memoirs, for instance, start from the 1950s and some reviews and director's notes are from 1950s and 1960s. The large body of writing that you see in the second section has 'happened' in the 1970s, but some have been taken from later years. So while the year and the source – wherever available – will be mentioned with the article, it still might appear confusing. The contributors too have been concerned about the fact that the views their articles represent are the ones they had at that point in time and might have undergone a change over the years. So these articles have to be read in that particular perspective and not as the current or absolute views of the scholars contributing.

While most articles in the last section have been written in the last five years, only the articles of Sadanand Menon and Mangai have been penned after the death of Badal Sircar, more as tributes to this great theatre person. Another element that is missing in this whole collection, in my view, is a true critical evaluation of Badal-da's work. I had hoped to get someone who has witnessed his work more or less first hand from the very beginning, in doing this assessment. Unfortunately I could not get such a piece right till the end due to the busy schedules of people I thought were most suited to this task. I have therefore attempted to partially address the lacunae in my introduction, drawing from whatever limited exposure I had to his practice and from whatever he had written and spoken, about his work.

This work would not have been possible without the rich material I got from the Natarang Pratishthan archives, Natya Shodh Sansthan, National School of Drama (NSD), UP Sangeet Natak Akademi Archives, Central Sangeet Natak Akademi, Seagull Foundation, Enact to name a few organisations and numerous experts and friends who gave their time to make suggestions, write the pieces, give interviews and share their insights. I am aware that the project has got inordinately delayed but (selecting material, translating it, editing it repeatedly took most of the time) I sincerely hope that it will help in giving an understanding of the journey that Badal Sircar made through his plays, his theatre, his musings, his theories and his *parikrama*s.

This will be my humble tribute to this rare, dedicated, committed and restless artist; a dreamer who created a new template for theatre practice for an India that he wanted synthesised.

Kirti Jain
New Delhi, 2016

INTRODUCTION

Part One

Early years

Badal Sircar[1] was born in a Christian family on 15 July 1925 and was named Sudhindra Sircar. His father Mahendralal Sircar was a professor in the Scottish Church College and later became the first Indian principal of this college run by the British missionaries. His mother, Saralmana Sircar was a voracious reader and a strict disciplinarian who had great ambitions for her son. His uncle, who had to often wade through knee-deep water when he came to see the young child in the rainy village where he was born, named him Badal, and that name came to stay.

Badal Sircar's family history and family traits give some clues as to the kind of person he finally became. On his father's side, his grandfather's younger brother, Bipin Chandra Sircar became a Christian missionary who despite extensive travel in the West as a missionary, retained firm roots in India and Indian culture. He believed that even if one converted to Christianity it was important to retain one's Indian identity. Hence unlike most Bengali Christians, whose middle names are generally Christian/English names, this family followed a different

1. The Introduction draws heavily from an interview of Badal Sircar taken by Amol Palekar and Sandhya Gokhale in Pune on the occasion of Badal Sircar Natya Mahotsav in 2004. Wherever the source is not mentioned the quotes are from this interview. (*Source: Natya Shodh Sansthan, Kolkata*)

path. Badal Sircar's father and his brother, deeply influenced by their uncle, embraced Christianity and were very religious.

On his mother's side his maternal great grandfather converted to Christianity because he wanted to marry his classmate, Virginia Mary, who was studying medicine at the same time as him. Though Virginia was a qualified doctor and one of the first three lady doctors of India, she more or less left medical practice after her marriage with Badal Sircar's mother's grandfather. Badal Sircar's mother probably inherited the reading habit from her and she passed it on to him. Due to the influence of the family Badal Sircar was a serious Christian in his early years. He read the Bible, went to Sunday school but soon started questioning what the pastor was saying, as his science education started presenting him with contradictions. 'If Darwin said Man evolved and the Bible says God created Adam and Eve—what should I believe?', he questioned himself. Unable to get convincing answers from religion, he finally stopped going to church and was consequently asked by his father to leave home, which he did in due course of time.

As a child he had become interested in reading through a trick of his mother. She once offered him one anna per chapter to read twelve chapters of Louisa M. Alcott's book. He trudged through the book and earned the twelve annas. But for the next book she refused to pay him anything. However, by then he had already got attracted to reading and would read whatever came his way and in whichever language. As part of this he read Shaw's *Arms and the Man* which was part of his sister's collection of books. In the privacy of his room he would read aloud all humorous roles in Bengali plays, and even though he became very interested in acting, he never got an opportunity to perform on stage. For his first play at the age of 15, he says proudly that he was the playwright, director as well as the actor.

'During the holidays, in 1941, I had adapted *Cinderella* from my sister's textbook and enacted it, with cousins and friends, before a family gathering, casting myself in the plum male role. Rarely, can a theatre personality claim the distinction of beginning as playwright, director and principal actor. He wrote another play which was a Bengali adaptation of Galsworthy's *The Roof*, which he gave to Sukumari-di, his mentor and a friend of his sister, for her comments. 'She gave such a scathing criticism of the play, with every minute detail noted, that I did not write another play for fourteen years. And when I did start writing I remembered her comments clearly and avoided the same mistakes. So her criticism helped me immensely.' There was a strong theatre team in the engineering college too. Somebody took him to the seniors to act and they asked if he would do female roles. He ran away and for four years he watched theatre but never acted in the plays.

In 1941 he cleared his matriculation and joined Shibpur Bachelor of Engineering College (Shibpur B.E College) in Kolkata from where he graduated in 1946. He had opted for engineering, thinking that it would not involve too much hard work, but having chosen it he was miserable as he just did not take to it. He did not want to borrow any money from the family so he had to start looking for jobs while studying. It is during this difficult period in his life that he got deeply involved in Marxist politics with the same passion as he had with religion earlier. These were the days of the undivided Communist Party of which Badal Sircar became an active member and made many friends. In the process he gradually got detached from his family.

Politics and town planning

In July 1947 he took up his first job near Nagpur in a construction company. He was there for about four months and was very unhappy as he missed Calcutta, his politics, his friends and all that intense action. He soon left the job and returned to Calcutta. However, he remembers that it was in Nagpur that he heard about India getting Independence and being partitioned. After returning to Calcutta he again looked for employment but could not procure a government job or any other with a decent remuneration in the city. By 1949 he had also got married and therefore had the additional responsibility of looking after his family. As he did not want to leave Calcutta, he settled for an ill-paid teaching job in an engineering institute in Calcutta. 'Whatever I learnt of Civil Engineering was while I was teaching here but I still did not like it.' He therefore immersed himself in politics as a part-timer. On the political front he got involved with trade unions that exposed him to the conditions of mill workers. He was a member of the Central Strike Committee. His involvement with politics was so intense that he felt that 'if the Party goes we will have to commit suicide.' But soon after the debacle of the railway strike he was suspended. He was also disillusioned with the Communist Party as he felt that there was no space for questioning and democratic decision-making within it.

Around the same time, he says:

> I happened to read... a small book of the Penguin series on Town Planning. And I was completely fascinated by it. Coincidentally my alma mater announced a course—A two-year Evening Diploma in Town Planning at this very time. I decided, that the evening time I gave to politics I (would) now give to (the) study of Town Planning. A teacher suggested books on the subject and soon I had read more books on the subject than the teacher! I was totally engrossed in the subject. It became my first love, theatre was only the second. But Town Planning did not have many jobs, and as a married man with two kids I needed a job.

He therefore went to Maithan (in the Dhanbad district of Bihar) in 1953 for a job with the Damodar Valley Corporation (DVC). He worked at the Maithan dam project on Barakar river till 1956. With his characteristic humour he informs, 'My record is that I have never stuck to a job for more than three years. There was a logic behind this action. Since you make a sufficient mess of the job in three years, it is better to leave it than stay to clean up the mess.' At times he is known to have left a job without finding another job.

The playwright emerges

In Maithan, in the absence of political activity, he resorted to an interest that he had developed in childhood—that of acting. He formed a club with his office colleagues called the Rehearsal Club, where the rule was that they would rehearse plays but never stage them. This decision did not last for long and ultimately provided the first platform to him as an actor. However he was not satisfied with the available plays, which led him to write/translate/adapt plays and start his career as a playwright. His first play in 1956, *Solution X*, based on the story of a Hollywood film *Monkey Business,* won him a first prize in a play competition.

After leaving the DVC job at Maithan, Badal Sircar went to London in 1957 to take an evening course in Town Planning and had to work to meet his expenses till he returned to India in 1959. He was thus exposed to the performances of great actors like Vivien Leigh, Charles Laughton, Michael Rodryth and Margaret Collins etc. He was also impressed with the theatre practice in London and he saw among others, three productions of Joan Littlewood—*The Hostage*, *A Taste of Honey*, and *Oh! What a Lovely War*. One of the performances that had a lasting impact on him was the performance of Racine's play *Phaedre* in a Theatre-in-the-Round. This was perhaps his first exposure to a performance of this scale outside the proscenium space and its impact has been mentioned in his memoirs. This probably was to play an important role in his conceptualisation of the Third Theatre. During this period he also maintained a diary with snatches of dialogues and poems that reflected his personal existential crisis. These disconnected pieces of writing were 'the beginnings of the most inspired play written in the sixties—*Ebong Indrajit* (*And Indrajit*). It is the *Waiting for Godot* of the Bengali Theatre'.[2] It was written in a play format later, at the instigation of one of his friends.

On returning to Calcutta in 1959 he formed an organisation called Chakra Goshthi. The members of this organisation met every Saturday and had heated discussions on subjects ranging from literature, theatre, music to science. It was under the banner of this organisation that some of the early plays of Badal Sircar were staged before the general public. But at this time his interest in theatre seemed just casual and as Samik

2. Rustom Bharucha: *Rehearsals of Revolution: The Political Theatre of Bengal.* Seagull Books, Kolkata, 1983

Bandyopadhyay has aptly commented about the group: 'A serious group of people who did not take theatre too seriously.'

Badal Sircar was very fascinated with comedies; thus his first few plays were comedies. Between 1956 and 1964 he wrote six plays, all primarily domestic comedies or science fiction fantasies: After *Solution X* (1956), *Baro Pishima* (1959, *The Elder Aunt*) and *Shonibar* (1959, *Saturday*, based on J.B. Priestley's *An Inspector Calls*) were written in London, *Ram-Shyam-Jadu* (1961, *Tom Dick and Harry*), *Ballabhpurer Roopkatha* (1963, *The Fairy Tale of Ballabhpur*) based on the story of an English film *You Are No Angel*, and *Kobi Kahini* (1963, *The Tale of a Poet*) were written to be staged by Chakra Goshthi.

Again in 1963 he visited France on a scholarship to get practical training in Town Planning, where with a lot of spare time in hand he wrote four more plays in the nine months that he was there. These included a serious play, *Sara Rattir* (1963, *The Entire Night*) and a comedy, *Ballabhpurer Rupakatha* (1963, *The Fairy Tale of Ballabhpur*). But with a dwindling bank balance he had to start looking for jobs to sustain his family. There were unfortunately no jobs in Town Planning and he was quite sure that he did not want to settle down anywhere other than in Calcutta. So he looked for remunerative jobs through various Asian and African embassies with a clear plan of working abroad for a while, saving some money, returning to Calcutta and then doing theatre. He finally got a job in East Nigeria and left with his family in 1964. He sent his family back soon as the Biafra Civil war broke out but he stayed on for three years. 'In fact, when I fled across the Niger Bridge in a cab carrying a suitcase and a last-minute bag containing my plays, I had escaped the Nigerian war by a whisker,' exclaims Sircar.[3]

It was in Nigeria that some of his most well-known plays were written. These include *Baagh* (1965, *Tiger*, inspired by Murray Schisgal's *The Tiger*), *Baki Itihas* (1965, *The Other History*), *Pralaap* (*Delirium*, 1966, inspired by James Saunder's *Next Time I will Sing to You*), *Tringsha Shatabdi* (1966, *The Thirtieth Century*), *Pore Konodin* (1966, *Some Other Day*), *Jodi Aar Ekbaar* (1966, *If There Were Another*

3. 'A Mellow Autumn' by Gautam Chatterjee. *The Hindu*, 2008

Chance, inspired by J.M. Barrie's *Dear Brutus*) and *Pagla Ghoda* (1967, *The Crazy Horse*).

A very pleasant surprise awaited Sircar on his return from Nigeria. His play *Ebong Indrajit* that was published in the journal *Bohurupee* in 1965 while he was still in Nigeria and staged by the group Shouvanik in the same year, had become an instant hit and earned him countrywide fame with multilingual translations and productions by leading directors taking place all over the country. He was conferred the Sangeet Natak Akademi award for this play in 1968. Badal Sircar the playwright was born.

Search for a new language

After returning from Nigeria Badal Sircar continued to work as an engineer and Town Planner, but his interest in theatre grew steadily. In spite of his growing popularity as a playwright he wanted to be involved in active theatre. Not surprising, since he got into playwriting because he wanted plays in which he could act. He initially worked in Bohurupee but did not think that the group was suitable for his kind of theatre. He then started his own group Satabdi in 1967 with his friends and associates. On 18 March 1967 Satabdi began its journey from the Rabindra Sarobar Manch in Kolkata. 'Satabdi was formed as a predominantly amateur theatre group that had no pretensions apart from wanting to entertain a middle class audience. It performed the most inoffensive comedies in the most predictable manner possible, using all the conventions of the commercial theatre.'[4] Additionally, since most of the plays written by Badal Sircar till date were written keeping the proscenium theatre in mind, all productions of Satabdi were performed in the proscenium format. But soon he started growing uncomfortable with it. The discomfort was partly to do with the dwindling audience as a result of the competition theatre faced from cinema and partly with the limitations that proscenium theatre imposed on the actors and director. He felt that theatre was not exploiting its full potential

4. Rustom Bharucha: *Rehearsals of Revolution: The Political Theatre of Bengal*. Seagull Books, Kolkata, 1983

as a live medium of communication and that 'the proscenium stage was stifled by barriers of distance and levels. Most strikingly that of light and darkness. As if we (actors) were surrounded by a make-believe world of sets, costumes and spotlights while the viewers watched us from the hiding.'

It is at this juncture, in 1969, that he was invited by the Government of India to visit three East European countries, namely USSR, Poland, Czechoslovakia for eight weeks under the Cultural Exchange Programme. He got the opportunity to see some of the most exciting and innovative theatre in the world—Yuri Lyubimov's productions of *The Good Person of Setzuan, Galileo* and *Ten Days That Shook The World,* and a rehearsal of Gorki's *The Mother* at his Taganka Theatre in Moscow; Jari's pantomime and Cinoherni Klub Theatre's productions in Prague; and most important of all theatre events, Grotowski's *Apocalypse Cum Figiris* in Poland. These ideas were fresh in his mind when he decided to stage *Pralaap* for a reorganised Satabdi in 1969 and the impact of this exposure in his subsequent work cannot be ignored. Though he claims in his treatise *Third Theatre* that 'Not much of those (ideas) reflected directly in our production of *Pralaap* and our subsequent productions of *Sara Rattir*, *Shesh Nei* and *Ballabhpurer Roopkatha*, except one vital principle—the concept of the Poor Theatre'. He continues:

> The term (Poor Theatre) is borrowed from Grotowski; but his concept of the poor theatre is that of going against the enrichment of theatre by borrowing from other art forms and techniques, such as background music, lighting, sets and costume; of impoverishing theatre to the extent of reducing it to the unadorned body of the performer, of going to the root of theatre—the rituals. We gradually reduced the use of sets, lights, costumes and background music, decided never to use mechanical device like tape recorders and projectors; but we also adopted the concept of Poor Theatre in the literal sense—that is inexpensive theatre. Our group was poor, so are our countrymen, but we wanted to *utilise* poverty and turn it into an advantage

> instead of allowing it to be a restriction. None of the productions mentioned above cost us more than Rs 100 for sets, stage props and costumes taken together. And it paid off, for this was the first time our sets (or the absence of them) were being praised by the audience and the critics alike.

He was now concentrating more and more on the actor's body—a process no doubt derived from Grotowski's acting methodology.

The shift in his theatre language can be seen with the production of *Sagina Mahato,* an adaptation of Gour Kishore Ghosh's play in 1971. 'Though it was initially performed in a proscenium theatre, it emphasised the physical elements of acting – mime, dance, movement – more than the speech of the actors. Sircar also attempted to break down barriers in theatrical time and space by emphasising the simultaneous action of his play and its consequential mode of narration.'[5] But this production did not realise its full potential till it was staged in an ordinary lecture hall of All Bengal's Teachers' Association. Here the actors and the audience were sharing the same space.

> Though the chairs in the hall were arranged in such a way that there was a central arena for the main action of the play, there were passages between and behind the rows of chairs that enabled the performers to move around, between and in front of the audience. Despite the freewheeling use of space, Sircar admits that the blocking of the play was rigorously determined by him. His actors did not have the freedom to explore the space according to their stimuli and perception.[6]

However this convinced him that any performance just needed performers and a bare space, it did not require a separate stage. Another accident where the lights failed during performance also gave him a

5. Rustom Bharucha: *Rehearsals of Revolution: The Political Theatre of Bengal.* Seagull Books, Kolkata, 1983

6. Rustom Bharucha: *Rehearsals of Revolution: The Political Theatre of Bengal.* Seagull Books, Kolkata, 1983

clue to stop depending on stage lighting for impact. This was then the beginning of the exploration towards Free Theatre.

The Third Theatre

So a new journey had begun and he now had to grapple with these discoveries to create a new form. But how could that be done without plays that could respond to his new ideas? He understood that he would have to write new plays to give shape to his ideas of theatre. This would definitely be a challenge as all his plays so far had been written with the proscenium stage in mind and a conventional structure of the play with focus on plot, characterisation etc. Howard Fast's novel *Spartacus* that he had liked immensely long back but was not confident of turning into a conventional play was what struck him as an ideal choice for the new emerging form. As Rustom Bharucha observes:

> After writing the first draft of his play *Spartacus* (based on the famous novel by Howard Fast), he did not proceed to designate the roles and rehearse the actors according to the physical demands and motivations of their characters. Rather, he submitted his script to the entire group of actors who 'confronted' it by improvising sections of the dialogue and finding visual equivalents for his words. The rehearsal became a workshop.
>
> It was a fascinating experience for Sircar to watch his play being molded, edited, tested, and ultimately transformed by his actors, who discovered their own potentialities as performers in the process of discovering his play. For the first time in his career, Sircar realised the value of a workshop; not only did it engage all the members of his group in a collective creative process (including those who considered themselves 'bad actors'), it also enabled his actors to confront and reject many of their inhibitions and psychological blocks.
>
> The process of discovering *Spartacus* was greatly facilitated when Anthony Serchio, a director from the La Mama Theater in

> New York, conducted a number of workshops. He taught Sircar's actors important exercises devised by Grotowski including 'the cat', a series of exercises that enables an actor to relax the tensions in his muscles and vertebral column. The workshops convinced Sircar that he needed more experience as a director to conduct the physical training of his actors.[7]

At this point of his journey in 1972 came two very fortunate interventions. He was granted the Jawaharlal Nehru Research Fellowship for his project on a new language of theatre which was to result in his treatise called *Third Theatre*. The second was an invitation by Richard Schechner to observe the rehearsals and workshops of the Performance Group in New York. Schechner on his previous visit to India had seen a performance of *Sagina Mahato*, had got an inkling of the direction of Badal Sircar's area of exploration through informal conversations and had therefore extended him this invitation. Assisted by the fellowship amount he received to fund his visit to the US, Badal Sircar was with Schechner's group through their rehearsals, workshop process and performance tour to several cities in the US and was very impressed with the involvement of actors at every stage of the rehearsal process. This was also his first exposure to Environmental Theatre. In his book *Third Theatre* he comments on the production of *Commune*:

> Although there was a central performing area, the performers quite often used areas within, behind, and over the spectators. The 'environment' encompassed the whole space...and the spectators constituted part of the environment. In other words, the experience of any spectator did not come only from the performance and the decor of the 'stage'...but from other spectators as well. The spectators were never *manipulated*, but their participation was apparent by their presence in the *space* encompassed by the *environment* of that particular theater. Altogether it was a new *language* of communication.

7. Rustom Bharucha: *Rehearsals of Revolution: The Political Theatre of Bengal*. Seagull Books, Kolkata, 1983

We see Badal Sircar explore a similar relationship between the actors and spectators in his subsequent productions, though how far he succeeded in keeping away from manipulating the spectators we will analyse later in this piece. He also learnt several techniques, games and exercises that he used later for training his actors as also in the numerous workshops he conducted all over the country. Rustom Bharucha mentions that Badal Sircar attended some of the discussion sessions between the director and the team of actors during the rehearsals of *The Legacy of Cain* on the interrelations of money, war and love and was impressed by their commitment and understanding.

> He was also drawn to their idea of politics, which had less to do with the propagation of particular issues than with their exploration of 'basic political philosophy' concerning 'man's consciousness and responsibility': While emphasising that his theater and philosophy 'differ considerably from those of the Living Theater,' Sircar acknowledges that the 'purpose' of his theater (which he never defines but which, one may assume, is the awakening of social consciousness in the spectators) corresponds 'almost exactly' to that of the Becks (Julian Beck and Judith Melina). For both Satabdi and the Living Theater, theater is more than a profession or pastime or passion: it is a way of life.[8]

The Third Theatre of Badal Sircar was thus a synthesis of two distinct kinds of theatre. One was the urban middle class realistic theatre, played in the proscenium, bound by demands of unity of time and space. The other, the rural theatre that was a freer theatre, more informal and communicating directly with its audiences. His Third Theatre was in effect a theatre of liberation in more senses than one. At one level it attempted to liberate theatre from the boundaries imposed by the proscenium, by the conventions and norms of naturalistic representation that included the elaborate paraphernalia

8. Rustom Bharucha: *Rehearsals of Revolution: The Political Theatre of Bengal*. Seagull Books, Kolkata, 1983

of sets properties, lights and elaborate costumes. In this attempt it also sought to strike a direct communication with the audiences like that in traditional rural theatre. It was also a liberation from the economics of doing theatre in the cities which entails hiring of space, publicity and printing etc. And it was a theatre that sought to liberate both performers and the spectators from their masks and inhibitions to not just understand themselves better but also to understand the world around them and be better prepared to change the unjust practices and inequalities existing in it.

Consolidation of the Third Theatre

Once back from the US charged with new approaches, strategies and tools, he felt better equipped to crystallise his own approach to theatre. As he himself says 'This was my first experience of the workshop process. I came back and started workshops with my actors, gradually evolving my own methodology. A whole new world opened in front of me. I was getting invited from all over the country and I learnt so much from each workshop working with different kinds of groups.' This was 1972 and many of us in different parts of the country were fascinated by the new approach to theatre that Badal Sircar propagated through his workshops. What was also very infectious was his intense idealism and commitment that attracted a large number of young people towards his kind of work.

However, back in Calcutta, where he had left the rehearsals of his play *Spartacus* midway, he had to look for a new working space to carry on his work. He finally rented a room of 850 sq ft on the second floor of The Academy of Fine Arts, an active cultural centre of Calcutta. With a capacity of about seventy spectators it was a room well suited for small performances and workshops. This he named Angan Manch. In his own words 'As soon as I selected Angan Manch I knew this is the theatre where I want to perform. Some of the group members left because they were more enamoured of the proscenium. We regrouped and continued to work.' Satabdi also undertook a membership drive to ensure an audience gaining 325 members each of whom paid

Rs 6 as annual membership fee and were promised at least three new productions every year and one show every week, a promise they kept in spite of several members leaving. Here the group also announced their decision to do away with tickets and create a community of theatre lovers comprising of performers, organisers and spectators. This is where *Spartacus* was rehearsed, evolved and finally performed opening up completely new dimensions of theatre language and experience not known to the audience before this and it started a new chapter in the theatre journey of Badal Sircar. This was the time that he also felt the need to envisage and perform a play like *Prastaab* (*Proposition*), to underline the necessity to eliminate concerns of money from life and theatre. Rustom Bharucha comments:

> *Prastaab* (*Proposition*), a one-man show performed by Sircar, voices the essential credo of the Third Theater. In many ways, its denunciation of money is so violent, so absolute, that one is almost tempted to reject it as an appallingly simplistic statement. It is difficult to speak of *Prastaab* as a theatrical event because it defies all notions and conventions of entertainment. One can speak of it more accurately as a *human act* that incorporates a deeply personal statement by Sircar.[9]

Most of his plays post-*Spartacus* were written for this format of theatre, what he called the Third Theatre or Free Theatre. Around 1974-75, Sircar's treatise *Third Theatre*, appeared in bookstalls with three editions getting sold out very fast. Third Theatre had come to stay.

Besides these formal shows at the Academy of Fine Arts, Satabdi decided to start performing at Curzon Park where another theatre group Silhouette was already performing. Some more groups joined in making this virtually a new theatre movement. These performances happened every Saturday sometimes to audiences as many as 3,000 in number. Badal Sircar and his group continued to perform here for a long time and he says that he never regretted the decision to perform at

9. Rustom Bharucha: *Rehearsals of Revolution: The Political Theatre of Bengal.* Seagull Books, Kolkata, 1983

Curzon Park. On the contrary, performing here gave greater credence to his idea of Free Theatre which did not require any paraphernalia or expenditure on publicity for getting audiences.

In an interview to Subhendu Sarkar, Badal Sircar refers to an incident at these performances:

> On 20 July 1974, Prabir Dutta died when the police lathi-charged. There was no provocation from the audience or the actors. The performances were discontinued. I always thought that we should resume performing there. That would be the correct attitude to establish our right to perform at Curzon Park. A committee was formed and we decided to perform *Michhil.* Actors from other groups took part in it. Keya Chakrabarty volunteered to act. I respect her for exhibiting courage. The show was successful. Almost 10,000 people watched the play. When the performance was over, they kept asking whether we would be back next week. We couldn't say anything, as there would be no protection next time. After a discussion, all the members of Satabdi unanimously decided that we should continue to perform at the park. We resorted to the tactic of guerilla warfare. All of us moved separately and converged on the park at a fixed time. There was a huge crowd. We thought something was wrong. Later we found that those were spectators waiting for us. After that, we continued performing on Saturdays till the announcement of the Emergency. Of course, performances were suspended after the Emergency.[10]

On the personal front, in the meantime, he first took on a job as the Chief Town Planner at the Calcutta Metropolitan Planning Organisation and then left it when he was offered the Jawaharlal Nehru Research Fellowship in 1972. Despite the fact that he loved Town Planning, he resigned from the job because his conscience

10. Subhendu Sarkar: Facets of Third Theatre, Conversation with Badal Sircar; *Two Plays*; *Indian History Made Easy; Life of Bagala.* Oxford University Press, 2010

would not allow him to continue at a place where his plans were neither discussed nor approved—just shelved. Later on he joined one of his closest friends who had become an eminent economist in his organisation called Comprehensive Area Development Programme—a quasi-government body. Badal Sircar says 'since I was doing theatre I agreed to join only part time at Rs 1,000 a month. This was about rural planning. This gave me the opportunity to know the villages of West Bengal (through) extensive travel for projects in every part of West Bengal. And after this I did no other job.' The impact of this exposure is quite evident in the later plays of Badal Sircar. From a playwright who strongly asserts that he can only write about the cities, we have numerous plays after this exposure that talk of the lives and plight of the rural population. His later turning to work with the rural and tribal population might also have been due to his experiences and knowledge gained during this period of travel to rural areas.

Parikrama: Contact with villages

In March 1985, Badal Sircar and his group took another step by joining in Parikrama, started by Angan Theatre Group. Several groups got together in Parikrama, and about 17 people would travel to remote villages covering Nadia, 24 Parganas, Hooghly and Howrah belts and perform their plays in improvised spaces for villagers, initially for two nights and three days with performances lasting from morning to night. Since this proved too tedious it was reduced to one night and two days. Badal Sircar has very insightful stories to tell about his encounter with the village audiences which can be read in his interviews in the book. This practice of travelling continued till late into his life as and when his health allowed him to do so. Performing in open spaces and in the villages led him to believe that the content of the plays had to be the foremost concern of his theatre. 'Content is the starting point, form comes later; first we decide the play then explore how to do it.'

Theatre workshops: Spreading 'Third Theatre' methodology

The other significant part of Badal Sircar's activity has been to conduct theatre workshops in all parts of the country to familiarise interested groups with his Third Theatre methodology. One of his earliest workshops had been in Manipur in 1972 on the initiative of H. Kanhailal, organised by the Manipur Sangeet Natak Akademi. It was:

> A three-week workshop in Imphal ending in a work-in-progress performance of *Spartacus* in the Manipuri language translated by Rajkumari Binodini Devi. Kanhailal too participated in that workshop. The performance of *Spartacus* was held in an open space with a roof supported by wooden pillars and the invited guests sat on mats. The ordinary people stood behind the fence, watching from outside. We had a cast of forty-two, with fourteen slaves. All of them got into the spirit of the play as the workshop had been successful. When the revolt scene came there was spontaneous applause from the people who were standing outside. The respected guests didn't clap. I have often noticed that in villages people applaud the most when there is no speech, where there is only a burst of energy in sound and movement. It's when the slaves revolt for the first time in the gladiatorial school of Capua. The message was conveyed.[11]

This made him realise the effectiveness of workshop process in getting the amateurs too involved and charged with the content of the play.

In the early days, Badal Sircar's workshops evoked a lot of excitement and curiosity. Hoards of youngsters would flock to his workshops and were closeted for hours going through the rigorous routine that he chalked out for them. And those who did not get the opportunity to attend these workshops never got to know what happened in these

11. Subhendu Sarkar: Facets of Third Theatre, Conversation with Badal Sircar, *Badal Sircar Two Plays*, Oxford University Press, 2010

workshops. There were strict rules about no observers being present during workshops, thereby creating greater mystery and speculation around his workshops. I believe that he was planning to write about his workshop methodology towards the end of his life. That would have been a valuable document as no significant documentation has been done of the basic methodology of his workshops and how they changed with each group and region. Lack of these records is indeed a loss for both theatre practice and scholarship.

Generally, he modified his workshop methodology depending on the group of people he was working with. But the essential aim of his workshops was not to train actors but to help human beings drop unnecessary masks and inhibitions that society forces on them. Therefore he had conducted workshops with very diverse groups, directed plays and helped participants understand the process of playmaking. He worked with amateur and street theatre groups, with social and political activists and also with religious groups in small towns of the country including marginalised and illiterate groups like cleaning women and maids. A large chunk of his workshops were with students – in colleges and universities – with art students and students from different disciplines. In all cases he had succeeded in infusing a sense of purpose and seriousness towards theatre apart from infusing confidence in themselves. And in many cases the workshop impacted in a significant way to give a new direction to the work the participant may have been doing before encountering Badal Sircar's passion, conviction and commitment. An interview with two students of fine arts at Santiniketan included in this book will give an idea of the impact of his workshops on the lives of young people and professionals. In India he had travelled from Kerala, Tamil Nadu in the south to Pune, Gujarat in the west and Lucknow, Delhi, Azamgarh in UP in the north. As he himself said, 'Apart from Arunachal Pradesh, Mizoram, Nagaland, Haryana, Goa and Kashmir I have conducted workshops in each and every state of India. Of course, I'm speaking about the India of my time. Now there are some new states which didn't exist then.'

He had also travelled to Bangladesh, Pakistan, Laos, Bangkok, Ireland and the UK to conduct these workshops and direct plays.

He introduced his approach to theatre in many countries through his theatre workshops. And the impact is most visible in the neighbouring countries who got a glimpse of some of the methods of Grotowski, Peter Brook, Richard Schechner and Augusto Boal, apart from his own exercises, through his workshops. He had worked with several theatre groups in Pakistan and the work of those groups which were more or less forced to do a guerilla kind of theatre due to the political situations prevalent in their country, shows a clear imprint of Badal Sircar's brand of political theatre. One of the groups, after coming in contact with Badal Sircar continues to work on Augusto Boal's theatre methodology introduced to them by Sircar.

The impact of his work in Bangladesh was more immediate as he could make several trips, could also take his productions for the audiences in Bangladesh and as a politically charged people, his methods made an immediate connection with the theatre community. As Dr Jamil Ahmad, an eminent theatre director and scholar from Bangladesh rightly points out, that the first tour of Badal Sircar in 1973, soon after liberation, virtually kick-started the Group Theatre movement in Bangladesh. According to him it was surprising that a people not yet initiated into theatre bought tickets to see his plays which ran thirty-four shows at a stretch, to packed houses. Subsequently seventeen of his plays were performed by various groups in different parts of Bangladesh. His first workshop was in 1989. Jamil Ahmad making a very perceptive observation about the impact of Badal Sircar on the theatre of Bangladesh mentions that while over the years one does not see the direct continuation of the Third Theatre movement due to different concerns of its people but a lasting impact can be seen in the formation of the Gram Theatre, which attempted a kind of synthesis of the traditional and urban theatre and the Mukta Natak movement which put into practice a theatre of the working class which Badal Sircar had wanted to do but could not practice. In a sense these two significant theatre movements are a legacy of Badal Sircar's Third Theatre in Bangladesh.

In 1985 he went to Britain and conducted workshops with non-theatre people—largely social activists who had got very impressed with his work and therefore invited him to work with their group. He stayed for three months conducting workshops in London, Leeds and Glasgow. Some of the participants were already involved with Fringe Theatre and continued to do that while some others are actively using theatre techniques learnt from Sircar in their work with communities. He went to Britain four times, the last time was in 1992 to conduct a workshop at the Drama Department of Birmingham University which culminated in a production of *Manushey Manushey*—a non-verbal script that can be adapted to any context as it looks at the callous nature of man as against those who are downtrodden and exploited.

He has particularly fond memories of his last workshop in Laos in 2003 at the age of 78. The workshop was organised by the United Nations Economic and Social Commission for Asia and the Pacific to use theatre in the AIDS and 'Substance Abuse' awareness programmes. The participants had nothing to do with theatre, but were very responsive to Badal Sircar's methods and approaches. The fact that Badal Sircar went out of his way to conduct such workshops points to his social commitment and using theatre to bring social change. These workshops were also a means of earning his livelihood since as a full-time theatre worker he had no other source of income, his own theatre being literally the poor theatre.

Collaboration with other groups

All this while he continued to work with his group Satabdi, doing new productions, call shows and travelling with his plays to the villages. There were other groups that followed in Sircar's footsteps who also worked closely with him and often on his plays. Two groups that Satabdi has closest ties with and works in collaboration with till date are Pathasena (Army of the Road, started in 1979), based in the suburb of Sorsemukhi; and Ayna (Mirror, started in 1988) of Kanchrapara, which is an hour-and-quarter train ride away from Kolkata. These three groups have similar organisational structures and share more or less the same philosophy.

As he says in his interview with Subhendu Sircar, 'We have been working with Pathasena and Ayena for years now. Pathasena was previously involved with the proscenium theatre. After having watched our performance at Calcutta Theosophical Society Hall, they decided to embrace the non-proscenium format.

Once Tarun (Poddar), Mukul (Chatterjee) and Ashok (Chatterjee) attended my workshop. Later they formed their own group, Ayna. They allow new members only after training them through the workshop process.'

Sayoni Mitra details in her article:

> They (the three groups) take turns performing Friday shows at the Loreto Day School in Central Kolkata, and at the bimonthly Saturday afternoon shows in Nandan, a middle-class cultural hub in the city. Satabdi, Ayna, and Pathasena have a ready repertoire of Sircar's plays, which makes it easy to interchange actors if any performer from one of these groups is unavailable for a show. Badal Sircar is still very much the life force of each of these groups. He has directed three plays with Ayna. At one time, he would attend Sunday morning rehearsals with them and return to attend Satabdi's evening rehearsals in the city. When this hectic commute was no longer physically viable for Sircar, the group opted to send two of its members over to his house every week to evolve a smaller play. Pathasena, based too far out of the city, has not had as much of Sircar's directorial involvement. But he has conducted the occasional workshop with them as well as helped in their production of Rabindranath Tagore's famous play *Raktakarabi* (Red Carnation). A difficult play by any reckoning, Pathasena entirely self-directed the production, receiving help only in script editing and characterisation from Sircar. Prepared after much hard work, Pathasena's *Raktakarabi* is now a 'landmark production of Third Theatre according to Sircar.[12]

12. Sayoni Mitra, Badal Sircar: 'Scripting a Movement'; *The Drama Review* 48,3 (T183) Fall 2004. New York University and The Massachusetts Institute of Technology

Even though his active involvement with the group started diminishing with his advancing age, Satabdi was only identified with Badal Sircar. With him as the chief ideator of the group, and one who took on every task from writing plays to shifting the sets, it is not surprising that one rarely hears of other full time members of Satabdi such as Dipankar Dutta, Kalyan Ghosh, Krishna Ghosh, Preeti Dutta, Shanta Dutta and Tapas Mukherjee. "It is true that Sircar has written or been involved in the evolution of an overwhelming proportion of the 44 plays Satabdi has done.

He has also directed all but five of them. But things are slowly changing. Bishakha Dutta directed her own play, *Shanaborir Kathokatha*, for the group. *Sada Kalo* (c. 1994), based on apartheid in South Africa, received much acclaim under the direction of Dipankar Dutta. Initially the play had a cast of 14, which was then reduced to three (Dipankar, Kalyan and Tapas) for *parikrama*s. Sircar admits that he was initially skeptical about whether the theme of apartheid would be understood or relevant to all, but was happily proved wrong when both versions of the play were very well received by urban and rural audiences alike. 'Dipankar had real talent,' he lauds. But this actor/director with great potential passed away in 1996. 'It is a loss that we are still trying to get over.'[13]

In the last year of his life, he received several honours, and the once angry man who had spurned or was cavalier to such honours was actually excited at being felicitated. It was a sort of vindication of his stand that after years of being marginalised and away from the limelight, the theatre community did have to give him his due and he was graceful enough to accept these recognitions of his contributions. His was a life lived fully to the last according to his convictions and impacting on thousands of lives around him.

Part Two

As we go through his life we find that his journey from a person writing plays for fun, to a serious playwright, to a director-actor and to

13. Sayoni Mitra: 'Badal Sircar: 'Scripting a Movement'; *The Drama Review* 48,3 (T183) Fall 2004. New York University and The Massachusetts Institute of Technology

a theatre visionary or activist happened at a very fast pace. And, as he himself claims, these turns were guided by a series of circumstances, though the seeds of the changes that came were definitely there within him. The years from 1956-64 were the years when he was mostly writing domestic situational comedies. It is from 1965, with the publication and staging of *Ebong Indrajit*, that his serious journey in theatre took off and was more or less like a roller coaster ride. The period from 1965 to 1972 must unquestionably be the most exciting years of his life, with new influences, challenges and discoveries at every step.

He formed his group Satabdi in 1967; toured to east European countries in 1969; contemplated moving away from the proscenium and restructured the group to work towards Poor Theatre; post his US visit and the Nehru Fellowship in 1972 he consolidated his ideas of the Third Theatre. In a short period of eight years—his creative journey had taken major leaps, so much so that he had more or less arrived at what he would continue to do for the rest of his life. The changes that came in his work were arising organically out of his experience of life and art that he was practising and observing. His subsequent work for the next four decades was further exploration of the potential of what he had spearheaded. In that sense there is no major shift in his outlook to theatre post-1972.

Badal Sircar's earlier comedies and fantasies are delightfully innovative and witty. One gets to see the lighter and humorous side of Badal Sircar where he could let himself go and just write for pure entertainment. Even though most of the plays of this phase were adaptations of western plays, in their structuring and adaptation to the Indian milieu Badal Sircar shows great ingenuity. This quality of pure and uninhibited enjoyment that one sees in this phase never really showed up much later as he seemed weighed down by a responsibility and probably passion to write plays for social change and empowerment. This is a great pity because modern India has not seen many playwrights with talent for comedy and had he continued, even if in his spare time, he would definitely have provided a body of plays that are needed for garnering audiences for the amateur theatre movement.

The next phase of his writing, from 1965-72 – and this is the most significant body of his work as a playwright – seems more autobiographical, in the sense it concerns itself with questions and issues that bothered him as a socially and politically aware individual. This is also the phase where he has written the maximum number of original plays starting from *Ebong Indrajit* to *Baki Itihas, Pagla Ghoda, Sara Rattir, Shesh Nei* to name a few. Most of his plays of the earlier phase and later plays were either inspired by or loose adaptations of other plays, mostly western. While he himself says in one of his interviews that he is no good at making new stories but has no problem in turning a good story into a stageable play, it remains a fact that some of his best and most discussed plays have been those which he created from scratch, because in all these the content carries urgency and seems much more rooted, and its relationship with the form, which was always different, seems very organic. In the 1970s, the pace at which he was writing plays and the kind of variety of forms and structures in which he poured his content was staggering and one can easily say that it placed him almost on top of the four greats of the time—namely Mohan Rakesh, Vijay Tendulkar and Girish Karnad. None of the others showed such an easy command of the theatrical form. He seemed to be playing around with different genres, garnering them at will—as and when it suited him. While he was still working within the proscenium, he was questioning the rules that guided the theatre of illusion.

While I will not get into commenting on plays of this phase as it has been done in several articles in 'The Beginnings', I do want to reiterate what several people have articulated, that in his move towards Third Theatre he more or less stopped writing plays that allowed for layered or multiple interpretations and therefore for other groups to take up for production. This indeed was a great loss to the Indian repertoire of plays. Here I would also like to refer to a prevalent trend or tradition in Bengal—that of playwright-director or playwright-actor. A large number of playwrights in Bengal direct their own plays or play the central roles in their plays. It could also be the case that actors took on the responsibility of penning the plays they would like to act in. This dual role might be instrumental in providing a deeper understanding of theatre as a medium, but it definitely limits the playwright in terms of freedom to express. His knowledge of the limitations of his own group, space and actors starts governing the choices he makes while writing. As Badal Sircar admits in an interview to Subhendu Sarkar:

> Initially there was a shortage of women in our group. That's why you will find only a mother and a daughter in my early plays. My wife used to play the mother's role and her sister, the daughter's. Later I have written some plays with Mou (Sanghamitra Bhattacharya) in mind. She is a member of Ayna, a group that works with us. Because of Mou, I could write plays like *Ka Cha Ta Ta Pa* and *Bagalacharitmanas*. And yes, characters have been created keeping myself in mind as well. But Satabdi has also produced some plays that I wrote or adapted thinking that they would never be performed.'

The same limitation is visible in almost all later plays of Badal Sircar. With the exception of *Michhil* and *Bhoma* almost none of his other plays could be taken up for staging by other groups. Even when they were not devised plays they were more like production scripts than plays with an independent life. Had he continued primarily as a playwright it is certain that he would have got much greater recognition than he actually got inspite of his lifelong tireless work in theatre. But then he would not have been himself! He was certainly more inventive as a playwright, had a great sense of humour with a disarming quality of being able to laugh at himself, more perceptive, poetic and philosophical. These qualities are not that visible in his theatre.

One other question has always bothered me about his writing and theatre of the 1960s and 1970s – that relating to his relationship with the Naxalite movement raging in his time – in view of the fact that Badal Sircar remained very politically inclined right till the end. Though he got disillusioned with the party and its leadership fairly early in his life, and considering that during the active period of his playwriting, the Naxalite movement was at its peak, it is very surprising that there is no reference to that movement, even obliquely, in any of his plays or in his discourse about that time. True, he was out of Calcutta for the most part during those years, but he was very much in touch with the youth of the time, so I wonder why it does not get reflected in his work. More so, since he was constantly complaining about the apathy and complacence of the Calcutta middle class and its youth, surely their active engagement and protest for the cause of the marginalised rural populace could not have gone unnoticed by him. Here they were not only taking responsibility for the plight of the poor but also acting upon that class guilt at the cost of their lives. In fact one feels that had he taken cognizance of that movement, his early plays may not have had the kind of despair and angst that they reflect about meaninglessness of the middle class lives and the plays may not have required the recurrent reminder for taking responsibility for social inequities and exploitation because this is precisely what the Naxalites were doing through their political action. His protagonists like Indrajit and the woman in *Sara Rattir* do protest against the middle class values and lives but this protest is within the boundaries of mundane middle class routine – its relationships and morality – unlike the young Naxalites who were courageous enough to not just question but also fight against the status quo. Yes, one tends to identify more with Badal Sircar's characters and the limits within which they rebel, and that might be the reality of the majority of the youth, but was it fair to ignore the idealism and the courage of those youngsters who sacrificed their comfort and lives for a revolution towards social change. It is also possible that Badal Sircar did not subscribe to the kind of violence propagated by this movement. Yet his not taking notice does seem surprising. Had he done that the reality he portrayed might have been more nuanced and layered and even varied. All protagonists might not have been the timid, trapped individuals or types that they seem in most of his plays of that period.

Coming to the next stage of his journey, arguably the most significant stage, it is interesting to note how his temperament, socio-political concerns, experience of practising theatre in difficult circumstances and chance overseas trips—all came together gradually to make him question the kind of theatre he was practising and subsequently to the idea of the Third Theatre or Poor Theatre or Free Theatre. So, while all the above factors play the role of catalysts or external stimuli, he was essentially looking for a medium that would allow him to interact more closely with the audience, to engage them actively in debate and dialogue about their role and responsibility as citizens, and to find methods where he would be able to practice theatre without having to depend on funding. At one level the search was for discovering the strengths of theatre as a medium as against a popular medium like cinema, and at another, consciously or unconsciously, was a desire to make a difference in the state of things as encountered or understood during his stint in politics. It is not accidental that at this stage he is choosing to write plays like *Sagina Mahato* and *Spartacus*—plays about the marginalised, the underdogs, the exploited, and about blatant injustice. All the intensity and passion of these plays and their productions comes from his political standpoint and the protest that he wants to register. Along with the protest was the desire to change, by giving voice to the oppressed. The rest of his work follows this very impulse—though in different ways.

At this point I would like to look at his quest for Third Theatre also in tandem with a parallel quest for Third Cinema articulated almost at the same time. 'Towards a Third Cinema', a manifesto written by Fernando Solanas and Octavio Gettino in 1969,[14] introduces the idea of a liberal, revolutionary cinema that works actively towards using its format and appeal to rebel against 'the System'. Interestingly, it is voicing concerns and approaches similar to those voiced by Badal Sircar in his search for the Third Theatre even though the stated objectives of the two are different. I do not know if Badal Sircar had heard of this thesis but it certainly points to some similar debates in the international arena regarding the purpose and mode of art. Let me give some quotes from the article on The Third Cinema mentioned above:

14. Fernando Solanas and Octavio Gettino: 'Towards a Third Cinema'. Tricontinental by OSPAAL, 1969

> Culture, art, science, and cinema always respond to conflicting class interests. In the neocolonial situation two concepts of culture, art, science, and cinema compete: that of the rulers and that of the nation—The culture, including the cinema, of a neocolonialised country is just the expression of an overall dependence that generates models and values born from the needs of imperialist expansion.[15]

Badal Sircar is also articulating his concerns about the modes of cultural expression that came into existence due to the reality of a colonised India. He says:

> One of the most important characteristics of the socio-economic conditions of India is an unfortunate dichotomy between urban and rural life.... As a result, the culture of the cities found its roots in Western soil and there was almost a clear break from the traditional indigenous culture. The culture of the countryside, however, did not die and the two cultures ran parallel, thus extending the urban-rural dichotomy to the cultural field.

In his essay 'The Changing Language of Theatre' he talks of himself (in third person) as a prototype who:

> ...while searching for a new language for communicating more effectively in theatre, he wants to do something about this dichotomy also, however inadequate and limited his attempts may be. His exploration, therefore, includes a search for a free theatre that will not be limited to an urban audience belonging to the middle and upper classes, nor tied down to backward values unrelated to the life and problems of the working masses of the country. He realizes gradually that a flexible, portable and inexpensive theatre is needed for that, a third theatre, at least for the time being.

15. Fernando Solanas and Octavio Gettino: 'Towards a Third Cinema'. Tricontinental by OSPAAL, 1969

You will find in Badal Sircar's writings a gradual rejection of the proscenium and the realistic theatre, a bourgeois construct taken from the colonisers. He arguably was not propagating revolutionary theatre but with his political bent of mind and leftist leanings he was definitely wanting to change society through his theatre. Or to be more precise—break their complacency and passivity towards social responsibility.

Badal Sircar felt that the relationship of the performer and spectator should be independent of concerns of money. For instance he felt that selling tickets for the performances would necessarily turn the audience into a consumer. And to do away with this practice he felt it necessary to make the theatre very cheap so that one would not need and depend for funds on the government, business houses or the audience. This dictated his move towards the Free Theatre or The Poor Theatre. The article on Third Cinema states a similar concern:

> In bourgeois art man is accepted only as a passive and consuming object; rather than having his ability to make history recognised, he is only permitted to read history, contemplate it, listen to it, and undergo it; man is viewed as a consumer of ideology, and not as the creator of ideology.[16]

Third Cinema is the cinema of liberation 'that recognises...the great possibility of constructing a liberated personality with each people as the starting point—in a word, the decolonisation of culture.' As they started making this alternative cinema they realised that they 'had at hand three very valuable factors: 1) The participant comrade, the man-actor-accomplice who responded to the summons; 2) The free space where that man expressed his concerns and ideas, became politicised, and started to free himself; and 3) The film, important only as a detonator or pretext.'[17]

16. Fernando Solanas and Octavio Gettino: 'Towards a Third Cinema'. Tricontinental by OSPAAL, 1969

17. Fernando Solanas and Octavio Gettino: 'Towards a Third Cinema'. Tricontinental by OSPAAL, 1969

So did Badal Sircar as he started practising his Third Theatre. 'The participant comrade, the man actor accomplice' were his actors who shared his ideology and who participated in creation of the performance. The performance provided the free space to the actor and spectator to express his concerns and ideas and begin the process of freeing himself. And that as Badal Sircar himself states repeatedly, the performances were very often merely a pretext to start a dialogue, a process of exploration of society and self.

> The man of the third cinema, be it guerrilla cinema or a film act, with the infinite categories that they contain (film letter, film poem, film essay, film pamphlet, film report, etc.), above all counters the film industry of a cinema of characters with one of themes, that of individuals with that of masses, that of the author with that of the operative group, one of neocolonial misinformation with one of information, one of escape with one that recaptures the truth, that of passivity with that of aggressions.[18]

Badal Sircar in his 'Changing Language of Theatre' says:

> The playwright may find that what he wants to say cannot be effectively said through a story with characters who have definite identities. A character may be too limiting in his individuality, a story may be too specific to suit his subject. For example, he may want to deal with the problems of people like himself, urban middle-class people – a minority in society no doubt, but an important minority – who he knows intimately. He may be more concerned with their problem in general than those of certain individuals and, therefore, he may find that prototypes rather than characters would be more suitable to express that the problems are not of one but of many.

18. Fernando Solanas and Octavio Gettino: 'Towards a Third Cinema'. Tricontinental by OSPAAL, 1969

'The effectiveness of the best films of militant cinema show that social layers considered backward are able to capture the exact meaning of an association of images, an effect of staging, and any linguistic experimentation placed within the context of a given idea.'[19]

Badal Sircar talking about his experiences of taking his work to rural areas is constantly pointing out how the illiterate villagers understood his complex plays and the imagery of the performance much better than their urban counterparts. 'Furthermore, revolutionary cinema is not fundamentally one which illustrates, documents, or passively establishes a situation: rather, it attempts to intervene in the situation as an element providing thrust or rectification. To put it another way, it provides discovery through transformation.'[20] Almost the same could be said of all of Badal Sircar's work—be it his plays, his Third Theatre practice, or his workshop methodology and objectives.

I have quoted at such length from the article on Third Cinema because I find it quite extraordinary that work in two different genres, across two continents and completely different contexts and histories have such common resonances in their approach to their mediums at approximately the same time. This similarity underlines another significant point that whether he admitted it or not his political predilections and commitment to change or desire for a total socio-political revolution are reflected in all the strategies that he finally adopts to create his theatre. That was indeed the driving force of his theatre practice and remained so till the end.

I would not be talking in any detail on the Third Theatre as all his interviews, some of which are part of this book, his writings and other articles have addressed this concept in detail. Scholars have critiqued his playwriting too, but what seems to be missing is a critical look at his work in theatre. It is important to do that because he insisted that he be looked at as primarily a theatre worker and not just a playwright. As I was going through a large body of writing on his work, this area

19. Fernando Solanas and Octavio Gettino: 'Towards a Third Cinema'. Tricontinental by OSPAAL, 1969

20. Fernando Solanas and Octavio Gettino: 'Towards a Third Cinema'. Tricontinental by OSPAAL, 1969

of his theatre practice I found missing. Rustom Bharucha, in his chapter on Badal Sircar, in his book *Rehearsals of the Revolution* does give very detailed accounts of the performances/ productions of the Third Theatre—almost like performance scripts. These are very valuable because they are the only detailed readings of these unconventional performances. But this writing belongs to the period when the Third Theatre was still a novelty and theatre scholars and spectators were still trying to find a critical language to read his work or formulate a response to this kind of theatre. It belongs to a period when Badal Sircar's work was growing with each production and crackling with the energy of any new found movement that is full of passion and belief in its purposefulness and capacity to change the way people look at theatre and even life. It was a period when Badal Sircar was travelling the entire length and breadth of the country to single-handedly familiarise people with his philosophy and methodology of theatre making and the entire theatre community of the country was discussing this alternative language of theatre created by Badal Sircar. And one must admit that his passion and his belief in his work was very infectious and particularly attractive to young minds who were looking for methods of meaningful interventions in the practice of art, for ways of contributing to social change through theatre. Numerous theatre groups in small towns all over the country adopted his methodology, staged his plays and were able to sustain meaningful but amateur theatre activity without too much demand on the resources. His was a methodology which truly suited the Indian theatre and gave a tremendous boost and impetus to the amateur theatre movement. He felt that 'the basic tool of trade of the art of the theatre is the human body. It is the presence of the body that ultimately distinguishes theatre from cinema.'

> Sircar emphasises the attitudes, gestures, and movements of the body of the performer. And it is by the imaginative use of bodies that he creates various 'stage realities'. As an illustration, it will do well to remember *Gandi* ('Circle', 1978), Sircar's adaptation of Brecht's *Caucasian Chalk Circle*, where the performers create a broken bridge, mountain, river, fire, and wind with the help of

> their bodies. By recognising 'human body' as the most important element in theatre, Sircar steadily reduces the use of sets, props, and costume. He also discards the use of mechanical devices like tape recorders and projectors. Thus his theatre becomes 'Poor Theatre', a term appropriate to the occasion.[21]

This new theatre language that he evolved, privileged content and empowered untrained young theatre actors to make socio-political intervention through theatre. It not only allowed for great flexibility in terms of performance infrastructure – be it ill-equipped performing spaces, or street corners, but also a legitimacy/respectability to such Free/Poor Theatre.

It is only when his Third Theatre practice stabilised, and had acquired a more or less fixed form and format, a set process, that one starts noticing the problems, or contradictions in his work. While he asserts that Third Theatre is all about ensemble and collaborative work, he seems to be the dominating spirit in his own team. He says that agreeing on a theme of a play had to be a consensual process, but he himself admits that the plays were written by him and then discussed. Rarely were there any dissensions from within the group, which does not necessarily translate into the fact that everyone wanted that particular text or idea to be taken up at that point in time. As the chief ideologue of the group and its undisputed leader there was very little chance that people would express disagreement with him. The very fact that when Satabdi underwent an overhaul in favour of giving up proscenium performances most of the members left the group, which clearly points to the fact that Satabdi meant Badal Sircar. He was derisive of people who were in favour of performing in the proscenium as he felt they were in theatre for 'success, fame and career'. Which actor wouldn't want fame and success? His were unreal conditions and therefore participation and retention of good actors was difficult. This is not to say that he didn't want to be democratic, or didn't value the opinion of other members. He did and vehemently so. He genuinely

21. Subhendu Sarkar, Introduction to Badal Sircar; *Two Plays: Indian History Made Easy; Life of Bagala*. Oxford University Press, 2010

believed that all decisions of the group were consensual because they were taken after long discussions, but the various interviews with him or his group members and his own articulation about his process prove otherwise. A member of his group while asserting that Badal Sircar believed in evolving a play through improvisations by the members was seen conducting the rehearsal recently, insisting on complete imitation of Badal Sircar's design of the production. Some of his actors and workshop participants informed that he never made the cast aware of the reasons of a particular choreographic decision, or choice of music or methods of concentration etc. As a result the performers were very often unable to keep the belief, or involvement or sustain energy for repeat performances. As Suvobrata Roy Chowdhury, a workshop participant puts it:

> Through the theatrical process he was a total dictator. He would never explain his processes…he just wanted us to be spontaneous without being told about the tools of the trade…(his) theatre process was quite different from the workshop. Theatre belonged to him. He was doing theatre, we were the bodies. Basically we were bodies he was using…he couldn't generate a thinking mind within us…. I feel that this is where Badal-da failed to create a dedicated Badal Sircar theatre. Because today we can ask who will take the position of Badal Sircar? Who will create new plays of the third form, using the tools he uses? Because he would never explain the tools.

This participant is pointing towards a very interesting dichotomy in Badal Sircar's approach when he was conducting his workshops and when he was directing plays. Much as he believed in evolving performance through participation and consensus so that the acting would be a 'state of being', he could not translate it into practice during rehearsals, though the workshops were definitely very participatory and improvisational. If performers were indeed just 'used as bodies' as claimed by some participants and if the nature of participation in a production tended to be mechanical and manipulative there is hardly any possibility of inner truth being presented by the actor. In other words, the performers would find it difficult to reach and sustain the kind of commitment and belief that Badal Sircar himself had in creating and working on the piece since only he knew why they were doing what they were doing and what it signified. He actually did not empower or equip them to discover their own impetus, action and aesthetics. This is a serious contradiction in his own process of work as perceived by or visualised by him.

There could be several reasons for this contradiction. One of them definitely was that in the conditions that theatre in Calcutta happened at his time and even now, he was largely working with untrained actors. Additionally, with his choice of working outside the proscenium, and imposition of very stringent standards demanding complete commitment, the members who joined the group were definitely committed to his ideology but not so much to improve standards of acting. Sircar's energy then must have been expended in bringing them to an acceptable level of performance than to equip them with the tools of the trade. This also impacted on the quality of performance in his productions, thus defeating his claim that theatre has to meet the artistic standards first and foremost for it to fuel change.

Another reason could be that as a person who had facility in writing his scripts, with a zeal for a particular kind of content, commitment to a definite process and method as a director, keen on acting in most of his plays, it is unlikely that he would find it easy to give creative space to any other member—a condition necessary for true collaborative work. As he mentions in one of his interviews, 'It was also a question of uneven talent'. But this may only be his reading of their capabilities, or rather just a comparative reading in relation to himself. Yet it must be said in his defense that when one is spearheading any change, and leading a movement, being dictatorial is almost imminent and therefore pardonable as only the initiator has the instincts required to lead the movement and decide its direction. Unfortunately, this is probably also the reason why his collaborators in his group and those running similar groups have not been able to innovate or develop on the methodology established by Sircar. They probably started depending too much on him for all artistic decisions to learn to take those decisions independently.

Badal Sircar trained his actors to act in a particular way, to use their body and all its tools to communicate the meaning/s of the text, and also to define the space as an ensemble. This required internalising the content of the play to the extent that it became an integral part of them to therefore find intense and direct communication. This worked well in intimate spaces particularly when the performers had undergone an entire workshop process that allowed them to evolve the performance and gave them space for a one to one communication with the audience. While explaining the essential language of his theatre in his essay, 'In Changing Language of Theatre' he talks of how the demand on the actor is different in his productions:

> In the conventional naturalistic theatre, the performer changes his identity to that of the character in the play. It is done through costume, makeup, bearing, movement, gesture, facial expression, mannerism—everything copied and applied; in short, faking. This is generally known as 'acting.' But now (in his theatre) the performer comes down, comes close, appears as the human being he is to the human being that the spectator is. Now he can no longer fake; now he has to take off his mask and be himself.

He goes on to say in another interview with Sharad Nagar (in 'The Third Theatre' section of this book):

> To my mind there can be two distinct kinds of acting. One is acting by enactment and the other is acting by a state of being. We can learn the technique of acting in such a way that I can communicate the theme, the mood, the emotion of the play. At the same time I can remain uninvolved in the content of the play as a performer. Now, in our theatre, the starting point is content. Which means that our primary thing is what we have to say. What we feel an urge to say. Acting by enactment is not

> possible by us. We have to use our own feelings, own reactions to the theme.

These are very significant formulations regarding the kind of acting desired in his work. He was possibly wanting to break away from the Stanislavskian acting and move towards a different kind of involvement of the actor-involvement with the comment of the play. However the problem in his formulation is with his conviction that other actors or acting was fake while his actors were revealing their true selves. Did he really believe that the actors in his productions did not have any mask? By virtue of being a performer you are putting on a mask of carrying a certain message to the spectator, in a given space and time. The performer's own reality cannot be the reality that he is required to communicate to the audience at a demanded time and space, however much he might have internalised the message or the content. And to that extent even an actor in a realistic play could have internalised the reality of the character to a degree that he starts believing it and living it out as his own on stage. Both have to put on an act, and have the belief depending on the process of the preparation of the production. Both are equally vulnerable on stage because in all good acting you expose some part of your real self in making the character or the content your own. In fact at the time Badal Sircar was experimenting with his methodology and also later, significant efforts were being made by several other directors to make the process of acting more subjective, more exploratory and find varied and subtle modes of expression—like a gesture, or an image or an object, that would communicate the inner meeting point of the actor and character. It is possible that Sircar, when talking of realistic acting, is referring to the superficial naturalism of the early years, not taking into account the other experiments of his time.

Badal Sircar wanted his performance to be a 'human act'—an act of direct sharing between the performer and the spectator and trained the actors accordingly. But it often made the audience, not used to such direct communication, quite uncomfortable, but as Sircar asserted that it was his intention to 'take the audience out of their comfort zone and push them towards action'. Here too he made the erroneous assumption that if you are directly reaching out to the audience and involving him/her in the performance that he too drops his masks. In fact a spectator is much more likely to drop his mask in the anonymity of a group rather than when he is publicly confronted. Getting into the private space of the spectator without his prior consent or willingness will only build bigger barriers than break them. If a spectator was unwilling to readily participate in the performance, then Badal Sircar was fairly judgmental of him taking him to be socially irresponsible. His actors too reflected the same judgement in their persistence that the spectator give an immediate response. This reading of the spectator's response seems simplistic, not taking the complex social, psychological, spatial dynamic of such a situation into consideration. His own view of theatre was formed of many such generalised formulations which either he chose not to question or did not get the time to question and examine. I do believe that he was too self-critical to not have been aware of the inadequacy of his formulations but I have not come across any material that suggests that he questioned or revised his views on various aspects of his theatre practice—that is the process, the acting style, design of the production, treatment of space and relationship with spectators once he had established the Third Theatre. Theatre scene was changing rapidly in the country and many exciting turns were inspired by his initiatives in theatre. But his own theatre did not respond to the changes and therefore almost remained at the level it had reached by the late 1970s.

One possible reason for him not reviewing his work as much as he should have could be the response of the Calcutta theatre community to his work. After the initial excitement towards his plays of the 1960s, and then to his ideas about the Third Theatre being shaped at the Academy of Fine Arts in the early 1970s, the theatre establishment started turning indifferent and at times even hostile once he had moved to the Theosophical Society of Bengal to practice Free Theatre.

As part of his idea of freeing theatre from financial concerns he stopped selling tickets and publicising his plays. As his theatre activity started losing its novelty and became less visible, the critics and scholars started posing questions regarding why he was not continuing to write plays of the kind he was writing earlier? Or why were his members leaving his group? Or did he regret his decision to move to the Third Theatre since it did not give him the same kind of recognition? From his responses to these questions that were bombarding him from all directions, it seems he felt duty-bound to defend what he was doing. This is not to say that he didn't believe in what he was doing, but these queries with their implied criticism, only pushed him to a corner where he aggressively asserted that this was exactly what he wanted to do and would not want to change his focus in any circumstances. Unfortunately this meant not giving him the opportunity to review his own work critically and it therefore stopped evolving. It got stuck in a groove, a set pattern which proved lethal for a theatre which had established itself through its passion, its excitingly flexible format, its structure which was meant to give space for change at every level. As early as 1983 Rustom Bharucha in his book has said of Badal Sircar's work, 'While continuing to challenge the norms, conventions, and economic structure of the commercial theater, it has established its own norms, conventions, and economic structure. Like many alternative theater movements that succeed, the Third Theater seems to have institutionalised itself. It tends to repeat the same ideas using the same techniques. What was once daring has now become familiar.' This is also borne by the comparative impact of a production of *Michhil* (*The Procession*) that I had seen in the 1970s and I saw again around 2000. The first one was full of a volatile energy, had the spirit and vulnerability of experimentation and therefore the full concentration and participation of the whole team. That was a very exciting experience, also because it was something very new and path-breaking at that time. But seeing the same production 30 years later I was truly dismayed because the design was an identical replica of the earlier production without the conviction of the original and the energy that comes from a fresh involvement with the concerns of the text. Theatre can never be revived—it has to be revisited. But Badal Sircar's work had frozen in time. I am sure he was aware of this but did not have the time to evolve new patterns and structures as he was doing everything himself—writing, workshopping, managing, directing and acting. He probably could not even see much theatre outside his own work that could provoke him towards new performance idioms and methods. It could also possibly be what Safdar Hashmi says in an interview to Eugene van Erven (published by Sahmat in 1989 as, *The Right to Perform: Selected Writings of Safdar Hashmi*) that 'Badal Sircar has created a cult; a personal myth around himself which makes it difficult for himself or anybody else to establish a critical relation with his work.'

Undoubtedly, the workshop process that he introduced, a synthesis of several methodologies that he came across, is the best and most telling illustration of Badal Sircar's belief, philosophy and methodology. And it is in this area that he has made the most significant and lasting contribution as a theatre practitioner. His workshops across the length and breadth of the country and beyond focused on creating the notion of how theatre can be done, how the collective works in theatre, how non-textual expression can be created and how strongly it communicates, how physical expression has to come from your own understanding and experience of life, how politics is manifested in each and every choice you make in a group etc. I do not know of anyone else in the country at that time who was utilising the workshop process towards preparation of productions, a process that is common practice today. While his theatre practice became repetitive, his workshops remained comparatively energetic and useful as he worked with people from different walks of life. He changed the exercises and games with each group of participants building the workshop around their needs and capabilities, working towards helping them realise their own potential. Talking to several participants of his workshops one gauges that his idealism, his intense belief and energy were very infectious and really enthused people, especially the young, wanting to get out of the growing cynicism, towards positive action. His intervention did change lives and the direction of the work people were doing before they met him. In a sense he is the only theatre person in the country who has impacted on the lives and work of so many artists and inspired them to practise art that will create awareness of the socio political reality of our times. There was an almost messianic quality about his persona which drew a great many people around him but which also partially worked against him as following this messiah became increasingly demanding and difficult. In a workshop, 'Badal describes his role as that of a catalyst agent; the work is generated by the performers/participants themselves. Badal's role is to: enable the participants to discover themselves as people by confronting their inner resources, tensions, and moments of communion.'[22] However here too, the basic framework and repertoire of his exercises, games and improvisations remained the same and limited. From the 1990s when more and more directors were taking the improvisatory path to directing plays there was a constantly growing repertoire of games and improvisations in circulation, some originally devised by these directors and some others drawing from international theatre practices. This allowed the directors to bring out varied expressions from their actors and allowed them to develop newer theatre languages. Unfortunately Sircar's basic exercises did not change significantly with time and hence theatre workers exposed to these other languages started getting disinterested in his work. His own theatre too, as mentioned earlier, stagnated and appeared outdated since new ideas were not being harnessed.

However, there was a close connection between the workshop process and the production process. As Sanchayan Ghosh, an artist and designer who attended Sircar's workshops, articulates in his interview in this book:

> I think Badal-da's workshops are his politics and the productions are extended imageries of his workshops. Like for our *Manushey Manushey* production, most of the actions evolved out of workshops. It is the memory of the emotions generated in the workshop that helped us to generate the same kind of emotions. It was not emulation of the memory but a reliving of the memories.

22. Rustom Bharucha: *Rehearsals of Revolution: The Political Theatre of Bengal.* Seagull Books, Kolkata, 1983

There is yet another area where his workshop methodology could prove to be very useful—that of Theatre-in-Education. Jo Trowsdale, a British scholar, in her article 'Sitting in Badal's Circle: Artist and Pedagogue; the Theatre of Badal Sircar,' talks about the significance of Badal Sircar's methodology in the practice of Theatre in Education—an area that has not been recognised in India. She says:

> The work of Indian theatre practitioner Badal Sircar represents a socially committed model of physically based theatre which has significance for drama educators.
>
> His work in Third Theatre bears many relations to existing Educational Drama practice, yet there is still more to be learned from his example...Badal emphasises the necessity to work in a physical form. In the West we are more familiar with a psychological form, in performance and in educational drama. Badal's work suggests that the physical work of the body, experienced through participation and through witnessing, engages us more fully and directly, at an instinctive gut level. As such it is the means to holistic mind-spirit-body experience of theatre. It is also the means of communication with the illiterate rural populace of India. The language of gesture, image, rhythm, movement and montage are immediate and are read instinctively. This is an alternative to the literary model of theatre which dominates much of formal education. A literary model is not only disempowering for many children, but does not draw upon their own instinctive and experienced understandings....
>
> The work of Badal Sircar, like that of Boal, offers an important opportunity to reconnect the Drama-in-Education tradition with the avant-garde in theatre. There are common themes across the two domains and by paying attention to artists like Badal, drama educators can find a way to reconnect their practice with a strong and developing area of arts practice.[23]

23. Trowsdale, Jo. 'Sitting in Badal's Circle: Artist and Pedagogue'; *The Theatre of Badal Sircar: Research in Drama Education*; vol. 2 issue 1. 1997, pub. Taylor and Francis

Summing up one can say that Badal Sircar, made an indelible mark on Indian theatre history – as playwright, theatre practitioner, ideologue and activist all rolled into one. The large body of his plays – both original and adaptations – would be the envy of most other playwrights of the country – in terms of the range of subjects, forms and styles. He single-handedly created and popularised a brand of theatre all over the country and also overseas which empowered small amateur theatre groups to practice theatre without much infrastructure and training and do so with a strong social commitment. He took on board the challenge cinema posed to the popularity of theatre and tried to identify the specifities and strengths of theatre as a medium to meet that challenge. In the process he succeeded in giving a new theatre language that broke out of the proscenium, where the primary tool was the actors' body and the objective-direct communication with the audience. He also succeeded in fashioning a very meaningful model for non-party political theatre and street theatre-both in content and form/forms. He was no scholar or theoretician but he evolved ideas and concepts that he reached through practice and grassroots work and a questioning mind. He was truly a phenomenon, not given due recognition in his life time for his committed theatre activity, for making theatre accessible to thousands across the country, and fighting a lonely battle to liberate theatre at various levels. Even if his contribution is not acknowledged the impact will remain in the works of innumerable theatre workers of the country and his ideas will continue to enrich the intellectual discourse in Indian theatre.

THE BEGINNINGS

MEMOIRS OF BADAL SIRCAR

Some Excerpts

Pratibha Agrawal's *Pravasi Ki Kalam Se* – a Hindi translation of the original Bengali memoirs of Badal Sircar – translated in English by **Gargi Bharadwaj**

DIARY
10.11.57

Gradually it is dawning on me that my soul is getting increasingly blunted. The fierce and compelling anger against the suffocating pressures of my surroundings which earlier destabilised me is no longer there. No protest, but peace. The peace of being in harmony with my surroundings. Nothing hurts anymore, nothing causes pain. The sensation of pain has been lost and now it seems that the sensation of happiness and joy will also be lost.

The Kolkatawala me and the Khaparkhedawala me—how diametrically opposed the two were! Forceful desire, suffocating loneliness, solitude. Did all that symbolise my defeat? Was it devoid of any feeling of strength, intensity? To desire with such intensity that the humiliation of defeat and anxieties of the future would appear trivial—was there nothing positive in that desire? Who knows? Sometimes I wish I had retained the mad desires of a 22-year-old instead of the present 32-year-old man—lifeless, duty-bound and bogged down by responsibilities.

Am I still a human being? Or am I just a living being out of the ordinary! A preordained journey of life—studying, employment, progress, saving money, managing a family and household etc., etc. Not just this. The kind of equations that would be established with others in future would have to be looked at dispassionately, in order to maintain peaceful equilibrium. Peace. That is the most desired. Not happiness or joy, for they are filled with both torture and conflict.

Thirty-two years. Is there still time to start afresh? Today it feels as if living is just a duty. Where is the attraction? The meaning and joy of living? Joy it seems had been abandoned in previous births. I try to keep myself alive by rearranging whatever little joy is left in the regimented frame of life.

... Will anything ever change? Will there ever be any change in my carefully regimented, hurdle-free and peaceful journey of life?

The fault, dear Brutus, is not in thy stars, but in thyself! The fault, dear Brutus ... the fault!

The germs of a terminal sickness are already present in my body. Inherent. I used to maintain that I represent the near-dead part of a dying social order. I have no words of consolation; there is no anaesthesia to numb the feeling of pain. One will have to tread consciously, slowly, towards death.

Today my ego is suddenly aroused when I think of so many who feel the pain of my absence, who love me, who desire me. This is precisely the joy of living. To be loved and to experience deprivation are what lend meaning and value to life.

Foolish!

Not in thy stars, dear Brutus. In thyself. Thyself.

DIARY
10.7.59

The exams are over and I've passed. According to the norm I should be at peace and celebrating. So I am peaceful and enjoying life. Events like exams reduce life to a single track. If the question arises why I exist, the answer that comes to mind immediately is—to pass an exam!

And after passing one exam? Another. If there isn't another? Then one enjoys the present state of bliss – this state of bliss – anticipation of which helped me pass each day before the exams. After the exams were over there arrived the inevitable anxiety of failing or passing. And having passed, I am now wandering about in a puzzled state of excitement, only to be faced with the question: What next?

After mundane issues like exams had been dealt with, the basic questions of life start resurfacing. Why do I exist? If I exist, then for what? What am I doing? What have I done all this while? What after this? Even if I do something, why do I do it? What is its purpose?

Self-importance is engrained in human nature. So is it in me. I rate myself quite high. Then there are others, friends and family, well-wishers and some fools too, who, to a large extent, are in agreement with me on this. And they can all ask in one voice—what is it you lack? A wide range of people perceive things differently and speak differently. For some I am a scholar, having passed many exams. For some I am a good man who can easily attract and charm people. And for some others, I have immense talent. It's true that this talent has not yet found a direction, but some day it will certainly surface—like chicken pox. Some are straightforward and say: 'Though I don't know who you are and what you are capable of, you are surely a good man and that is the ultimate meaning of your being.'

I naturally believe whatever people tell me. Only those who think I am bad anger me. It feels as if I have not been understood. I pity those who don't say anything for not having recognised my talent.

If this was indeed the truth, there would have been no problem. Belief in oneself is like belief in God—sufficient enough to go through life without complications or questions. But when I piece myself together – pieces of myself as perceived by me and others – and try to decipher this whole, everything gets mixed up.

Not that I am seeing myself for the first time today. I've been seeing myself in different ways for a long time. In different stages of life, in different situations, in contact with different people. Seen and known myself every day. And this knowing has become so enormous, that it now seems unfamiliar.

Does man need faith to survive? Belief in God? In ideals? In work? In fellow human beings? In revolution? In oneself? In love? How can I say which one of these beliefs motivates me today? Belief in life? Does that exist at all?

Calcutta-Howrah, Calcutta-Nagpur, Calcutta-Maithun, Calcutta-London. And back to Calcutta. Who knows where next? The past has been moving like a wheel. Yet not exactly like a wheel. Every circle constantly superseding the previous—that is the tragedy. The tragedy of knowing. I receive it, I understand, it ends, I discard it. And I receive it again. How much novelty can there be in a lifetime? Don't all the letters from Calcutta replicate this very circle? Aren't they sullen with this repetition? Am I also not just a part of this wheel? Will I ultimately not be just a part?

Even then, the desire for an impossible, miraculous happening does not end. It feels this isn't everything. This can't be the end, there will be something more. Something that will blur everything that preceded it in its blinding brightness. A self that forever dreams, boundlessly! The effect of the dream doesn't seem to vanish even after waking from sleep.

I have achieved whatever there is to achieve. And what came out of it? Nothing! This is so true. That one will get more and that getting will set one apart—this hope is just as false. Because of dreams, the past and the future are opposites. Only by turning the face of the future towards the past can one end the dream. Alternatively, this can be done only when dreams blur. A hundred and eighty degree angle turns to a zero degree angle. Instead of getting lost while staring into the unknown, blurred future, the present can be made more specific. Put differently, one may as well die!

To die is eternal bliss. How many are blissful and content in death. Having shaped the future into the past and having become one with that, they have died in bliss. One day I too will die this way. Why not just exit now?

LETTER
9.9.63

Manu,

... completed the play. It was a bit rushed towards the end. If possible, I will rewrite the end.

I am unable to conjure any opinion about the play. One room, one night and three people—this is my play. I've called it *Sara Rattir (All Night Long)*. It cannot have any other name. It has the form but not the nature of a play. The form: three scenes, fifty-six pages, therefore it might even be called a long one-act play. Its nature: more readable than do-able. And that's why the descriptions in the brackets are not only stage-directions, but a lot more. All I can say is that like *Ebong Indrajit*, this too is very personal.

It is said that my plays are repetitive. I say the same thing again and again. This criticism may get reinforced with this one. The reason: here the repetition has not just happened; it has been *made to* happen—consciously.

But I am reviewing the play even before reading it out. Whatever the play might be, I feel utterly delighted after finishing it. There is always the fear that I might not be able to complete whatever I begin. But this play has been completed.

I am happy that the play is complete but what will I do today? Reread the end and feel that I wouldn't be able to change it. Whatever is written is now there to stay.

Haven't I been repeating myself? Why am I unable to narrate the play? I will not be able to write another play like *Baro Pishima*. My capacity to entertain, to make people laugh seems to be disappearing. Writing is becoming increasingly colourless and heavy. The capacity to relate a real incident realistically is also diminishing. It is taking the form of allegory, becoming more like poetry. The form seems increasingly strange and awkward. And the most dangerous thing is this—that despite all the imagery and ornamentation, real people are emerging more explicitly. Writing is becoming more intimate, increasingly personal!

DIARY
12.9.63

I received the letter today. Dated the 10th, it reached today.

I am drawn towards *Sara Rattir* time and again. What had I intended to write and what it finally became! It was neither here nor there! It seems that I played a superficial game and trivialised a complex and deep issue. From the perspective of containing this monotonous city life, it seems a neat game, but what right did I have to do this?

Have I turned so banal?

This tired old man is my creation. This old man is me.

To invoke. To invoke what? My muse? Rot! My old dreams? My past? All that had been sweet in my past? All that had been something of worth, while being in my past?

But why invoke? Why don't they come themselves?

Do I want to translate it all into poetry?

Why am I beating about the bush? Am I afraid of the truth? Why do I want to conjure up something which is not there? Why do I want to go on living a life which is not mine? For others? For them? But isn't it a staggering lie?

Yes, it is, That is why life is a lie, a big lie.

Other people. Another person's perspective. Another person's notion, imagination, dream. Another person's desire, belief, love, longing, despair, pain. These are all extremely valuable. They come at a very high price. And it must be paid. There is no other way out.

And none of this is mine.

They love. I need love. They dream. And I thrive in dreams. They want. They demand. They desire. Not me. But something they want me to be. Something they need me to be.

And I live to live up to their dreams, their desires. Because I want to.

DIARY
21.10.63

Manu,
(12:05 at night)

It's over. Just now. Release for Raghuda and for me too. God! Hasn't he troubled me endlessly this month!

Raghuda who? In a way he could be called the hero of *Ballabhpurer Roopkatha*. The play could well have been called *Raghuda*. Went through so much himself and made Bhupati bear it as well. Didn't trouble me any less.

The play is complete, but not done. There are huge gaps in between. The poetry isn't well integrated. As a play, I haven't written such a half-baked one before. But the film I saw in London dominated my mind due to the freshness of its story. A humorous plot grips me if it is even slightly different from the usual. I know what it takes to capture this within the limits of the stage. Even so, in *Ram-Shyam-Jadu* I somehow managed to capture it, but in this one I just could not get the grip of things. As a result there is plenty of nonsense and glib talk. Unable to find solutions to so many problems, I kept searching for a way to escape from it all.

Two female characters: mother and daughter. That same tender age, like *Ram-Shyam-Jadu*'s young girl. Tell me, what could I do? A Bengali comedy, a *roopkatha* (fairytale) at that. How would it work without including a young girl? Wouldn't the readers (or audience) of a *roopkatha* get angry if there was no young princess?

I finally reached a crossroad where six or seven paths meet. In this city there are many turns where several paths meet. All roads seem angular and pointing, like stars *(Mor Tara)*. There is no other city that is a greater maze than this one. I am sitting at a coffee table set along the footpath. It's been almost twenty minutes and so far no one has come to ask me what I want. I have to sit for another hour. Let them come at leisure. This is the advantage in Paris. Pay around a rupee and get a table-chair set for yourself on hire along the road—one can sit there as long as one likes. Along with it one gets a free mug of coffee or a beer—'free', doesn't cost anything

Despite their daily threats that it will soon become extremely cold, today was pleasantly warm, or rather, pleasantly less cold. There is an abundance of trees, but they are all completely bare. Don't I talk about bare trees very often? Here, during winter, the sight of completely bare trees hits you more than the extreme cold. Oh, how I dislike them!

I thought I wouldn't touch the play for a month but its construction seems so loose; the humorous lines are so few that there is no respite without going through it immediately. I am done after writing *Sara*

Rattir and *Ebong Indrajit*. But if I have to make this play work it will have to be beaten into shape!

Last night I went to Cartier Latyaar (Latin Quarter) for dinner. I saw two boys using an artist's chalk to draw on the footpath. 'Thank you' was written next to it in around fifteen different languages. It's a usual sight here. I said, 'If you like, I could add two more languages to it.' I was given a piece of chalk. I wrote 'thank you' on the footpath in Bengali and Nagri.

DIARY
26.11.63

Word, line and note. Depending on these three toys, I am slowly trying to fill in all the gaps of my life. Except for basic survival needs, the heart does not crave or worry about anything else.

Is there nothing left for me to desire? Only a satisfactory job and the play of word-image-sound?

I spent all of last night conceptualising the theatre. The coming together of word, image and sound. The imminent light seems possible only here. I do not understand line and note, but even then there is a desire. I desire to bring them together, to create one unified complete whole.

LETTER
28.11.63

Manu,

To be honest, I didn't have to do any work in the last two weeks. One or two lectures, a minute-or-two-long meetings, and two phone call—that is the work done in the last fifteen days. Maybe because there is endless time in hand; that's why the inability to do anything. The one thing that has been done is that the gaps in *Ballabhpurer Roopkatha* have somehow been filled. Now at least, it can be read out (to others) at one go.

I didn't see any theatre or film during the long vacation. Didn't feel excited enough. All I saw was the museum. I got cards made and now have the right to enter without paying money. I have been to three museums six-seven times over. I have seen paintings. Some days it even happened that after shutting my eyes at night, all I saw was colour—the shapeless sheen of thick oil paint. Seems there can be no picture without colour, but my strength lies in the pencil. I now understand why painters come to Paris. There is an abundance of paintings. Starting from the primitive to the post-modern times. So many diverse threads, varied perspectives, genres, many forms of self-expression. Even after being here for so many days now, it feels I haven't seen half of what there is to see!

I don't attempt to create images anymore. It's not my age to capture colours anymore. That's why I only look at colours—as much as possible.

I think more about writing. But what use is thinking? As of now, there is a new problem. The *Ebong Indrajit* thought process and *Ballabhpurer Roopkatha* thought process stand in opposition to each other. As a result, I am unable to think on either of them in any depth. Then sometimes I decide—no serious thoughts anymore. I will only attempt to amuse. And a little later I find that there is no humour whatsoever. I have even thought of writing something other than a play but to no avail. I don't even feel like thinking about it. The medium of a play is now so deeply seated in my mind.

The thought of doing theatre and theatre projects often becomes almost obsessive. On such days I am unable to think of anything else. Against all reason, logic and intellect, entire evenings are spent imagining somewhat impossible ideas related to theatre. I calculate. I make drawings of the set. I give shape to the production in my mind. I think of lighting. I think of the stage.

LETTER
1.12.63

Manu,

For the last many days I have been attempting to write something new. I have thought on each of the foreign plays I have read and all the foreign films I have seen, but could not really proceed in any direction.

Even then, I am unable to take them out of my mind. These long days of leisure – during my French scholarship – it feels criminal to not begin anything here. Days together from six in the evening till midnight have passed without doing anything. Not even being able to think of one particular thing for long enough. Stories, events, humorous situations, characters all came in glimpses but have not been sustained. I haven't been able to decide anything— whether the play will be humorous or dark, long or short, based on a foreign story or a celebration of my own imagination.

I also thought of my old writings. Why did *Baro Pishima* become more popular? Maybe a domestic background, familiar characters, over familiar incidents etc., have lent it an authenticity due to which even the lack of a narrative does not bother the audience. The story of *Ram-Shyam-Jadu* is far more powerful but the characters seem to have lost their truth in the process of taking the narrative forward.

But if this is true (I don't know, maybe it isn't) then *Samavritta, Solution X, Ballabhpurer Roopkatha* etc., should lose out even more. And lose out they will, for sure. All of them begin from a known story. In unfolding this story within the limits of the stage and offering a solution to the problem at hand, the characters and what is called the 'atmosphere' of the play are both lost.

Except *Baro Pishima*, all the plays that are my own – *Shonibaar, Ebong Indrajit,* etc., – are in another category altogether. One part of this week-long internal deliberation was whether I should write another story-less play like *Baro Pishima,* based on just a context and a few characters? Much like *Baro Pishima* that had the background of amateur theatre and a few characters like Buaji (Pishima), Anu, Yogeen, Nitai and Ananth. Shambhu, Phuphaji (Pisheymoshai) etc., came in later, for the sake of the story, whatever the story is.

This didn't really come to my mind. Even if it did, I didn't allow it to stay with me. Last evening suddenly this thought occurred to me quite forcefully. The humorous situation of a foreign story, not the story itself, but a few characters centred on a small, nearly schismatic part of the story crowded my mind. And a few more. I wrote a small note or two in my copy. Character. Situation. A background that I am a little familiar with. A beginning. An inkling of a possible end. Nothing but just an inkling, that too quite insignificant. I tried to recall whether I had this strength when I began writing *Baro Pishima*?

Eleven-thirty at night. I put the familiar third bracket on a blank paper and wrote the description of the room. Two characters. Some conversation. After that six more pages. Quarter to three at night, I went to sleep.

Finished the first scene about an hour ago. Twenty pages. Nearly without an obstacle. Without the fuss of a story, the conversation developed easily. Maybe there is some scope for a little humour even (although it's not something that should be said), at least more than the first act of *Ballabhpurer Roopkatha*. But a fellow playwright has said, 'The final act of a play is special.' Therefore, he who is unable to write the first act properly, should give up this attempt altogether.

At least a consolation, if nothing else. Even if the thought of chronic 'wastage of time' did not evaporate completely, at least I produced twenty pages. After writing four pages of *Ebong Indrajit*, it lay incomplete for six months. *Baro Pishima*, after half the play. And *Ballabhpur* after five pages, for two months. Half of the first act of *Ram-Shyam-Jadu* took exactly four years. Are twenty pages any less then? Maybe it will finish one day. I can recall at least four such plays right now that even after five to twenty-five pages of writing, just lay untouched from nine months to nine years. There must be more such plays. Let them be. Why only look at the bad side of things always? What do you say? Especially on the day when one has just finished the first act of a new play.

DIARY
6.12.63

Just finished *Kobi Kahini*. Bang on the stroke of midnight. I started it last Saturday on 30th November. Then I had conceived and decided to write it. It had never occurred to me before Saturday evening that I will sometime write a play around a completely imagined story. A mere idea of a poet's impersonation from an ordinary Wodehouse book. The name of the book, even that I do not remember, what to say of the story?

I am experiencing a deep sense of satisfaction and pleasure. This time I did not stop in between. Nor was I stranded when faced with an unexpected hurdle. At the end, there was no pain of limping through it, not even the restlessness of not having evoked humour. As if everything kept flowing smoothly, from beginning to end, in just six days.

And see the irony! Until last Saturday evening I was upset at my inability to write a play like *Baro Pishima* anymore—on a self-imagined plot around a domestic household.

Let whoever say whatever they want about my plays. For me the experience of writing each new play is different and exceptional. Each play is, as if, a history in itself.

LETTER
7.12.63

(As it struck midnight a long time ago)
Manu,
Record break!

I completed a full-length play in six days. Not a copy of a foreign story, but self-imagined and conceived. I've called it *Kobi Kahini*.

I feel (at least there is a sense) that people will laugh. Thinking of myself as the director, this is how it feels to imagine the staged play. There is no point thinking of anything as the writer. Frivolity, yes, but it feels that I haven't just created laughter out of running and jumping around, like *Solution X*. I am myself quite impressed by one or two situations.

... Fifty pages I had written—until then there was no definite idea of the end. Everyday I thought, now I will fall prey to anger.

Aah, why can it not be read out to someone just after writing?

Shall I read them both at the Chakra on a Saturday? That'll take 45 hours. But after reading one, how will I keep waiting all week? Can it not be a whole night session like last time? A Shivratri sitting.

... Four scenes. Seven men, two women. Oh gosh, again the young tender aged girl!

But in one thing I have succeeded this time. No soft scene! No marriage. The boy is in love but he hasn't been left to dwell uselessly in love. Maybe this was the fear in the last scene, so no opportunity for the young Mr Lover to enter there. This wasn't right. He should have been made to enter at least once.

Tell Shyamal Da that he has already been selected for major roles in both these plays. In fact, the main role in this play. I have a part in *Ballabhpur*. In this play, regretfully I don't. But there is no soft scene, so it's possible to wear a wig for Sanat's role and…Putul, as always, is the mother. You are out. There are two and two—four oldies but there is little possibility of entering, pushing Shyamal Da and Prateep.

Let me be lost in imagination tonight. If it's certain that a play will never be staged, it cannot be written. Leave imagination. That it is possible to write a play without visualising a stage in front of you, is beyond my understanding. That I will be able to write anything other than plays doesn't seem feasible. Gradually I am getting entangled in this.

Thirty to forty professional groups in London and Paris, stage eight shows each week—the thought makes me cry.

Learnt town planning, but no one wants it. Wrote plays, and no one wants that. Tell me, what should I do?

No, these sad things are creeping into my mind again. Let these things be for tonight.

…In the afternoon I saw a file in a shop in which separate pages of the play can be arranged together. I was just short of buying it. But thought maybe it wasn't a good idea to buy it before completing the play. Natya-Lakshmi (the goddess of money for pursuing the art of theatre) could even get angry and not let the play to be completed. Now it seems maybe it would have been better to have bought it!

LETTER
16.1.64

Manu

…Went the other day to the museum after many days. Numerous images/paintings again. Numerous colours.

…went to (watch) theatre last Sunday. To a Theatre in the Round. One theatre like this is regularly active in Paris. Gave a lecture once at the Chakra on this 'Theatre in the Round', remember? I'd seen one in London and read about it in books. The performance takes place at the centre in a circular space, surrounded by audience sitting on all four sides, as in a circus. In a way I'd just gone to see the hall. It was the story of a court-martial and if you didn't understand the language then everything was blank.

But everything wasn't blank. I understood very little of the dialogue, could only thrash out some impressions of the story. That's all. Along with that, surely some special experience. The play was adapted from English to French—*Caine Mutiny Court Martial*. Whatever points I'd heard in favour of the Theatre in the Round had only been understood theoretically. Only now did I realise how much more the audience could be involved through this medium, instead of the conventional proscenium theatre stage. No set, no stage décor. Three wooden tables, six wooden chairs, some paper, that's it. Nothing else. Even then it felt as if I was witnessing live people. Just the way I had witnessed at the Calcutta High court as jury – giving testimony, counsel and lawyer's arguments – this too was like that. I had never even imagined that actors could come so close to the audience. Yes, two things are very critical—intense acting and, you can well understand, no prompting at all.

Three hundred people can sit in the room but in no more than six rows. The actor is not far from any seat. From the third row it felt as if I was sitting in the counsel's room. The same door that lets the audience in and out before the performance is later used by the actors to enter and exit. The audience are lead from the stage itself to their seats. Stage, meaning the floor (level) itself—with a gallery of chairs laid out all around.

Naturally, that evening again went by in strange visualisations. I have laid the set for *Ebong Indrajit* on stage many times. This time I laid it in the round (in my imagination). Saw that very little space is required. And liked it too. There is no need to make Amal-Bimal-Kamal stand in a line. They can stand in a circle—that might be even better. To cut the long story short, I feel this is more effective than the regular stage. By the way, this requires a lot of thinking because there is a lot of freedom in laying out the set.

But what's the use of this visualisation? Whoever will stage *Ebong Indrajit*?

LETTER
25.2.64

Manu,
The stay in France was a long vacation. Nine months. Yet, most part of this stay was spent with a sense of a lack of time. Numerous futile thoughts and worries clogged the mind.

Watched a play in London. It was surprising. A new trend has begun on the London stage that wasn't visible five years back. It's called – *Oh! What a Lovely War* – an anti-war play. This shouldn't really be called a play because actually it isn't a play. It has a serious content but presenting it through the medium of humour, song and dance was beyond my conception. Profuse examples of serious issues presented through the medium of humour are to be found in the history of theatre – but this was unadulterated musical comedy – the lowest level of drama.

Wit is most crucial to this medium, yet the frightful absurdity of the First World War has been communicated in an extremely powerful manner. The Second World War has not been touched and there wasn't even any need to. So it feels that if this is the image of the First World War, then where will the absurdity of the Second take us?

This is not a written play. By the look of it, one understands that it has been given shape on the stage, at least most part of it. The creator of this is a middle aged woman called Joan Littlewood. Her theatre factory named Theatre Workshop is located in the workers' settlement in East End, London. I had first seen its play *The Hostage* at East End's Stratford Theatre about five years ago. It's only appropriate watching there. Saw one more – *Taste of Honey* – saw it this time. It seems that there is so much more beyond whatever we understand of theatre, whatever we have understood till now. If we think and if we do, then it's all possible to do.

Don't think that after watching this, it occurred to me to write something. Doing this kind of thing is so beyond my capacity that no ideas (come to mind) on this. Only one thing comes to mind—there is much more potential inherent in theatre than the importance I give to it. Without depending on the written play, without becoming a part of literature also, theatre can survive. That its survival is possible, is now quite apparent. As if theatre is now coming to fore as a complete art in itself. Such an unknown and wonderful face of theatre has crowded my mind that my head spins with excitement.

LETTER
1.1.64

Manu,
... after watching theatre here, it seems that the play is (meant) for acting. In the (kind of) theatre we pursue, we simply mount the play somehow, but we are not able to go beyond that. These people develop and explore the play through acting and experimentation, more than the spoken word. Surely, it's not appropriate to compare their professional stage with our amateur stage.

I went and watched Ionesco's play. Two short plays. I hadn't read either. I had read three-four other plays in English. That he is continuing to write plays without caring for old structures, contrived meanings and conventional rules had attracted me to Ionesco. At that time, one couldn't imagine that these strange/awkward plays could be meaningful when staged. On watching, I was spellbound. I understood that there are (also) people who stage such plays. And wonder of wonders, in spite of being in French it was understandable! Even laughed at some playful moments. Not on seeing others laugh, but understanding it myself.

And the hall. That too was an experience. Theatre Centre is heaven in comparison. This stage was only a little bigger than a half of that stage. After much pushing, hardly sixty seats could be accommodated in the hall. The ceiling was low, like regular houses. The painting and whitewash inside had probably not been done in the twentieth century. Seats etc., also belonged somewhat to the past century. The lobby at the entrance was tiny and then the hall was opened (to the public) only five minutes prior to the show. As a result the audience was kept waiting, standing along the passage. The show began fifteen minutes late. I was in the seventh row out of the total eleven rows. Even after getting a discount (on the ticket), I had to pay ten and a half rupees. The audience in the front row could easily rest their elbows on the stage and watch the play. I don't know if that row is the cheapest or not but thankfully, my seat wasn't there. No provision of luxuries like washrooms etc. Not even a single seat was vacant.

No set. It's already difficult to move about on such a small stage. Light—straight on and off. Characters—six in the first one and three in the second. Time—45 minutes each, so an hour and a half.

But (I) felt I would have been deprived had I not seen it.

Basically, humour has been captured. At least in these two. But humour not in any superficial way. Laughter—beyond the absurd. No hint of reality therefore; (and) even though it was satirical it is difficult to call it a satire. Since it moves towards the absurd there is no sharpness, or sense of attack; yet, some truth, a greater reality emerges from within this absurdity and confronts (us).

For the time being, I have started experiencing a certain self-satisfaction in relation to *Ebong Indrajit*—after watching theatre here. Only one mistake—that of making it serious. If it is re-written using only humour, it'll be a great job. It's not completely impossible, maybe that's (what is) appropriate. This thought came to my mind before watching Ionesco; there is proof of this in the diary entry of last November. That noting is even prior to watching *Oh! What a Lovely War*.

People in Europe have gone through the World War. They have seen many people die. Suddenly all together, many violent deaths. Even now these people live close to these sudden untimely deaths. They remember. In our world, people die of drought, disease, starvation. But we don't see, don't understand, don't even feel. Those who write don't experience that death. Those who die, don't know how to write. Here those who write, die, and those who are dead, are the ones who write. That's why it's possible to laugh at the big truth, the utter serious truth here. Not only possible, but as if that's the only way out left (now). Like if one is not very far off from death, then the luxury of tragedy becomes intolerable.

There was humour about the war in *Oh! What a Lovely War*. I was stunned at first. Now I have slowly begun to understand. A little bit. How can I understand it all? I have not seen (the) war.

The victorious juggernaut of industry and capital, the expansion of affluence covering everything—Europe's soil is being stuffed with shrubbery. The soul of Europe has become habituated to cohabit with death. And it laughs. It laughs at life because it is having to laugh at death. And it is dancing. Dancing in a frenzy, forgetting the world, having immersed itself. Our prayer dances, all-night-long dances of adivasis, aboriginal dances of Africa – whatever elements of self-immersion (are present) in these – Europe is fighting tooth and nail to acquire.

Got entangled with dance. Dance is the other side of the same thing. They don't want to think—neither about death nor about life. For those who don't have another option but to think, those who can't forget—they are laughing. The laughter of *Oh! What a Lovely War*.

It doesn't work to write at night. Scattered, mutually opposing, useless ideas. Even then, ideas. Seems as if even now they are going round in my mind. Good, I wrote *Ebong Indrajit*. *Sara Rattir*—that too was a good thing to do. *Ballabhpurer Roopkatha*, *Kobi Kahini*—there was nothing in those but even then it was good practice. Feels that I have progressed a little. Bit by bit, scattered, contradictorily—but even then I have moved a little. Amal, Bimal, Kamal and Indrajit are dancing. A choral dance. Indrajit's rhythm is a little different, a little complex. But his physics, cinema, literature, his examination, interview, office, his bride and groom, man and wife, boss and mistress, playing cards—as if everything fits into a dance drama.

Don't know if Badal Sircar will write another play or not. If he does, then that play should be one in which people laugh their hearts out. And think. And laugh even more after thinking.

DIARY
13.1.64

Why are you bent upon writing like this Badal Sircar? What is the need? Why this desperation? Do you want to run and jump time? And win? You can't. Only time will succeed.

When you just can't live without it, then write. There is no need to manufacture writing. Let go of this eccentricity of a theatre project. Forget about the Journal. Theatre, journal—there is no value of these things by themselves. They'll happen in their own time, by themselves. And then they wouldn't let you be without writing.

Not happening by itself? What do you have to do? Will you be able to fight this immense vacuum? Hasn't someone called Don Quixote attempted that already? Then why (must it be) you again?

The fight will go on anyway. Till the time you believe in living, the fight will continue. Accepting very many things and not wanting to accept many others—this is what being alive means. To be living means to accept death while not wanting to accept it. To live is to fight.

Until you finally decide to commit suicide, the fight will go on. Don't worry. What purpose is it to swing your sword in empty space? If one has to live then no worries, no fuss, no tearing hurries.

DIARY
23.01.64

Nigeria. Africa. One more continent. At least three years.

If I get it, will have to take it. Will have to understand whether I am a town planner or not. Before moving around the country in unemployment, I will have to accept the job in Nigeria if I get it.

Plays? Theatre? Chakra? Contacts? Calcutta? No solution. I have been pushed to the wall. Everything will have to be postponed for three years. For three long years.

Thoughts about Shankar churned in my head last night, after eleven. Had to wake up this morning, that's why did not linger on it longer. Today I can stay up all night. But today Nigeria has messed up everything. I am unable to think anymore today. Conversely I am thinking what will happen if I write about Shankar.

But is Shankar's story not separate from Nigeria? Shankar's story began on the first night of the journey itself.

But there is still an uncertainty. The journey is uncertain.

Who knows, by the time the journey becomes certain, it might be more difficult to write. If it becomes certain, that is.

One more picture emerged. The news of someone's suicide I read in the newspaper. Writer's imagination. First image—very first scene. After that, a woman's opinion. Second image—the second scene. Last scene—the dead man's ghost.

Twelve-thirty at night. One more evening has passed. Unproductively.

BADAL SIRCAR

Middle-Class Responsibilities

Samik Bandyopadhyay

Though it is difficult to trace a Badal Sircar style running through all the 21 plays that he mentions in the bio-data I have before me, a commitment to the milieu of educated middle-class life in Calcutta might define the common basis of almost all his plays. The choice of this particular area of experience can be explained in terms of an intellectual humility, a sense of the limits of knowledge and experience: 'I do not know the oppressed masses. I do not know the workers slaving in the coal mines. I do not know the peasant toiling in the cornfields. I do not know the *bedey*s playing with snakes, the Santhali chieftain, the fish killers of the big river. Those whom I see around me have no shape, no colour, no substance. They are undramatic. They are—Amal, Bimal, Kamal, and Indrajit.' That statement of a credo by the Lekhak in *Ebong Indrajit* provides an insight into one of the typical Badal Sircar situations—the confrontation between the structure of mediocrity and the lonely individual struggling to rise above the mundane. Sircar takes care to keep his Indrajits earth-bound in their submissions and compromises; his dreamers are not exceptional, but men slightly different. The anti-romantic sense of reality is carried into the plays in bits of irony: Indrajit's wanderlust redefined by the Lekhak as 'an *Introduction to Geography*. Recommended by the Directorate of Public Instruction as a text book for class six;' 'The Tiger's passion for knowledge delimited to a problem with simple arithmetic.' Sircar's 'other' men stand out in a spiritual non-conformism, rarely worked out into gestures or actions. *Baki Itihas* closes on Sharadindu, checked in his attempted suicide, sitting with his forehead on his 'firm wrists. His body is rigid with pain, the pain of living the rest of his life with a consciousness of the rest of history.'

Attached to the city of Calcutta in more ways than one (ranging from ancestral connections and growing up in a big house in one of the older sectors of the city, to a professional interest as a town planner), Sircar has an intimate feel of the urban conscience of this city, has a profound understanding of the middle-class intelligentsia so passionately worked up time and again over political issues and situations apparently remote, and indulging at the same time, effortlessly, in a continuum of humdrum desires and aspirations. *Ebong Indrajit, Baki Itihas, Tringsha Shatabdi* and *Shesh Nei* constitute a Calcutta quartet through which Sircar probes into the Calcutta middle-class mind. Sircar's indifference to the tradition of the professional theatre in Calcutta has proved to be an advantage; for the traditional professional theatre here has been catering for the last hundred years at least to a strangely mixed audience not particularly urban in its character. In a desire to appeal to the sentiments of those who come on short visits, to appeal to the sentiments of those in North Calcutta as part of a schedule which includes the city zoo, the city botanic, the city museum and a number of temples architecturally nondescript, the professional theatre has tried to cling to the lowest common denominator in its choice and handling of themes. Fortunately this theatre has never really existed for Sircar. His early connections with non-professional theatricals has given him almost an instinctive sense of the theatre as entertainment, but he had to forget even that before he could write *Ebong Indrajit.*

One of those theatre memories that I shall cherish for long is the first time I heard Badal Sircar give a private reading—of the play, *Ebong Indrajit.* Here was a play which was ruthlessly authentic, which reflected doubts and uncertainties that the post-World War generation shared, side by side with the more common pursuit of success; a play that I could not relate to the familiar body of Bengali plays. Introduced to

Sircar that evening, I persuaded him to read out for me and my friends all the plays he had written up to that time. *Ebong Indrajit* had virtually nothing in common with the set of early comedies that I discovered only after *Ebong Indrajit*. The comedies were consciously derived from screen comedy; and the fun lay more in elaborately contrived situations – a trio of good-natured criminals using a snake to get rid of undesirables, a scientist experimenting with an elixir that should restore youth or may be childhood and the scientist's wife taking the neighbour's child for her husband restored to childhood, and an amateur group placating an orthodox aunt who would not allow theatricals in the house – than in comic style. Sircar remains strangely earthbound even in the comedies, even when he reaches out for fantasy—in the jealous wives in *Solution X*, in the excitement and small tensions that go into the preparations for the performance in *Baro Pishima*.

Ebong Indrajit is a work of style, of levels; an area of middle-class consciousness is explored through abstractions of situations and attitudes. Sircar avoids both facile optimism and faddish pessimism, but is able to capture a more authentic state of mind—the sense of waste through which an enlightened middle-class youth passes as he fails to bridge the gap between his sense of a mission or a purpose and his life of trivialities to which he is doomed, and the consequent sense of an otherness that only lacerates him. He tries to submerge himself into the mass inertia—he tries to become a Nirmal; but he still remains different in his rejection of the grossest material values that determine the limits of the existence of his fellow beings; the Lekhak says, '... we have a road. We shall walk. I don't have anything to write, yet I shall write. You don't have anything to say. Yet you will speak. Manasi has no point in living, yet she will live. We have our road, we shall walk.' Indrajit refers to the myth of Sisyphus, but a ready identification with Camus' reinterpretation of the myth is not called for; the myth rediscovered is an element in the middle-class conscience of the urban intelligentsia, and it comes up just like that. A confrontation with a relentless reality leads to a recognition that 'we do not have a *teertha*. We have our *teerthayatra*.' Structurally *Ebong Indrajit* has a freedom in the casualness with which Sircar juxtaposes the two points of view, the poetry in Indrajit and the Lekhak sharply counter posed against the cryptic monotones of Amal, Bimal, and Kamal. The unusual structural freedom may be explained in terms of Sircar's claim that he had not conceived it as stage drama at all.

The three comedies after *Ebong Indrajit* do not seem to belong to a single phase of creativity. They represent an uncertain groping, maybe a waiting even. I consider *Ballabhpurer Roopkatha* as Sircar's best comedy. It is a spoof on ghost stories, and manages to place a 400-year-old ghost in the house of a young dentist, creating trouble for the latter by philandering with the daughter of an industrialist who is interested in buying old houses. Colloquial nuances in the references to the familiar ghost provide for quite a number of laughs; and the newly-rich industrialist's passion for old houses to prove ancestry, a passion for possession that extends even to bats and ghosts, has the necessary satiric line that adds to the richness of the comedy; the creditors dressing up as attendants to a landowner who does not afford attendants any more, bring in an element of masque which is comic in its shabbiness, its conscious derivation from the historical line in the traditional professional theatre, and the running fear that they might get caught.

Baki Itihas is Sircar's second major problem play after *Ebong Indrajit*. Basanti who is a storywriter and Sharadindu who is a lecturer in Bengali literature form a typical couple, representative of the world of the educated middle class in Calcutta. Sircar accumulates details from the elaborate arrangement of the entire flat with its kitchen, its drawing room, its dining space, the importance of the bookcase in the setting as described in the stage directions to the slight discord over an unpaid electricity bill with which the play opens. The news of a suicide by a chance acquaintance whom they remember faintly sets them on a pastime—story-writing. Thinking of spending the Sunday on an outing to the Botanics, or Diamond Harbour, or on a social call, they hit upon the least troublesome alternative of all—writing stories on a suicide, speculating on the reasons that must have been there. The two stories are theatrically presented in the same manner: while Basanti's story is obviously Ibsenic, Sharadindu's is of a sensational-psychological kind: they quarrel over the merits of the stories; and there is irony in the way the death of a man provide matters for light-hearted literary conversation with the inevitable suggestion of a common tendency towards self-centered indifference to the world outside. The last Act is a confrontation between Sharadindu and the dead Seetanath. Sircar does not try to rationalise the encounter; for all practical purposes, it is an encounter between two living men and at the same time a confrontation between two Sharadindus, the public self and the private self. Seetanath hands Sharadindu an album of pictures culled from newspapers – a parallel to Sharadindu's own collection of newspaper clippings (in his case of news and editorials) – and Sharadindu discovers a whole history of oppression and torture and cruelty – from the myths to history, from the building of the pyramids, the Christians thrown to the lions, the German concentration camps, to Hiroshima and Vietnam – 'the rest of history.'

Sharadindu says, 'History is not this.' Seetanath banters, 'What is history? A history of passing examinations? The comfort in the company of a lively bright and enthusiastic wife?' Seetanath challenges him, 'What about the rest of history?' Sharadindu cries out, 'But what can I do about it?' Seetanath's tone is now different, cold and quiet:

> No. You can't do anything. I couldn't do anything. Nobody can do anything. Oppressions, killings, riots, wars – all these will continue, men will commit these – yet man has nothing to do. The man who is satisfied with two meals a day will pierce another man with a bayonet. The scientists who cannot bear the pain of an animal will create a weapon to kill a million people. They are all men. Like you. Like me. They have all tried to live on one or another meaning they have given to life.

Seetanath finds an absurdity in a life of continued custom, a life blind to concern and responsibility and asks Sharadindu a question that he has already asked Seetanath. 'Why have you not committed suicide?' And Sharadindu tells Seetanath in a moment of intense drama, 'Go away, Sharadindu'; and Seetanath has to remind him, 'I'm

Seetanath.' Sharadindu makes the same movements as made by the two Seetanaths in the two stories—preparations for a suicide. But the drama comes full circle with Basudeva's entrance with the news that Sharadindu is finally going to become an assistant professor, a promotion. Sharadindu tries to come back to the security of his reality, in the last few minutes of the play. Sharadindu is torn desperately between his craving for contentment and his sense of 'the rest of history.'

Structurally *Baki Itihas* achieves a peculiar tension between the apparently regular construction framed within a typical Sunday with the reference to a party in the evening and Basudeva bringing the news of the promotion on his way back from the party and the disturbing pattern of reality and an objectification of conscience confronting each other. The point of the play reaches the spectator or reader more sharply through that tension.

Badal Sircar's statement of the 'philosophy' of *Tringsha Shatabdi* as 'the responsibility of all mankind for the events of our times' (as quoted by E. Alkazi in his director's notes in the brochure for the Dishantar production of *Hiroshima)* links *Baki Itihas, Tringsha Shatabdi,* and *Parey Kono Din (Sometime, Later).* On his return from Nigeria in 1967, I remember Sircar describing the three as a trilogy, and in the first reading of *Tringsha Shatabdi* Sharadindu and Basanti reappearing as the central couple. While *Baki Itihas* probes into the first strings of a reawakened conscience, *Tringsha Shatabdi* takes it a step further in the intellectual exploration of the reality, in the investigation. My latest interview with Sircar gave me the impression that *Tringsha Shatabdi* originated as a documentary play, which he framed with a 'quotation' from Sartre's *The Condemned of Altona,* a 'quotation' in terms of the drama that underscores the point of responsibility, and brings in at the same time the international relevance of this attitude of responsibility, and can draw in for the more sensitive reader or spectator associations from Hochhuth's, *The Deputy* or Miller's *After the Fall* or Weiss' *The Investigation.* Sircar thoroughly resents now any overemphasis on the documentation at the cost of the local and contemporary relevance. In the choice of his witnesses for the

Hiroshima catastrophe Sircar is careful to choose only those (with the exception of Einstein, who provides a necessary climax to the series of 'appearances') who were cogs in the insensate machinery or the victims and who share in common with their middle-class 'judges' a blind helplessness, the incapacity and powerlessness to check the ruthless course of institutionalised and organised and politicalised violence or torture. Sircar manages to suggest the sheer size of the crisis and its aftermath and yet keep it within human dimensions, within individualised modes of suffering enabling a redefinition of the issue in strikingly everyday middle-class terms:

> You and I are passengers in a bus, backseat customers. The driver drives on recklessly at a speed of eighty miles per hour. But we don't have the right to tell him: 'Soft, keep your eyes open. There's a child crossing! Be careful!' We don't have the right to ask him whether he has a licence, whether he is sane. We have to look out of the window all the time, keep our eyes away, and say, 'How beautiful!'

Porey Kono Din, Sircar's only science fiction play, gives the Hiroshima experience another dimension, the issue of responsibility a further complexity, as the playwright brings back a group of travellers from the future to study human suffering in a village destroyed by a meteor in 1926. One of the travellers – Clea – experiences pity as she falls in love with the young protagonist of the play. But there is something inevitable and inescapable in time past—a subtle variation of that sense of helplessness and inertia that a tension between Serin, who hears a music in suffering and is fascinated, and Shankar who must stand in the ruins and the flames crying and speaking in starts:

> If I ... If ... I knew ... knew somehow ... maybe ... I could have checked it ... stopped it ... somehow. Or some thing ... I could have done, could have held ... them ... forced them ... so that ... so that there would have been ... at least not that amount ... that amount of suffering ... something ... ohh ... I'll ...

> write it down; I'll tell people … tell people … tell everyone. This time … I couldn't do anything … now … the people … tell everyone. … This … time … I … couldn't do anything … now … the people now … they can't be saved. But later … later someday … in the future … later … later sometime … later, sometime …

Stylistically, *Porey Kono Din* is the first Badal Sircar play with a strong non-verbal content; the crisscrossing of the two segments of time and the fictional content of the future make the mundane colloquialism that Sircar handles with such precision elsewhere ineffective. Language wise, he breaks the colloquialism with an offstage narration by the protagonist himself in a chaste formal language (in Bengali sharply different from the colloquial in the separate forms of the verbs), which serves to bring in a tone of history, impersonal and formal and past-oriented. Sircar exploits the magical properties inherent in a fictional future in a recourse to the cinematic:

> Clea's hand on handle - reposing on the surface of the door. A well-built arm, sparking in the light. A moment. Then Clea, she passes the door in calm measured steps;

or—

> …as Shankar descended into the spell, the lights had started taking on a smoky tint. The room almost dark. Shankar and Clea were floating on the dim light. Now it went totally dark. Shankar comes upon Clea listening to Serin's recording of the music of suffering in the Great London Fire of 1664. The window was no longer there.
>
> The wall was lost in a thick spiral of fog—a spiral of innumerable moving shadowy figures. Only shapes, no clear images. The moving shapes rolled and disintegrated and turned, one after another, in the moving spiral of fog, they merged into the music of sounds, into the shrill cry to build an image of the final and ultimate catastrophe. The world was sinking in the overwhelming horror manifest in the shadows, dances, sounds,

> and music mixed up with the agonized writhing of the human race and its shrieks distorted by pain.

Badal Sircar has a personal way of treating foreign plays that come his way; he has never tried to adapt a play in the sense plays are adapted in Indian languages from foreign sources. He prefers describing these plays as 'inspired by' rather than adaptations of the original plays. He does not keep the play by him when he works on the derived play and depends on his memory or an early reading; a method that allows him greater creative freedom.

This is the approach that has gone into *Baagh* from Murry Schisgal's *The Tiger*, *Jodi Aar Ekbaar* from J.M. Barrie's *Dear Brutus*, and *Pralaap* from James Saunders' *Next Time I'll Sing to You*. In these plays he allows a crust of foreignness in the circumstances. In the kind of communication into which the characters enter, and in the very central experiences—a man acting like a tiger to kidnap a girl and then submitting to the girl; a spirit giving a group of characters a second chance to organise their lives and the characters remaining equally discontented in their new relationships, and a group of actors improvising a play which tries to be ruthlessly objective but the experience turning out to be one of disconnected tensions and sheer tomfoolery.

While *Baagh* and *Pralaap* touch connections in contemporary reality, *Jodi Aar Ekbaar* (*If There Was Another Chance*) remains in a sweet never-never world made more obvious in the common speech verse of the characters, and the more rhythmical chants of the Buddha Jin, a mythical child dressed up as an old man appearing on horseback and speaking most of the time to percussion *bol*s of a particularly lively kind.

These 'derivations' show a greater concern with style while the issues are only lightly touched; while a strong intellectual passion tears its way through the form itself in the problem plays concerned with suffering and responsibility, the group of 'derived' plays use conscious stylisation or carefully modulated and worked out disruptions and conventional structure.

Interview with Badal Sircar

Samik Bandyopadhyay: In the first place, how did you come to playwriting?

Badal Sircar: Quite early in my life I came to prefer plays to other forms of literature. Right from my days in school, I was a prolific reader of plays. My readings in drama covered a wide range—from the Bengali classics of Girishchandra Ghosh, Kshirodeprasad Vidyavinode, and Dwijendralal Roy to Bernard Shaw and Galsworthy. One of my earliest exercises in playwriting was an adaptation of Galsworthy's *Roof* in 1945.

I had little direct experience, however, of the theatre as performance on the professional plane. As a student I had not seen a single professional performance. In the fifties (1950s), I saw two productions by Sisirkumar Bhadury –*Sadhabar Ekadashi* and *Michael Madhusudan* – inadequate as productions, but redeemed by great acting. The one thing I really liked was Manoranjan Bhattacharya's performance as Rammanikya in the former. As an actor, I acquired some experience as a comedy actor in domestic theatricals, and tried my hand at adaptations from stories. I came to have a really positive interest in playwriting only in the early fifties, when I came to act in amateur groups. *Solution X*, virtually my first worthwhile play, came in 1956. It was directly inspired by a film I had seen – *Monkey Business.* I had seen it only once and had missed most of the dialogue, a factor that proved to be advantageous, for I had to write my own dialogues. It was an exercise in bringing a plot with a wide span into the limits of a single set.

In 1957, I went abroad for the first time, and was exposed to a rich field of theatre. In the UK I saw two Joan Littlewood productions—*The Hostage* and *A Taste of Honey.* (And) *Long Day's Journey into Night* with Alec Clunes as the Father, *Party* with Charles Laughton, *Duel of the Angels* with Vivien Leigh, and phenomenal hits like *My Fair Lady, Irma La Douce* and *The Mouse Trap.* On my return in 1959, I became more active in the theatre—acting, writing and directing plays for Chakra, a group some of us had set up in 1960. In the plays I wrote around this time, I had the thought at the back of my mind that I had to feed the theatre in which I could work. But I never really tailored my plays to suit the resources of Chakra.

Bandyopadhyay: How would you assess your early plays?

Sircar: *Baro Pishima,* written in 1959, has proved to be quite popular with various amateur companies. But I have never thought highly of it. It has an authentic atmosphere of the theatre about it as its redeeming grace. *Samavritta,* my only crime play, was inspired by the film version of *Scapegoat,* in which I had missed the dialogue again.

Bandyopadhyay: How did you come to write *Ebong Indrajit,* which is such a sharp departure from the line of your earlier plays?

Sircar: All the poems in *Ebong Indrajit* (except *Keno tumi haanchbe? Keno tumi kashbe?* Why would you sneeze? Why would you cough?) were written in London in 1957-59, almost as a diary. The play was written in Calcutta in 1962, but in the same spirit. I had not conceived it as a play; it was almost a private piece of writing, and a temperamental predilection for the dramatic determined its form. Even after I had finished it, or even when you took away a script to have it published for the first time in Bohurupee, I never considered it stageable. As a matter of fact, I produced *Samavritta,* after I had completed the play *Ebong Indrajit.*

Bandyopadhyay: How was *Baki Itihas* written?

Sircar: I know you think a lot of *Baki Itihas,* but it is not one of my favourites. I haven't read the play after December 1965, when I read it out to Sombhu Mitra and his company. I don't feel like reading it. And if I have the choice, I'd always prefer reading out *Sara Rattir* to reading *Baki Itihas.* In Nigeria, planning a short vacation in Calcutta, I thought of taking back something for my friends, and I wanted to write a play. Kurosawa's *Rashomon* inspired the basic idea of a number of versions of the same situation. But I almost gave up the play after having completed the first episode. A friend liked the incomplete script, and I came back to the play after a long gap of time. I had to reject the first draft of the second episode. But then the going was smoother. *Baki Itihas* was difficult writing.

Bandyopadhyay: I remember you were back in Calcutta for a few months in 1965, and you read out *Baagh* to me a day or two before you left Calcutta to go back to Nigeria again.

Sircar: I had read Murray Schisgal's *The Tiger* and *The Typist* in Nigeria, and had once thought of adapting the former. But I could not imagine fitting it into a Bengali context. Back in Calcutta on a vacation in 1965 I saw the Nandikar production of *Phool Phootuk na Phootuk,* an adaptation of the last act of Wesker's *Roots.* It was not perfectly transplanted to the Bengali context, it remained incongruous in parts, and yet it clicked. That reassured me. If this was permissible, why should I not try? I did not have Schisgal's play before me when I wrote *Baagh* in Calcutta. I'm not sure whether you would call it an adaptation, or a play inspired by the Schisgal play.

Bandyopadhyay: Back in Nigeria, you had one of the busiest phases of playwriting.

Sircar: On my return to Nigeria I found that my attitude to playwriting had changed. On my short visit to Calcutta, I had found *Ebong Indrajit* being staged with commercial success and directors interested in my work. Sombhu Mitra had already taken up *Baki ltihas,* there was a demand for my plays. In the past I could leave an unfinished play lying about. But now that would not do. That would explain the prolific playwriting – six plays, of which the first four came in the first three months – in 1966-67 in Nigeria.

Bandyopadhyay: Did you come to have a greater interest in form from your greater involvement in playwriting? How otherwise would you explain the various kinds of plays you wrote in this phase—a documentary play, a science fiction, a verse drama…?

Sircar: I have never tried to experiment with forms for their own sake, or try to work in a variety of forms. For me, the theme has always dictated the form. But the process has never been quite simple. For example, I had liked Maxwell Anderson's verse plays *High Tor* and *Winterset;* written poetry myself between 1943 and 1957 and felt quite confident in handling verse. But I had to wait till I had found my theme in *Dear Brutus* before I could write *Jodi Aar Ekbaar*. In James Saunders' *Next Time I'll Sing to You,* what I appreciated was the possibility of a play without a story. In fact, I have never been able to build a story. The only original story I have ever handled is *Kobi Kahini,* and I still wonder how I made it. But once I had adapted Saunders's structure in *Pralaap,* it came to reflect my philosophy, not Saunders'. I discovered for myself the possibility of communicating serious thought and ideas through humour. If people had cared to enjoy the play without searching for meanings, they would have found the meanings alright.

Bandyopadhyay: *Tringsha Shatabdi* in 1966 was a more committed play than your more sceptical earlier works.

Sircar: In Nigeria I read *Formula for Death: E=mc²,* and thought that this book should be translated; people had to be made aware of the gruesome implications of the Hiroshima experience. But I have never liked translating. In the mid-1950s I had served on a jury, and the idea of a courtroom drama had haunted me ever since. I conceived my organisation of the Hiroshima facts in terms of a courtroom play. I wanted to emphasise the relevance of those facts to an average contemporary Bengali: that would explain the Bengali context. I thought of it as a sequel to *Baki ltihas;* you will remember the characters had the same names Sharadindu and Basanti, when I first read out the play to you. I had never thought it could be staged, even though some of you had talked of such possibilities after my first reading.

Bandyopadhyay: *Shesh Nei* was your last original play. After a reading of the play, you told some of us, 'It *is* a punch of *Ebong lndrajit, Baki ltihas,* and *Tringsha Shatabdi*'. What did you really mean?

Sircar: That statement has caused a lot of misunderstanding by now. I'd like to clarify. *Ebong Indrajit* is in a sense a personal play. While it would not be true to say that Indrajit is Badal Sircar, it would be futile to deny the affiliations it has with me. I had isolated a part of myself, almost in a scientific and philosophic manner and exaggerated it to a point of intensity. Hence it does not express the whole of me or us, but retains an authentic connection with my personal history. *Baki Itihas* is rooted in a similar isolation and intensification. It concentrates on the question of guilt that has no place in *Ebong Indrajit*. Its third Act has something of Indrajit. If I ever rewrite the play, I'd like to change it, to concentrate on the guilt. *Tringsha Shatabdi* moves from the question of guilt to that of responsibility, from facing guilt consciously to a recognition of responsibility, as evident in the very central act of sitting in judgment. In all the three plays I had treated segments of a single human experience, but all the time I had desired to capture within the scope of a play the entire experience.

I captured a complete image of my past in *Circus*. But it came out rather crudely and ungrammatically. *Shesh Nei* was a revised and diluted version; at the same time it was more theatric. To the treatment of guilt and responsibility it brought the concrete nearness of total man; it humanised the abstract issues to a far greater extent. While *Ebong Indrajit* dealt only with reactions and effects, *Shesh Nei* could project more of a single, sentient man. It explored the same pattern of a development of consciousness in Sumanta's commitment at the end. But the sharp point of the earlier plays had to be abandoned to project a wider totality.

Bandyopadhyay: From your last play *Sagina Mahato,* it seems you are more interested in the moment in nonverbal and visual values, in theatric values to be more precise, than in idea or the merely dramatic.

Sircar: My first experience of the Theatre-in-the-Round in London in 1957-58, and again in France in 1963, gave me a vague feeling that this was better theatre than the proscenium-bound theatre. The closeness of the spectators was the first point in favour of this theatre. A number of factors – my exposure to the works of Joan Littlewood *(Oh! What a Lovely War)*, the Theatre on the Taganka Square in Moscow, and Jerzy Grotowski in Poland, my conversations with my filmmaker friend Barin Saha, and a number of books – led me on to think in terms of a consciously theatrical theatre, consciously opposed to the cinematic and (made me) more conscious of fundamental theatric values and a more intimate theatre at the same time. My thinking on these lines was further clarified when I had to give a long series of radio talks from the Calcutta centre of All India Radio, and I decided to give a series on the theatrical theatre. I thought of doing *Sagina Mahato* in the round, only after I had completed the script; after a few proscenium performances by my own company Satabdi, I tried it out in the round for the first time on 24 October 1971; and a single performance proved my thesis.

An audience of slightly more than a hundred people sat around us, as we performed on the floor. We could see all our spectators; we could touch them if we wanted to. At times we moved in from their sides, or even went behind them. I must say I have never felt such silence or concentration on the part of the audience. At one point the lights fused; the actors went on in the dark; the hall lights came after 30 seconds—a few neon tubes, inadequate for a stage performance. The acting continued in this for five minutes before the stage lights came back again. Yet all this time the audience retained its concentration; there was not a murmur, there was not a sound of someone fidgeting in his chair. If there had been the least of a sound, we could not miss it: we were too near our spectators! At the end of the performance not a single spectator mentioned the mishap. That first experience has given me enough courage to continue my work in this area of the theatre. Even if I am wrong, I can explore it; I can justify my work in the theatre only when I am able to do something that no one else is trying to do at the moment.

Bandyopadhyay: What are you working on at the moment? Any new play?

Sircar: It's a new project. I'm planning an intimate theatre in Calcutta – a small theatre, which will be a rendezvous till one hour before the daily evening performance – (serve as both) meeting place and a theatre. The chairs will be rearranged in that one hour for a performance in the round. I have visualised the project in great detail; some funds and all kinds of assistance will be necessary initially; but with a slight push at the beginning, I'm sure it will be a tangible and useful and effective proposition. The entire project, as I conceive it, is an exciting endeavour to make the theatre a more intimate and informal experience. I expect no profits financially, but a lot in terms of more meaningful theatre activity.

Published in Sangeet Natak – *Issue no. 22, 1971*
Journal of the Sangeet Natak Akademi
Courtesy: Natarang Pratishthan Archives

THE THEATRE OF BADAL SIRCAR

Sumanta Bannerjee

I

> I do not want to accept the notion that we Bengalis are fond of weeping and ashamed of laughing. On the contrary, I want to say—we can laugh even at moments of extreme pain, we can express the greatest tragedy by means of laughter, we can present the most complex problem through laughter and come to terms with it. The value of laughter to me is therefore not at all insignificant. If laughter is healthy, if I can make others laugh without resorting to mere buffoonery, mannerisms or grimaces, I do not think such laughter can be pointless …
>
> **Badal Sircar**

Badal Sircar's foray into the theatre world began with comedies. I remember having seen the first public production of his play almost forty years ago—way back in September 1960, when his *Baro Pishima* (written in 1958) was staged in a hall in Calcutta. A humorous comedy of situations, the play was produced by Chakra, a group which was brought together by Sircar, with the help of his friends and relations. The following year, the same group staged *Solution X*, another hilarious comedy written by Sircar in 1956. At around the same time he came out with two more comedies – *Shonibar* (1959) and *Ram-Shyam-*

Jadu (1961) – and he never gave up his penchant for light-hearted comedies. He could explore the agonising process of self-discovery of a young couple in *Sara Rattir,* while at the same time write a boisterous play about the ludicrousness of a bunch of eccentric characters in a dilapidated mansion in *Ballabhpurer Roopkatha*—both written in the same year, 1963. In fact, the sense of the comic never allowed Sircar to remain grim even in his serious drama. It is lit up by flashes of witty dialogues or surprising twists of incongruous situations. The heavy dish of the metaphysical anguish in *Ebong Indrajit* is peppered with the light-hearted spicy comments of Amal, Bimal and Kamal. The funereal gloom hanging over the characters in *Pagla Ghoda* is lifted occasionally by the breeze of the smutty jokes exchanged by them over drinks. The comic came back in its own right in Badal Sircar's later plays written in the 1970-80 period, which saw the beginning of a new phase: the Third Theatre. In the plays of this genre, he brought a hard glitter to the comic, which earlier he had treated with romantic delicacy. There is a bitter mixture of savage humour and serious political discourse in these plays.

The comic in theatre fascinated Sircar from his childhood. As he narrates his earliest memories of the Bengali plays of D.L. Roy, Girish Ghosh and Kshirodeprasad Vidyavinode, which he read as a young boy, he tells us that the humorous characters in these play struck him most. As he grew up he was drawn, among others, to the comedies of Shakespeare, Sheridan, Shaw, and Moliere.

When he began to write plays, it was this tradition of the gaiety of the old comedy that influenced him to a great extent. His earlier comedies were written in the 1950s. The locations and the characters were from the Calcutta middle-class milieu. The primary objective was to provide social entertainment and relaxation in those environs. In fact, Sircar's first theatre group, Chakra, grew out of his amateur activities in staging plays with friends and neighbours in a housing complex in Entally in East Calcutta, where he was living in the early 1950s. The plot of one of his first comedies, *Baro Pishima*, is about preparations for staging a play by young residents of such a middle-class urban housing complex. While preparing the staging, everything goes awry with the arrival of the baro pishima, or the eldest aunt of the girl who is to act in the role of the heroine. The aunt is an overbearing prude who would not hear of her niece acting on the stage. The entire comedy of *Baro Pishima* hinges on the ingenious manipulation of a series of intricate situations to hoodwink the domineering lady, and finally ends with the winning over of the aunt. It is the stock plot of old comedies—a story of funny and surprising situations, the suspense about the unpredictable, the overcoming of difficulties, and the denouncement with the reward of worthiness in the form of the engagement between the heroine and her secret admirer. But Sircar works off this plot by giving it a new twist. On the stage itself, he brings the theatre in confrontation with a real-life situation, where the characters also have to play-act at another level. The intrigues that go on behind the scenes of a play within the play form the staple of *Baro Pishima*.

It is interesting to note that Sircar returns to this play-within-a-play device in his later comedies too. The cast appearing on the stage play dual roles—one for the audience, and another for the characters in the play. Thus, in *Ballabhpurer Roopkatha* (1963), an eccentric businessman wants to buy a house that will have to be old and look dilapidated. And for good measure, he is prepared to add more to the price if it is a haunted one! The hero, who owns such a house, in order to impress the buyer, knocks together a mini-play, where his friend pretends to be the manager of his estate, and his servant and neighbours his retinue.

Similarly, in *Ram-Shyam-Jadu* (1961), the gang of three robbers, pretend to be what they are not, and end up by acting as the benefactors of the victim whom they initially wanted to rob. In *Solution X,* again, at a certain stage the characters deviate from their defined roles, and act as children, albeit unwittingly. A drug for metamorphosis (called 'Solution X' in the play and meant to make people young) invented by a forgetful middle-aged scientist, creates boisterous havoc in his life as well as that of his wife and other associates. As in *A Midsummer Night's Dream*, they change for a brief while. The drug makes them behave like children as long as its effects last, making them unaware of the hilarious effects that their bedlam has on the other characters in the play. The twist is at the end, when it is discovered that the change in the behaviour pattern of these characters is not due to the original Solution X as invented by the scientist, but to an accidental mix of the chemicals which was brought about by his little son while playing in his laboratory.

Social concerns also keep cropping up in the middle of these fantastic situations. As early as 1959, Sircar wrote *Shonibar*, where a middle-class clerk, burdened with office work, passes through alternate phases of fantasies about promotion in office and nightmares about retrenchment. In *Kobi Kahini* (1964), the spectators see the lineaments of contemporary society, where a poor school teacher gets bewildered by the chicanery of self-seeking rival politicians during an election, and is soon embroiled in their petty trickeries. In these comedies the comic becomes something more than mere humorous exaggeration, and it approaches the level of the serious, where no careful spectator can fail to read the bitter cynicism under the mask of the comic—a mood that was to return with a sharper political perspective in the later phase of Sircar's 'Third Theatre.'

Sircar most often deals with stock situations and stereotypes as characters in these plays. At exactly the proper moment, coincidences and accidents happen; the characters display their appropriate faculties, and all ends as it should happen. He uses the all too familiar devise of intrigues to keep the audience in suspense and lead them on to the happy ending. But it is his acute observation of contemporary types in Bengali middle-class society, combined with superb theatrical dexterity and brilliant wit, that have made this group of lightweight comedies a durable part of the Bengali stage.

II

> ... I have composed three plays in my life, during the writing of which the feelings and views were quite different from those experienced when conceiving my other plays. It was as if I was writing [these three plays] in a delirious mood of giddy rapture without planning any direction for their development. As if a ghost was shaking me by my neck and making me write. From this point of view – whatever the

critics might say – these plays have a different meaning for me. The three plays are: *Ebong Indrajit, Sara Rattir* and *Pagla Ghoda.*

Badal Sircar

Ebong Indrajit (written in 1963, but published for the first time in 1965) established Badal Sircar in the Indian theatre with his own brand of drama of ideas, written in a style which was to be his characteristic. It was to be the forerunner of a series of plays composed during the next decade or so, the dominant preoccupation of which was the crises of middle-class values in the 1960s. Moving beyond this was the disconcerting awareness of the predicament of a human existence which was out of harmony with its surroundings.

The ideas that recur in these plays have an almost obsessive air about them, like Pirandello's passionate insistence on a few favourite themes. Sircar's plots centre around the fundamental human paradox of ambitious aspirations and pitiful limitations; the unequal contest between the individual rebel and the inhospitable universe; the tragic split between freedom and intellectual integrity on the one hand and love on the other; loneliness; role of memory in life; guilt and responsibility for past deeds; and the ever present haunting fear of the nuclear blast that will put an end to the world. All these ideas are shot through with doubts and questionings. They suggest the impossibility of defining reality, or pinning down individual characters, and challenge the prevailing concepts of order and stability. They also raise a fundamental question that relates to the theatrical depletion of the tragic hero or heroine. Does the fatal flaw that makes the tragedy inevitable in their lives lie in themselves, or in the circumstances in which they happen to be situated?

These ideas shape the form of Sircar's plays of this period. The theatrical conventions of the naturalistic drama are destroyed. In keeping with the nature of these ideas which stress contradictions, uncertainty and the tragic-comic absurdity of human life, all semblance of logical construction, of the rational linking of idea with idea in a sequential structure, is almost abandoned. Instead, the irrationality of experience is transferred to the stage. Events change, but the characters (of the cast enacting their roles) remain the same, merely changing their names. Sometimes they move through mechanical, machine-like repetitions of actions and utterances – symbols of the dehumanising process of the industrial – commercial value system. He adopts devices like the play-within-the-play, the play-outside-the-play, breaking into long dramatic poetry, etc.

An important aspect of the formalistic innovations in the plays of this period is the use of dramatic monologues in verse. Having written poetry in the past, Badal Sircar found it easy to solve some of the problems of speech in verse. This was also in keeping with the past tradition in the Bengali stage, where characters often broke into the verbal rhetoric of poetic dialogues or soliloquies at crucial dramatic moments. By bringing back poetry to the theatre after many decades, Sircar to some extent was also satisfying the cravings of an audience that had been brought up on the vacuous formality of rigid prose in the theatre for much too long. Sircar's monologues in verse are of course totally different from the high-pitched melodramatic outpourings of the romantic characters of the late nineteenth-early twentieth century Bengali plays which are still popular on the commercial stage. He expresses individual and social concerns in a poetic idiom which has rhythm that is close to contemporary speech. The sudden switch from prose dialogue to verse reflects the shift of mood and feeling of the character. Very often such poetic shifts are meant to help the audiences to share the ambience of the dark labyrinths of the human soul which only poetry can express, or understand the symbols of fantasy through which the plays speak at a certain stage.

Those who were acquainted with the contemporary western philosophical trends and the new theatre movement that was developing under their influence in Europe in the 1950-60 period, might have found the presentation of these ideas and the dramatic devices chosen by Badal Sircar in his plays to express them, rather blasé or unoriginal. The theories of existentialism of Sarte and Camus were already familiar to the Calcutta Coffee House regulars. The Theatre of the Absurd had arrived, and the plays of Beckett, lonesco, Adamov and Genet had reached the bookstalls. In fact, in 1965 (the year when Sircar was writing *Ebong Indrajit*), Mohit Chattopadhyay came out with his first absurd play *Kanthanalite Surya*, where the hero imagines that a sun has got stuck in his windpipe and he cannot bring it out—symbolising a mediocre person who imagines that he has all the qualities of a genius within himself, but cannot express them. The Calcutta theatre-lovers, therefore, were familiar with the arguments that Sircar posed in *Ebong Indrajit*. When towards the end of the play, Indrajit compared his efforts to the futile attempts of Sisyphus to lift the huge stone to the mountain top from where it always rolls down, the discerning spectators could immediately get the message and trace its source in Camus' *Le Mythe de Sisyphe*. Even the theatrical devices were old hat. The play within-the-play, the symbols and the fantasies, the poetic monologues, were worn out in the West—what with the experiments made a year ago by Maeterlinck and Pirandello in devising techniques to express their metaphysical idea, or by Eliot, Auden and Isherwood in their poetic drama.

Thus, it appears to us today as if Sircar was again using the same stock plots and stereotypes as he had earlier used in his comedies. While in the past they were borrowed from the old English and continental plays and earlier Bengali theatre, in his serious plays the situations, the characters and their dialogues seemed to be modelled on the ideas of contemporary European philosophy and dramatic literature.

But as with his comedies, even in these serious plays of his, Sircar brought in a new abiding flavour where the hands of a superb playwright and theatrical technician were evident. The theatrical speech was at once colloquial and poetic. The handling of the situations was ingenious and innovative. The characters in these plays were located in the urban Bengali middle-class environment of the 1960s—a period which was an important watershed in the history of post–Independence Bengal. Although Sircar's ideas might have been influenced by the West, the concerns and anxieties that they expressed were authentic, since they were being experienced by a generation of perceptive youth in Bengal, as also in other parts of India at that time. All these shook the Indian theatre goers into a new realisation of the possibilities of the drama as a means of expressing the complex spiritual anguish of the times. As Satyadev Dubey was to explain later, while describing the impact of

Ebong Indrajit on the audience: '... It was about the Indian reality as they knew it, was a theatrically effective and crystallized projection of all the prevalent attitudes, vague feelings and undefined frustrations gnawing at the hearts of the educated urban middle class.'

Let us get back to the historical context when these plays were being written and staged—first in Calcutta, and later in other metropolitan cities (during the late 1960s–early 1970s period). More than a decade after Independence, the 1960s appeared to the urban Indian middle-class as an age that offered too much for a few instead of enough for the many. The idealism of the years immediately following Independence had dissipated and degenerated into corruption among the political leaders and cynicism among the common people. A generation of unemployed educated youth had grown up finding their ideals and hopes crashing in disappointments. It was not merely a question of jobs for them. It was a crisis of values. As in other parts of India, in Bengal also they were torn between the norms of moral integrity and responsibility, with which they grew up as children in their middle-class homes in the 1940-50 period on the one hand, and the new norms of unscrupulousness that they were required to follow in their youth to survive in the commercial world of the 1960s on the other. Here they had to come to terms with bribery, nepotism and various other forms of corruption. Those who could not cope with these came to feel that they were unnecessary, unwanted and useless, whether in their homes, or in their careers, or in their personal relationships. A sense of utter loneliness and inexplicable alienation gripped them. Yet, their hopes and desires were still glowing like dying embers.

It was this generation that discovered in Badal Sircar's *Ebong Indrajit* an indigenously designed experimental drama that gave voice to their inarticulate cries, and a certain shape to their confused ideas. Indrajit and his friends pass through various stages of life—from classrooms to office corridors. For Amal, Bimal, Kamal and others, there is safety only in conformity and obedience, in comfortable jobs and common-place marriages. They are caught in the web of defined roles, where they accept everything – from consumerism to corruption – without questioning their dehumanising effects. Indrajit cannot fit himself into their roles. Unlike the heroes of romantic drama, or political agit-prop plays, Indrajit does not convert Amal, Bimal and others to his views. He remains an individual rebel who struggles against obedience and conformity and wants to pass beyond the circle of routine. In the course of this unequal struggle between himself and the hostile environment, Indrajit himself changes. In the end, he emerges as a more discerning, intellectual and undaunted human being. Though he may never see his dream of a world made after man's desires, he rides on his dream. He ascends for the sheer exhilaration of the ride, not for reaching the destination. The playwright, who is a character in *Ebong Indrajit*, and acts as Indrajit's alter-ego while writing a play about him, ends by defining the role for the hero: 'Remember—it is not the pilgrimage, but the road to the pilgrimage which is our destiny.'

The appeal of Badal Sircar's plays of this period among the perceptive sections of the Indian urban middle-class audience, lay in his ability to rescue some pattern and significance for human life out of the utterly dismal scene of disillusionment and failure that surrounded that audience. The adventure of self-discovery through confrontation with the grim reality, and defiance of it at every stage, was projected by Sircar as the individual rebel's only way of triumphing over the hurdles created by society.

We meet such a war-worn rebel in the old man in *Sara Rattir* (1963). He has faced human destiny at its worst, challenged its malevolence, and gazed steadily at the heart of the pain. In his own words: 'All through the night, I have remained awake, have watched, have learnt…I have sharpened my two eyes on the whetstone [of experiences] and made them razor-edged. Being on my guard against dreams, I have remained alert, awake all night with my two sharp eyes open.' In his isolated house there arrives a young married couple during a stormy night, seeking shelter from the rain. The two are tied together, yet kept apart by their different versions of love and freedom, and isolated by moral emptiness. The old man's razor-sharp probe cuts through the façade of their domestic peace. Under his sad and relentless questioning, the two discover each other and realise how distant they are. The woman becomes aware of the emptiness that gnaws at her heart, her tiredness with comfort and peace in her home and her restless desire for a glimpse of bliss. She experiences a few moments of ecstasy when she discovers herself and articulates her deepest desires in the company of the old man during that night. But bliss cannot co-exist with peace for long. It evaporates with the end of the rain and the breaking of dawn. She has to come back to the mundane world and return to her home with her husband. But she will remember this night forever. She will treasure those moments of self-awareness.

It is this sudden insight into the undiscovered aspects of one's existence during a particular experience that jolts another couple in *Baki Itihas* (1965). After reading an account of a suicide in a newspaper, the husband and the wife imagine various possibilities that could have led to the suicide. Each decides to write separate versions, the wife stressing the financial and emotional problems of a middle-class home as possible reasons for the suicide, and the husband, being of an intellectual bent, discovering a morbid psychology behind the act. But there can be other reasons beyond these individual *itihas* (or the 'other history') which are beyond the history of the petty interests that shape the views of life of the middle-class couple, and that lead them to write their stories—the history oppression of mankind, of slavery, of Hitler's persecution of the Jews, of Hiroshima, of Vietnam. By introducing this wider dimension of world history, Sircar seeks to lift his audience to the higher plane of social and political criticism.

The issue of suicide comes up again in *Pagla Ghoda* (1967) where the characters explode into flashes of agonising self-confession in the span of a single night. Four men sit over drinks in a hovel in a cremation ground, keeping vigil over the burning body of a girl whom they had brought there for cremation. There is a play of reality and illusion, with the dead girl appearing in the midst of their talks and reminding them of their past guilt and responsibility in relation to their respective women lovers. These women were let down by the men and driven to death. Recalling these relationships in their lives, the characters in the play fight between themselves over claims of innocence and a sense of guilt, moments of self-swindling and self-confession. At the end the dead girl reappears. Unlike the women in the lives of these characters, this girl was never loved by any man. Losing all hope of receiving love, she ultimately committed suicide. But she did not know that one of the four characters – Kartik, the pharmacist in the medicine shop – was her silent admirer who, however, could not muster enough courage to express his love to her. Saddened by the girl's desperate act and also feeling guilty of not saving her by proposing to her at the right time, Kartik in the last scene is about to commit suicide by taking poison. But he throws it away when he remembers his own words with which he used to comfort the love-lorn girl before she died: 'If you remain alive, everything is possible.'

The question of responsibility and guilt reappears in one of the last plays of this phase, *Shesh Nei* (1970). It is the same context of an unequal contest between a rebel and a hostile social environment. In an imaginary courtroom trial, the hero faces the prosecutor who accuses him of a number of crimes—indifference to his mother, deserting his career, throwing away the chance of promotion in a job and abandoning the women who loved him. As he faces each of these characters who complain how he has wounded their feelings, he defends himself by reasserting that the prospects that they offered him would have imprisoned him in a role model, from which he has escaped by choosing poetry as his means of expression. He plucks victory from the very jaws of defeat by turning the tables on the prosecutor and challenges the prevailing concepts of crime and innocence, legality and illegality, justice and injustice. Summoning as witnesses the pavement dweller, the agricultural labourer, the retrenched factory worker, he asks the judge: where is justice in their existence? Who are the criminals? They, or those who make them suffer? Thus, the onus of responsibility is shifted from the individual to the unfair social order. The tragic flaw of the hero lies not solely within himself, but in circumstances. Such being the case, there can be no judge to pass sentence. The entire court proceedings lose legitimacy. Each individual is the accused and the judge at the same time—compounding his/her own responsibility with that of society. It is a continuous process of self-evaluation and social criticism. There is thus no end to the trial—*shesh nei*.

In almost all his plays of this phase (1963-70), the protagonists, despite their bitter disappointments in life, the collapse of their ideals and their reconciliation to defeat, continue to live with a purpose, although without any illusion, at the end. They try to rescue from the wreck some human value that one can yet cling to. And at the end, they hold up for us that value like a drowning man clutching at a life buoy.

One notices also an increasing concern with contemporary political issues in some of these plays. Soon after *Baki Itihas*, in *Tringsha Shatabdi* (1966) Sircar raised the questions of collective responsibility in the specific context of the dropping of the atom bomb on Hiroshima and Nagasaki. In a symbolic presentation, the twentieth century is here put in the dock and asked to face the thirtieth century and explain the inhumanities perpetrated by the people of the century.

Significantly, in the same year, 1970, when Sircar wrote *Shesh Nei* (which also has political overtones), he decided to adapt a political novel to the stage. The novel was *Sagina Mahato* by a Bengali writer, Gour Kishore Ghosh. It was about the life of a worker who became a trade union leader, the changes in his mentality and lifestyle brought about by the policy of expediency followed by the leaders of his party, and his painful efforts to survive. The play was first staged in Calcutta on 24 October 1971, by Sircar's theatre group called Satabdi. Badal Sircar considers the date as an important landmark in his career as a dramatist and producer. Its production was marked by a new experiment—the Theatre-in-the-Round, where the proscenium stage was abandoned in favour of an open area where the audience sat all around the performers.

It was these plays with a political message, and particularly, the formalistic innovations in the staging of *Sagina Mahato*, which paved the way for Badal Sircar's transition to the next phase in the 1970s—when he chose a new style as well as a new audience. He began to take up topical themes of socio-political importance, and experiment with them in unusual forms which required no elaborate stage for their presentation, and had direct and live communication with the spectators.

This is the first part of the article published in Theatre India *Issue 2, November 1999, NSD journal*
Courtesy: Natarang Pratishthan Archives, New Delhi

PLAYS IN A NATIONAL PERSPECTIVE

Round-Table Discussion

Samik Bandyopadhyay

In November 1996 Natya Shodh Sansthan, Kolkata, organised a Round-Table Discussion around some plays of Badal Sircar as part of a much bigger project of creating a dialogue between playwrights and practitioners, around processes related to some significant plays that had been shortlisted by the Sansthan.

The session (28-30 November 1996) was introduced and conducted by **Samik Bandyopadhyay** and attended by **Badal Sircar** and directors **B.V. Karanth, Shyamanand Jalan, Satyadev Dubey** and **Rajinder Nath,** among others. Excerpts from a Synoptic Report of discussions in one of the sessions

Opening the discussion on Badal Sircar's plays, Samik Bandyopadhyay said that around the 1970s there was a resurgence of the idea of an 'Indian Theatre,' trying to address the problems of a post-Independence sensibility, shaping or defining itself. Since the theatre movement and theatre activity had reached a critical problematic situation, theoreticians, academics and even bureaucrats decided to define 'Indian Theatre,' and impose their theories on the theatre community. Fortunately, these ideas did not last. In the course of their work at the Natya Shodh Sansthan (NSS), they noticed several plays, Indian and foreign, old and new, classical and ultra-modern—which would re-emerge repeatedly in different parts of the country. Worked upon by different directors, these would develop angles with different meanings and perspectives. They thought of undertaking an exploration of these particular plays. Different people in different contexts have repeatedly sought them out and worked on them. Thus, these texts contain a value, a potency, which offered this challenge.

Bandyopadhyay explained that they wanted the invited playwrights and directors to engage in a dialogue over the texts. They decided to begin with the directors, to get their reactions to the text—what drew them to the text, their ideas as they worked on them, and how their vision of theatre came to engage with the texts.

The playwrights were asked to share, in retrospect, what they thought of while writing the plays, what impact they hoped to achieve and the subsequent history of the plays, which does not remain the same once they are staged, as they become part of the public domain.

Explaining the pattern and format of the seminar, Bandyopadhyay said that they could (a) explore the value/worth/relevance or the meaning of the texts in terms of both the text as it was made and the text as it grew in the production/theatrical process; and (b) open up a kind of a dialogue between the playwrights and the directors, which could go beyond the archival process to further creative interaction.

Bandyopadhyay requested Karanth and Dubey to share their experience of discovering *Ebong Indrajit*. Karanth recalled how he found it surprising 'that though this play was reputed to be of an intellectual sort, and we were told that people would not understand the play, I found for myself that people in small places such as Udupi, Sagar, Davangere, Chitradurg, understood the play....What enthralled the audience most was when a few actors, shouting, rushed to the stage from amidst the audience. None of them had ever seen a play like that.'

For a later production at the National School of Drama (NSD), as an exercise for the students, in a version rewritten by Balraj Pandit, who also wrote some very good poems (it was a lyrical play) for it, Karanth was more experimental: 'For me Indrajit is an individual character with a distinctive identity. All the other characters are routine and unimpressive—they are merely numbers. Indrajit is different. So in my production sometimes Amal becomes Indrajit, sometimes Vimal becomes Indrajit, sometimes Nirmal appears as yet another character.'

In other words, Karanth saw the possibility of an Indrajit implicit in every character.

Karanth recalled that in his initial reading of the text, he had found the Writer most important, not Manasi and Indrajit. But later, for his NSD production, he called the play *Amal, Vimal, Kamal,* and gave priority to the human relationships in the play: 'But no human relationship is static. This is the essence of all relationships…it is just that we undertake journeys in vain, not reaching anywhere.'

Karanth referred to another Kannada production of *Ebong Indrajit* directed by a 'young college student, Narasimhan,' in Mysore, performed in a college courtyard, with no stage lights at all. Lights from the classrooms served as the only lighting arrangement. He laid a lot of stress on the Indrajit-Manasi relationship. His interpretation was striking because of its simplicity.

Two other productions of the same play made by Karanth – one for Darpan (Lucknow) and a revival in Kannada – failed. The text itself was widely recognised in Kannada literary circles as a very good play. Karanth even today feels a strong connection with *Ebong Indrajit*: 'I gained recognition in Karnataka due to the production of *Ebong Indrajit.*'

Speaking after Karanth, Dubey said: 'I've come here because it gives me an opportunity of re-examining my life. This forum gives me an opportunity to explore my past and *Ebong Indrajit* has been a very major part of my life in the past.'

Dubey recalls his first direct access to Sircar's text through Pratibha Agrawal's Hindi translation of *Ebong Indrajit*:

> You cannot forget certain things that become so important in your life and one of these was the translation of *Ebong Indrajit* that she sent me. I loved it and I took her permission.
>
> *Ebong Indrajit* was such a discovery.... I feel so much in love with the play, that despite the fact that I had done a lot of productions, odd productions even, *Ebong Indrajit* became an obsession—so much so that I just could not imagine a production for years and years…and of course this also set me out in search of Manasi…till I suddenly realised that Manasi was just round the corner—Sulbha Deshpande! Why am I looking elsewhere?

Dubey referred to a later press report claiming that Sircar had 'disowned' his earlier plays including *Ebong Indrajit*:

> [A]nd I got furious...For me it was like denying my entire existence. It was like sort of having a brother and then being told that he was never your brother...So for a long time, Badal-babu and I were not on talking terms, for I could not forgive somebody when he had destroyed my life...for taking away something that was so much a part of my existence...This was the sort of extreme, you can say, perverse, attachment that I had with *Ebong Indrajit.*

Sircar clarified:

> I never rejected *Ebong Indrajit.* It only proves the power of the Press ... I have never ever rejected my old plays and certainly not *Ebong Indrajit* ... I guess someone may have asked a question—I was working in the Third Theatre by then. I must have said that our group will not do *Ebong Indrajit* or such plays now. That is not our priority. That doesn't mean that as a playwright I rejected *Ebong Indrajit* or *Baki Itihas* or *Sara Rattir* or *Pagla Ghoda.*

Dubey said: 'Badal-babu means more than Shakespeare or the Greek playwrights to me because he has been more a part of my life. It is as simple as that.' Explaining what he called his 'obsession' with *Ebong Indrajit,* Dubey said:

> It was, in its own way, an assertion, a very peculiar kind of an assertion. Even when people asked, 'What is this walking on the road?' It was all there, ultimately, in that last poem—most people saw it as a poem ... It becomes a positive thing that at least you're walking, and of course you have shades of Tagore in it. So all those cultural resonances were there ... the constant echo of the surroundings, not what you might call a cognition of the very object .... What I have always loved in plays and in

poetry are the echoes which surround a piece of dialogue—and therefore the dialogue becomes more evocative.

Criticising Sombhu Mitra's production of *Baki Itihas,* Sircar said:

> Sombhu Mitra is a great director and a great director has to, at times, reinterpret the play. That's one thing. But sometimes it becomes an obsession. [The director feels] if I don't change something, then I become a lesser director. I mean, it becomes a case of changing for the sake of changing. Now Sitanath and Kanak, Saradindu and Basanti are four separate individuals. Basanti imagines something and writes about the causes of Sitanath's suicide. Then Saradindu imagines something. But none of them is satisfied. The third act again is Saradindu's play.... It is in Saradindu's mind. For so long he was thinking, but now he is identifying himself, his own experiences, with Sitanath's. But that also does not explain the real reason for Sitanath's suicide. In fact, that is not important in the play at all.
>
> Now if you use the same set of actors for both the couples, in the third act, when Saradindu is still there, one new actor has to come in. When the new actor comes, he immediately becomes Sitanath's ghost. I never meant that and I think Sombhu-babu knew that I didn't mean it. [There seems to be an attempt to give] the real reason for Sitanath's committing suicide. Then Saradindu is nowhere in the play! Thus it changes the entire meaning of the play. It has a stunt value, with the same actor doing Saradindu and Sitanath, and the same actress doing Basanti and Kanak, but that does not remain my play anymore.

Referring to Rajinder Nath's production of *Baki Itihas,* Sircar said: 'I felt he was very faithful to the text, he is always faithful to the text. I admire him for that...He understood the play and did it.' Kumar Roy, lead actor of the Bohurupee's *Baki Itihas* directed by Sombhu Mitra, explained how major emphasis was placed on the third Act where Sitanath confronts the middle-class existence of this professor of literature and his amateur writer wife, in their complacent round of domestic chores and Sunday outings. The rest of history, of human beings exploiting and mistreating human beings in violation of the norms of social justice, was not part of their consciousness, till they were awakened to an awareness of this 'other history'. ...at the end of the play, when the news comes that the man has got a better job, there is uncertainty over whether it was going to happen or not, a point with which the play had initially begun, matching the uncertain existence of individuals.

Next Shyamanand Jalan described the first step of his production of *Ebong Indrajit* as a kind of entry into the meaning of the text as the playwright had conceived it:

> First of all we wanted to understand the play and Badal-da was kind enough to come and talk to us...We got so enamoured that we wanted him to continue throughout the re-hearsals, but he refused. But we went to the central idea of the play. The central idea of the play is, as he has explained and Pratibha-ji has written in the book [her translation], the state of not having hope...or, as he described it at that time, non-hope. That was one thing, and there was a second thing...that has now got diluted and we have become habituated to it—terrorism and loss of life, and all that. In the early 1960s people were quite concerned with [the threat of] the wiping out of the world because of the atom bomb and the hydrogen bomb. But that sort of fear has become dormant now; we have accepted that these things can happen...But it was new at that time, in the 1950s and the 1960s, and it was playing on our minds. And therefore, the total philosophy of *Ebong Indrajit* and the total content of *Ebong Indrajit* became very personal.

Jalan touched upon the problem of language, the existence of different kinds of Hindi, and the problem of transmitting a Hindi that was too literary, too elitist, to an audience which was not elitist:

> Pratibhaji's Hindi is a bit too Sanskritised. How to convey through that Hindi the meaning of the play to an average audience—that

> question had to be addressed...Grappling with this problem we discovered movements...The whole production of *Ebong Indrajit* was geared towards the discovery of images...of inflexions... of ways of speaking, of standing, lighting, to convey the mood and the thoughts. And for this we used circular movements. This was the first attempt on my part to convey the whole thing not through words but through movements and images.

Jalan insisted that it was the visualisation in moving images that made his *Ebong Indrajit* production meaningful and effective in terms of communication:

> We were not doing a play. We were conveying something to the audience—some meanings, some observations, some thoughts, in a language which they did not fully understand. And the thoughts were not very easy, they required a certain receptivity on the part of the audience, a certain intellectual standard to grasp them, and therefore we had to convey them very simply.

Recalling the audience response to Anamika's production of *Ebong lndrajit,* Jalan said:

> Our best audience and best response was at the show at Kalamandir, Calcutta, before a Bengali audience. That gave us so much strength because we were talking in Hindi and we had a 100 per cent Bengali audience and they responded to it...The two other performances which come to mind were in Allahabad where we had professors and students and writers in the audience, and in Kanpur, where the audience was diametrically different—an audience of shopkeepers.

Dubey's production of *Ebong lndrajit* had Sulabha Deshpande as Manasi, Dubey as Indrajit and Amrish Puri as the Writer. Dr Jabbar Patel recalled the great impact of this production, the brilliant acting by Sulabha Deshpande and Dubey: 'Dubey's use of space (I still remember

Sulabha and Dubey walking with a platform behind them, and the use of different light groups as they walked); and the use of different speech patterns; and above everything else, the way the whole thing was held together in a beautiful fusion.'

Shiv Kumar Jhunjhunwala's first production of *Baki Itihas* in 1976 left him with a sense of dissatisfaction with the feeling that he had not been able to explore the play, particularly the psychic side of the human mind, its different layers and how human beings tend to get involved in their small personal tragedies rather than the larger tragedies happening elsewhere. It was this dissatisfaction that drove him to produce it again ten years later, 'prompted' by the Gulf War, more like a personal statement in protest against the war: 'I added one or two lines in the end in which I referred to the Gulf War.'

Dubey upheld Arvind Deshpande and Sulabha Deshpande's interpretation of *Baki Itihas,* in which they followed Sombhu Mitra's scheme of the same people playing both the sets of characters. For him, Sitanath coming again is the writer's imposition. He also recalled a production in Gujarati of *Ebong Indrajit,* directed by Praveen Joshi, with Arvind Joshi, his brother, playing Indrajit, and Sarita, a brilliant actress, playing Manasi, with the sets designed by M.S. Sathyu. The set was full of mushrooms, and yet their style was a sort of Gujarati realism as in professional theatre: '...I remember being able to sit through the play, not getting bored, but I said, yes, it is a different play which they are doing...But it didn't do well. The first production of *Ebong Indrajit* in Bombay was the Gujarati production. I did it two years later.'

Responding to Dubey's request for more details about *Ebong Indrajit,* Bandyopadhyay briefly narrated how the first production was done and how a smart member of Bohurupee had published the play in the *Bohurupee* periodical. It was picked up by Gobindo Ganguly. Liking the play, he had gone to Sircar for permission. But Sircar was not in the country and he wrote to Gobindo-babu that he had given the permission to Sombhu Mitra, but that if Bohurupee did not have a problem, Sircar had no objection. Sombhu Mitra got the impression that Badal-babu did not have faith in him and was keeping his options open. So Sombhu-babu declined and Gobindo Ganguly did the play. For Bandyopadhyay, this first production was responsible for bringing Sircar to light in a way. Bandyopadhyay said: 'I am in total agreement with Girish [Karnad] that all Badal-babu's directorial work with his earlier comedies was extremely amateur in the worst sense of the term, with one or two good pieces of acting by Badal-babu himself and one or two others. So even Badal-babu, I think, didn't take himself seriously as a playwright.' Summing up the different aspects that led to the popularity of *Ebong Indrajit,* Bandyopadhyay reiterated (a) the Souvanik production, (b) the interest of other people, (c) the Hindi translation by Pratibha Agrawal, (d) the production by Jalan, and (e) Dubey's acting in Jalan's production that made watching the plays a wonderful experience.

Bandyopadhyay mentioned two historically important and interesting points about *Ebong Indrajit* going against the mainstream of Bengali theatre, for which Sircar was 'deliberately rejected by the Bengali theatre.' Bandyopadhyay added that for a long time no director or group in Bengal would touch Badal-babu's plays, although Badal-babu had earlier explained that he had no objection to any director trying his plays out. It was only Bohurupee that staged *Baki Itihas, Pagla Ghoda* and *Jodi Aar Ekbaar.* Bohurupee even invited Badal-babu to do *Pralaap* and he remains the first and only outsider who, despite not being a part of the group, was invited to do a Bohurupee production of his own play. There was, however, only one show of *Pralaap* and there was a strong resentment against Badal-babu.

Bandyopadhyay remarked that Utpal Dutt had made cruel and even obscene attacks on Sircar without having seen any of his plays or productions. Charging him with blindly following Richard Schechner and Julian Beck of the American theatre who used nudity and obscenity on stage, Dutt had given gory details of sex orgies and acts like shitting on stage, that had become popular in American theatre. Badal-babu was labelled as a part of this school. Bandyopadhyay reiterated that all his life Badal-babu had remained an outsider in the Bengali theatre circles: 'He doesn't belong to the mainstream Bengali theatre.'

Bandyopadhyay explained that the Souvanik production conveyed Sircar's predicament of being an outsider, because visually and even sound-wise, what came through was the real pain and anguish of a

Bengali middle-class, thinking person. This anguish reflected the frustration of the early 1960s, of this man who would not give up his ideals despite the early idealistic visions of Independence crumbling, of radicalism selling out and the crisis mounting. That pain, that anguish, that bitterness, was lost in the obvious symbolism of a railway track, a green signal and loud overacting.

Karnad had some interesting comments about *Ebong Indrajit* and repeated that he wished to thank Anamika Kala Sangam for giving him the opportunity to watch the Bengali production. He further explained that during the 1960s there was a debate among theatre persons as to how to get away from the well-made play. Dubey on reading (Karnad's) *Yayati* had commented that it was a well-made play. *Yayati* has properly structured scenes. The whole question was how to get away from the scene divisions and the early Ibsenite structure of the play. Karnad added that even *Tughlaq* has these scene divisions.

Karnad emphasised that given these circumstances, *Ebong Indrajit* was a tremendous stimulant for him. After seeing the Bengali production in Calcutta, Karnad had gone back to work with the Madras Players who did plays in English. They had been producing plays like *A View from the Bridge* by Arthur Miller; but soon they tired of producing such plays and felt that they should do modern Indian theatre. Karnad's first choice was *Ebong Indrajit.* Karnad had directed the play along with a friend, Ammu Mathew. He had not seen Dubey's production, nor had he seen Jalan's. As a result, Karnad explained, his production was very influenced by what he had seen on the Bengali stage.

Talking about his directorial stance, Karnad explained that not being a theatre director, 'I did not follow all the literalness or the overdone things, but the general pattern of movement…And somewhere while directing the play, I said this is how it is…the fluidity of movement that one is talking about.' After this venture, Karnad had written *Hayavadana* within a year. He felt that there was a direct connection between *Ebong Indrajit* and *Hayavadana.*

(This was the end of the pre-lunch session on 30th November 1996)
Courtesy: Natya Shodh Sansthan, Kolkata

ON THREE PRODUCTIONS OF 'EVAM INDRAJIT'

A Comment

Pratibha Agrawal

The fact that a creative work that appears sufficiently simple on the surface can actually be extremely complex and that it can allow for completely different interpretations by different people, became very clear as I watched three different productions of Badal Sircar's *Evam Indrajit*. The rendering of a play depends more or less on two primary elements—content and form. The content is entirely that of the playwright. The director internalises it as much as possible and confronts it, to then transform it into a performance, using his imagination. Just as the contents belong more to the playwright, the form belongs more to the director. The playwright writes the play in a definite style, in a given structure, but the director has full liberty to transgress that.

Let's first look at the content of *Evam Indrajit*. What is the primary objective of the playwright? Does he want to merely portray the activities of the common man or does he want to say something else through it? Does he want to focus on Indrajit's desire to embrace death over life or does he want to give more importance to Manasi's thought that inspires continuing on the path of life? Is it an ordinary path that he is talking about or is it that pilgrimage on which the poet had been initiated in his prime and which he does not want to give up even at the end of his life's journey? Are the poet and Indrajit two parts of the same character? Is the dejection, suffocation and weariness of

Indrajit actually the dejection, suffocation and weariness of the poet? Is it an inevitable destiny that one has to pull on with life like Amal, Bimal, Kamal? Or like Indrajit, to dream big and fail, losing all hope and faith and reject life completely? Or like the poet, knowing full well that the road is endless, still accept the destiny of walking on? Is the closing of the play optimistic, pessimistic or something in-between—an optimistic pessimism of sorts?

These are some of the legitimate questions that arise on reading the play, and all the three directors have tried to answer them in their own individual ways, according to their imagination. While there have been several productions of this play in Bengali, Gujarati and Hindi, I will be discussing the three productions that I have seen, namely those by theatre groups Souvanik (Bengali: Calcutta), Anamika (Hindi: Calcutta), and Dishantar (Hindi: Delhi). I first saw this play in original Bengali around three years back—in a production where Govind Gangopadhyaya was the director as well as the lead actor. The production was very effective and stayed in the mind for long, so much so that I was drawn to see two more performances. Govind-babu had definitely emphasised the optimistic viewpoint—life has to be accepted inspite of all its travails and unhappiness; that we have to carry on without the assurance of a bright future, simply because there is a road ahead and stopping midway means death. Govind Babu had expressed his viewpoint very effectively, though, in the process the inner conflict of Indrajit got lost somewhere. Indrajit wavering between life and death, restless, agitated, floundering in taking a decision—these aspects somehow went missing. A red light present on stage from the start, turned green at the end as Indrajit decided to live on. This was a rather crude method of suggesting a very serious import. Despite such shortcomings, one cannot deny that the overall presentation left a mark and is, in fact, responsible for the recognition of the play *Evam Indrajit* and Badal Sircar at the national level.

The second production was by Anamika, directed by Shyamanand Jalan. He was more concerned and proactive about trying to unravel the meaning and content of the play. His long-protracted discussions with

Badal Sircar are a testimony to that effort. He found it a play primarily dealing with the frustrations and conflicts of youth; he did not see any ray of hope in the portrayal. For him, the mention of pilgrimage or the road to the destination, referred to in the last poem, was not significant. What was central, according to him, was the reference to the myth of Sisyphus—the pain of the Herculean effort that he has to make even while knowing its meaninglessness. For him, even though the Poet and Indrajit were not the same, neither were they split selves; yet they were alike, the suffocation and frustrations of Indrajit were the frustrations of the Poet too. The outcome of this interpretation was that the characterisation was very powerful.

The play got established for its serious content, and its theme emerged as very disturbing. But it was also very heavy. What is the point in accepting life in a predicament of complete helplessness—isn't it as good or as bad as death! I can't tell you how depressing the closing scene seemed during rehearsals, before it was staged! It felt as though the Poet, Indrajit and Manasi standing on stage, were not human beings but the ghosts of the cursed Sisyphus himself; they were living corpses! But by the time the play was actually performed on stage, the deep pessimism and meaninglessness ceased to be depressing. Acceptance of life was simply an acceptance of life, not of death.

I do not know how this shift came about, whether due to the inner inspiration and understanding of the director or the views of critics and viewers, but according to me the shift was in the right direction. After all, if there is not even the slightest hope left, Indrajit's choosing death over life would be more logical.

This very logic was played out by Mohan Maharishi in the Dishantar production. In his view, Lekhak and Indrajit were two aspects of one character—the Lekhak expressed whatever he wanted to say, through Indrajit. And what he wanted to say was again full of deep despair, devoid of any hope or faith whatsoever. It was about a person who had lost his centre of gravity, who in his efforts to rise like a meteor had failed miserably. This was a man who was scorched in his own fire. What was the point of living such a life! That is why at the end of the play the Lekhak strangles Indrajit (imposed by the director)—as though fed up with and weary of everything, he forcibly put an end to everything.

To reach such a climax the director skipped several pages of the last part of the play. The road and the journey, the pilgrimage and the path leading to the destination, had all become meaningless for him. I felt that this was unnecessarily stretching the reach of the play. Frankly speaking, it amounted to blatant injustice to the text. The last part of the play is very significant from the point of view of the meaning behind the play. Skipping it is actually like taking away the spirit from the body. Maybe this error in judgment happened due to ignoring the poems in the play. This was probably the reason why neither the meaning of the play nor the characters of Indrajit and the Lekhak came across with any intensity or passion in this production. Somehow the production did not work in spite of having talented actors like Om Shivpuri and other such members in the team. Even though Indrajit was not strangled in the Calcutta performance, massive editing in the last part made it soulless. The end remained weak.

Without speaking about the form and structure of the play and the productions, the discussion will remain incomplete. The playwright has presented very realistic situations in an unrealistic form. So, while there is a realistic touch to most situations, dialogues and characters, it requires great imagination to present them on stage. The play has several locales. To present them realistically with scene changes for every locale would make it very clumsy. It is important to have one common design for all. That would also allow for a greater play of imagination—both from the director as well as the audience. Similarly, barring Indrajit, all actors are playing more than one part. With simple, basic variations, presenting a completely different character is the second requirement and the third is mime. All the three directors carried this out successfully. In Souvanik's production, the sequences with mime were very lively and effective. Govind Babu had used some common properties like dusters and playing cards, etc. Shyamanandji had completely ignored these and Mohan Maharishi had provided the Writer with all the properties required for writing. It is a kind of play (probably all plays can be done this way) where the director can decide to use or completely do away with properties.

In this context Anamika's production deserves mention. Here the director tried out some effective devices, most significant of which was to freeze the actors at points. The impact of this device was that at times it communicated the stillness/stability in life, at another its unchanging or mechanical quality, and yet another its continuity. Similarly, circular movements helped us experience various eternal concepts of life on the move—the continuity of life without any definite beginning or end, the moving earth, and the force of a continually self-propelled life. By juxtaposing seemingly meaningless dialogue with music and overstated modern dance movements, the meaninglessness of our lives was highlighted very effectively. It is also true that throughout the play movements and gestures were a little too exaggerated; false laughter that was meant to indicate the hollowness of life seemed overdone at times; not enough attention had been paid to minute details of mimetic movements; often the characters were unnecessarily noisy. Yet one can say without hesitation that Shyamanandji has understood the play the most and has successfully employed several experimental devices.

From the point of acting, possibly Souvanik's production was the best because their teamwork was very good. Amal, Bimal, Kamal and Mansi were natural and lively. Govind-babu left a mark as the Lekhak. But Indrajit did not have the intensity expected of him for this role. Maybe the characterisation was responsible for this lapse. In Shyamanandji's production all characters, except the Lekhak played by the director himself, seemed weak. In fact, they appeared amateurish in comparison. Indrajit was louder than required, as though he was trying to convince people through the power of his voice. At many instances Mansi's conflict and struggle seemed contrived and imposed. Amal, Bimal and Kamal could have been more natural. Although the actors' acting prowess at Dishantar was in general of a higher standard, they did not have the power to move the audience to a show of emotions. Barring some moments, even an actor like Om Shivpuri could not impress due to the interpretation of the director.

I am confident that this play will become more popular and that directors with greater competence will be able to explore newer dimensions in their productions in future. They should not make the mistake of leaving out the poems from the script. The creation is a very powerful one on its own. There is great pleasure and satisfaction in reading it, producing it, or watching it as a play. It makes you encounter the truth in all its dimensions and depth.

Translated excerpt from the introduction to the published play
Translator—Pratibha Agrawal
Publisher: Rajkamal Prakashan, 1969

SIRCAR AND INDIAN THEATRE

Satyadev Dubey

It is difficult for me to write about Badal-babu now because I have, lately, had the chance to get to know him personally and it has been a great experience to discover what the writer intended consciously and what one got out of reading or seeing his plays. It has its humorous aspects also. For instance I have always found *Ballabhpur Ki Roopkatha* a very fine piece of theatre (whose plot, perhaps, is derived from some insignificant novel by P.G. Wodehouse) and I have repeated ad infinitum that only an Indian writer could think of using a Kalidasa-reciting ghost in a farce. Because for me the most memorable bits of the play have been the Sanskrit verses which neither I nor the majority of the audience understood. Both in Anamika's production in Hindi and the Theatre Unit's production in Marathi, it is this situation which becomes the high point of the play.

Badal-babu himself didn't know enough Sanskrit to choose these verses—somebody sent them to him with the English translation and only then did he incorporate them in a situation he had already conceived. Similarly, in *Baki Itihas* he wrote the third act first (it is there that he grapples with his basic preoccupation) and then had to work backwards to find two acts that would go with it.

This, among many other things, goes to prove that Badal-babu is not just a playwright, but essentially a man of the theatre. If he had been only a playwright, *Ballabhpur* and *Baki Itihas* would perhaps not have been written. It is when considerations of good theatre come in that these two works become acceptable. (I will not waste words in explaining this subtlety. One either understands it instinctively or one does not.)

It is fated that some writers become the vanguard of movements. It is not that other writers have not broken new ground, created new idioms and tried to express the reality around them; they have done extremely progressive work but because they are ahead of their times or, more usually, the thinking intelligentsia is lagging behind, their work has to wait for proper evaluation. It is ironical that a progressive piece of writing when discovered later can be mistakenly labelled fashionably imitative.

But Badal-babu's entry into Indian theatre was beautifully timed. Perhaps he made the final breakthrough when a considerable amount of modernity had already been ushered in and the new directors who responded so happily to him had already achieved an identity. Dharamvir Bharati's *Andha Yug* (written in 1955) and *Sangmarmar Par Ek Raat* had already heralded the birth of a modern idiom in Hindi both in dramatic verse and prose. *Andha Yug* had proved its vitality in the Theatre Unit production in 1962. (The 70 mm production of the National School of Drama followed and not preceded it as some sycophants would like to advertise.) Anamika of Calcutta had already done Rakesh's *Ashadh Ka Ek Din* in 1959. The adaptation of lbsen and Chekhov for the Bengali stage had been accomplished and the practitioners of modern theatre all over India had started finding their inspiration in Sombhu Mitra and Tripti Mitra. Nandikar had come into existence in the 1960s. All over India a decided shift in favour of modern Indian language plays was discernible. Tendulkar had already been discovered for the Marathi stage by directors like Damu Kenkre in the 1950s. Adya Rangacharya made a definite break from his past style in the early 1960s and Karnad's maiden play, *Yayati*, was also written at that time. Badal-babu wrote his *Evam Indrajit* in 1962. At the end of 1964 Anamika held an All-India Drama Festival and Symposium where people discovered each other and the Kannada playwright, Adya Rangacharya. Shortly after that *Evam Indrajit* was performed in Calcutta.

It was in 1966 that Adya's *Suno Janmejaya* and Karnad's *Tughlaq* (written in Kannada in 1964) were performed in Delhi. Bombay saw the former and *Yayati* in the same year. It was slightly before or after those two plays that *Evam Indrajit* was performed in Hindi, in Delhi. Despite the mutilations the script suffered in Delhi, the play was taken to heart by everybody and in no time all over India people were talking of Badal Sircar and his *Evam Indrajit*. Since then the play has been produced in Gujarati, Hindi (by Anamika and Theatre Unit), Kannada, English (by the Madras Players) and other languages. With Sombhu Mitra's production of *Baki Itihas*, Badal-babu soon became the most talked of and performed playwright with amateurs.

What was there in Badal-babu's writings to which people from every part of the country responded? What is that indefinable something else which makes Badal-babu the most representative among Indian playwrights?

Badal-babu obviously brings to his playwriting a clarity of mind which is all too rare. This clarity is reflected in the construction of his plays and the precision of his dialogue. The precision of dialogue never negates its evocative quality. His characters are rooted in their environment and are recognisable human beings lacking totally in enviable heroic qualities. But the unheroic in them becomes appealing on the human level with out destroying their credibility and vitality as stage characters. They speak about a reality which has immediacy for this generation.

It is *Evam Indrajit* which distils the best qualities of Badal Sircar and also goes beyond him. It provided for us the shock of recognition similar to what Hemingway provided for his generation. It is the one play which accommodates and expresses practically all the major concerns, aspirations and problems of the new, rootless, urban generation and invests it with deep, autumnal sadness.

Published in Enact – *59.1971*
Courtesy: Natarang Pratisthan Archives, New Delhi

'KAVI KAHANI'

A Play Review

Rajinder Paul

To Agredoot of Delhi goes the credit of introducing two comedies of Badal Sircar, *Ballabhpurer Roopkatha*, staged as *Ek Tha Raja*, and *Kobi Kahini (Kavi Kahani)*, to Delhi audiences. Badal Sircar, started as a writer of light comedies and kept on winning innocuous little, feather-weight competition prizes. Even after having become a 'heavy' as it were, he takes himself as seriously as a writer of comedies as the Delhi audiences take him as the writer of *Evam Indrajit* et al

Thus the credit. Garlanding ceremony over, the production, if one is allowed to change gear so quickly, started off in neutral gear. It went on and on with R.N. Raja as the clerk writing an election speech for Mani-babu in stone-crushing Hindi. However, with the entry of Kimti Anand (that dependable actor in various guises that one sees on the Delhi stage), the farce or comedy wears the appropriate costume.

The plot also starts heaving complicated sighs. And satire comes up. Modern poetry, the elections, the Samaj-serving *bhadra mahilayen* and all the rest. Samarjit Sanyal is presented to us as the Kavi in question. Mani-babu's daughter, Lily, is of course interested in writing poetry and is conversant with every syllable that Samarjit has scrapbooked. So is her mother Supriti. Our poet comes and resides in the election rocked house of Mani Mazumdar. The poet is of course fake. It's part of the election stunt. But before he parachutes himself down the bathroom window with the help of a sari, he provides some of the most interesting and incisive moments. Kulbhushan Kharbanda in the role of the hoax Kavi adopts all the self-righteous, stuck-up, opinionated attitudes a matinee-idol writer would adopt.

Lily (Kamini Chandioke) and Supriti (Meena Williams), the daughter and mother...provided ample fun. Another actor who was good was Devendra Mohan as Sanat. His slow, tortoise-paced gait and gestures suited the nervous, scared school teacher-on-probation. Rajendra Kumar as Mani-babu did as well as he possibly could.

Dina Nath's direction as usual depended a lot on slapstick. There's nothing wrong—only if the play can carry it or if it can carry the play through. Otherwise it provides a kind of unwanted unevenness because all the actors can't adopt a particular style. But the play as a whole was good fun. This I think was mainly due to the verbal wit and sharpness of the lines. In that the translator, Mr Ashok Bhattacharya, must have played a prominent part. Ashok Bhattacharya certainly has a gift for razor-sharp dialogue.

The article was published in Enact – 59, 1971
Courtesy: Natarang Pratisthan Archives, New Delhi

'MIDSUMMERING'

A Review from Kolkata

In the 1960s Badal Sircar hit the headlines as an avant-garde dramatist of the first rank with his existentialist exploration of alienation and the human psyche in *Ebong Indrajit.* His most recent serious work has been a Grotowski-influenced experimental *Spartacus,* but in between, for more than a decade, Sircar has been more concerned with the world of comedy. And truly he is a fine comic artist (both as playwright and actor) of class and distinction. If *Baro Pishima* was an enjoyable farce and *Abu Hossain* a cleverly modernised, richly comic adaptation of a Girish Chandra classic, Sircar seemed to have reached the height of his comic style in the hilarity and wit (verbal and situational) of *Ballabhpurer Roopkatha.*

Badal Sircar breaks new ground with his latest comic offering *Jodi Aar Ekbaar* produced and staged by Bohurupee. His previous plays were in prose—this one is in verse that is light and bright and falls skipping on the tongue. Sircar achieves an easy, colloquial, everyday melody in the lilt of this kind of verse and shows himself in perfect control of hilarious rhyme. Our ears are not much attuned to this kind of spontaneous-seeming stress and fall of the accents and the rhymes, which might make the verse play seem artificial at the outset. Those habituated to the nineteenth century bombastic and florid style of verse may stumble in making the change from the heavy sonorities of the early days to the light touch of Sircar's tripping rhymes. But verse is just a convention and we all get used to it—especially if the playwright handles the convention in such an utterly entertaining style as Sircar here does.

Jodi Aar Ekbaar takes the old theme of 'if' and gives it a novel form. A group of guests arrive at a seaside resort and put up at Happy Lodge run by a fun-loving manager. On a particular day every year the tribals at the resort village offer homage to Buddha Jinn - the local god - who comes down dancing among the mortals for that one day. The god grants every man his heart's desire, but the tribals know that no good comes from his boon. The city-bred couples at Happy Lodge are bored with their lives (and each other). Everyone thinks that s/he has made a mess of his/her life, and if only they were given a second chance they would choose partners they really loved and live the lives they really wanted to live. The manager invokes the good Buddha Jinn to grant this boon. Everything changes, everyone gets his or her heart's desire, and riotous complications follow. Behind all the fun and games of this bright entertainer, behind all its pleasant and pleasing comedy, behind all its jolly fantasy, there lurks a serious thought—that man is never satisfied with what he has, that he is forever restless and wants to return and take the road not taken.

The production values and the performances match the easy assurance and fluent spontaneity of the play. The stage is simply but effectively set. Kumar Roy's décor creates the hotel patch out of bamboo strips and a minimum of furniture leaving a large stage area free for mime and dance. A raised platform points to the beach, a hint of the blue ocean is suggested in the background, while a rising moon adds to the atmosphere. Tripti Mitra does not act but concentrates on directorial work. The dramatic unfolding of the action is carried forward with an easy-paced tempo; the actors' movements are beautifully coordinated and the interpersonal lyric dialogue equally well-handed; the mime and dance sequences nicely timed.

Author not known (Anonymous)
Published in Enact *-111-112, March-April 1976*
Courtesy: Natya Shodh Sansthan, Kolkata

Reviews

'IF WISHES WERE HORSES'

From a conversation between
Dnyaneshwar Nadkarni and **Amol Palekar**

On 5 December, Calcutta witnessed a momentous theatre event when an original Bengali play by one of its stalwarts was revived in the city after two decades. The Marathi version by Amol Palekar of Badal Sircar's *Pagla Ghoda* was the inaugural offering at the ninth Nandikar National Theatre Festival. The conversation was held on this occasion

'Two decades ago, Badal Sircar plays were very much in vogue in Marathi theatre,' says Amol Palekar. 'Our Bengali colleagues used to joke that we Maharashtrians had weaned away their playwright from his native soil.'

Palekar believes that Sircar was never accepted in Bengal to the same extent that he was in Maharashtra. This is true as far as the late 1960s and early 1970s are concerned. One remembers a young Amol Palekar, then a bank clerk, translating Sircar's early play *Vallabhpurchi Dantakatha (Ballabhpurer Roopkatha)*, staging it with Satyadev Dubey, and acting in it. It is a charming play, quite unlike the ones Sircar wrote later. It helped launch both Palekar and his newly-discovered Bengali genius in one dramatic gesture.

A number of Badal Sircar plays were performed in Marathi between 1969 and 1977. They included the slender and formalistic *Evam Indrajit*, the thought-provoking *Baki Itihas*, *Ant Nahi*—which portrayed the trapping of a sensitive intellectual, *Juloos* (fleshed out by

Palekar in his production from a skeleton script) and *Saari Raat*. Some of the translations were essayed by Palekar himself; others by well-known litterateurs such as the late Sadanand Rege and P.L. Deshpande.

During these years Palekar used to invite Sircar to Bombay to conduct workshops. There was truly a dynamic atmosphere prevailing in the experimental Marathi theatre at that time, and men like Badal Sircar, Vijay Tendulkar and Amol Palekar were leading figures in the revolution. 'Dubey and I staged Badal-da's *Pagla Ghoda* first in 1971,' Palekar recalls. 'Kumud Powar acted the key female role in the Marathi version, while Tarla Mehta played the lead in the Hindi version. While I remember much else from the first version, what really stands out is the manner in which Chandrashekhar Kamarkar used to say, "Tara O Maa!"—just an exclamation, as he along with others waited to burn the body they had carried to the cremation ghat. Amrish Puri, then yet to be swallowed up by villainous roles in films, was an asset to the Hindi staging of the play.'

Sombhu Mitra, who had produced other plays of Badal Sircar, presented *Pagla Ghoda* with his daughter Saoli in the key female role. One remembers her gliding around the stage, suitably spectral.

'Sombhuda made some changes in the play,' says Palekar:

> He recruited four or five different actresses to play the women in the flashbacks whereas we, in our current production for Saarth and the National Centre for the Performing Arts (NCPA) in Bombay, as also for our original staging, have only one actress, Chitra Palekar, playing all the roles. This tests her versatility, besides providing a dramatic thrill to the audience, which sees a single actress assuming these various personae.

And now, Paleker's achievement has become even more newsworthy, as the latest production of *Pagla Ghoda* was the inaugural offering at the ninth Nandikar National Theatre Festival, which began last week in Calcutta.

Palekar points out the peculiar propriety of the Marathi *Pagla Ghoda* being selected as the festival's opening entry. 'It is a Marathi Badal Sircar play that is at last representing him in Calcutta,' says Palekar. 'There has been a sort of parting of ways between Badal Sircar and the more or less settled avant-garde theatre in Bengal.' Playing the central role, Chitra Palekar gets into her stride in the garb of the other aliases. These flashbacks are related to the four men we see in the foreground.

The exploration of the psyche of the dead girl through the agency of a flesh-and-blood actress moving on the stage as if in an evil dream is one of Badal Sircar's most telling innovations. Chitra Palekar fully lives up to the emotive needs of this other-worldly appearance.

As the quartet drinks away, its members also open their hearts and briefly enact the tragedies they have encountered in their lives. We see an engrossing spectrum of emotions and experiences in these flashbacks. Not all the relationships are legitimate. For example, the one binding Lalu Sheth (Palekar has not replaced the burly Rahul Solapurkar in the part) with a woman outside the marital orbit is very touching. However, the most important of the four men is Kartik, the compounder (played with surprising authenticity by Hemu Adhikari). Tragedy-stricken, he is about to commit suicide towards the end, but changes his mind in a life-asserting gesture.

The title of the play, *Pagla Ghoda*, is to be traced back to a children's nonsense rhyme used by Badal Sircar. The legendary Marathi poet, the late Chim Tryam Khanolkar, translates this rhyme from the original Marathi thus:

Together spread the mango leaves
The mango leaves
Strikes the hunter, gallops the horse
Rani, Rani, make way
Galloping comes the mad horse.

True to the innovative spirit of his production, Palekar also uses verses by the veteran poet Indira Sant. They are used as an alternative for Badal Sircar's dialogue:

I want something, I want something
I want some kind of pain

Pain - whose wound will always be fresh
Deep pain which will reverberate through me.

(Translated from the original Marathi)

'When we thought of reviving the play,' explains Palekar, 'we were no doubt convinced of its contemporary validity. I think the play still rings true and probes deep into tragic experiences. At the same time it is a very human document.'

Badal Sircar's *Pagla Ghoda* tries to map out the significance of life in the background of a scene associated with death. The very fact that the four men on the ghat are unloading themselves of their innermost feelings suggests a process of purification—the same process involved in the burning of a dead body.

Badal Sircar's plays, as they were staged here more than twenty years ago, indicated a unique experimental thrust. Soon, however, Sircar underwent a transformation and moved away even from that theatre which in his writings, he calls the 'Third Theatre.' He was either greatly influenced by the ideas of the American dramaturge, Richard Schechner, or greatly influenced him. Whatever the process, Badal Sircar took first to the streets, and then to the fields and mines in the hinterland. Every week he and his dedicated troupe trek miles and stage their partly impromptu plays among the masses.

Amol Palekar, on his part, has run the whole gamut of Badal Sircar's dramaturgy. *Vallabhpurchi Dantakatha, Pagla Ghoda* and *Juloos* project three totally different phases in Badal Sircar's work. Palekar has now come full circle and created a production that fits in appropriately with the impact of Palekar's return to the stage.

Many, many years ago, a Maharashtrian company staging an Urdu melodrama took Calcutta by storm. With a much more sober play – and one from the theatre armoury of Bengal itself – Palekar and his colleagues are bound to repeat the feat.

Published in The Illustrated Weekly Of India; *12th to 18th December 1992*
Courtesy: Natya Shodh Sansthan, Kolkata

'EVAM INDRAJIT'

Shyamanand Jalan

On watching Badal Sircar's plays being enacted on the stage, one felt the urge to rebel. It seemed that these plays demand a liberation being denied to them. My rebellion translated itself into my production of *Evam Indrajit.* Liberating it from the rigid technicalities of presentation, we tried to project the soul of the play before the public. The fact that people kept sitting and watching it indicated that we had been successful to some extent. To begin with we thought that the common audience would not endure it, but we discovered that the so-called 'common' audience did like it. Whether they understood it or not, we felt that they definitely experienced it.

First of all, I only try to get a sense of the play. I do not try to understand or analyse it. I read it rapidly and then lie down with closed eyes. Some strange ideas and shapes start forming in my consciousness. If then I feel strongly the 'desire' to produce it, I get engaged in its presentation. Even then, I do not read it repeatedly. After selecting some colleagues, we sit and read together; we try to feel and understand it. Then we start playing with it. We enact a small scene, deliver a few dialogues, examine one or two gestures and continue reading. All this becomes like a game for us. And by the time the play is memorised, we have a vague form and image in our minds.

We actually start understanding the play when we start run throughs. But even at this stage the comprehension lacks specificity.

> It is not necessary that behind hopeless acceptance there should be an identified feeling or emotion, i.e. despair or asceticism. The passage of time and the conditions prevailing at that time create new states of mind. The meaning of the word 'love' had different connotations four hundred years ago. Today, or forty to fifty years ago it had a different meaning altogether. At that time, platonic love would have had no meaning at all.

These words *(see above)* of the playwright Badal Sircar had suddenly revealed the mystery about *Evam Indrajit.*

Having arrived at the twilight of life
My mind and heart should not forget
The basic mantra
There is no pilgrimage only the journey
There is no aim, only a road
You have to walk the pilgrim's path
That is the aim, that is the destination

These are the last lines of *Evam Indrajit* (see above). His selection of words to express his state of mind, disturbed me then as it does today. With these words he has given us a direction, but he has also confronted us with a dilemma. How does one express that 'basic mantra' as an actor? How does one evoke from within, the unnamed, undefined emotion? Merely experiencing that emotion is not enough. After all the aim is to communicate the experience. In striving to express the un-namable, we repeatedly made errors and continue to make them. At times Mansi starts weeping and at others, Indrajit. Often the Writer starts dominating.

Then there was the question of stage, the audience. To take a neutral stance, as suggested by the playwright may not work for the audience. If after half an hour the audience starts yawning and looking around, then how can dialogues and situations be delivered with neutrality? It remained our job to enliven and colour them.

My production was trying to discover a way out of this maze of questions. How can a man, who realises that life is meaningless, continue to live without deceiving himself? Then what should he do? Should he die? Commit suicide? Like Indrajit was contemplating? Or should he deceive himself in the hope that the sun will shine once again? But today hope has disappeared from the life of a thinking and sensitive man. The moon and the sun are no longer a mystery. There is no heaven or hell. Under the earth and below subterranean regions, lies the land again. Above the head there is air and then void and rising higher still, perhaps there is the same air and maybe more land. Even before we begin pushing the stone up the mountain, we know it will not stay there, but will come rolling down. And even if it does, what purpose will it serve? With what hope can man survive today—man who is the product of the nuclear holocaust?

So what should he do? Should he die?

Then? What is the use of dying? If both dying and living are meaningless, then why not live? Perhaps…

No, 'Perhaps' is also no longer an alternative; we have come to know its hollowness, we no longer have faith…

'Perhaps' is hollow, but it does exist…like a dream.

With a view to bring into focus the central thematic concerns of *Evam Indrajit,* we have used various devices, the main device amongst them being the mixed theatrical style. At places it was realistic and at some places it was stylised. This play was not tied to the concept of time and place and units of character, nor did we tie the presentation to these concepts. We tried to discover the basic philosophic intent in every sentence and character in order to manifest it. We presented it in a form in which we could reveal the central idea powerfully. I have assumed that the whole story is that of the 'Writer' himself, and towards the end Indrajit becomes the 'Writer.' We have simply projected the central theme and did not comment on it. Nor did we ridicule the ordinariness of the ordinary man. Our efforts were to maintain the sensitivity of the play.

We have conceived the choreography of the play and the characters keeping in view the central idea. Our idea was to affect the audience through the sounds and visuals, rather than words. Therefore, we have used circular movements at several places.

Stage sets were simple. We needed a few different levels. Having created these levels, Khaled Chaudhary, the designer, wanted us to reveal the thematic substance through visuals. Golden doors, golden arches and caves were conceived. These were doors within doors, stairs within stairs, but ultimately the same land.

In the case of music, we tried off-stage sounds in place of music, only words, only rhythms which could evoke an appropriate atmosphere in some particular sequences and enhance the pacing of the play.

As far as costumes were concerned, we conceived Amal, Kamal and Bimal as a single character. They were not in uniform clothes; they wore a variety of clothes found in daily life. The only difference was that the costumes were exchanged between the three characters in different acts. Mansi was in a light, rose-coloured sari and Indrajit was in black and dark blue. To make the 'Writer' a part of the environment of the play, we have dressed him in brownish tones.

Courtesy: Director's Note, Aaj ke Rangnatak; *1973*
Publisher: Radhakrishna Prakashan

'SAARI RAAT'

Amrish Puri

I am not getting into the philosophical import of the play or into a discussion on its various interpretations, but I would like to state honestly that so far no other play (with the exception of *Pagla Ghoda*) has disturbed me as much as *Saari Raat*. I have got lost in the characters of the play, particularly the woman's character, every time I have read it. Any woman who desires the ideal state of completeness can achieve it only in a dream. Ultimately she has to face reality, she can't escape that. She wants that something, some miracle would get her to her beloved Ranjan. For Ranjan she is willing to sacrifice anything, any time – her husband, her world, her peace – but she must experience bliss.

In my view Ranjan is no one other than an adult Indrajit.

I would like to say a few things about my production of this play—

- I had got my actors to speak the dialogues at an easy and natural note. We had seated the audience as close to the stage as possible, without using the last few rows in the auditorium. We did not use mikes so the audience was able to enjoy the natural quality and subtleties of dialogue delivery.

- To communicate the suggestive quality of the dialogues we had tried to pack them with additional meanings.

- In the beginning the couple enters in normal light, and later we tried to create an atmosphere of fear through light and sound effects. This helped in creating a mysterious and magical atmosphere around the old man.

- Throughout the play the old man kept his eyes open. He closes his eyes at the end, as if he too is dissolving with the night, disappearing. Incidentally at the end of the play, through lights, we attempted to make the old man invisible, which highlighted him as an unrealistic presence.

- To maintain a suitable atmosphere in the play we collected quite a variety of properties and set props.

- The most important element of the set design was the window. The woman was made to get attracted to the window, repeatedly. The scenes between the old man and the woman were placed near the window. Since the man was not a part of this action, he was not allowed to come near the window.

- The entire performance was without an interval, which helped keep the audience totally involved.

The first production (in Hindi) of *Saari Raat* was staged by Theatre Unit, on 19 September 1972 at the Tejpal Auditorium, Bombay. There were six shows at the time. Participating artistes were –

Off Stage:

Direction: Amrish Puri; Producer: Satyadev Dubey; Lights: Dilip Kolhatkar; Sound: Dharamsee Merchant/ Pradeep Deshpande; Set Design: Damu Kenkre

On Stage:

Old Man: Amrish Puri; Wife: Sunila Pradhan; Husband: Gajanand Bagera

Translated from the Director's Note in Pratibha Agrawal's translation of the play
Publisher: Vidya Prakashan Mandir, 1981

'ABU HOSSAIN'

Vimal Lath

I had liked Badal-babu's Bengali production of *Abu Hossain*. Girish Ghosh had written the play in a style that was prevalent in his times. But Badal-babu, by adding the prologue, removed all the difficulties that the text presented. That is why he could do away with Arab costumes, classical singing, elaborate set design and hoards of women actors. Abu Hossain romances in shirts and pants, Harun Al Rashid makes an entry in a suit and hat, Roshanara and her friend sing away in nylon saris, a well-built young man with his chunni-covered head enacts Salima's role, by shifting some wooden blocks from one place to another a change of scene is achieved etc., etc.

Even so, this production that was being done in the name of the new theatre movement, seemed somewhat dissatisfying. Other than the period costumes of the old king and his minister, there was nothing in the production to suggest that it was a distortion of a play by the well-known Girish Chandra Ghosh, or that there was an attempt to create a fusion of the old and the new.

Pratibha-Ji (Aggrawal) felt that the play had the potential of being performed in Hindi so she translated the play. When she read it out one day, frankly one did not feel particularly enthused to take it up for production. Girish Babu had written the first scene of the first act, in blank verse. Pratibha Ji had also translated it in blank verse. My suggestion was that the whole play should be turned into blank verse and she immediately agreed. The script that we got after this was a completely transformed one. It seemed that someone had put new life into the play and the dialogues seemed to flow seamlessly from one to the other.

Then there was hardly any difficulty for the director, with a good script in hand and Satabdi's production in mind. This play did not require communication of any philosophical content like in *Evam Indrajit*, neither did it have to sugar coat some biting topical satire for the audience, nor did it have to weave a web of symbols around the supposedly intellectual psychology as in the non-dramatic texts prevalent these days. The play was very simple that could be understood by children even. All that required to be done was to create a fusion of the old and the new in a way that it becomes wholesome entertainment for the viewers. So, the director's work did not really require any exercise of the mind.

Yet the question remained—how to create this wholesome entertainment? Will dialogues dotted with English, mouthed by an Arab character dressed in pant and bush shirt tickle the audience? Will the twenty-four songs of the play sung to film tunes not degenerate into a crude parody? And what about the amalgamation of the old and the new?

I found a solution in the traditional costumes of the Arabs. Abu Hossain dressed in a puffy salwar, shirt, jacket and cap suddenly says in the middle of normal dialogues: 'No, I will befriend you only for one night. Stranger, I have been hurt badly. My father died of a heart ailment and I don't want to take any chances' or the minister says to Harun Al Rashid: 'You gave opium my lord? In this day and age? LSD would have been better!' It seemed that this kind of mixing of old and new references and language did not allow the play to degenerate into a mere parody, but instead created a spicy feel to the text.

Arab music also helped solve some of the problems. For scene changes where just one stool (that was turned around to serve as the throne or a bed or a step) a wooden frame and two curtains were shifted around by the characters dressed in Arab costumes, in full view of the audience, with Arab music playing in the background. The atmosphere created provided a mixed flavour of the old and new.

The most difficult scene in this play is that of the mad house. Badal-babu's imagination has completely transformed this scene, and the character scheme is not that of conventional mad people. Actually through these inhabitants of the mad house Badal-babu has pointed towards the inconsistencies in the fields of literature, history, economics, science etc. in today's world. He, in fact, says that today man is living in a madhouse. The fifth madman is specifically important as he represents a violent streak that wants to destroy the entire world in one go. To communicate this message to the audience without reducing the scene to a joke, it is played in the auditorium around and between the audience. The stage has been extended into the audience from the centre and the sides, which makes it more effective.

So these were some of the general problems and their solutions for a person directing *Abu Hossain*. Now, it might not be out of place to mention some of the problems faced specifically by a director working for Anamika. The commitment that Anamika has made for the past four years of staging a play every week, is enough to rattle any director. And when that play is *Abu Hossain,* with its cast of 45 characters including seven female roles, for which 21 amateur actors have to be brought together every Sunday, the challenge becomes even greater. In a non-Hindi speaking city, finding suitable actors for such a large cast and then keeping them together till the play opens is a big enough task, to constantly keep changing the cast for the ongoing shows due to unavoidable circumstances, is really difficult. Starting from 30 December 1973, till now this play has had 14 shows and has had to undergo at least ten changes in the cast for almost all the major and minor roles. When the play starts regular shows I wonder if I will have any hair left on my head.

Translated from the Director's Note in Pratibha Agrawal's published translation of the play
Publisher: Radhakrishna Prakashan, 1974

PLAY:
Ebong Indrajit (Bangla) (1965)
PLAYWRIGHT:
Badal Sircar
GROUP:
Souvanik, Kolkata
(Nemichandra Jain Collection, Natarang Pratishthan Archives)

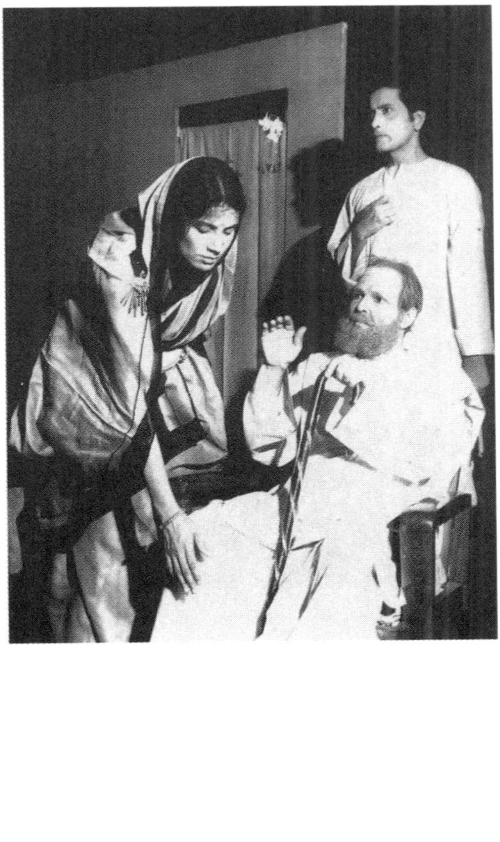

ACTOR:
Tripti Mitra, Shobhen Majumdar and Kumar Roy
PLAY:
Baki Itihas (Bangla) (1967)
PLAYWRIGHT:
Badal Sircar
DIRECTOR:
Sombhu Mitra
GROUP:
Bohurupee, Kolkata
(Natya Shodh Sansthan)

ACTOR:
T. P. Jain (Sharad) and Kulbhushan Kharbanda (Sitanath)

PLAY:
Baki Itihas (Hindi) (1968)

PLAYWRIGHT:
Badal Sircar, Translation: Nemichandra Jain

DIRECTOR:
Rajinder Nath

GROUP:
Abhiyan, Delhi

(Nemichandra Jain Collection, Natarang Pratishthan Archives)

ACTOR:
Shyamanand Jalan (as Lekhak), Satyadev Dubey (as Indrajit and Chetna Tiwari (as Manasi)

PLAY:
Evam Indrajit (Hindi) (1968)

PLAYWRIGHT:
Badal Sircar, Translation: Pratibha Agrawal

DIRECTOR:
Shyamanand Jalan

GROUP:
Anamika, Kolkata

(Natya Shodh Sansthan)

ACTOR:
Satish Anand (Sitanath Chakraborti), Sheila Dyson (Kanak)

PLAY:
Baki Itihas (Hindi) (1969)

PLAYWRIGHT:
Badal Sircar, Translation: Nemichandra Jain

DIRECTOR:
Pyare Mohan Sahay

GROUP:
Kala Sangam, Patna

(Nemichandra Jain Collection, Natarang Pratishthan Archives)

ACTOR:
T. P. Jain (old man) and Sudha Chopra (Wife)

PLAY:
Saari Raat (Hindi) (1970)

PLAYWRIGHT:
Badal Sircar, Translation: Pratibha Agrawal

DIRECTOR:
Rajinder Nath

GROUP:
Abhiyan, Delhi

(Nemichandra Jain Collection, Natarang Pratishthan Archives)

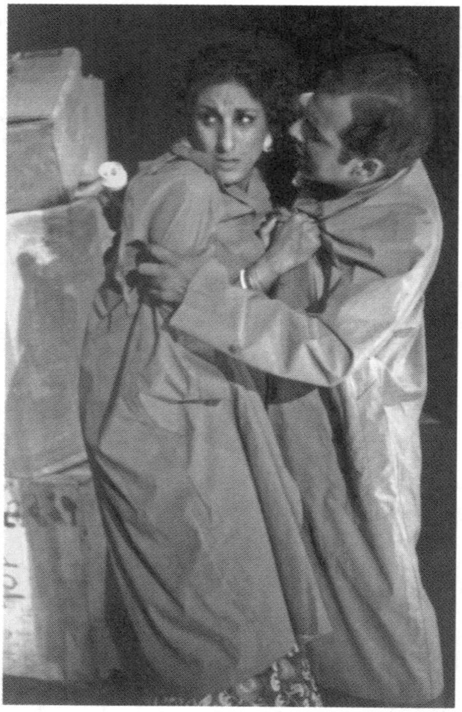

ACTOR:
Sudha Chopra (as Wife), Shyam Arora (as Husband)

PLAY:
Saari Raat (Hindi) (1970)

PLAYWRIGHT:
Badal Sircar, Translation: Pratibha Agrawal

DIRECTOR:
Rajinder Nath

GROUP:
Abhiyan, Delhi

(Natarang Pratishthan Archives)

ACTOR:
Amol Palekar and Hemu Adhikari

PLAY:
Pagla Ghoda (Marathi) (1971)

PLAYWRIGHT:
Badal Sircar, Translation: Arvind Deshpande

DIRECTOR:
Satyadev Dubey

GROUP:
Theatre Unit, Mumbai

(Natya Shodh Sansthan)

ACTOR:
Shyamanand Jalan (Satu) and Yama Agrawal (Lakshmi)

PLAY:
Pagla Ghoda (1971)

PLAYWRIGHT:
Badal Sircar, Translation: Pratibha Agrawal

DIRECTOR:
Satyadev Dubey

GROUP:
Anamika, Kolkata

(Natya Shodh Sansthan)

ACTOR:
Amol Palekar and others

PLAY:
Ballavapurchi Dant Katha (Marathi)

PLAYWRIGHT:
Badal Sircar, Translation: Amol Palekar

GROUP:
Aniket

(Natya Shodh Sansthan)

ACTOR:
Kumar Roy, Debatosh Ghosh, Kaliprasad Ghosh and Shanti Das

PLAY:
Pagla Ghoda (Bangla) (1971)

PLAYWRIGHT:
Badal Sircar

DIRECTOR:
Sombhu Mitra

GROUP:
Bohurupee, Kolkata

(Natya Shodh Sansthan)

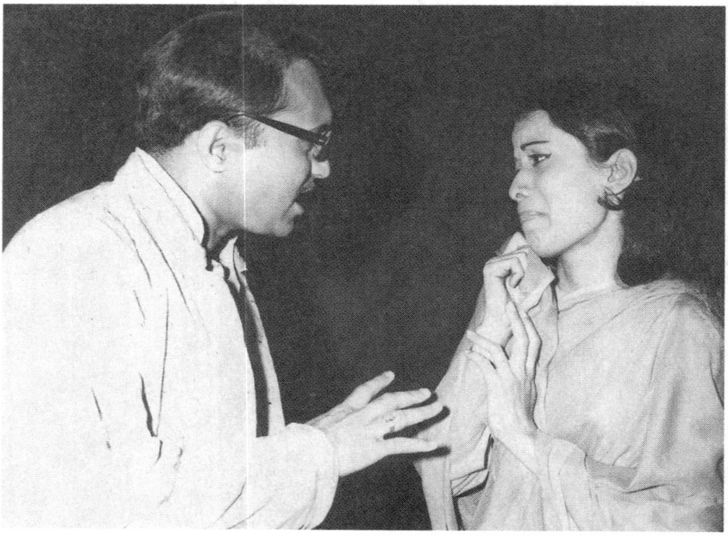

ACTOR:
Suren Fatarpekar (Shashi Babu), Kumud Pawar (Malati)

PLAY:
Pagla Ghoda (Marathi) (1971)

PLAYWRIGHT:
Badal Sircar, Translation: Arvind Deshpande

DIRECTOR:
Satyadev Dubey

GROUP:
Theatre Unit, Mumbai

(Nemichandra Jain Collection, Natarang Pratishthan Archives)

ACTOR:
Sulabha Deshpande and Kamalakar Sarang
PLAY:
Saari Raat (Hindi) (1972)
PLAYWRIGHT:
Badal Sircar, Translation: P.L. Deshpande
GROUP:
Avishkar, Mumbai
(Avishkar, Natarang Pratishthan Archives)

ACTOR:
Aditya Vikram and Yama Agrawal
PLAY:
Saari Raat (Hindi) (1974)
PLAYWRIGHT:
Badal Sircar, Translation: Pratibha Agrawal
DIRECTOR:
Shivkumar Jhunjhunwala
GROUP:
Anamika, Kolkata
(Natya Shodh Sansthan)

Actor:
Harish Bhatia (Purush), Aloka Mehndiratta (Stree)

Play:
Evam Indrajit (Hindi) (1976)

Playwright:
Badal Sircar, Translation: Pratibha Agrawal

Director:
Atulvir Arora

Group:
Abhinet, Chandigarh

(Nemichandra Jain Collection, Natarang Pratishthan Archives)

Actor:
Jaydev Hattangadi talking to his actor Shrikant Dadarkar

Play:
Abu Hasan (Hindi) (1976)

Playwright:
Girishchandra Ghosh, 'Distortion' by Badal Sircar, Translation: Pratibha Agrawal

Group:
Avishkar, Mumbai, Maharashtra

(Avishkar, Natarang Pratishthan Archives)

ACTOR:
Sunila Pradhan and Amrish Puri

PLAY:
Saari Raat, (Hindi) (1977)

PLAYWRIGHT:
Badal Sircar, Translation: Pratibha Agrawal

DIRECTOR:
Amrish Puri

GROUP:
Theatre Unit, Mumbai

(Natya Shodh Sansthan)

ACTOR:
Ernest Albert (Purush) Usha R. Sharma (Stree)

PLAY:
Saari Raat (Hindi) (1978)

PLAYWRIGHT:
Badal Sircar, Translation: Pratibha Agrawal

DIRECTOR:
Atulvir Arora

GROUP:
Abhinet, Chandigarh

(Nemichandra Jain Collection, Natarang Pratishthan Archives)

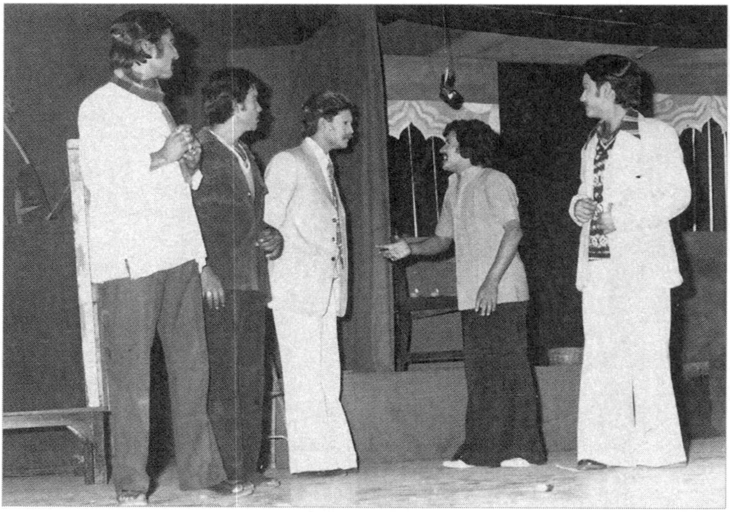

ACTOR:
Mazhar (Ram), Nandlal (Shyam), Raghubar Dayal (Shukdev), Nandkishor(Jadu) and Raj Bahadur (Jaydev)

PLAY:
Ram-Shyam-Jadu (Hindi) (1978)

PLAYWRIGHT:
Badal Sircar, Translation: Pratibha Agrawal

DIRECTOR:
Madan Mohan Shrivastava

GROUP:
Rupayan, Jamshedpur, Bihar

(Nemichandra Jain Collection, Natarang Pratishthan Archives)

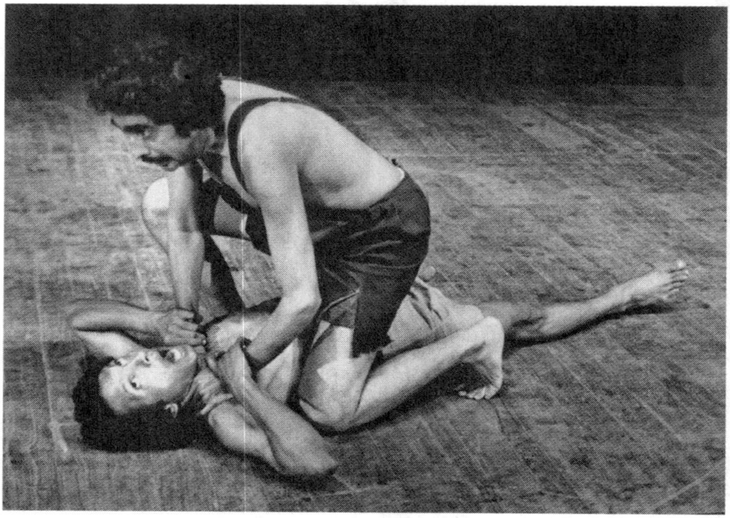

PLAY:
Spartacus (Hindi) (1978)

PLAYWRIGHT:
Dramatised in Bangla by Badal Sircar from Howard Fast's novel. Translation: Rati Bartholomew and Virendra Saxena

DIRECTOR:
M. K. Raina

GROUP:
Prayog, Delhi

(Natarang Pratishthan Archives)

Play:
Baki Itihas (Hindi) (1981)
Playwright:
Badal Sircar, Translation: Nemichandra Jain
Director:
Sanakhya Ebotombi
Group:
National School of Drama, Delhi
(National School of Drama)

Actor:
Ashutosh Awasthi (Dr. Sinha), Jitendra Shrotva (Dr. Somen) Nahid Jamal (Roopa)
Play:
Solution X (Hindi) (1982)
Playwright:
Badal Sircar, Translation: Yama Shroff
Director:
Jitendra Mittal
Group:
Yayavar Natya Mela, Lucknow
(Nemichandra Jain Collection, Natarang Pratishthan Archives)

Left:

Actor:
Seema Bhargava and Kailash Kaushik

Play:
Kavi Kahani (Hindi) (1984)

Playwright:
Badal Sircar, Translation: Ashok Bhattacharya

Director:
Sabina Mehta Sood

Group:
Shri Ram Centre Rep., Delhi

(Shri Ram Centre, Natarang Pratishthan Archives)

Actor:
Seema Bhargava, Pratima Kazmi, Sanjeev Sahay and others

Play:
Kavi Kahani (Hindi) (1984)

Playwright:
Badal Sircar, Translation: Ashok Bhattacharya

Director:
Sabina Mehta Sood

Group:
Shri Ram Centre Rep., Delhi

(Shri Ram Centre, Natarang Pratishthan Archives)

Actor:
Dinesh Thakur (Sitanath) and Minakshi Thakur (Kanak)
Play:
Baki Itihas (Hindi) (1987)
Playwright:
Badal Sircar, Translation: Nemichandra Jain
Director:
Dinesh Thakur
Group:
Ank, Mumbai
(Nemichandra Jain Collection, Natarang Pratishthan Archives)

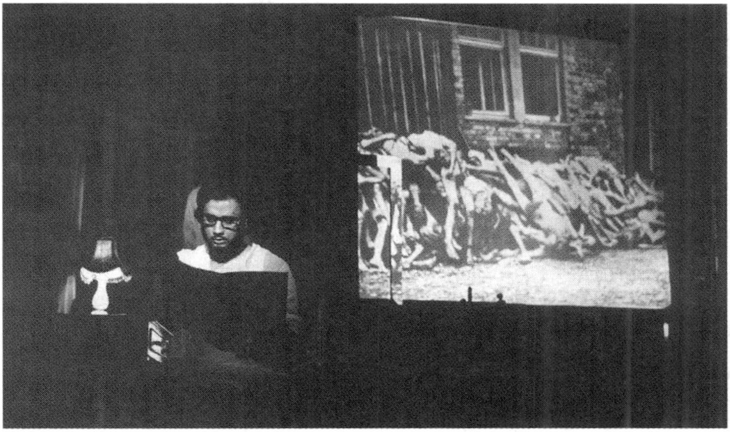

Actor:
Dinesh Thakur
Play:
Baki Itihas (Hindi) (1987)
Playwright:
Badal Sircar, Translation: Nemichandra Jain
Director:
Dinesh Thakur
Group:
Ank, Mumbai
(Nemichandra Jain Collection, Natarang Pratishthan Archives)

ACTOR:
Arijit Guha, Ramaprasad Banik and others

PLAY:
Jadi Aar Ek Baar (Bangla)

PLAYWRIGHT:
Badal Sircar

DIRECTOR:
Tripti Mitra

GROUP:
Bohurupee, Kolkata

(Natya Shodh Sansthan)

ACTOR:
Anupam Shyam (Satu), Amit Banerjee (Shashi), Shrivallabh Vyas (Kartik), Vipin Kumar (Himadri), Seema Biswas (Girl)

PLAY:
Pagla Ghoda (Hindi) (1988)

PLAYWRIGHT:
Badal Sircar, Translation: Pratibha Agrawal

DIRECTOR:
Satyadev Dubey

GROUP:
National School of Drama Rep.

(Nemichandra Jain Collection, Natarang Pratishthan Archives)

Actor:
Vimal Lath (Abu Hasan), Kalpana Tiwari (Sakhi), Snigdha Vahi (Roshanara), Narendra Agrawal (Mansoor) Tridip Dugarh, Govind Fatehpuriya and Ramavtar Bagla (Vaitalik Gan)

Play:
Abu Hasan (Hindi)

Playwright:
Girishchandra Ghosh, 'Distortion' by Badal Sircar, Translation: Pratibha Agrawal

Director:
Vimal Lath

Group:
Anamika, Kolkata

(Natya Shodh Sansthan)

Play:
Baki Itihas (Hindi)

Playwright:
Badal Sircar, Translation: Nemichandra Jain

Director:
K.P. Singh and Shail Choyal

Group:
Seva Mandir Abhinaya Goshthi, Udaipur, Rajasthan

(Nemichandra Jain Collection, Natarang Pratishthan Archives)

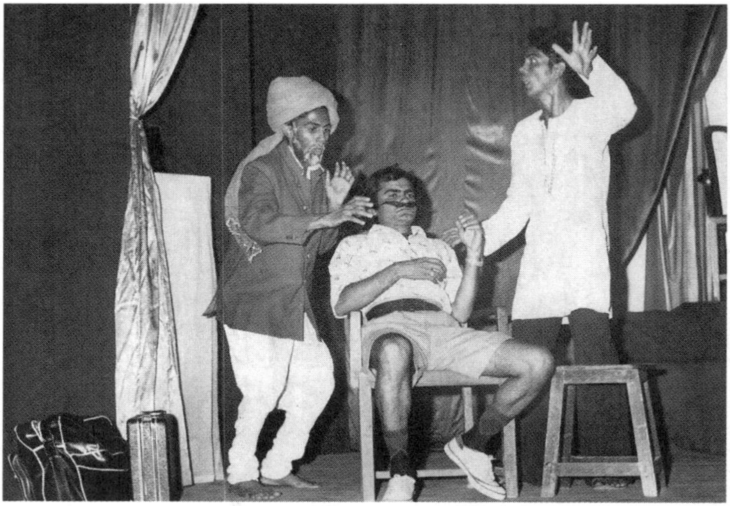

Play:
Ballabhpur Ki Roopkatha (Hindi)
Playwright:
Badal Sircar, Translation: Pratibha Agrawal
Director:
Afsar Hussain
Group:
Rangayan, Bikaner
(Nemichandra Jain Collection, Natarang Pratishthan Archives)

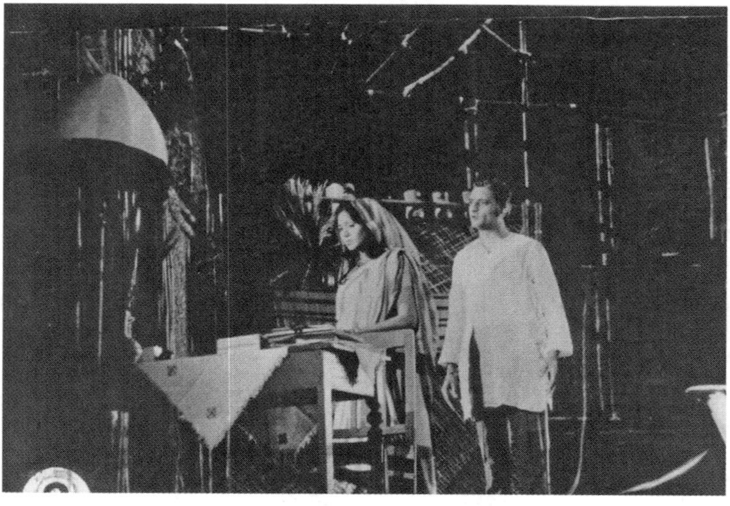

Play:
Baki Itihas (Hindi)
Playwright:
Badal Sircar, Translation: Nemichandra Jain
Director:
Bansi Kaul
Group:
Darpan, Kanpur
(Nemichandra Jain Collection, Natarang Pratishthan Archives)

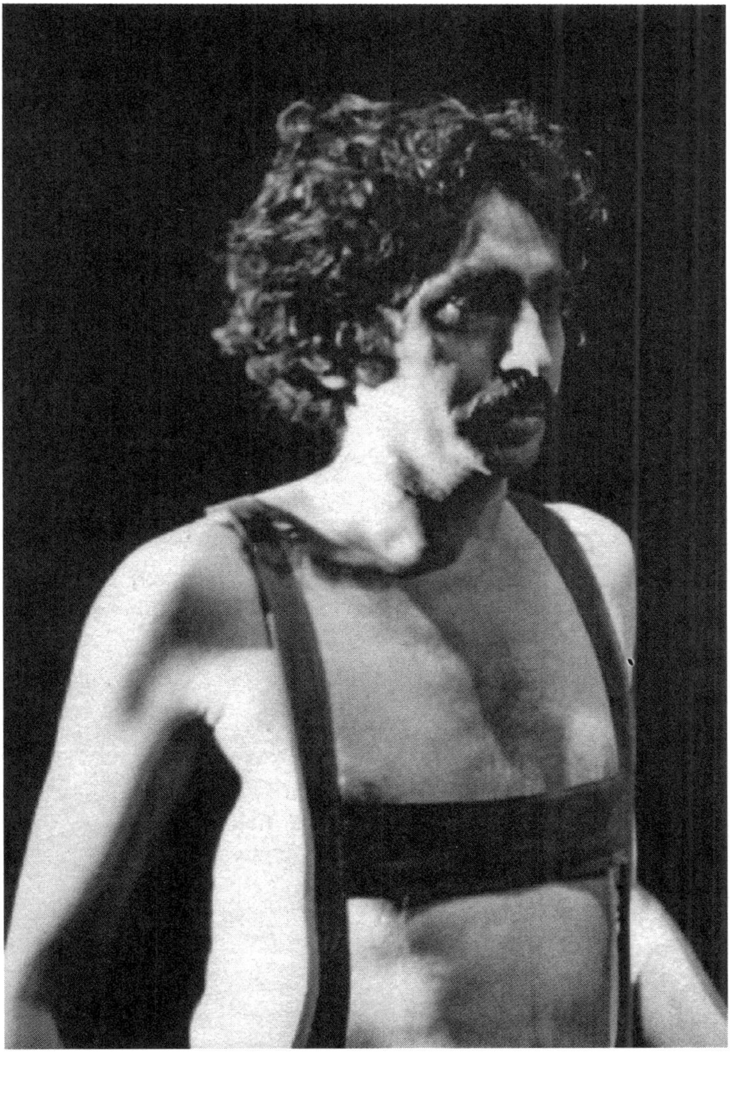

Play:
Spartacus
(Hindi) (1978)

Playwright:
Dramatised in Bangla by Badal Sircar from Howard Fast's novel, Translation: Rati Bartholomew and Virendra Saxena

Director:
M. K. Raina

Group:
Prayog, Delhi

(Natarang Pratishthan Archives)

THE THIRD THEATRE

WORLD THEATRE DAY MESSAGE
1982

Badal Sircar

I *believe* that theatre is 'Human Action'. The event of theatre can take place only when two parties of 'Human Beings' – performers and spectators – gather at the same place on the same day at the same time and stay together for a period of time. Theatre is 'Here', 'Now'.

I *believe* that to ensure human action, the barriers between the performers and the spectators should be removed as far as possible. The proscenium theatre is full of barriers, barriers of distance, of levels, of light and darkness, and hence I do not believe the proscenium theatre to be the proper medium for 'Direct Communication' that the 'here, now' of theatre can offer.

I *believe* that human action is possible when theatre is 'Free'. The condition of having to pay for entry to theatre establishes a buyer-seller relationship which, however much in vogue and considered essential in most societies, is certainly not a 'Human Relationship'.

I *believe* that 'Free Theatre' is possible, even in societies based on buying and selling. The costly items of theatre-stage and auditorium, sets and props, spotlights, audiovisuals and gadgets, are not essentials of theatre. The only essential tool of theatre is the Human Body. People donating voluntarily (as they often do in political parties) will help realise whatever little they need to run their theatre from voluntary donation after the show, without making payment a precondition of entry to theatre.

I *believe* that theatre is for the sake of Man, and therefore is for the sake of Human Society. When a society cries for change, theatre becomes Theatre of Change.

I *believe* that Theatre, like all arts, can be an Art only when it is Honest, that is when genuine beliefs and feelings are communicated. This is possible only in Free Theatre. When art becomes a commodity, genuine beliefs and feelings are gradually replaced by elements of saleability.

I *believe* that theatre should be based on Cooperation, as the future society should also be, and not on competition.

(The emphasis is that given by the author.)
Issued by Bhartiya Natya Sangh, affiliated to ITI, UNESCO
Courtesy: Natya Shodh Sansthan, Kolkata

THE CHANGING LANGUAGE OF THEATRE

Badal Sircar

When I try to talk about the language of theatre, the first question that I have faced is, who am I? That includes a series of questions—where do I come from? Where do I belong in the complex social structure of this complex world? What are my times? What is my language? What is my theatre? What is the language of my theatre?

All this sounds egoistic, but it is not. The questions are relevant because I am bound in space and time. I am not independent, I am not absolute, I am not universal. My thoughts, my actions, are limited to the life I have lived, the experience I have had, the choices I have made or have had to make, so far. To talk about the language of theatre, I can only talk about my language in my theatre. I could easily have said 'we' instead of 'I', for there are many others like me in the present company, for example. I can be taken as prototype of a particular class in a society at a particular period.

Let us do so; let us take a typical person like me. An Indian, a city man, born and brought up in Calcutta – a monster of a city – but a monster that is alive, throbbing with vitality and viciousness, may be with a vision too. A middle-class man. Perhaps his father was a professor in a Calcutta college, his grandfather a school teacher in a village, his great-grandfather probably had some petty land-owning interest. An educated man, which means he has gone through the English system of teaching mills – the system being English all through, the medium of instruction being vernacular in most parts – which will be very apparent if he ever tries to deliver a lecture in English before an august company such as this. He got his education because his father could afford the college fees and could support a dependent up to the mature age of 21. The level of his education is high in the context of a country where 70 per cent of the population is illiterate, but very low in terms of the knowledge a man can really acquire.

Where does he belong in 'time'? Let us assume that his basic education was completed in a colony under the British rule, and he became a wage-earner a little before Independence. And he is still alive; still going, strong or otherwise, in 1982.

His language, philologically speaking, is Bengali. Culturally speaking, it is English; for the culture of his class in the cities of this country was English, still is English.

This person, this typical middle-class, urban-educated Bengali is, at a given moment, the result of all the choices he has made in his life prior to that moment. The choices were not wholly independent; they were determined and limited by his surroundings, his class roots, his times. But even within that framework there may be wide variety, and that makes him an individual even when he is a prototype.

One of the choices that he makes in one phase of his life, let us suppose, is theatre. Like many such choices, it may have initially been just a pastime. An occupation for his leisure hours, it gradually acquires more and more importance in his life; acting in sporadic amateur performances at first, then directing and, finally, trying to write plays, because he wants to produce plays.

Being a city man, he naturally accepts the city theatre in the first instance. To be more specific, he chooses the theatre prevalent in Calcutta at the time, say in the early 1950s; and he adopts the language of that particular theatre. He may be vaguely aware of other kinds of theatre prevailing in the rural areas of India but, having little exposure to them, the question of exploring in that direction does not occur to him.

As a matter of fact, when we use the term 'theatre', an English term which we have more or less incorporated into our languages, do we not always visualise the city theatre? A large hall, with rows of seats for the spectators, all facing the same way? If we are the spectators, we find ourselves facing a wall that looks like a huge picture frame, with the 'picture' covered by a heavy curtain. When the action begins, we are plunged into darkness and the curtain is removed, exposing the area of action which is virtually another room with a raised floor on the other side of the picture frame. All the light is in that room, all the action, all the speech and sound. The make-believe world of theatre is there, the make-believe life; and we watch and listen, sitting in another room, passive and patient, hiding in the dark. The world of action beyond the frame is real and unreal; it is not reality but an illusion of reality. The people in action are people like us, but also different from us, detached from us. They did not come through the same doors that we used, and they will go out by a different one when the event is over. Even now, they are not aware of our presence or pretending that they are not—which means that they are ignoring us or that we are useless to them. But at the same time we know that we are not useless; whatever they are doing, they are doing for our sake. Without us, they would be useless.

When our prototype chooses the theatre, it is this theatre that he chooses; the proscenium stage, that is the stage beyond the frame known as the proscenium arch and the auditorium with rows of numbered seats, the sets and the spotlights, the costume and the makeup, the greenrooms at the back of the stage and the lobby at the front of the house, the publicity of the show and the booking office with tickets of different prices. Let us suppose that he carries on for nearly twenty years apparently without any change in his attitude towards such a theatre.

Nevertheless, the forces of change were there, throughout the period, working within, almost secretly.

'Change' is like a magic element. A person belongs to a given world at a given time, but the world changes in time and he changes with it. The world changes him but he, along with the others, also changes the world. Herein lies his power. He is a product of a particular society in a particular period, but he can influence the change of that society by every single choice he makes, every single action he takes. He is not alone. The choices made, the actions taken by many people like him ultimately change the world, for better or for worse.

So despite his continued acceptance of the prevalent city theatre, questions arise in his mind with his increasing involvement in theatre. When he begins to write plays, more questions crop up. How much can one express in theatre? Can one express everything that one thinks and feels about? What are the limits? How much of a play is literature? What is the relationship of a written play with the performance of the play? What is the difference between the language of a play and the language of the theatre? What is theatre, for that matter? How does one communicate through theatre? How much of the theatre is entertainment, how much is aesthetics and how much a means of communicating messages? What are the similarities with other art forms? What are its distinctive features? What is theatre in the Indian setting?

One can go on adding questions, but that is not necessary. The answers that are found are seldom full or final; but the process of asking questions and trying to find answers is the process of 'change', and that is what really matters. The change comes from a growing awareness—not just of theatre, but of theatre in relation to life, society and time. The process is complicated and many-faceted, even confusing; only when the answers are not stored in the mind at an abstract level but are tried out in action is confusion gradually dispelled, helping a pattern begin to emerge.

The exploration begins by looking closely at the thing at hand and that is the city theatre of the present. A writer writes a play—that is the beginning. As such it is a piece of literature written in a particular language which is to be read by others knowing that language, just like they read a poem or a novel. But then comes a director who transforms the written play into audio-visual scenes with the help of several performers. Let us call this the score, as some theatre people do. When the performers project the score to other people, it is no longer a piece of literature to be read and enjoyed privately and severally, but an event to be audio-visually experienced by a group of people assembled for that purpose—the spectators. This event is the performance. If the play is the beginning, the performance is the end and the score is the connecting link. And all these three elements taken together – the play, the score and the performance – constitute what we call theatre.

The playwright therefore has to think of the final event, the performance, right from the beginning. He has to deal with two media simultaneously—literature and theatre. His language has to be a special language, different from that in other branches of literature, for it must be translatable into audio-visual scenes which can be projected by a group of performers to a group of spectators. These two groups assemble and stay together for a span of time by mutual agreement, and the play in its entirety must be expressed in audio-visual terms within that span of time.

The playwright can do this through a story. He usually does, and has been for quite some time.

In order to be translated into theatre language, the story has to be expressed through the interaction of a number of inter-related people – the characters in the play – mostly by means of dialogue. Here, the language of the playwright is the language used by different persons in the story. The playwright is actually copying from life. The characters of his play are most believable when they speak, behave and react in exactly the same way as the spectator would expect them to, under the circumstances created by the story of the play. Those circumstances must also be believable, that is, something that can happen in real life. The *settings* of the events of the story should be as close to the real-life situation as possible. But just a copy of real life does not make theatre; the playwright has to screen out those inevitable details with which life is encumbered, which are not relevant to his story, which are not interesting. He may decide to omit two hours, three days, several months or even years from the life of the people in his play. This time lapse is indicated by a gap between two consecutive parts or 'scenes' of the play, usually created by closing the curtain or by making the stage dark. The change in the locales of different events is also indicated in the same way.

This kind of theatre, as we all know, is called the naturalistic theatre. The performers' task in such theatre is to speak and behave in the manner of the characters of the play, and the director prepares the score accordingly. The idea is to make the spectator believe that the people on the stage are not performers but the actual people of the story; that the stage is not just a raised platform but the actual places where the events of the story occur. In short, *an illusion of reality* is to be created in the mind of the spectator, so that he can identify with the characters in the play in terms of his own experiences in real life, feel for them, be moved by the events in their lives.

In naturalistic theatre, the language of the play and the language of the theatre have the same point of reference—real life as we find it; and hence the two languages are not much different if the copy from life is authentic. It is a game of recognition. The playwright knows the man he has put in his play as a character, the director recognises the man and helps the performer recognise him. The performer copies the man in his performance, facilitating the spectator to also recognise him.

The proscenium stage is very suitable for this kind of theatre. One can take the advantage of the distance between the performer and the spectator, and of the separation of the acting area from the sitting area of the spectators, to create the desired illusion of reality. The stage lights play an important role in making the fake look like the real. That is why magicians, also known as 'illusionists', always prefer the proscenium stage.

Several questions crop up. To what extent can such illusion be created? Does the spectator really forget that it is the stage, and that the people on it are performers? Whatever illusion is created, how much of it is through the willing use of the spectator's own imagination rather than through what he actually sees and hears? Does not the spectator come prepared to be deluded, obeying an unwritten law of theatre?

And now, here is the new art-cinema. Can theatre really compete with cinema in the matter of creating illusions? The answer obviously is 'never'. The images of the cinema are the images of reality where photographs of a snow-capped mountain, a foaming sea, a pulsating city street are taken. Even the indoor sets look real, because much more money can be spent in constructing those sets and the camera can hide many defects and leave out unrequired details. In that case, is it not better to depend more on the imagination of the spectator, at least in the matter of the settings of the events in the play? Why not, for example, put up a free-standing door frame to represent the door instead of trying to show realistically the entire wall with a door in it? Such things are being increasingly done now-a-days in the naturalistic theatre.

But once one emerges from the bounds of the necessity of creating an illusion of reality, the emergence need not be limited to the sets alone. One can come out of the story, come out of the characters, come out of naturalism altogether. The playwright may find that what he wants to say cannot be effectively said through a story with characters who have definite identities. A character may be too limiting in his individuality, a story may be too specific to suit his subject. For example, he may want to deal with the problems of people like himself, urban middle-class people – a minority in society no doubt, but an important minority – who he knows intimately. He may be more concerned with their problem in general than those of certain individuals and, therefore, he may find that prototypes rather than characters would be more suitable to express that the problems are not of one but of many. He can use four prototypes with rhyming names like Amal, Vimal, Kamal, Nirmal to emphasise their generality. He can give one of them another name – say Indrajit – to show that this person is in some ways different from the other three; but Indrajit is also a prototype, not a character. To express the problems of Indrajit effectively, he may put in somebody, one of the dramatis personae, who is neither a character nor a prototype but a kind of alter-ego to Indrajit. As a story would be too specific to project the universal nature of the problem, he uses a cycle of typical events from their lives instead—examination, interview, marriage and career. If he does so, then the exploration begins for a new language of theatre and he soon comes to the fundamental question—what is theatre?

Looking for the answer to that question, the first thing he realises is something he had always known but had never understood the full import of; the fact that theatre is a live show. The event of theatre does not take place unless two parties of human beings, the performers and the spectators gather at the same place on the same day at the same time, and stay together for some time. The performers are here and now, although the story or the theme of the play may be there and then.

As soon as our prototype realises this, the spectators acquire a new importance for him. Can we – he asks himself – afford to put the spectators at a distance? At a different level? In darkness? Have they not come to meet us? Are they not an integral part of the theatre event? In the light of these questions, the architecture of the proscenium theatre appears to be all wrong. All spectators on one side means pushing the last row too far. Why not put them on all sides? The higher level of the stage makes the performers superior and detached. Why not come down to the same level? The spectators hiding in the dark render it impossible for the performers to get any direct feedback from them, or for the spectators to get feedback from one another. Why not put them in the light so that we can see them and they can see one another? Everybody looking in one direction and seeing the action beyond the picture frame creates a two-dimensional image. Why not be in the same space with the spectators to make it a three-dimensional reality as theatre really is?

Theatre is live. In theatre, direct communication is possible. That is the strength of theatre. That is where cinema can never compete with theatre. Theatre is the meeting place of two sets of human beings; something happens between them—a human act. Theatre is a human event, cinema is not.

It is said that the source of theatre is ritual. Ritual is a theatre in which the whole community participates. The play is not written but is known by the whole community; the score is also known; the roles are distributed according to convention. In ritual, everybody participates but there are some performers who have special roles—'shamans', guides and initiators, trance dancers, high priests, chosen seniors. They are allotted special action and speech, special costume, special makeup. It is true that ritual is mainly result-oriented—it is performed to ward off calamity, bring rain, increase fertility, initiate a child into adulthood, transform single status into married status etc., but ritual is also entertainment. The elements of fun and fiesta are there for the entire community. Theatre can also be result-oriented, as theatre committed to a particular cause is. Such theatre desires to change the thought and belief of the spectators, lead them to some action. In this respect, theatre is moving closer to ritual, inter-weaving efficacy and entertainment. But to attain efficacy, asks our prototype, do we not need the greater participation of the spectators? Can we afford to monopolise all the action and give them a passive role as is done in the conventional city theatre? Is there no way of including them a little more in the event of theatre, as communities do in ritual?

In theatre, communication can occur in four ways: performer to spectator, performer to performer, spectator to performer and spectator to spectator. Of these, the first two ways are very clear to all of us. The performers always project to the spectators; that is what theatre is for. The performers communicate with one another, for they are interrelated in their roles in the play; even when there is no story and no characters, they work as a team, complementing one another in action and speech. But when we speak of the other two ways of communication, we begin to panic. We think that the spectators communicating to the performers or to other spectators would mean chaos. And so it would, if we assume that communication is limited to language. The attention of the spectator, concentration, the reaction to the performance reflected in his facial expression or the tension in his body—all these can be a form of feedback to the performer or to another spectator. And once the performer recognises the presence of the spectators by coming nearer, by putting them in the light, other opportunities of voluntary and spontaneous participation on the part of the spectators can be included in the theatre.

This process of exploration, of asking questions and finding possible answers, does not remain limited in his mind simply as a thought process. Being actively involved in theatre all through, he tries out many of the answers in his practice even within the framework of the city theatre. The language of the plays he writes, the language of the performances he directs or acts in, goes on changing.

For instance, when he comes to realise that theatre is a live show, he naturally begins to depend more on human beings—both performers and spectators. That brings him to a further realisation that the basic tool of the art of theatre is the human body. Coming out of naturalistic theatre confirms this realisation. All the paraphernalia of the conventional city theatre – sets, props, spotlights, costume, make-up – are they really essential? They may be helpful, they may be necessary for some kind of plays, but is any of them the essential tool of the trade of theatre? In other words, will theatre cease to be theatre if any or all of them are absent? Without the human body, without the active presence of the human being, theatre will not exist.

So even in his proscenium-theatre practice, the emphasis on sets, props, costume, makeup and lighting gradually gets reduced, whereas the dependence on the human body increases. The language of the plays he writes changes accordingly, although they are still written with the proscenium stage in mind. Even when he writes a play which has a story and identifiable characters speaking naturalistically, he prepares a structure that is far from naturalistic. Continuity of time and separation of space are not respected; the action flows from one time to another, one space to another, without any break, without changing sets or props. Even events occurring at two or more different places at two or more different times are enacted simultaneously. Sometimes space is expanded, sometimes time is telescoped. As sets and props are suggested rather than shown, so are events and actions suggested by signs rather than actual actions—like a series of abstract movements and gestures, like a burst of body energy and sound energy. He does these because of his increased dependence on the human being—the performer's body on the one hand, and the spectator's imagination on the other.

And if the magic of change really works, the final outcome for him is to come out of the proscenium theatre altogether. It is a difficult step to take for a city man like him who has accepted the proscenium theatre for so long but, once he takes the step, the language of his theatre begins to change rapidly. A kind of consolidation of all the little changes that have occurred so far in his thoughts and actions begins to take place.

Let us presume that he took that step ultimately, say in the early 1970s, and he now tries to describe the theatre he chose.

This is an intimate theatre. The performer is able to see the spectator clearly, can approach him individually, can whisper in his ear. The performer may even touch him if he wants to. The action can take place in front of the spectator, but may also be behind him or by his side. The mistaken notion that each spectator must be able to see the entire action at all times, no matter if he sees it from a distance of 200 feet, is dispensed with. The language of this theatre involves *being within* and *experiencing*, not viewing and hearing from a separate distant sanctum. It involves projecting individually to another human being and receiving his feedback here and now, not projecting to a dark amorphous mass and pretending to be unaware of the fact that the mass is composed of human beings.

Experience is the key word in every art. The appeal of an art form is principally, if not solely, through emotion and not through intellect. The function of a novel is not just to tell a story to the reader but to create a world through the feelings and associations aroused in his mind. A good painting does not just depict a scene or an incident but moves the viewer emotionally. Does that not apply to the language of theatre as well?

These words – 'communicating through emotion', 'theatrical experience' – what are their implications in the new theatre?

The demand of the spectator in the new theatre is not of an illusion of reality but of reality itself, the reality of the presence of the 'performer'. For, this theatre does not involve only a change in the interrelationship of the spaces occupied by the performers and the spectators; it involves a basic change in the relation between the performer and the spectator as two human beings. That leads to a change in the language of performance. In the conventional naturalistic theatre, the performer changes his identity to that of the character in the play. It is done through costume, makeup, bearing, movement, gesture, facial expression, mannerism—everything copied and applied; in short, faking. This is generally known as 'acting' .But now the performer comes down, comes close and appears as the human being that he is to the spectator—who is also another human being. Now he can no longer fake; now he has to take off his mask and be himself.

Being one's own self is one of the most difficult tasks today, in our civilisation. The so called civilised man is taught to wear a mask from his very childhood. 'Do this', 'don't do that', 'behave properly', he is told all the time when he is a child, and he tells himself the same when he grows up. His behaviour, his movements, his facial expressions, his gestures, his speech—everything gets constrained and conditioned, and what he presents to others is not his real self but an external appearance, a façade that will protect him and help him in this unkind society revolving around competition. He uses only a part of his body to express his emotions and that suffices to express the little of himself that he wants to present to others: the code of this civilisation is not expressing, but hiding. In what is known as the 'naturalistic' theatre, the performer copies this very unnatural and highly artificial behaviour and speech of another person who is in a similar condition—he takes off his own mask only to put on the mask of somebody else.

But the new theatre demands a different language of performance altogether. The performer has to take off his mask and lay bare his real self. In the 'civilised' world, theatre is probably the only public place where this is at all possible, and now the performer can take advantage of it. It is also a great risk to take, for he is vulnerable without his mask, without his protective armour. But the risk has to be taken because that is the only way to appeal to the spectator to take off his own mask. When that happens, theatre becomes a real human event, a real meeting of human beings; not mask to mask, armour to armour, but man to man.

By all this, the importance of the intellect is not being belittled; one acquires knowledge through intellect and knowledge is extremely important. But knowledge without feeling makes one pedantic, as feelings without knowledge can put one in an ivory tower or send one to the mountains to meditate. The integration of knowledge and feelings is what can be called consciousness, and it is consciousness that can induce and guide any meaningful action that can in turn change the world for the better. We know that people in this world die of starvation, that people are tortured behind prison walls, that the planet earth can be destroyed totally by a minute fraction of the stockpile of nuclear weapons: all this is knowledge. But unless we feel the full import of that knowledge, we do not take action.

Let us come back to the consciousness of the person we are talking about. He realises now that the changed language of his theatre gives him the means for a man-to-man, gut-to-gut communication of feelings. He does not deny that it has been done sometimes in his proscenium theatre also but his own experiences, both as performer and as spectator, tell him that the communication has to work against heavy odds, has to cross many barriers and only the greatest of plays, the greatest of performers, can achieve such emotional impact. In the new theatre, he feels a freedom that he has never felt in proscenium theatre.

He has another realisation which is very important to him. He finds that by dispensing with the costly stage and auditorium, the paraphernalia of non-essentials like sets, props, spotlights, costumes etc., and by depending on the human body, he has freed his theatre from an abject dependence on money. In a society based on buying and selling, art unfortunately also becomes a commodity that can be bought and sold, and he was forced so far to accept that condition. But now the possibility of creating a Free Theatre opens up. And that brings him to one of the first questions he asked himself right at the beginning—what is theatre in the Indian context? So let us go back to the beginning of the process of change and examine it in another light.

Right from the beginning he is aware, however vaguely, that the theatre he is choosing is not the only theatre of India, nor the most prevalent or popular in terms of the number of spectators. It is not even a theatre born in this country. There is great variety of theatres, grouped under the general heading of 'folk theatre' or 'traditional theatre', having different forms and names in different regions. India, therefore, does not have one theatre but two distinct kinds. The first kind is indigenous and is prevalent in rural areas, whereas the second kind has been imported from a western country, namely Britain, a little over a century ago; and even if we say that it has acquired Indian citizenship, it is still very different from the first kind and is contained in the urban areas. These two theatres have been running parallel for over 100 years without any significant give and take.

This state of affairs is not surprising. One of the most important characteristics of the socio-economic conditions of India is an unfortunate dichotomy between urban and rural life. This dichotomy is not limited simply to disparities in economic standards, services available, educational levels, cultural developments and so on, but is something more fundamental. Its root lies in the historical fact of India having been a colonial country for so long. In the first phase of colonial exploitation, the products of the highly developed cottage industries of India were purchased at unfair rates by the East India Company and paid for by the money collected by taxing the Indian people; and cities like Calcutta, Bombay, Madras were created to serve as centres for collecting and exporting such products to Europe. The capital accumulated through this exploitation enabled Britain to complete her Industrial Revolution. Then, of course, it was not in the interest of Britain to import Indian products but, rather, to sell her own industrial products in India. Hence, first, the Indian cottage industries that tended to compete with the British industries were systematically destroyed and next, India was converted into a backward agricultural country to serve as a gigantic market for British industrial goods on the one hand and to supply raw material to the British industries on the other hand. The establishment of the zamindari system was a very effective means to achieve these ends. The cities and ports of India played a greater role in this phase of foreign exploitation, and the urban-rural dichotomy in the economic field became much more pronounced. Cities developed and thrived literally at the cost of the villages.

The effects of this dichotomy in the cultural field were also very pronounced. English education was introduced to serve British colonial interest, and quite naturally, the facilities were first provided in the cities. Those who could take advantage of the English education in the first instance belonged either to the families of landholders under the zamindari system, or to the families of businessmen, brokers, usurers etc., who acquired wealth in the process of colonial exploitation. As a result, the culture of the cities found its roots in western soil and there was almost a clear break from the traditional indigenous culture. The culture of the countryside, however, did not die and the two cultures ran parallel, thus extending the urban-rural dichotomy to the cultural field.

This perspective of the theatre situation in India gradually develops in the mind of our prototype through the period of his activities within the confines of the conventional city theatre; and, while searching for a new language for communicating more effectively in theatre, he wants to do something about dichotomy also, however inadequate and limited his attempts may be. His exploration, therefore, includes a search for a Free Theatre that will not be limited to an urban audience belonging to the middle and upper classes, nor tied down to backward values unrelated to the life and problems of the working masses of the country. He realises gradually that a flexible, portable and inexpensive theatre is needed for that, a Third Theatre, at least for the time being.

And now, when he finally breaks away from the proscenium theatre after so many long years, he finds that he has not only found a way of communicating directly in theatre, thereby utilising the strength of this live art form, but that the solution to the problem of creating a flexible, portable and inexpensive theatre – a Free Theatre – is also at hand, because he is no longer dependent on the money required for the costly inessentials of the proscenium theatre. His theatre can now serve two purposes, can move in two different directions. Firstly, through an intimate theatre, an intense emotional communication is possible and, secondly, theatre can go to a place where people are not waiting for them specifically. Both these theatres can be free in principle as well as in effect, for they can function on the basis of voluntary donation. Payment of money need not be a condition of entry. This is very important, not just because most of the people in this country cannot afford to pay the price of the tickets but, principally because a human act like theatre should let people meet freely on the basis of equal status so that their relationship can be *human*.

Although the philosophies of the two kinds of new theatre are the same, the respective languages differ considerably. The environment of the intimate theatre obtained by the arrangement of sets, the individual approach made possible by proximity of the spectators, the intensity of communication, the subtlety of projection—all these are not to be had in an open-air performance in a village or a park where, sometimes, thousands of people gather. But this may be more than compensated for by the fact that his theatre can now reach the working people of villages and slums who would never have come to his intimate theatre in Calcutta. So if he is reluctant to leave any of the two theatres, there is no other way but to work hard to develop and master both the languages.

So here he is our prototype, the language of his theatre changed fundamentally, and still changing. The language has changed, but not because he wanted to change it for the sake of the change. His exploration has never been motivated by a desire to experiment alone. He has never believed in maxims like 'art for art's sake' or theatre for the sake of theatre'. The entire process of change involves a philosophy, and he believes that the new language can only be established if it takes the shape of a movement. And when he looks around, he finds that slowly but surely the movement is beginning and gathering momentum—in the suburbs of Calcutta, in the small towns of Bengal, in other parts of India, even in some villages. He is by no means the initiator of the movement; the problems of the day, the need of the hour are inducing many people at various places to change the language of their theatre independently, just as has happened, and is still happening, in his own life.

Theatre by itself will never change the world for the better, but let us allow theatre to stake a modest claim in the process of that change. And let us wish that the language of theatre continues to change everywhere accordingly. As for the man, well, he is only a prototype to show the universal nature of the process, as in a play, so we can forget him now.

Maulana Abul Kalam Azad Memorial Lecture, 1981
Courtesy: Seagull Books, Kolkata

OUR STREET THEATRE

Badal Sircar

Every major language contains many words that have different meanings for different people, depending particularly on the 'class' or milieu the person using or reading the word belongs to. The word 'theatre', for example, evokes in the mind of the educated urban middle class or the 'upper class' person, the image of the proscenium theatre with its stage, auditorium, spotlights, sets, and all the paraphernalia. For him, the predominantly popular theatre of India will have to be qualified by the adjective 'folk' or 'traditional' to have the proper image evoked.

Likewise, the term 'Street Theatre' should actually mean the innumerable theatres we find in streets and public places presented by acrobats, jugglers, magicians, animal trainers, quack-medicine sellers, wandering singers and dancers, who all do it for their living. But to an educated middle class city person like me, as well as the readers of this article, the term brings forth the image of some persons like us stepping outside the precincts of the conventional indoor theatre and its ticket-buying audience to present theatre free of cost for the public in general in the streets and other such public places.

Why the 'Street'?

There must be a fairly definite reason for an educated urban middle class person for choosing to do theatre in the streets instead of the secure and well-equipped world of the conventional indoor stage and auditorium. Although some may do it for the sheer novelty and adventure of it (a valid enough reason), most of those who are at present wholly or partly in 'Street Theatre' have a more defined purpose. Almost invariably, these are not the people who have taken up theatre simply for the sake of the art form. They have something definite to say, some definite knowledge or consciousness or feeling or experience, to communicate to others; they have found theatre to be a very effective means for such communication. The very nature of what they want to communicate determines to a large extent the people they want to communicate to. In other words, to such people the content of the theatre is the primary and the most important factor and the content decides the choice of the audience. Again, for such people, the form of the theatre is determined by the content as well as the audience chosen.

In India, as in any other underdeveloped country (or 'developing country', if you prefer the euphemistic term, or 'third world country' if you prefer the American classification), Street Theatre therefore, is on the whole a purposeful theatre in the context of the connotation of the term 'Street Theatre' we assumed in the beginning.

If we wish to express in one word the predominant nature of the contents projected by those of us who are involved in Street Theatre, it would be 'change'. Somebody who is not satisfied with the existing state of affairs would want to change it to something better. The change he or she seeks may be specific and limited—such as passing or opposing a legislative bill, succeeding in a particular movement, putting this or that political party in power through the election; or it could be a drastic socio-economic political change. In either case, the person in question would like as many people as possible to think and feel the same way about the issue as he or she does. Oftener than not, the person finds that if the ideas and feelings are shared only by the people of his or her own class, the desired change may not come. Reaching beyond the class therefore, is foremost in the mind of this person. If he or she happens to be in theatre, or chooses theatre as the means of communication, the person can't afford to remain content with the middle class and upper class ticket-buying public coming to the conventional city theatre. One has to come out of the theatre hall and go where the people are – people of one's own class – who cannot afford to or do not care to come to the theatre hall, as well as people belonging to rural and urban working classes. This is how the content determines the audience, and how the content seeks new forms—one of which may be the form of the Street Theatre.

Which 'Street'?

So far as the form is concerned, 'Street Theatre' may be defined as a theatre performed free in a public place where people normally gather. The place may be a street, a public park, a market place, a railway station, a compound of an office or an institution, a gathering place in a village, or any such similar place. I mention the word 'free', which means that any payment made is absolutely voluntary—usually donation collected after the performance by 'passing the hat' (a towel or 'chaddar' in our country). As this donation is given *freely*, it is really *participation* by the audience, not payment for *buying* entertainment.

Street Theatre is always Free Theatre, but Free Theatre is not always Street Theatre. If a theatre performance is made for invited guests only, it is free, but is not Street Theatre. Besides public park and other places, our theatre group Satabdi performs once a week in a room where there is an accepted custom of paying a donation of one rupee, but that is not a precondition of admission. Anybody who cannot afford to pay even that one rupee is welcome to the performance, provided there is room for him. In this respect, our theatre in that room is free, but it is not Street Theatre. Street Theatre by and large is a theatre performed for people who have not come prepared for a performance. But here the definition tends to become a little tricky. If a particular public place is chosen by one or several theatre groups for performance on a fixed day of the week at a fixed time, then soon there would be an audience who would come prepared for the performance as well as those who are not so prepared. This was the case of the Saturday afternoon performances at Surendranath Park, (formerly Curzon park) Calcutta, which began in the early 1970s and quite often attracted an audience of one to 3,000. Even here, the prepared audience has always been less in number than the unprepared audience, and should certainly be defined as Street Theatre.

Again, Street Theatre is not the only course open to the theatre worker who is concerned primarily with the content. Many theatre groups, including ours, perform at various places like a village, a slum area, a college lawn, by invitation. In such cases the hosts organise the audience. Although admission is free in most of these cases, the audience comes prepared for such performances, and these do not really fall into the category of Street Theatre, even if they are held in open public places.

Form of Street Theatre

The reason for my attempts to define Street Theatre is not just academic and theoretical. The preparedness or otherwise of the audience makes a fundamental difference in the matter of determining the form of the particular theatre.

Coming prepared for a performance means a definite choice. I have chosen to come to a particular place specifically to see a particular performance and I am agreeable and psychologically prepared to give it adequate time and attention. It also indicates a previous knowledge—I knew the specific date, time and place of the performance, hence the question of publicity is included. The theatre for such prepared audience can be longer, more complex in theme, more sophisticated in structure, choreography and acting, more exploratory and experimental than that for an unprepared audience. In other words, more risks can be taken and consequently there is the chance of more gains in the matter of effective and intense communication. The only problem is that it does not reach the people who will not come, who are disinterested, who are unwilling to go to any place even smelling of theatre. That is the most important reason for doing Street Theatre—to reach the people who do not or cannot come to a specific theatre place and that is why it is better to stick to the definition of unprepared audience, even if they, like at Curzon Park, do not constitute the entire audience.

If somebody is unprepared for theatre, it is the business of the Street Theatre worker to make him prepared through the performance itself. This is a major factor in determining the form of the Street Theatre. The first step is to gather the initial audience. Beating a drum and announcing loudly that a performance is to take place is a common practice. I have seen it done by a group in Chandigarh performing at a shopping centre, and also in a Karnataka village where the entire group went round in the village in a procession with drums and gongs, the children following. The children in fact are the greatest allies of Street Theatre, particularly in the matter of initial gathering. One group that used to perform every Sunday in a public park in North Calcutta – the older part of the city – used a novel method. Adjacent to the park are middle class households as well as a large 'bustee' (slum hutments). The bustee dwellers constituted the majority of the audience, and although they knew about the Sunday performances, they did not have watches or clocks to come by the stipulated time. So the group members spread out along the fence of the park, each at least thirty feet away from the next man, and in a well-rehearsed loud voice in unison announced the performance. To me, it was almost a theatre by itself. Singing, preferably in chorus to project more and to cover deficiency if needed is another sure way of gathering an audience in our music-loving country. This is the practice of many Street Theatre groups in West Bengal. As it takes time to gather a sizeable audience, it is better to have a short skit before the main performance—a kind of 'curtain raiser' although there is no curtain!

But drawing initial attention of the people is far less difficult than keeping their attention throughout the performance. It must be remembered that many of them cannot afford to give it much time as they are unprepared for the theatre. Some will give time, but at a cost—like being late in going home or places of business, or foregoing some important errand. (One of the regulars from the audience at Curzon Park used to be a young 'paan-beedi' hawker who refused to sell anything during the performance even if asked for, thereby losing money that he could ill afford). Street Theatre therefore should be short and precise and interesting, loud and clear throughout. It should be as dramatic and as full of theatrical surprises and action, as possible. Humour is a great help; so are songs and dances, or dance-like movements. Use of very simple, portable and inexpensive props and costumes is also very effective. Clowning. I mean real clowning, is an asset.

A Street Theatre can be a well-rehearsed written script, or it can be improvised. Improvisation however needs a framework and demands great skill on the part of the performers. I have seen a Street Theatre in Pune, which tended to become too long and ultimately somewhat boring because enough attention was not paid to this aspect. It was regrettable, for the theme was good and the audience was good. Whether the theatre follows a script or is improvised, rapport with the audience is very necessary. This needs imagination as well as experience. A lot can be learnt from our folk theatre in this respect: the way the performers there relate directly with the audience is wonderful. In the Chandigarh performance mentioned earlier, there was a scene of garlanding a minister. The garland was made of empty cigarette packets (quite colourful) and a young spectator, about 12 years old was asked to do the garlanding. He did it very solemnly and the audience loved it. Once of our plays is structured like 'madari-ka-khel' where the children are asked to applaud, and the 'bachhalog' always do it with gusto.

There are times when, and places where Street Theatre has to become guerilla theatre. In countries under dictatorship, or where brutal repression of progressive movements and thoughts is carried out behind the garb of democracy, the need for change is the most acute, and Street Theatre in such conditions can be the only form of theatre where something worthwhile can be said. Guerilla theatre must be very short and precise, making a single point with as much impact as possible. The performers must be capable of discussing the issues with the audience after the performance where conditions are favourable, as well as of winding up and dispersing quickly if the need arises. Preliminary activities like gathering an audience are not possible; the performance must start with a bang. Hence choosing a spot where there would be some people right from the beginning is important. The number of spectators is bound to be small, advantage of that should be taken by making the theatre intimate and intense. The idea is to have a number of short performances at different prefixed spots, the performers dispersing and re-assembling each time.

Is Street Theatre an Art?

Some people argue that although Street Theatre is necessary to propagate something, it is not really art. This concept is based firstly on the mistaken notion that anything done in a 'proper and decent' theatre hall automatically becomes art, and anything outside is non-art by definition. Secondly, the term 'propaganda' is associated with non-art by some people who think that art should have an ivory-tower purity. This second notion is strengthened by the productions of some social or political workers who choose theatre as a tool to propagate, but are too lazy or too impatient to master the tool. As a result, their theatre is neither art nor propaganda. Whether theatre would be art or not depends on the theatre workers, irrespective of their working in theatre halls or working in streets. And as for propaganda, every theatre, in fact every art, is propaganda, as it propagates something or the other. Street Theatre propagates change, the so called 'pure' theatre propagates status quo.

As theatre does not become art automatically if done in a regular theatre hall, so does it not become art automatically if done in the streets? Theatre, like any other art, demands not only talent, but also hard work in training, which many people indulging in theatre seem to forget. The term 'Street Theatre' is composed of two words. Our primary concern should be the second word—theatre; otherwise the very purpose of this purposeful theatre will be defeated, however strong and important the content may be.

Courtesy: Sangeet Natak Akademi Journal. *Issue 69, July-September 1983*
Courtesy: Natarang Pratishthan Archives

ON THIRD THEATRE

Interview with Badal Sircar

Samik Bandyopadhyay

Unpublished interview done in 1989 for the Nehru Shatabdi Smarak Samaroh organised by Sangeet Natak Akademi

Samik Bandyopadhyay (SB): Would it be correct to say that when between the late 1960s and early 1970s you made the shift from the proscenium theatre to the concept of the Angan Mancha, the choice for it was a very definite choice, and determined more from an urge to explore the redefinition of theatrical space in terms of the relationship between audience and performance, than from a clear ideological/ sociological position on the function of theatre or a passion to grapple with issues that demanded a different theatre, as it has defined itself more clearly in your later work?

Badal Sircar (BS): I think you're correct. At the point at which I moved out of the proscenium theatre, the limitations of the proscenium theatre, limitations in terms of communication and in terms of the relationship between performers and spectators within which it operated, provided the vital, immediate provocation. The content of the theatre or the desire to create a free theatre – flexible, mobile, transportable, inexpensive and possible to carry to the villages and small towns with ease – were not so much in view then. But to leave it at that would be leaving it as a half-truth. You have to understand my personal growth into theatre or a little about how I came to and accepted theatre. It was not as if I had rejected the proscenium theatre on the score of its inadequacies in terms of communication, and then grafted on to the new theatre certain elements of what you may call content or philosophy or ideology. It didn't work that way at all. It can't work that way in fact. There was a time in my student days when I was directly involved in the kind of activity to which our theatre is now geared, but not through theatre. Then, like many of those involved in it in the same way, from the middle-class of Calcutta, I too came to withdraw myself from it, to shrink from it, so that when I chose theatre, it was more of an alternative occupation, not really believing that theatre can be used as a tool for social change.

Creating good theatre was then the main objective to express certain truths but not directly concerned with social change. This was the result of not believing in theatre totally. When I came to the proscenium theatre, I hadn't realised the strength of theatre. I wasn't aware of what theatre can do. In other words, there was already deep down an awareness of the limitations of this theatre. It was from that awareness itself that there eventually came the questions of communication, utilisation of space, re-defining the spectator-performer relationship; and the gradual realisation that the distinctive feature of theatre is that it is a live show and it offers scope for direct communication, man-to-man communication. And therefore, that the barriers between the two parties to the process, viz. spectators and performers, should be minimised, and if possible, eliminated. With that realisation, I left the proscenium theatre.

Almost simultaneously with the break, I could feel a new strength in my theatre, and I could at once see a link between what I was trying to achieve in my other direct activity and the theatre that I had now re-discovered. I could see that theatre could do it. So you see, it was not as if the content came later. It had been there all the time. Have I been able to make it clear? The split between my political role and theatre, which had remained outside it for so long, was bridged with that realisation and the philosophical polities of our theatre were consolidated.

SB: In other words, there was a divide in your work when you first came into the proscenium theatre, between your political/ideological commitment or concern and your work in the theatre. I remember your remarkable achievements in those days in light comedy or farce or plays of wit. You could see that these could be combined only when you found your own theatre. But could you tell me in more concrete, experiential terms, how and when you recognised the strength of this other theatre in the course of your first Angan Mancha experiments/exposures?

BS: The story of *Spartacus* would be relevant here. I had read the Howard Fast novel long ago, and had liked it immensely. I had read it many times, and had occasionally toyed with the idea of making a theatre piece out of it, only to turn away from the idea almost instantly: how can theatre ever encompass that enormous canvas? But with the slow growth of an awareness of the power of theatre, there came the thought: well, it may not be impossible after all, for everything is possible in theatre, but it needs a talent greater than mine. I won't be able to do it. But when I was thinking of breaking out of the proscenium theatre in the late 1960s and had started thinking on the new form, but hadn't figured it out as yet, I thought even I could make an attempt with *Spartacus*. That was when I first thought of it, before the first trial show of *Sagina Mahato* in the Angan Mancha setting and I wrote *Spartacus*. And as I was telling you, *Spartacus* from its inception, had to do more with the political objectives I sought outside theatre than with creating merely good theatre. It was no longer an ordinary satire like my earlier *Kobi Kahini*. It was a departure. Not one of those interesting, amusing stories. I wrote *Spartacus*, the first play I wrote for the Angan Mancha, in the new form. I wrote with this acting space in mind. All my earlier plays I had written for the proscenium theatre. With active involvement in producing/directing from the very beginning, I have never been able to write a play without the acting space clearly defined in my mind. If not consciously all the time, at least subconsciously, I have a clear visualisation in my mind of where and when a character sits or stands or moves directorially. I had already seen and studied the space where we would eventually stage *Spartacus*, the room at the Academy of Fine

Arts, and I had all its dimensions, its entrances and exits, in mind. But we didn't open there with *Spartacus*, but with *Sagina Mahato* which I had written for the proscenium theatre, but thought that it would come out much better in the Angan Mancha.

SB: Even in its new setting, *Sagina* ultimately remained a spectacle with its novelty lying almost entirely in its interesting use of the space. It was with *Spartacus* that the audience identified and related to a new theatre for the first time. For me at least, it was only with *Spartacus*, that I started reacting and relating to the new relationship with the performance, as I could feel myself as part of the slaves – a slave myself – and thus it was more of a departure. How concretely did the impact of *Spartacus* on the audience affect you? Did you feel that the audience was discovering itself through the performance, as you took part in the performance yourself?

BS: That I can't actually say, for my way of thinking was different. But what I can say is that *Spartacus* had been my favourite play for its theme and for its partial success in bringing at least part of the gigantic canvas into the frame of theatre. It was a favourite with our group too. We took a whole year to produce it. We really worked hard on it. It would have probably taken us four hours to present my first version of the play. There was an interesting process in the way the play was condensed through workshops and rehearsals, with the dialogues giving way to non-verbal modes of expression. *Spartacus* was thus a landmark for me as a playwright, and for my group as a team. I have never been able to envisage the response of the audience in advance, but I could feel that with *Spartacus* we had made a giant leap to a closer relationship with the audience. At the start I had the fear that the audience would not take to this form so easily, but with *Spartacus* we did communicate a lot. What's more, those who form the core of my group now, the most serious and the most motivated and therefore the most serious members, came to our group not from any urge towards theatre. In fact, they had nothing to do with theatre as such, but (they came) from the feeling that they'd like to be part of the group that staged *Spartacus* the way it did. They didn't want to act at all. In fact they were forced to act later. It was *Spartacus* that provided that core with its philosophical foundation and strengthened it. The way it brought these people to our group could be an evidence of what you were suggesting, the beginning of a tangible process of breaking down the barriers between performers and spectators.

SB: The way you describe it, wasn't it then a part of the audience itself being motivated by the performance to become a part of the performance? In other words, many of those who joined your group after *Spartacus* joined as audience rather than as performers. As you said, they were not keen to take part in the performance as such.

BS: Maybe.

SB: Between *Spartacus* and *Bhoma*, your next landmark, wasn't there a radical change in the personnel of your group? A massive exodus, and the emergence of an almost new group with *Bhoma*?

BS: Not quite, For the process had actually started when we had decided to give up the proscenium theatre for good. There was an overlapping period of about six months. Even when we had booked the Academy hall for the Angan Mancha for two years, we still had plans to perform in the proscenium theatre once in a while, from our old repertoire. We were, in fact, abandoning the proscenium theatre at a point of time when we had tasted success with plays like *Ballabhpurer Roopkatha, Abu Hossain* and *Sagina Mahato.* It was not as if we had failed in the proscenium theatre, and were therefore opting out.

SB: As a matter of fact, you broke out of the proscenium theatre exactly at the point where you had touched success.

BS: We had just started getting 'call shows'. So many of them.

SB: It would have been different if you had opted out of the proscenium theatre at the end of your stint at the Rabindra Sarobar auditorium, where it had not clicked. Because then it could have been explained away in terms of simple frustration.

BS: We had, in fact, met and resolved to abolish the old Satabdi before we plunged into it. We began from scratch. There were a few from the old Satabdi of course, but the majority were newcomers, that's how it began. *Spartacus* was reviewed after this change over with a predominantly new cast much before *Bhoma*. There followed yet another exodus of several members bearing the old hangover. All this had taken place as we moved through *Michhil* and *Tringsha Shatabdi* towards *Bhoma*.

SB: Ultimately how many of the old Satabdi stayed on from the proscenium days to the present? No one?

BS: Just I. There's one more person from there in the present group. Sandip had joined at the fag end of the proscenium days, but had not taken part in any of the proscenium productions.

SB: So, for all practical purposes…

BS: It's just me.

SB: The change between *Spartacus* and *Bhoma* was marked on two levels. On one level, the character and spirit of the group was more clearly defined with the exit of those who temperamentally and ideologically belonged to a different theatre. It was quite understandable that the Angan Mancha would be served exclusively by those who were committed to it. On another level, your experience of working with the comprehensive Area Development Programme and your exposure to a whole new area of experience, as in *Rangabelia*, served to lead you on to other issues and another theatre and *Bhoma*.

BS: What was new in *Bhoma* was the experience it recorded. The politics behind it was already there in *Spartacus*. But *Bhoma* was the first product of my direct personal experience of the reality of rural

India. The first few lines of *Bhoma* explain why and how it came to be written—'What I hadn't known yesterday I know today, and I have friends who do not know it, even today, and I would like to communicate to them the little that I have just come to know about life in the village.' Thus *Bhoma* was written for people like us, aimed at our kind of people, not meant to be performed in the villages. But when we took *Bhoma* to village audiences, they found a point of identification in the issues it touched—underground water, agriculture, their problems, land relations and its departure from the gods and goddesses and kings and rulers of earlier theatre. There was nothing new for them in it in terms of information. It was all familiar stuff. They knew it all. I had learnt all that from them anyway. I hadn't written *Bhoma* for them. All that I had put into *Bhoma* had been put in for people like me, for their edification. To that extent a new dimension had come in with *Bhoma*, not in the field of philosophy or politics, but in the field of knowledge and experience, and naturally the philosophy in its turn had been better defined and further consolidated, as it has gone on happening from play to play. *Bhoma* was followed by *Sukhpathya Bharater Itihas*.

SB: There was yet another development between *Spartacus* and *Bhoma* in terms of theatre language from the more sculptural flair for abstract formulations in *Spartacus* to the more enlivened and varied human movements in *Bhoma;* a further reduction of the word content with the use of repetition and visual clarification/elaboration, for underlining as a new theatre idiom. In this development of our language of theatre were you drawing on other theatre or life experiences? Did your Manipur experience help you in any way?

BS: Not consciously. If you speak of precision of language, I'd say I'd achieved it already in *Ebong Indrajit*.

SB: When I speak of language, I refer to the physical expression of theatre, of the formal organisation of the thing, rather than your words. For with your words, you've always been precise. In *Baki Itihas*, for example, complex psychological experiences are communicated in the minimum of words. On the verbal level, *Baki Itihas* is extremely precise. *Tringsha Shatabdi* is very precise. But I'm asking you about the physical language of the theatre, its formalisation, its meaningfulness.

BS: When I wrote for the proscenium theatre, I had a fairly well-defined notion, at the time of writing itself, of how the characters would be moving on stage because the naturalistic theatre is extremely limited in terms of movement. In modern civilisation, movement in our day-to-day life is extremely limited, and it is the job of naturalistic theatre to copy this life as faithfully as it can. The word 'naturalist' is in a way a misnomer, for the behaviour that it copies is unnatural in the civilised world; when I came to write *Bhoma* the whole question was open. In the naturalistic theatre, in the matter of movement, you can't really go beyond very few alternatives. Whether you'd stand at downstage left or at downstage right would be considered an alternative. You can stand, sit, walk about, lie down. You can't go beyond these for in civilised life we don't go beyond these. But in a play like *Bhoma* I can't visualise the entire movement at the time of writing. I can visualise only a small percentage of it for here the process really starts when we put it to work in the rehearsals or what we call the workshop. For it offers a thousand and one possibilities. So I'd say the two languages are not determined simultaneously at the time of writing.

In fact, *Bhoma* has a peculiar history of writing. I didn't write it as a play at one go. The experiences that had affected me deeply, disturbed me, enraged me had come out almost as a personal diary in the form of scenes detached; spread over a period of three years. The scenes lay with me.

SB: Were they all from your *Rangabelia* experience?

BS: I began a little before that, from when I went to Ramachandrapur for a day and a half every week. That's when my exposure to the rural reality really began. I was just back from Nigeria, and didn't have a job. Ajit suggested that I could start studying and serving in the villages. I went round that entire area in Bongaon Ramachandrapur, Singjole and had my first first-hand exposure to rural poverty, land relations, what it meant to be a landless *khatmazdur*. While working for the CITU, I had come to know of the plight of the small industrialists in Tangra or on Belilius Road, from a survey report. Dev Kumar Bose, a scientist friend from my Scottish Church College days, now a member of the State Planning Board, gave me a copy of a report prepared by a commission appointed by the President of the US. All these bits and pieces were accumulating. Members of the group were also asked to write down their own pieces. Not many of them wrote. Mira wrote quite a few. The *Rangabelia* scenes with *Bhoma* came to be added to them later. *Bhoma* was not originally supposed to take up all that space in the play. The scenes were read out to the group and it was decided to weave them together into a play through workshop activity. It is thus different from all my other plays. It was not received or written as a play at all. When the scenes were written, I had no idea of the production design of the performance, or how the body language would be put to use. There was only a strong faith which came from my experience with *Spartacus* that a lot of things would be solved in rehearsal, how certain lines would be spoken, who would speak them, how they'd be chorally arranged. This faith persists with me even now. With my latest work, the poetry montage *Janmabumi Aaj*, I had the same faith. I didn't know what shape it would take, but I was confident that a way would come out of our workshop process, with our team.

SB: Can we then draw the theoretical inference that you are moving away from a theatre, that is the modern experimental theatre in India and elsewhere too, that believes in the primacy of the director, who has the secret with him, and it is his job to impart that secret to his actors to make them realise his own vision which has been there with him clearly from the start anyway? You start with an idea but as playwright/director you really don't even know what shape it will ultimately take. It has to evolve and define itself through the workshop process.

BS: When I first got seriously involved in theatre and was saddled with the entire directorial responsibility in the 1960s, I was quite enamoured with the western process of production notes with diagrams and notes on blocking on the page on the left, and models made with toothpaste tubetops—leading to what would be the director's works entirely. The actors were quite happy with the process, for they found that the director had thought out everything for them, they didn't have to think at all. Through the years I have come to a diametrically opposite position. Now almost deliberately I do not make any production plans before the rehearsals. When the content became so important in our work, the direct, personal involvement of every performer in the content itself became absolutely essential. It wouldn't be possible any longer for the actor to act as a tool or as a pawn in the hands of the director. And once a director accepts this process, things become easier for him for now he has the advantage of drawing on other people's thinking to enrich his own thinking.

In a rehearsal process, when we start from a scene in a script, it may be that we offer the first suggestion. But the performers and those watching as Satabdi members, may reject it as unworkable. Our actors have his expression 'I feel like a fool' which means 'I'm feeling uncomfortable,' or 'there's something wrong with it,' or 'it's not coming out.' Then there are other suggestions that are executed. If there's too much of discussion, I try to stop it, and say, 'Fine, let's try it out?' We go on trying the alternatives till there's a point at which everyone present agrees, 'It's clicked'. But then we come home and make no notes at all. With the constraints under which we operate, our next rehearsal may be seven days later. And then there's a controversy, one group claiming, 'This is how we did it', and another group protesting, 'This is how we did it.' We let the discussion run for a while, but then when we find the two or even more groups adamant, every group depending on memory, we stop the discussion, and decide to start from scratch. What happens is that those expressions or movements that we have really liked come back to us, with or without modification.

SB: In other words, an automatic sifting takes place.

BS: Yes. But we never keep notes. In several plays, we start from the choreography from a workshop base, which trains us for mutually dependant spontaneous teamwork, the use of space, trust, both physical and mental, and imparts to us a realisation of the potentials of the body, that confidence. From *Manushey Manushey* onwards, we have not been beginning from the script, we don't do any casting, and we start from a theme or the language. In the poetry montage, for example, I would read the poem out, and they are left, within a framework, to do whatever they want to do—sound and movement. The workshop base wouldn't let them turn whatever they do to chaos; they can bank on their earlier experience to discipline it. While reading, I have responded to their improvisations and my reading has been affected; my pauses, my emphasis, my repetitions, my paraphrases have been determined for me. I lay down the frameworks from time to time – 'Don't use any sound at all', 'use slow motion only' – we set constraints on ourselves, 'absolutely free' simple frameworks and they can do whatever they like within these minimal frameworks. This is a process that allows the theme to grow into the blood of the actor so that the poem by Birendra Chattopadhyay or Manibhushan Bhattacharya doesn't remain a poem by any of them but becomes the actor's own. He can say, 'I wrote it'. Once this is accomplished, we try to bring it into a discipline and only then we choreograph it. Earlier we would begin with the choreography. But now the workshop process in more integral and creative.

SB: Did you start moving into the open space altogether outside the theatre with *Bhoma* for the first time?

BS: No. The process had started earlier, when simultaneously with our performances in the Academy of Fine Arts Angan Mancha, we had started performing at Curzon Park, where Silhouette had opened up an open theatre space. When the Academy raised its rental for the Angan Mancha space two years later, we went out into the open space situation, and for two years we performed at Curzon Park, opposite the Hind Cinema, opposite the Academy, and at college and university lawns. We didn't stop to consider whether we could afford the new rental or not. We chose to move out into open space.

The Emergency was declared when we were preparing *Bhoma*, and we knew that its message or statements would not be tolerated by the Emergency regulations. Once the Emergency was declared, the groups performing Saturdays at Curzon Park closed down of their own accord. We continued for three Sundays more in the grounds opposite the Academy then the police intervened directly and stopped us. Then we had to start looking for a closed space again. *Bhoma* was staged underground fashion in several small lecture halls before being driven out of them one by one.

SB: So with *Bhoma* you were back in enclosed space. But as the Emergency was lifted, you were again traveling a lot into the villages and performing in the open, often at places where theatre hadn't reached at all, places entirely outside the theatre circuit. How were these people and places located?

BS: Not by us. By the hosts. In my work with the Comprehensive Area Development programme, I would come in touch with people from many villages. Some of them, knowing that I was involved in some kind of theatre, would invite us to perform in their villages. Or a spectator at our once-a-week performances in Calcutta would extend a similar invitation to us, the man himself and the village suggested unknown to us. These shows were all on invitation, never improvised of our own accord, as it now happens from time to time.

We would often perform in a village on a Sunday at around three in the afternoon, and come back to Calcutta by the evening train, due to constraints of time as our members couldn't afford to miss work on Monday. The attendance would be low, and the real peasants would be missing. The audience would be primarily the village middle class and the richer peasantry. We would explain it away in terms of bad timing, performing in the afternoon. But recently, during our first *parikrama*, we found our morning and afternoon performances in the villages equally well-attended, the audience comprising mainly of peasants and never less than five-hundred.

So now I feel that the fault lay with our hosts. Our hosts must have belonged to the middle class and the peasants would not be properly informed. If the peasants, the *khatnazdur*s, had known, they would have come. In our improvised shows now we see a lot of them, some of them coming in straight from the fields, with some of their tools in hand, bare-bodied. Obviously the people who came to our performances in Calcutta and invited us to their villages were not from the poor peasantry. They were the exceptions of course. For example, there was this brilliant student of chemistry from the Calcutta University who was fascinated by our *Tringsha Shatabdi* and other plays and invited us to perform in his village in Bardhaman where he had brought in the peasantry…

SB: …proving that this man had a rapport with the peasantry.

BS: What I have noticed, the remoter the village, the less the class barriers: there is more mixing among the classes at a social level, everyone knows everyone else. There is greater detachment and polarisation in villages near Calcutta, with the richer sections almost totally oblivious of the peasantry. In a village called Amlaguta in Singhbhum – you have to go there from Patangda near Tatanagar, an extremely poor village difficult to reach – they took me seven miles on a cycle. I sat on the rod, quite uncomfortable. I could see a social relationship between the richest and the poorest, all sharing a common Santhal origin, though they now speak Bengali, and have forgotten the Santhal language.

SB: The experience of the first *parikrama*, as you have just now hinted, was an eye-opener in several respects, and a landmark in your work. Would you try to assess it more categorically?

BS: Before I go into that, I'd like to touch upon something else to fill in a gap. While we were performing in the Angan Mancha in Calcutta and visiting villages and colleges and university campuses for what we term 'call shows' or invitation shows, a whole new movement was growing up in the suburbs of Calcutta, where there was no money for theatre activity, but many unemployed young people, middle class, with some education, having completed school at least, in other words, people with a lot of energy in store, who had now suddenly discovered a theatre they could tackle. The movement led to a string of Third Theatre festivals in the small towns, bringing together a number of these groups and receptive audiences in every case.

The reason was more economic than anything else. A lower middle class, with dreams of a house of one's own, has now acquired plots of land in these suburban towns, built houses on some of these, left others vacant. These people cannot normally afford to come down to Calcutta to see a play; maybe, at the most, once a year during the pujas. Travelling to the city, paying for the theatre tickets, and, because it's a very special occasion, a visit to a restaurant would cost a lot and make a big hole in their budget. They now find theatre at their doorsteps and it's free. There may be door-to-door collections, but you pay fifty paise or two rupees, and you can step out of your house with your family, and see the play. There is no other entertainment. These festivals gave a boost to the movement, by offering the new groups places to perform. They were not doing theatre for money, they just wanted to do it. Groups of singers or choirs grew up along with the theatre groups. A normal festival evening would feature half an hour of songs followed by a theatre performance of about an hour or a little more. There was a set pattern, even a set one for refreshments—bread with potato curry, and tea. The sponsors would pay for our second class train tickets. Nothing else.

SB: I have had fried eggs on some of these occasions.

BS: That came at the more affluent places and sometimes bananas. After the first spate of these festivals, running continuously for a week at a stretch, or on 15 or so consecutive Sundays, often in different spots in the same area, there would be a lull. We are now trying to review the festivals. The groups themselves are taking the initiative. We have such festivals lined up for the next few months at Madhyamgram (sponsored by Ritam), Kanchrapara (sponsored by Pathasena),

Krishnanagar (sponsored by Teerandaj) in its fourth year. We are taking the initiative for organising such festivals on six consecutive Sundays, at six different spots in the same region, so that the region is fully covered. You have been to several of these and you have seen how they happen. This becomes an alternative circuit for the Third Theatre groups and encourages the growth of new groups. This is the setting against which the *parikrama* was planned. It all began when I came back from Karnataka, from my first exposure to the theatre *jatha* organised by Samudaya, and spoke about it to my group. Debashis Chakraborty of Arena Theatre Group was the first to ask—'Can't we have something like that, Badal-da?' I had discouraged him initially, saying that here we are fighting among ourselves all the time and there's such a lot of politics that it is not likely to work here. But the idea stuck and when it came up again we accepted it readily. The initiative lay with Debashis and the group at Thakurnagar that he had been instrumental in building up. I needn't elaborate on the achievements of the first *parikrama*. You have edited a documentary record of it yourself. You know all about it. There were certain key points we realised—that there was never a lack of an audience; we were there entirely on our own initiative, and whenever we performed, during whichever part of the day, there was an audience, with minimal publicity support. All our notions of what the so-called, uneducated rural audience would understand of our urban plays had to be thoroughly revised. We had had the same experience with *Spartacus* in the past, which was always a sure success with village audiences, inspite of its sophisticated structure, absence of a story line and historical reference. Urban spectators who liked *Spartacus* still went on telling us that the masses wouldn't understand it. That was what had given us the courage to try poetry montage out on our *parikrama*. All the poets we had chosen were urban, but the poems came from powerful feelings and the subject was hunger, which is neither rural nor urban; in fact it is more of a rural experience. The poems chosen focus on hunger and children, though they had not been deliberately chosen to focus on those two themes. We were not even half-prepared, may be one-fourth prepared; still we dared to try it out in our village march. If the feelings are deep and authentic they communicate fairly smoothly. That was an experience. There was another important experience. The 75 young men and women from eight different groups, all from urban or semi-urban middle-class backgrounds, living and moving through numerous inconveniences, big and small, never showed signs of tension; they all seemed to be somehow high, so that they could laugh away every single hassle. That is no mean achievement. There were at least two groups that I came to know for the first time on the tour. I hadn't known of their existence. All these groups came together on the *parikrama*. This consolidation of the groups, even of those that had been working closely together for some time already, through this experience was something important for the movement, as it broke down ego barriers between the groups.

SB: Between the two *parikrama*s, the one important decision you took was to bring your once-a-week schedule of performances at the Theosophical Society Hall to a stop. In the last few shows that I went for, I did see full houses. So I wonder if the fall in attendance was a reason.

BS: It was a reason. I'll start with the negative reasons. The attendance was falling. In our earlier phase at the same place, we had had steady support from the students, groups from one particular collage at a time virtually capturing the shows—from Presidency College, Medical College, Calcutta University. But this time, the attendance was lower, part of the general situation of the serious theatre all over the country.

SB: When you shifted from the Sindhi Association Hall and returned to the Theosophical Society Hall in the University area, we thought you'd get your old student audience back.

BS: We were victims of an overall withdrawal of the audience from serious theatre. And then the authorities of the hall itself were making things unpleasant and difficult for us to throw us out. To these negative reasons we added the positive reason of what we had learnt in the course of the *parikrama*. We had already started asking ourselves whether it was worthwhile to perform for 25 people at a financial loss that we wouldn't have suffered if we had a full house. We had our doubts, but it still served certain purposes: it served as a post-office where people could contact us every Friday.

On the *parikrama*, when we discovered that even when we visited a place uninvited, with almost no prior intimation, started singing songs, and drew an audience immediately, of more than a thousand at a time, that stayed on for the three or four hours that a programme lasted, we felt all the more strongly that there was no point in performing for the Calcutta audiences. With this realisation, all that we needed was a single meeting where we unanimously decided to give up the regular Calcutta shows. Earlier I had been the most pessimistic asking for the closure, with the rest resisting. This time they all agreed but on the basis of a positive alternative programme for at least two *parikrama*s a year on different routes, and instead of Fridays on Sundays, regular shows in the villages on invitations, and in the Third Theatre festivals, and even trying it out in a strange village if on a particular Sunday we didn't have a show booked.

The group had had another experience in my absence which was found significant. Satabdi had a performance scheduled at Kanchrapara, which was cancelled at the last moment, after the group had reached the Sealdah station to board the train. The group was in no mood to come back. They went to Kanchrapara, chose a likely (or unlikely) spot, and improvised a show, which by the time it ended, had drawn 500 people, who stayed on after the show to know more about the group and its activity, entertain them with tea—creating in its course, a new base. There is also a possibility of Satabdi trying out such new places. It may fail at some places, and then we'd know where it could work, and where it couldn't and why. For the Calcutta audience, whom we do not underestimate, we have concentrated on theatre festivals, preferably twice a year—the first of these scheduled for 18 April 1987, an hour and a half every evening. We have not gone for advertising in the Press, have kept the performance free (of cost), and we appeal for a donation of two rupees, instead of the current one rupee. The publicity will be by word of mouth.

To answer another query of yours, the full houses you saw towards the close of the Theosophical Society Hall proramme were the result of the announcement we had made that these would be the last shows there. This was necessary to break down the middle-class (static) inertia of our potential audience: at the last shows at the hall we collected the addresses of all our spectators, whom we'd be trying to reach when we hold our Calcutta festival. We'd be distributing handbills, putting up a board for a month at the College Street Coffee House, and posters at ten points for this festival. The scale and scope of publicity will be the same as that for the Angan Mancha. I'm not saying that this will be a fixed principle for ever. If we go in for a single press advertisement, the two rupees rate, I know, will at once jump to three. That's what we are trying to avoid.

SB: So it was the experience of the first *parikrama* that finally made you take the plunge. Has the alternative programme started rolling already?

BS: We can perform in the open only in the dry season. So the real season for these shows stretches from after the Pujas, that is November to March–April–May. We are booked already for all the Sundays in January, and have started booking for February. Festivals have been lined up at Kanchrapara, Krishnagar, Halishahar.

SB: Playwise, in this last phase, I have found *Khatmat Kring* and the poetry montage a departure from the line of *Bhoma* and *Basi Khabar*.

BS: From my perspective, this feeling of doing something that I've never tried before, has come to me several times; it came to me when I did *Bhoma*, it came to me when I did *Khatmat Kring*. I had never used farce or slapstick humour for a theme like this…

SB: …and such a consistent use of black humour.

BS: …I started rehearsing even before the play had been completed. We started working on some of the scenes even before I knew whether the play would ever be completed. I told my group that the Bengali audience cannot cope with black humour. They like a serious theme seriously treated, or a comic theme comically treated. That is our orientation. So it would be rejected outright even if it were produced. It was a challenge. *Janmabhumi Aaj* was also a challenge. The new production I am working on is again a challenge. It's a play by a South African, Woza Albert, created in collaboration by the director, Barney Simon, and the two original actors, Percy Mtwa and Mbongeni Ngema, around the notion of Christ's second advent in South Africa. I have read the play and seen a number of stills – a fascinating work made out of the point of view of the common people of Johannesburg – 'scouring the Gospels and the streets of Soweto and Johannesburg'. The challenge lies in making something out of the Christ's advent myth which is not meaningful here, and in working on the serious issue of Apartheid in a black comic slapstick vein. This is being directed by Dipankar Dutt.

SB: So you have made a straight translation of the play and handed it over to the group? There was a phase in your work when you had focused on the rural-urban divide. Do you work now within any such fixed parameters, or just react from issue to issue, as you have taken up violence in *Khatmat Kring*, hunger and children in *Janmabhumi Aaj*, and the Apartheid in your work in progress?

BS: It's the second course. I have themes in my mind that I consider vital, but I can't write just like that. There are often plays or novels that I read and think I could make a play out of one of them. But I must be able to transplant it in India.

SB: Would you then say that the primary consideration is that it should make a point in India at this point of time?

BS: Right. The point of relevance is always there. There are many of my older plays for instance, that Satabdi never performs. It does not mean, as it is rumoured (it was Dubey who probably started it), that I disown my earlier plays. They are still true for me, as true as when I first wrote them. But there is a question of priorities as to what are the truths that we should bring to the forefront now. It is not the time to focus on the truth of *Evam Indrajit*. There we follow a framework with a wide range which allows us to produce *Nagini Kanyar Kahini*. We are not tied in any way to the formula of the so-called 'revolutionary' play.

SB: In 1985 and 1986, you have been to Britain twice, and conducted a series of workshops. How did this happen and what did you find there?

BS: In Britain, there's the section of middle-class youth that has turned away from what they call the 'middle fast life' of conformism and yet hasn't gone for drugs and the hippy culture in a kind of rebellion with a social or political – 'political' is what they call it – mission in view. There's even an organisation called the WCDS that offers them partial financial support to visit Third World countries. They don't come to see the Taj Mahal or the Himalayas, but get attached to a rural project. There are such young people, with no background in theatre, but looking at India for a form of theatre or music to serve their ends. They discovered our work by joining a workshop we were holding for workers in a voluntary agency involved in rural development. They went back to Britain, raised funds from like-minded groups, and sponsored my trip. The first time I was there for eleven weeks. On this second visit, I limited myself to eight workshops – minimum of 18 hours spread over three or four days – six outside London, two in London. There's likely to be another trip in 1987 for two months.

SB: Who are the people you are working with?

BS: The organisers are what I would call unemployment activists, living on dole and active against the dole-givers. They live in 'masses' with a common kitchen—a departure from the British cult of the home or the individual or privacy. They have taken part in the workshops. There have been people from fringe theatre groups too, a drama school graduate, a guitar-strumming tube station singer, even people who have nothing to do with theatre from a sense of curiosity about an Indian offering a course in theatre.

SB: What use have they made of what you have imparted to them?

BS: Of those who come out to India, Mike Hancock has made the best use of what I have imparted. The young woman in the group has become a 'whole timer' in a Nicaragua Solidarity Group, and has nothing to do with theatre any more. Paul Thomas is involved in 'theatre-in-education' using theatre games to carry information on world happenings to the schools. Mike has continued the work into street theatre, formed a small group, brought a bus and travelled for two summers living, sleeping and travelling in the bus with a few ten minute pieces. In one of the two that I have seen, they use a Mr and Mrs Smith and a Master of Ceremonies in a TV quiz format to poke fun at consumerism and the cult of violence and relationships.

There's the scene, for instance, where Mr Smith is given a revolver and asked to kill off his wife, and they kill each other off. In the other, a young woman is ordered about 'do this, do that' and dominated by her father, the school teacher, the priest, the next door neighbour and ultimately Mrs Thatcher and cowards. A stylised play. The plays are not great works but involve a lot of creativity. They have made their own interesting costumes, enormous Margaret Thatcher and Reagan puppets, death masks to attract people. But what an unfortunate country where the people are not drawn to theatre! Mike was with me on our second *parikrama* this year, and envied our people's openness to experience and performance. I remember the biting cold in which they performed with almost no audience around and I told them that I had to stand for ten minutes in the middle of a street with my eyes turned to the sky—simply to draw an audience around me. That's what they suffer from. But things have been better this summer, I'm told, with more fruitful post-performance discussions with the audience.

Courtesy: Natya Shodh Sansthan, Kolkata

Actor:
Badal Sircar, Debashish Chakroborty and others

Play:
Sagina Mahato (Bangla) (1971)

Playwright:
Dramatised by Badal Sircar (based on the novel by Gaur Kishor Ghosh)

Director:
Badal Sircar

Group:
Satabdi, Kolkata

(Natya Shodh Sansthan)

Actor:
Badal Sircar, Debashish Chakroborty and others

Play:
Sagina Mahato (Bangla) (1971)

Playwright:
Gaur Kishor Ghosh's novel dramatised by Badal Sircar

Director:
Badal Sircar

Group:
Satabdi, Kolkata

(Natya Shodh Sansthan, Natarang Pratishthan Archives)

PLAY:
Michhil (Bangla) (1974)

PLAYWRIGHT:
Badal Sircar

DIRECTOR:
Badal Sircar

GROUP:
Satabdi, Kolkata

(Natarang Pratishthan Archives)

ACTOR:
Badal Sircar and others

PLAY:
Abu Hossain (Bangla)

PLAYWRIGHT:
Girish Chandra Ghosh, 'Distortion' by Badal Sircar (Bangla)

DIRECTOR:
Badal Sircar

GROUP:
Satabdi, Kolkata

(Satabdi, Natarang Pratishthan Archives)

ABOVE AND LEFT:

PLAY:
Shesh Nei (Bangla)

PLAYWRIGHT:
Badal Sircar

DIRECTOR:
Badal Sircar

GROUP:
Satabdi, Kolkata

(Satabdi, Natarang Pratishthan Archives)

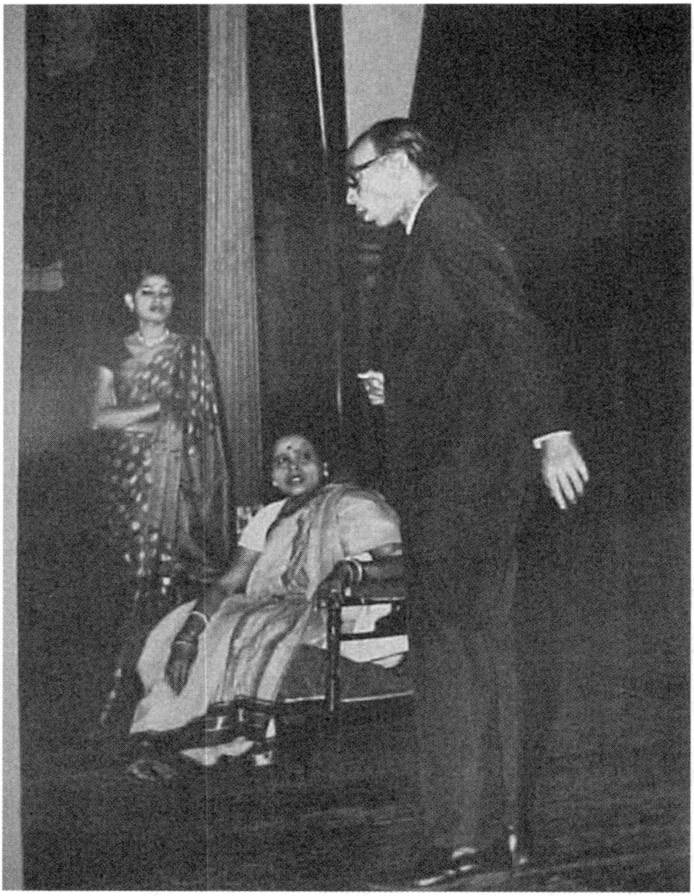

ACTOR:
Badal Sircar and others

PLAY:
Ballabhpurer Rupkatha (Bangla)

PLAYWRIGHT:
Badal Sircar

DIRECTOR:
Badal Sircar

GROUP:
Satabdi, Kolkata

(Satabdi, Natarang Pratishthan Archives)

ACTOR:
Badal Sircar and others
PLAY:
Gandi (Bangla)
PLAYWRIGHT:
Badal Sircar
DIRECTOR:
Badal Sircar
GROUP:
Satabdi, Kolkata
(Natarang Pratishthan Archives)

ACTOR:
Deben Ganguly, Murari Chakraborti, Chhaya Mandal, Apurba and Badal Sircar
PLAY:
Gandi (Bangla)
PLAYWRIGHT:
Badal Sircar
DIRECTOR:
Badal Sircar
GROUP:
Satabdi, Kolkata
(Natya Shodh Sansthan)

Above and left:

Actor:
Badal Sircar and others

Play:
Bhoma (Bangla)

Playwright:
Badal Sircar

Director:
Badal Sircar

Group:
Satabdi, Kolkata

(Satabdi, Natarang Pratishthan Archives)

Actor:
Badal Sircar

Play:
Bhoma (Bangla)

Playwright:
Badal Sircar

Director:
Badal Sircar

Group:
Satabdi, Kolkata

(Satabdi, Natarang Pratishthan Archives)

ACTOR:
Jyoti Murari Chakraborty, Deben Ganguly, Baidyanath Dulal

PLAY:
Michhil (Bangla)

PLAYWRIGHT:
Badal Sircar

DIRECTOR:
Badal Sircar

GROUP:
Satabdi, Kolkata

(Natya Shodh Sansthan)

PLAY:
Sagina Mahato (Bangla)

PLAYWRIGHT:
Gaur Kishor Ghosh's novel dramatised by Badal Sircar

DIRECTOR:
Badal Sircar

GROUP:
Satabdi, Kolkata

(Satabdi, Natarang Pratishthan Archives)

ABOVE AND LEFT:

PLAY:
Spartacus (Bangla)

PLAYWRIGHT:
Dramatised by Badal Sircar from Howard Fast's novel (Bangla)

DIRECTOR:
Badal Sircar

GROUP:
Satabdi, Kolkata

(Satabdi, Natarang Pratishthan Archives)

PLAY:
Hattomalar Oparey (Bangla) (1977)

PLAYWRIGHT:
Badal Sircar

DIRECTOR:
Badal Sircar

GROUP:
Satabdi, Kolkata

(Satabdi, Natarang Pratishthan Archives)

PLAY:
Michhil (Bangla) (2000)

PLAYWRIGHT:
Badal Sircar

DIRECTOR:
Badal Sircar

GROUP:
Satabdi, Kolkata

(Satabdi, Natarang Pratishthan Archives)

Actor:
Badal Sircar
Play:
Michhil (Bangla) (2000)
Playwright:
Badal Sircar
Director:
Badal Sircar
Group:
Satabdi, Kolkata
(National School of Drama)

Actor:
Badal Sircar
Play:
Michhil (Bangla) (2000)
Playwright:
Badal Sircar
Director:
Badal Sircar,
Group:
Satabdi
(National School of Drama)

Actor:
Badal Sircar
Play:
Michhil (Bangla) (2000)
Playwright:
Badal Sircar
Director:
Badal Sircar
Group:
Satabdi, Kolkata
(National School of Drama)

Actor:
Badal Sircar
Play:
Michhil (Bangla) (2000)
Playwright:
Badal Sircar
Director:
Badal Sircar
Group:
Satabdi, Kolkata
(National School of Dama)

Actor:
Badal Sircar
Event:
After presentation of 'Michhil' Badal Sircar addressing the viewers (2000)
Venue:
Madhyamvikrisht, National School of Drama
(National School of Drama)

PLAY:
Manushey Manushey (Bangla) (2000)
PLAYWRIGHT:
Badal Sircar
DIRECTOR:
Badal Sircar
GROUP:
Satabdi, Kolkata
(National School of Drama)

PLAY:
Dwairath (Bangla) (2003)
PLAYWRIGHT:
Badal Sircar
DIRECTOR:
Badal Sircar
GROUP:
Satabdi, Kolkata
(Natarang Pratishthan Archives)

ACTOR:
Badal Sircar

PLAY:
Michhil (Bangla) (2000)

PLAYWRIGHT:
Badal Sircar

DIRECTOR:
Badal Sircar

GROUP:
Satabdi, Kolkata

(National School of Drama)

Actor:
Badal Sircar

Play:
Michhil (Bangla) (2000)

Playwright:
Badal Sircar

Director:
Badal Sircar,

Group:
Satabdi

(National School of Drama)

Actor:
Badal Sircar

After presentation of Michhil, Badal Sircar addressing the viewers (2000)

National School of Drama

Actor:
Badal Sircar

After presentation of Michhil, Badal Sircar addressing the viewers (2000)

National School of Drama

'THIRD THEATRE FOR ME IS A PHILOSOPHY, AN IDEA'

Badal Sircar

An informal discussion was organised between Badal Sircar and the theatre workers of Lucknow by the UP Sangeet Natak Akademi at its studio in November 1988, when Badal Sircar was visiting Lucknow to conduct a theatre workshop with students of Bhartendu Natya Academy. Prominent theatre personalities present were Daya Prakash Sinha, Vishwa Mohan Badola, Atamjeet Singh, Bandhu Kushawarti, Dr Anil Rastogi, Rakeshji, Yogendra Nath Yogi and Late Ranbir Singh Bisht among others.

Badal Sircar answered all the questions posed by those present. The entire proceedings were recorded by the Academy. The transcription of this English recording was done by Nandini Mishra.

Q: Maybe I am wrong, but I think that of late your creativity as a writer has suffered some kind of a blockage. If I am correct, I think the 1960s and the '70s saw the best coming out of you. Now you are involved in a very exciting kind of theatre which has thrilled all of us, it has given us inspiration. But do you think as a producer you find that writing work suffers, as I believe it has in your case?

Q: Tell us about Satabdi. What sort of theatre does it do? Does it have its roots in the traditional? Or is it inspired by another theatre personality? Or it is your own creative innovation?

Q: When you see a performance of your play where you feel that the team has interpreted it wrongly, what is your reaction? Do you approve of such interpretations?

Q: As an appendage to the question asked by the lady about the interpretation and your being either satisfied or dissatisfied, I remember your remark after seeing one of your plays *Ebong Indrajit*. Perhaps you disagreed violently with the interpretation of Mohan Maharishi at that time. If I am not mistaken, your remark was that while the theme of the play you had written was life, he had made it death. Now I would like to ask you very pointedly, do you think there is such a thin line of demarcation between life and death as to allow a director to interpret it in such a manner without going out of the theme and content of the play?

Badal Sircar (BS): Actually, I had thought that from the questions I'll get something to talk about at length but it seems that most of the questions are quite specific which can be answered separately. So I think it would be better if I clarify certain things, because most people outside Bengal know me primarily as a playwright, through translations, first into Hindi then maybe into other languages through Hindi. Very few people really know that I am involved in theatre practice, active theatre even today. So there is some misconception. I want to make that clear first.

I got interested in theatre rather late in my life. I never thought I had any aptitude whatsoever for theatre. Therefore, during school or college days I never performed, never went anywhere near theatre except for watching. I liked to watch. Its only when I was working that gradually my interest developed that way. Rather late in my life. But late in my life means quite early in the time point, as many people here, particularly the workshop participants, were not even born at that time. It was in the early 1950s or so. I got drawn first by acting, of course in a very amateurish way. First acting, then taking some responsibility in direction and only then did I begin writing (plays). This too, because I wanted plays to direct, because there was a dearth of plays in my language. And I think that holds good for other Indian languages as well—a dearth of plays. So, the incentive to write plays was that I wanted plays which I would like to do.

This situation, on the whole, holds true even today. My incentive for writing plays is my theatre practice. So I do not consider myself primarily a playwright. Playwriting is secondary for me; theatre practice is primary. Many people, quite a few people, have told me, look you are a second grade director, and may be a third grade actor, but you are a first grade playwright. Well, not so crudely but that is exactly what they have meant. That by trying to direct plays you are abandoning something you can do, for the sake of something you can't do well. But I can't help it. Even if that is true I can't help it, because that is what I am interested in. I am not so interested in play-writing.

So, whenever I go and people who have heard my name but don't know much about me meet me, they invariably ask one question – which embarrasses me because I don't know how to reply – '*Aapne naya kuch likha* (Have you written anything new)?' It's a very stock question. It always comes. This question '*naya kuch likha*' presupposes that I am a playwright who is always writing something or the other and therefore the question '*Abhi naya kya hai*?'

But this is not true. It has never applied to me. When I write, I begin quite often with a scrap of paper or something, because I think it will not go beyond the first one or two pages. Quite often, it is cyclostyled sheets where one side is blank. You know that kind of scrap paper? Only if I find that it is going beyond two pages do I take a proper paper. All the time I am afraid that it will not be finished, and therefore I am always in a rush. So as to be sure it is finished in a rush. Most of my plays have been written in three to seven days at most. Those which took longer, were because of some block somewhere in the middle; I gave it up as a bad job and maybe after one or two years I took it up again and it got finished. But the rush is always there.

Ebong Indrajit was written in seven days, actually in seven nights, because I never thought of taking even one day's leave from my office. I have taken leave for many frivolous reasons, casual leaves just for an *adda* and gossip, etc. But for writing? No. Writing was so unimportant to me. I never thought of taking leave for writing. So after the day's work and other things, I would begin at 10 at night and stop at 3. Next day the same routine. Most of the plays were written that way. *Pagla Ghoda,* I think, was written in four days. *Sara Rattir* maybe took slightly longer, but even so, it would not be more than a week. *Kobi Kahini* was probably written in four-five days. I am saying these things to let you know my priority. But to Mr Badola I have a question—you said nowadays creativity in my writing has stopped. Does it mean that I don't write any more or he doesn't know about my present plays or he doesn't like my present plays? Which one is it?

Q: May I clarify this thing? My question was specifically referring to the kind of communication you had with the outside audience because you are essentially a Bengali writer and your work needs translation. It needs some kind of a journey outside the state, which I think it had during the 1960s and '70s and I have been a witness to that. You did write extensively and you wrote some things which did get noticed. Now okay, I do believe that you are creative, and you are busy in some other form of creativity in theatre—you are producing plays, you are directing plays, you are holding workshops. I am not saying that is not creativity. That's not what I meant. What I am trying to say is that we don't get to hear or read more of you. Now, I think even that is a blockage in terms of creative writing.

BS: My question was more specific than that. I was trying to find out what is the last play written by me that you are aware of?

Response: This is what I am saying. The point is that if we are not aware of them. I am.....

BS: Just a personal question. What is my last play you have read or seen?

Response: Your last play I have seen was *Michhil.*

BS: Nothing after that?

Response: Nothing after that.

BS: But I have written many plays after that. Like *Bhoma* that has been translated into Hindi. After *Bhoma* the only play translated into Hindi was an adaption of *Caucasian Chalk Circle* as *Ghera*. The plays written afterwards have not been translated into Hindi. Why I am asking this question is to point out that it is not true that I stopped writing. But it is true that while earlier plays got translated and therefore provided the link with theatre people and other people outside the state of West Bengal, these plays did not get translated and therefore the touch was lost. So there is an information gap also. That's why I asked this question. You read *Ebong Indrajit* and performed in it. You liked it probably. You read *Michhil* or saw *Michhil* done. Now comparing these two, if you reject *Michhil* then of course you can say that qualitywise the creativity has stopped or in *Bhoma* creativity has stopped. That is another question.

I have been doing a different kind of theatre since 1972-73. That will come in answer to Mr. Sinha's question, 'What kind of theatre does Satabdi do?' Probably I should answer that first. Then probably another factor will come in. The kind of theatre the theatre world of India is generally not interested in. So those who used to translate my plays into Hindi are no longer interested in translating my plays. Those plays have not got, to use a crude term, a market. A market means a city theatre market, the proscenium theatre market, the box-office market. It has not got any appeal. So that way I am out of link with the rest of West Bengal anyway. Now I have my own purpose, own reasons, own incentives, own urge for writing those plays and I personally do not feel that some of those plays at least, not all, are any worse than *Baki Itihas* or *Pagla Ghoda*. Only they are less liked. Let me put it in another way. I will not say good or bad or worse or anything like that because I am not the critic, not the judge. I feel an urge, I write. What I mean is, the plays I want to do, the plays I want to produce, I am proud of those plays. Like a play you have never heard about, *Khatmat Kring*. I am proud of writing it. I am proud of writing it more than I am proud of writing *Ebong Indrajit*. I make a definite statement of this. Or I am no less proud of writing *Bhoma* than I am proud of writing *Baki Itihas*, probably more.

And I will, if I can at all write, write a play like *Michhil* and *Bhoma* and not a play like *Baki Itihas* or *Pagla Ghoda* anymore. So that's a very subjective view I am giving. I know most of the theatre people in India are very disappointed. *'Badal-babu aajkal aap hamare liye nahi likhte hain, hamare liye.'* Probably it is wrong Hindi I am speaking. 'For us, you are not writing for us'. So there is a distinction between 'us' and 'them'. There is a difference—'*kiske liye*?' It's absolutely true. I am writing for us. Those people who were asking me for plays, they stand for a particular theatre. I don't write for them anymore. I don't want to write for them anymore. When they say you are not writing for us, they mean those plays which will succeed on proscenium theatre. No, I am not writing for the proscenium theatre! I have not been doing proscenium theatre for the last fifteen years. I am writing plays which if anybody produces on the proscenium stage will be maimed, will be crippled. Some do. Students do them for competitions, sometimes win prizes also. But they are not meant for that and much is lost when the plays are produced in the proscenium theatre. I am not writing for them.

Anyway, I think, at this point I should go to the question asked by Mr Sinha. I will state it very briefly without going into too many details. I left the proscenium theatre in 1972-73. I mention two years because there was an overlapping period. By the middle of 1973 I disassociated completely from the proscenium theatre. Now I do another kind of theatre. Very briefly, there are two reasons for that. One is related to the art form of the theatre, related to the question of theatrical communication. The second is the urge and necessity I felt for creating a Free Theatre. They came one by one actually. As a theatre man, as a person interested in theatre, as a theatre worker, naturally the question of theatrical communication was important to me, and being a city man I began my life by taking proscenium theatre for granted. But it is obvious to anybody in India that there are two kinds of theatre in India – or any other country similar to India – not one, because there are two kinds of cultures, not just theatre. And that is because India has been a colony for a long time, so there is a dichotomy between city life and village life. In a colony the cities develop at the cost of villages, not like in a country which we call a developed country, where the development of the city and the rural areas are complementary to each other and they depend on a general indigenous economic development. But our cities, I mean the modern cities, were created by the British, mainly for the purpose of exploiting our country. Therefore, the port of Calcutta, Bombay, Madras were created to take raw material from our country and to bring their extra produce back, using India as a market. So, from the very beginning the cities have had a very exploitative role. Even today, after forty years of Independence, I, at least, and you might not agree with me, don't find much difference from that colonial character. So city poetry is quite different from rural poetry, city painting is different from rural painting, city music is different and city theatre is also different from rural theatre.

Not only are they different, they run parallel. They don't meet. I mean if any form of folk theatre becomes popular in the city, we buy them up. We make the folk theatre people distort their theatre to please us. That is not meeting. There is no healthy give and take between the two. So, being a city man, born and raised in Calcutta, I naturally accepted the proscenium theatre as the only theatre. But I had my doubts, I had my questions. And these questions went on bothering me.

From the early 1950s I started in the amateur way of doing theatre sporadically, on and off. From the 1960s onwards we had a cultural group, not a theatre group, but because I was one of the founder-members of the group and I wrote some plays, I was interested in theatre, so some times we had productions. Then in 1967 we established our group, Satabdi, as a regular theatre group. We continued with this proscenium theatre. Earlier most people were going to the cinema, there was a competition, uneven competition. The cinema appeared to have a lot of strength. They showed so many things which in our theatre we couldn't show. But by that time I was so involved in theatre I could not accept that. That theatre has got no strength and cinema has got all the strength. So I tried to find out the distinctive features of theatre, which cinema will not be able to imitate. Fortunately at that time there was no television in India. Yes, I say fortunately. And no video, only cinema. So looking for the distinctive feature which could not be imitated by cinema, I found the obvious thing which everybody knows—that theatre is a live show, cinema is not. If it is a live show, direct communication, man-to-man communication, is possible. In cinema they can show a lot of things but always through images. Theatre can show only a little but what they show is reality. The human being that is present in the theatre as a performer is the reality, there. If he is ill there is a problem. There would be no problem in cinema if he fell ill, only the shooting date would be changed. This would be a problem for the producer, but not for the cinema itself. Maybe it would delay things. That is a point of strength. Man-to-man communication is possible in theatre. If that be so, then the barriers between the two parties, the spectator and the performer, should be minimal. This was my logic from the point of view of communication.

At that time I was not giving this logic to anyone else. It was to myself, as it was almost twenty years since I had been associated with theatre in some capacity or other, from 1952–53 to 1972–73; so it was not easy for me to cut my roots. But that question bothered me and I personally found the proscenium theatre full of barriers. I did not like the barrier of distance with everybody sitting on one side, and the last row goes so far (behind). If they sat all around like in the Bengali *jatra*, the last row with the same number of people would come nearer.

I found the barrier of levels – stage at a higher level, auditorium at a lower level, balcony still at another level – detachments, (a) separation. I found them as barriers. I found the barrier of light and darkness. The audience hiding in the dark and the performers on the stage in the light, in the acting area. I thought that to be the greatest barrier, because if direct man-to-man communication is possible in theatre then theatre is human action. Cinema is not human action. Two parties of human beings have come to the same place on the same day, at the same time. And something happens between them, some inter-communication – not just one way – (takes place) between them, because both parties are alive human beings. When something is happening between them, it is human action.

And here on the proscenium theatre, one party – we have kept hiding the party of spectators in the dark – and the performers are pretending, they are not there, denying their existence; and the spectators are asked to forget their existence, to hide. In a way, if I may be permitted to vulgarise a bit, we are giving the role of peeping Toms to the audience. You hide in the dark to see something private happening here, on the stage; we shall pretend that you are not there. That is the way I look at it. Certainly many of you here will not agree with me. And all of this done for the sake of naturalistic theatre, because in naturalistic theatre you have got to create the illusion of reality. And to create the illusion of reality, that darkness is needed, the spot lights are needed—so that it can help us imagine, help the audience imagine, that this is not the stage but the drawing room. And by creating that illusion of reality we begin to believe and identify ourselves. I thought about that too, but then again the second thought came—to what extent and proportion is the present day theatre naturalistic? None of our folk theatres is naturalistic. And if you consider the quantum of theatre in terms of the number of people seeing it, the folk theatre audience will exceed the audience of the city theatre many many times. And none of them is naturalistic. *Tamasha*, *nautanki*, *terukuttu*, *jatra*—none of these theatres is naturalistic.

As a matter of fact, naturalistic theatre came into being after the French revolution, when this new concept of bourgeois individuals was created. Before that naturalistic theatre didn't even exist, because that concept of individualism was not there. So although there have been great naturalistic plays, I am personally a great admirer of Ibsen, not so much (of) Chekov, but Ibsen personally, even today. That does not mean that I'll have to accept naturalistic theatre as the only way of doing theatre. And if I don't do naturalistic theatre, at least the kind of theatre I do now, I find naturalistic theatre very limited and it does not serve my purpose. I have not stated my purpose yet, but (I have realised) it does not serve my purpose. So, if that be the case why should I accept all these barriers? Why can't I minimise the barriers? If I perform in the city why don't I get down on the floor of the room, share the same space with the audience, same level – the floor – have the same lights? Let me see the audience, let me recognise their presence, let them see one another. Let us make it a real meeting of human beings. Of course the plays will have to be different. And that is why, so that I can do this in practice, I started writing plays where this direct communication is fully utilised.

That is why in my play *Spartacus* (taken [*sic*] from Howard Fast's great novel *Spartacus*), the crucified slave comes out of the cross, goes to one member of the audience and whispers in his ears 'I will come back and I'll be in millions.' Then another slave does that, then (the) third slave, then gradually those voices rise, and they all begin to say 'I will come back and I will be millions.' If you do *Spartacus* on proscenium stage this can't be done. It just can't be done. It adds something to me [*sic*], this direct communication.

This is just one example. I can even give an example from *Ebong Indrajit*. When I wrote the play, I had proscenium theatre in mind. That incidentally answers your question. Being involved in practical theatre all the time, I can't possibly write any play without imagining how it will come out. That thought will always be there. I think every playwright has to have the image of the performing area, whether it is the proscenium stage or anything or visualise it, otherwise it can't be a really successful play. In *Ebong Indrajit* the Lekhak – I think many of you know that play – calls somebody from the audience. That is not a stunt. Anybody who has seriously read the play knows it's not a stunt. It is vitally important for the play to show that Amal, Vimal, Kamal and Nirmal or Indrajit are prototypes, they are not characters with definite identities. There is no character as such in *Ebong Indrajit*. Therefore they should be just anybody, one of a group or class. So, calling them from the audience is vitally important for the play. In my transition period, I did one proscenium production of *Ebong Indrajit*, and after that I did our Angan Mancha production. Naturally the two choreographies were entirely different. In our Angan Mancha production, which is in a room, people are sitting. The Lekhak goes to the people one by one, looking into their eyes, one by one…till he comes to the actor who is doing Amal and who is sitting there and selects Amal [*sic*]. Then he goes on doing the same thing to more people, selects Vimal [*sic*].

Now I think you can imagine this is better than just calling out to the dark auditorium 'Listen please would you come to the stage' because I have seen, particularly when I was doing Lekhak after I selected Amal, although everybody knew through their intelligence, logically, that I will not select him (people at random). Everybody understood that there are plans—actors whom I will select are sitting amongst them. Even then most people, when I looked into their eyes, started getting a bit nervous (anticipating) that I will call them. It made a difference to me. Whatever I am saying—I am saying from my experience because I am not an academic man, I am not a theoretical man; everything is my experience.

And after I have chosen this path from 1973-88, there hasn't been a single moment when I regretted my step, not a single moment. Rather I got confirmed in my views more and more and more [*sic*]. Very subjective, very personal, but that is the case. This is the communication part. I just said we came out of the proscenium theatre for the communication part.

But there is another question. That is the question of a human being's consciousness, awareness, experience. Being born in a country like India, we cannot help being conscious that hunger exists, death by starvation exists. We have to be concerned about that. Maybe, being born in (the) United States of America some people can't imagine that people die of hunger. But *we* know it. We do not have to only imagine [*sic*]. We have seen these things. And there are so many other things which we notice in our personal experience or maybe through the privilege we have had – we middle-class people – of getting education. Yes! Getting education is a privilege in India. Most people haven't got it. I have got it, I am privileged. I belong to a privileged class. Through newspapers and books we learn other things also—we learnt about (the Second World) War, we learnt about the death chambers of Auschwitz, we learnt about the nuclear bomb, we learnt about the nuclear bomb being air borne twenty-four hours—we know all that. Not many people know, as I was telling the people in our workshop the other day.

I also came to know the other day that if half kilogram of plutonium is equally distributed amongst the entire population of the world – five hundred crores – everybody will have fatal cancer. Half a kilogram of plutonium! And the world now possesses 17,000 metric tons of plutonium. Each metric ton is one thousand kilogram. We can't help being aware of these facts.

I am not mentioning many other facts. I am not mentioning imprisonment, and injustice and torture and senseless killing which is happening again and again because your language is different from my language, because you wear a turban and I don't wear a turban, because the colour of your skin is different from mine, your religion is different from mine, although, maybe, you don't care about your religion and I don't care about my religion. Still I go and kill you. These things are there and at the same time, we know, even in such a society, human love has not been destroyed. Even today, solitary confinement is probably the worst punishment in jail. A man wants to hold the hand of another man. It is still there but his society is making a division between one human being and another all the time. All the factors are there, all this awareness is there and naturally an urge to change all these things or see them change. I can't change them, you can't change them, maybe all of us together can't change them. But if this gathering can become like those words in *Spartacus* – 'I will come back and I will be millions' – if we can become millions, they can be changed. But what is more important is that they have to be changed because we have come to such a pass that it is mass suicide for the entire human race…mass suicide. That is the position we have come to. Now, the man who becomes aware of these things is also doing theatre. He wants to do theatre. So the only alternative he has got is to put these things in the plays.

I am sorry Mr Badola I can't help that. I will be writing plays like *Bhoma* and in the other plays like *Baki Itihas* in which, according to you, I showed my creativity, you will find these elements. In *Ebong Indrajit* also, you will find that rudiment of consciousness. This question of atom bombs being airborne twenty-four hours is there in *Ebong Indrajit.* It is a recurring theme. And I think you know my play *Tringsha Shatabdi* which Dishantar produced under Alkazi's direction—it is there too. It is almost an obsession with me. There are other obsessions also. So I have got to write a play on that if at all I write a play.

As people become old, except in some exceptional cases, their creativity reduces. Now as I am getting older, that's what I believe. In my case it is certainly getting reduced. I am getting more and more dull (duller) and less capable. That is happening. But if I write at all, the subject will be important, the theme will be important. And I don't care whether the standard of artistic quality is reduced, provided I can talk about these things. I will have to write them. That's a compulsion with me. If I can't write at all, that's a different thing. Therefore if people ask me you are not writing for us, and if writing for them means I will have to forget these things, I will have to think which plays will be successful on the Hindi stage or the Gujarati stage or the Marathi stage or the Bengali stage. Well I am very sorry. I apologise, I will not be able to do that.

I am privileged in one more way. I didn't have to depend on writing for my livelihood. That's a very fortunate thing because I think nobody in India can survive properly simply by writing plays. Maybe by writing novels one can survive. But writing only plays or poetry, nobody in India can survive. So those playwrights who are affluent, you will see they are writing for the films also, not just (scripting) plays.

Anyway, to answer Mr Sinha's question about the way we are doing theatre a bit more fully (comprehensively)—we have been doing theatre in three different ways. One is what we call Angan Mancha. That is the name of our theatre. Our group's name is Satabdi, which is an intimate theatre, a room like this or maybe smaller than this, which can accommodate say 70 to 100 people, sharing the space, using room lighting. That's one. The second one is doing theatre in the open air. Open-air can be in a street theatre situation – as in Calcutta there was a park in central Calcutta (where we regularly performed) – we call it Curzon Park. The present name is Surendranath Park, where several groups used to perform every Saturday. And at one time, for several years, we had been having a gathering of 3,000 people! It became quite an institution in Calcutta. That's the street theatre situation, where, after the performance we used to collect donation by passing around the hat. We don't have hats so we pass a towel! The third way is that of sponsored shows. We Bengalis have given it a separate name – English but Bengali English – we call them 'call-shows' because we get called for shows. So that's the third way. This is what we have been doing.

Now, we tried to make it Free Theatre because we thought the changes in the society which we would like to see, those changes can be brought about not by people like us, the middle class; they will probably be brought forward by people for whom change is a life and death question. For us it is not. Not from the immediate point of view. I mean, we are very short sighted on the whole. We think only of tomorrow, or that kind of thing. So we give way to short-term interests. For our middle class people the short-term interest is to go to the next higher step of this staircase, although by doing so they will have to elbow somebody down to the next lower step. We middle class people have more or less accepted this competitive world. That is why the story of Henry Ford is considered very inspiring and is in every school text book. How poor he was and how rich he became. One man can become like that. Yes, one man can become like that but we forget the greater truth. That as a class we can never become Henry Ford. So in America the jargon that every American citizen can be the president of America is both true and untrue. It's true that one American has become the President of America but most of the Americans do not become presidents of the USA.

So most of us are after the short-term truth—my promotion, my examination, my career, my money and all that. But for those at the bottom of the staircase, for them it's a life and death question. Not the question of going to the next higher step but just going on living, not dying of starvation. They will be probably changing the society. So somehow we will have to establish a link with them. Not with a view to teach them but to retain our own perspective. We have got to establish a link and maybe there can be a give and take; we can learn something from them and maybe we can (in return) communicate (transfer to them) something of what we have got through our privileged education. I don't consider this teaching. I have no pretension that I have or we have the competence to teach the working people, but I consider it as an inter-change (exchange). That is where we will have to go.

Also, because from the communication point of view I have already left the proscenium theatre and stage, I found that now sets are irrelevant to me. Spotlights are also irrelevant to me because I am not trying to create an illusion of reality. Now, rather the human body, its energy, the human energy—that is more important to me. This is the basic tool of this trade. Without this, theatre is not possible. The human body, and of course the mind, the whole human being, those are the most important things. Now I am in a position to create free theatre also. So both the purposes meet at the same point. Because I don't need the auditorium and lots of rent, I don't need spot lights, so I can perform anywhere. I can do in kerosene lamp light, in daylight, on the ground, not even a raised platform. It may be a little bit difficult for those sitting behind to see, but anyway still I have got to do it whatever they can see. And as much as possible we go to the villages. That's what we are trying to do.

From 1972-73 to 1986 October, we had been performing almost regularly once a week, every Friday, this Angan Mancha performance in Calcutta. Even that we try to make free theatre although we had to spend money to hire the hall. I will describe the economics. It is very interesting. Free Theatre, according to me at least, means where payment of a certain amount of money is not the condition of entrance. If you pay two rupees or three rupees you are allowed in, otherwise stay out. And if you have three rupees you have the right to come in and demand entertainment from me; it's a buyer-seller relationship. That is not free theatre. But if you are invited to come and if you wish you pay something, in that condition we both are free and it's a more human action. So, even when the audience has the capacity to pay the money, we do not want to make it a condition. We want to keep the condition free. So after 1980 it used to be a donation of one rupee by convention; those who did not have one rupee did not have to pay anything. But there was one constraint—when the house was full, it was a small room (after all), then we had to ask them to come next time because we could not accommodate them. In the villages and other places automatically they are all free and we tried to collect our money as much as possible from just passing the hat.

Now, in Calcutta this hall used to cost us fifty rupees for rent. Based on the other expenses at the time we began in 1973-74, we found costs for each production to be seventy-five rupees, sorry, the show cost. And if hundred people come and give us one rupee each, there is a margin of twenty-five rupees. So Free Theatre even in a city is absolutely feasible. We ourselves did not believe it at first but it was proved to us that it's feasible. And we do not sell tickets as such. We ask for donations. Always at the same rate. Everybody is equal. We don't believe in somebody having the privilege of sitting in front because he has paid twenty rupees and another person sitting behind because he could not afford that and paid only five rupees. We do not believe in that. That's not human action in our opinion. So it's some donation or nothing at all, but first come first serve, wherever you want to sit. That's the condition.

So we don't sell tickets really. We don't publish souvenir programmes begging for advertisements. We do not go to any cigarette company or other company and collaborate with them to do our publicity. We do not even apply for any grant either from the government or any other place. And so far we have survived. And I believe that if we don't survive it will not be because we lack money. It will be for other reasons. Most probably it will be for the reason that there are precious few according to the present values who would like to do theatre like this (of this kind). Because this theatre cannot be done if one thinks of one's career or one's fame or money. This is almost like political action. If you think, if you feel an urge this should be done, you do it. If you think of your personal gains you cannot do it.

Therefore this theatre cannot be professional theatre. This is a very restricted field in a way. Anybody wanting to join our group, the first thing I try to do is to discourage the person. Do not enter this group. There will not be any career. We do not advertise in the newspaper, we don't invite critics, we do not publish any names separately anywhere. You will gain nothing, so don't come to this group. At the same time a lot of work is demanded. All the weekends of your life will be gone. Saturday-Sunday will mean either shows or long rehearsals. All the weekends you will have to sacrifice. My sister lives in such and such place so I go for a weekend trip. No, you can't do it if you come to this group, so why join? And they don't join, they don't come. Our group has been getting reduced [*sic*] gradually.

But those who join, I think they have done so after becoming conscious of this long-term interest. Long-term interest is not trying to go to the next higher step of the staircase, but to abolish the staircase altogether or at least to remain with those who want to abolish the staircase. That has been our Satabdi theatre. Now whether I got this theatre I have created from some other source like our traditional theatre or some foreign source, actually in some ways is irrelevant to me. I will take from any source if I think it will help the purpose. What is the purpose? The content is the primary point—what I want to say. If I find in any folk theatre that this particular form will help to project my content more effectively, more intensely, I will borrow it. If I find it in some foreign theatre, I will borrow. So I have no compunctions about begging, borrowing and stealing. And I don't even remember the sources. And naturally, when content is the most important thing, grafting is something which is out.

Folk theatre suddenly has become very important, almost a watch word to the city people. I think the city people are beginning to feel a bit guilty—'we have been very unjust to the village people, so at least let us go gaga over village culture. Let us do that.' If you utter the term folk theatre you cannot say anything. I once became very unpopular in a Delhi seminar. Now I don't go to seminars at all. The subject was: *Relevance of Folk and Traditional Theatre in Modern Theatre*, and it was a three-day seminar. For the first two days I heard. You know all sorts of praises and adoration of folk theatre, nothing about its relevance to modern theatre. There were great exponents, knowledgeable people. They were talking, describing in details and all that.

On the third day somebody – you know there are always some mischievous persons – said 'Badal-babu, you have not spoken for the last two days, so say something.' And that was the mischief. I said:

> Look I came here, I thought I don't know much about folk theatre and I will get to know something which will be relevant to my theatre which I can steal from here and use in my theatre. But all I am hearing are eulogies of folk theatre. Well, if I can't use anything of folk theatre in my theatre then tomorrow even if folk theatre is finished in India I don't care at all.

And immediately there was an uproar with people saying 'You can't say that!' I got provoked also, so I said 'I can say that. And you can say you don't agree with me. You ask me to say something, I said what I believe.' Well that's my attitude. So many people ask me your theatre is Grotowski's theatre, isn't it? Far from it. I learnt several things from Grotowski, from his books, but not much. And when I heard Grotowski has left theatre, I lost all interest in him. When he came to India I didn't even try to meet him although I met him in Poland. I saw his theatre in Poland. I didn't even try to meet him. I lost all interest. And as far as our theatre is concerned, I know it is far from Grotowski's theatre. Grotowski never cared for content. We start from content. So it's very different. It's very difficult to pin-point what is our kind. It's neither folk nor traditional. Which is why I called it the Third Theatre.

To me Third Theatre is a concept, a philosophy, a politics if you like. That is Third Theatre. Form is not that important. And in a way we are not committed to any particular form or any particular style. Taking the art form of theatre from point A to point B can be a very valid purpose for some theatre people, a very valid purpose. Creating impressionistic art instead of the old kind of art, old kind of painting is certainly a very valid thing. All I am trying to say is—that is not my purpose. My interest is not there, our interest is not there—taking theatre as an art form from point A to point B. But as we need that particular form which will project our content—content of that particular play most effectively. So we have to explore a lot, explore its form. And many diverse new forms sometimes. Every play of ours is a challenge to us in trying to find a form. I won't go into the details.

I think I have talked a bit too much. Now I will take the questions one by one and try to answer. I think I have answered Badola's questions as much as I could. I think now it is clear that it is not my wanting to direct in opposition to my wanting to write, or rather being creative in the field of direction at the cost of being creative in the form of my writing. As a matter of fact, I don't bother about creativity. I have got to do this theatre and say something through theatre because that is the only thing I know. So it is not a question of creativity at all. So even if I am a bad director, even if it is at the cost of writing a certain kind of play, I have got to go on doing it. It is not question of emphasising directing as against writing—that's not the question.

Now about the second question—(about) the theatre we had been practising. You can say it has been devised, but we had to devise part of it out of a need. And I do take workshops here and there. Some people do the same kind of theatre in other parts of India. That is true. Whether I keep in touch, I cannot myself keep in touch but many of my workshop participants who have done some follow up, who found my workshop or the kind of theatre I practise or preach useful— if they write then I keep up with the news. And throughout India all my friends are now workshop friends. And so I quite often create a scandalous situation, in Delhi particularly. All the intellectuals and stalwarts of theatre and the art world go to the Mandi House area. They find me with very young people in their early twenties or even in their teens. They are my friends and I don't think it is liked very much but I can't help it. They are my workshop participants and have become my friends. That happens all the time. So I would like to keep in touch but I cannot manage to do so.

Then there is the question about seeing my play being done by other people and my reaction to that. First of all, being in active theatre and naturally a part-time theatre, everybody has to work for a living. Remember, it is Free Theatre! So we can't pay anybody anything. They work in an office or something, they come in the evening and that time naturally is our working time which clashes with the show time of other people's theatre. So we get very little opportunity to see other people's theatre. That's a sorry state of affairs, but that's what it is. So I don't get much opportunity of seeing other theatre, and in Bengal I don't think anybody else produces my play. I am quite unpopular in Bengal. Probably I am more popular as a playwright in other parts, not in Bengal. These who do my plays—I have seen many and have different reactions to different productions. So it's very hard to reply in one sentence or give a definite reply. Naturally sometimes I have seen very amateurish productions. It's not possible to like that.

Coming to the second part of Badola's question – whether there is a difference between life and death – that's too philosophical for me, I won't get into it. If I remember correctly, we had a discussion throughout the night at Dishantar—a very interesting discussion for me after I had seen *Ebong Indrajit*. And that is the first production of *Ebong Indrajit* I saw in Hindi. Before that I saw the Bengali one by Souvanik which I do not consider my play. That was not my play. They did is as a stunt and made weird interpretations of all sorts. If I am permitted, let me tell a story. The director asked me why I chose the names Amal, Vimal, Kamal. I answered with the obvious response—that these names rhyme and to just show them as prototypes, thats all. They said 'Oh, we thought it is A, B, C, and I means *main*.'

I didn't understand at first! If you mean A, B, C, (then) Amal is 'A', Bimal is 'B' but is Kamal 'Camel' that it becomes 'C'? Kamal is spelt with a 'K' but they made it a 'C', for 'Camel'! And what does it mean anyway? A, B, C and I—Indrajit as 'I'! So these kinds of absurd, weird interpretations! All they thought was that it's a bit different so it will become a box office hit. And it did become a box office hit for Souvanik.

But the really serious production I have seen is yours—Dishantar's. Earlier I talked about how you threw away the last one-and-a-half pages of *Ebong Indrajit*. To me the last one and a half pages are vital. I won't go in to the question of life or death. So, therefore, yours ended in a kind of frustration, which by the way, is very dramatic. Frustration to us is very dramatic. But anyway, when I wrote the play I wrote it as a private piece of writing. I was very much into theatre at that time. Never thought of producing it. It was in my drawer for three years at least. I read it only to my friends. I never thought anybody should produce it or I should produce or publish it. Somehow it was drawn out and things started happening. I wrote it as a private thing. Therefore those last one-and-a-half pages is [*sic*] very important to me. It is not a question of interpreting my play or anything, but without that my play is not my play. I can't help it.

Pagla Ghoda was produced by Bohrupee directed by Sombhu Mitra, for whom I have great respect. When he asked me '*Yeh agar suicide kar le toh? Kartik*?' (Supposing he commits suicide? So I said, 'Then I will consider it is not my play [*sic*].' That was the total dialogue [*sic*]. I did not know what he was going to do. What he did is probably worse than Kartik committing suicide. Probably this thing will be relevant to only those who have read *Pagla Ghoda* or seen it. Kartik neither committed suicide nor did he deliberately decide to live (which is important to my play). He poured the poison on the ground, then suddenly, frantically, tried to pick it up and lick it, ending in indecision. I think this is worse than committing suicide. These things happen. What can I say? It was otherwise an excellent production.

In *Baki Itihas*, in the third Act, to me Sitanath is not a ghost. To me the third Act is Sharad meeting Sharad, not Sitanath—that is third Act to me. Now, for reasons of stunts, Bohurupee used the same actor and actress for both Sharad and Sitanath, Basanti and Kanak. Naturally in the third Act another actor had to be brought in; there was no way out because there was nobody else available. Only one actor for both Sharad and Sitanath. In the first two acts it worked well, but in the third Act Sharad has to speak to Sitantah. So a new actor had to be brought in. Immediately it is obvious when a new actor comes that he is the ghost of Sitanath, there can't be any other alternative. That spoils the play. I didn't want the ghost of Sitanath. I wanted Sharad speaking with Sharad. The second story was Sharad's imagination. The first story was Basanti's imagination. The third Act is also Sharad's imagination. Therefore the same actor should play Sitanath in all the three versions.

These things are done, what can I do? I can't do anything. I do not stop anybody from doing my play. When Shyamanand Jalan started directing my play *Ebong Indrajit,* he told me 'I'll discuss it with you.' I said 'Welcome.' We discussed it. 'You must come to every rehearsal.' I said 'Sorry I won't.' '*Ek saath karna hai.*' '*Nahin, tum direct karo.*' '*Agar tumhara play hum badal dein?*'

> *Badal do.* Change any line you want, add any line, throw off any line. I will retain only one right please. If anybody asks me afterwards—'How did you like Shyamanand Jalan's production (of *Ebong Indrajit*)?' I will tell him openly and frankly what I feel. You must not object to it. If I think it is a rotten production, I will tell the person that I found it a rotten production. That right I want to retain. But I will not restrict you from doing anything, throwing away my lines, adding lines, whatever.

These have been my conditions with the directors. I will never stop anybody's production. Souvanik's *Ebong Indrajit*—I have been saying all kinds of bad things, whatever I feel like. And as you see I am talking about Sombhu Mitra's production. That right I want to retain.

Now about this question on the Theatre of Synthesis. Actually it has a history. I got this Jawaharlal Nehru Fellowship. And there was an obligation that I would have to write and publish a book at the end of it. They told me they would not give the fellowship for writing plays because they thought I would be writing plays anyway. They would give it on the basis of a project. So I submitted a project to them. The name of that project was quite a long one, I don't know if I can repeat it correctly—Workshop for a Synthesis of Theatre as a Rural-Urban Link. That is what I did. And actually at that time, 1971 to '73, I was in a transitory phase. You remember in 1972–'73 I changed over? So in 1971 everything was boiling in my head. Naturally I wanted to do this. At that time the concept of Third Theatre didn't come to me. I was thinking of doing a theatre where direct communication could be utilised. So naturally, at first I thought about the first theatre – that is folk theatre – and I was doing the second theatre—that is city theatre. So this question of synthesis was predominant in my mind. That's how I submitted the project on Synthesis. But as I proceeded – since it was my work and I was not just doing it to oblige the people who gave me the fellowship – I dropped the idea. It's not a workshop of synthesis any more to me. I was not trying anymore to provide a link between theatre and city theatre. By that time I was fixed in my idea that it must be an alternative theatre. So that's why when the book was published it was called the *Third Theatre*. But still, as I was obliged to the people who gave me so much money for two years, I had put that name – Workshop for Synthesis – and by doing so, acknowledged my debt to them. That's why some people got confused (and asked) – 'Have you provided that link?' 'I have not, because I lost interest in that.' So that probably explains the name.

Q: You have talked about the Third Theatre as a political theatre. Can it be called political theatre as you interpret it?

BS: I think it's better that I make it clear [*sic*]. I made a statement that the Third Theatre is a matter of philosophy to me, so anybody doing theatre only as a career cannot do Third Theatre. In a way it is political action. That is the term I used. I think that is quite different from calling Third Theatre a political theatre—just a matter of correction.

Q: Please permit me to call it political theatre. That is my own individual view, because you have talked about the class-ridden conditions in society. It is possible that you don't call it a political theatre but your eye is on the conditions prevailing in society and you feel the need to change those conditions. My question is whether this Free Theatre or Third Theatre has a vital link with the people getting together and fighting to change society in different spheres of life; or whether you think about making a link and relationship with such people fighting towards a better society? Or are you saying that you are not interested in establishing any such links?

BS: I will answer this question directly. As a matter of fact, it would have been the ideal condition if this theatre had a direct link with people's struggles. That way our theatre would have thrived, and probably could have helped the people's struggle as such. But I don't find the conditions of my country...conducive for this. Therefore, I could not establish any link between my theatre and the people's struggle that way. But it can be linked. The people's struggle can again be interpreted or looked at in different ways. As I said, I consider our theatre to be political action, still it is not political theatre. Why? Because quite often words have associative meanings. Politics as a philosophy is really my personal belief. But when we use the term politics, immediately the image of a political party comes to our mind. That's a different thing. If I say 'political theatre,' people get the idea that we are linked with a political party. That will be wrong. It is not political theatre in that sense. But I definitely consider it political theatre because it is our politics. Ours – we the members of the group – our politics. We have a politics. Now if our politics as expressed in our theatre could have been linked with a greater politics in the countrywide struggle or something, it would have been wonderful. But I do not find any such struggle around me. I do not find that. A kind of struggle which I have experienced. Maybe some members present here also experienced that, but most – the majority are my workshop students – have not. In the years 1944–'45–'46, at the peak of the freedom movement, I remember Hindus and Muslims fighting together. I remember those days. There was a general surge in the people's struggle. Then in between we have seen, at least locally in West Bengal, the 'Food Movement' as we call it. It was there. There were other kinds of struggles also. But since the early 1970s to this day, all I find around me, whenever there is a people's participation, the movement is a chauvinistic movement. More and more chauvinistic ideas are inspiring people's participation. Whether it is Punjab or Assam or wherever, it is all these things—religious chauvinism, provincial chauvinism, language chauvinism.... All retrogressive things. So where is the people's struggle with which we shall link? So in a way, it is a very frustrating situation. It is not that we don't want to do it, we want to do it very much but we can't do it. The physical objective conditions don't exist. Now there are leftist parties. They have formed a government in West Bengal. Right? Well, what should I say? We go to the villages walking—three-day treks! If we get any opposition it is from the leftist party. Although what they were supposed to do is the same as what we want to do. They were supposed to bring social change. But we were actually prevented from doing our performance in one place by that (same) leftist party. And we are suspect because we do not belong to them. If we do not belong to them, automatically we are Naxalites. And to them Naxalites are worse enemies than those they call the bourgeois, this and that. That is the situation there. *Toh kahan milega hamara struggle jiske saath hum link karenge?*

Hindi translation published in Chhayanat, *100*
Courtesy (original English version): UP Sangeet Natak Akademi Archives

THE THEATRE OF BADAL SIRCAR

Sumanta Bannerjee

In continuation of the first two parts included in 'The Beginnings', the author looks at the second phase of his work as director, playwright and theoretician, in this four-part article

III

> Can we...afford to put the spectators at a distance? At a different level? In darkness? Have they not come to meet us? Are they not an integral part of the theatre event?...All the spectators on one side means pushing the last row too far. Why not put them on all sides? The higher level of the stage makes the performers superior and detached. Why not come down to the same level? The spectators hiding in the dark render it impossible for the performers to get any direct feedback from one another, why not put them in light so that we can see them and they can see one another?...Why not be at the same space with the spectators to make it a three dimensional reality as theatre really is?
>
> **Badal Sircar**

A theatrical problem which had exercised Badal Sircar's mind for quite some time during his experiments with a variety of technical devices in the 1960s in plays like *Ebong Indrajit, Baki Itihas*, or *Tringhsa Shatabdi,* was how to bridge the distance between the play and its audience, the performers and their spectators. This urge was further accentuated by the increasing infusion of political ideas in his plays. It grew out of the realisation that theatre should not only reflect the human condition but should also endeavour to make the audience aspire to change the present condition. It was necessary, therefore, to take the theatre to the people at large—in villages, city slums, factories, college lawns, office canteens, public parks etc. This was not possible through the proscenium stage. Sircar, through his group Satabdi, which was established in 1967, therefore began to evolve a flexible, portable and inexpensive theatre from the 1970s onwards, variously known as the Third Theatre, or the Free Theatre, or Angan Mancha in Bengali.

Just as in the case of his earlier plays, his development of the concept of the Third Theatre was also taking place against the backdrop of the contemporary scene. His plays of introspection were shaped by the concerns and conditions of the Calcutta middle-class youth of the 1960s to the early 1970s period, when the Naxalite movement was shaking up the status quo by raising a number of fundamentally important political and social questions. It challenged the traditional interpretation of Indian history by questioning the role of the national leadership in relation to the rural poor during the anti-colonial movement. It exposed the opportunism and expediency of the existing political parties in the history of post-Independence India. It defied the conventional middle-class-dominated conservative social norms and values. The exodus of a large number of these defiant youths from the middle-class homes to the villages, inspired by the Naxalite ideology of agrarian revolution, drew public attention to the hitherto neglected needs and aspirations of the rural poor. In the context of West Bengal, along with the politics of agrarian revolution, the rich cultural tradition of the numerous Bengali rural folk forms also attracted the attention of politically committed dramatists during this period. It may be recalled that Utpal Dutt took up the popular rural theatre form of *jatra* at this time to stage his political plays like *Rifle* (1968), *Jallianwala Bagh* (1969), *Dilli Chalo* (1970), *Sannyasir Tarbari* (1972), and *Mao Tse Tung* (1974).

Both these political and cultural developments of that period left their mark on Badal Sircar's concept of the Third Theatre. One must, however, add in this connection that from his writings on this concept in 1971 (when he had just started experimenting with it), it appears that he was more driven by the need to reach an audience directly, and thus more concerned with the technical device of the 'Theatre-in-the-Round' in order to gain that objective. It was only later that Sircar, in his writings on drama, came out more explicitly on the political messages that he wanted to convey through Third Theatre. In an article in a Delhi theatre magazine in 1981, on behalf of his theatre group Satabdi, he said: 'We believe that theatre should not only reflect human condition, but should also endeavour to change the present condition to something better. Hence we write, select or prepare only such plays that fulfill the above purposes.' Still later, in an introduction to a selection of his Third Theatre plays, he was more forthright when stating: '....In this theatre, the content is the main thing. The "form" comes later. We do not produce any play in this theatre which does not have any social or political message.'

But even before coming out explicitly in his articles about his political objectives, Badal Sircar in his plays for the Third Theatre had already begun to strike a political note. In 1972 he adapted Howard Fast's famous novel on the slave rebellion in ancient Rome, *Spartacus*, for his Angan Mancha. It ends with all the slaves rising together in a rhythmic gesture that symbolises Spartacus, their hero who had become a martyr. They speak in the voice of Spartacus, asserting that he will always be wherever people struggle till they achieve liberty, and that he will come back, reborn among millions of people. Significantly, Sircar introduced a lot of physical action in his play in the form of a variety of body movements—violent gestures to express the oppressive nature of the Roman slave-owners, contortions of the body to convey the pain of the torture suffered by the slaves, sudden acrobatic movements by the slaves to assert their defiance of their owners. This stress on the body was to become a major ingredient in Sircar's concept of the Third Theatre, where he tried to use physical gestures and movements, as far as possible, to supplement dialogues, and supplant conventional stage sets and props. We shall come to this aspect of the Third Theatre later.

As for his political message in the contemporary Indian context, *Michhil* (1974) was one of his first plays of the Third Theatre phase to express it. Sircar here picks up the all-too familiar trait for which Calcutta is famous – as a 'city of processions' (*micchil* in Bengali) – to show how this once radical demonstration of genuine popular urges has degenerated today into a ritual that is used by the ruling classes to confuse and exploit the masses. The play ends with all the people – the performers as well as the audience – forming a human chain, thus emphasising the need for collective effort to form a new *michhil* or procession, that would translate their dream of freedom from exploitation into reality.

In some of these plays of the Third Theatre, Sircar often employs fantasy, allegory and traditional folk to point a revolutionary moral. A fable is occasionally used to underpin the main theme. He introduces absurd and extravagantly comic characters, and the final outcome is a grand mixture of serious poetry, parody, caricature, burlesque and various folk media styles, with a sharp political message.

A typical example is *Lakshmichhharar Panchali* (1974). It is in the form of a traditional folk poetic debate known in the Bengal countryside as *tarja* or *kobi-gaan*, where two singers, or groups of singers, engage in a verbal duel by exchanging extempore verses on either mythological events or contemporary political happenings. In this play, an elderly *kobi* or versifier contends with a younger one. The debate between the two moves on to questions like why do the poor farmers lose their land and suffer illiteracy, why they cannot compete in a free market economy etc. It ends with songs expressing the determination of the poor to win the land they till, the things they produce, and distribute them equally among themselves.

The utopia envisaged at the end of *Lakshmichhharar Panchali* is brought to life in *Hattomalar Oparey* (1977). It is mixture of fantasy and social criticism. Two thieves, while escaping their pursuers, fall in a river, and arrive in a fairy tale state. All the people work here and enjoy the fruits of their labour. There is no buying and selling of commodities, no police to guard shops and houses, hotels offer free food and medical aid is available for all. In other words, it is a Communist society of the future. Out of sheer habit, the thieves try to steal, and to their utter surprise find that whatever they want to steal is given away free. Finally, the friendly citizens come to their help, and put their knowledge of stone and mortar (which they have acquired as thieves, to make holes in walls to enter houses) to use by training them as masons, and thus change their roles from house-breakers to house-makers. The end is a song by a chorus which praises the virtue of labour, the need for the availability of things for each according to one's needs and the equitable distribution of production.

Did such plays of the Third Theatre genre have the sort of impact on the audience that Badal Sircar envisaged? According to his own testimony about the experiences of his theatre group Satabdi during its tours in villages in West Bengal, they did have some impact. He quotes a very interesting observation made by a villager who saw one of these plays of the Third Theatre genre. When asked about what he understood, he paused, thought and then in a very unemotional cool voice replied: "We, the poor, don't have any problems in understanding; maybe the rich don't understand."

There is a certain simplification, sometimes bordering on propaganda, in the presentation of the final message in the plays of this type. Is this because of the model adopted by Sircar in the writing of these plays, or due to some inherent vacuity in his understanding of the political transformation? Clearly, the model is either a folk cultural form (as in *Lakshmichhharar Panchali*, where the two characters follow the conventional narrative style of the rural *kobi*s or versifiers), or the fairy tale (as in *Hattomalar Oparey,* where the protagonists arrive in a strange land like the heroes of old adventure tales).

While Badal Sircar's plays of this genre conform to the folk tradition's theatrical norm of the moralistic ending, they fail somehow at providing a sequential explanation for the sudden turn of events which leads at the end of his plays to the rise of the downtrodden. In the traditional fairy tales and folk theatre, such a turn where the victims of the evil forces ultimately triumph is usually brought about by a series of miraculous superhuman acts. Sircar, because of his political beliefs, skips over these stages of magical events. But it is these which are the ingredients of rural folk entertainment that lead to the logical denouement. Sircar, after having convincingly exposed the evil machinations of the modern-day demons, abruptly rushes to the moralistic end where he announces the ultimate victory of their victims—the oppressed poor.

Sircar's choice of such a style for his Third Theatre experiments was apparently dictated by the desire to reach a wider audience in the rural areas who had been brought up on these cultural forms. But there are several problems that a modern playwright faces while using such a model. First, he/she has to discard a lot from the traditional structure and select only those parts or sequences that lend themselves to the propagation of the playwright's message. This may create a jarring sense of discontinuity in the perception of the rural audience, who are used to the familiar sequential pattern. Secondly, the message – usually political, unlike the popularly accepted traditional religious and moralistic ones – is a new intrusion in this type of folk style-based theatre, which has to be made acceptable to the rural audience. Besides, too often the serious and complex nature of the theme may get over-simplified by, or even subdued to, the requirements of these traditional folk forms.

In spite of his sincere efforts to explain the basic logic of capitalist exploitation and imperialist domination in terms of popular perception, Sircar's tendency to end these plays with an abrupt denouement that often envisaged a fairyland utopia, or pledged a revolution of vague sorts, defeats the very purpose of the alternative theatre movement. Among its many other objectives, the alternative theatre aims at provoking the audience to question the status quo, as well as the various prevailing economic and political recipes to change it. Instead of allowing the audience to continue to wrestle with the brain-teasing questions that he poses in these plays, and help them find their own solutions, Sircar seems to be in a hurry to inspire them to adopt his own political vision, which somehow remains ambiguous.

Sircar however succeeds in a large measure in those plays of the Third Theatre genre, where he employs the urban form of documentary oeuvre and satirical skits based on historical and current social and political problems. *Sukhapathya Bharater Itihas* (1976), which deals with past episodes from Indian history, is an interesting example of this. The title literally means 'an easily-read history of India.' Located in a schoolroom situation but staged in an open-air scene, it is a satirical exposition (in the form of school lessons) of the history of British colonial exploitation of India.

Similarly, *Khatmat Kring* (1983) moves through a series of short satirical skits which juxtapose fleeting glimpses of political murders and street rowdiness in modern Calcutta with scenes of anti-Jewish Nazi propaganda in Germany in the 1930s and anti-Shudra acts of Rama in Ramayana. In a sort of stream-of-consciousness burlesque, one dialogue or an incident sparks off memories of similar historical events of the past, the association of one leading to that of another. As a result, the scenes keep on shifting rapidly from the immolation of Joan of Arc to the burning of a bride for dowry, from the competitive environs of a modern commercial office to the nuclear race in the international arena which leads to a future world where men have killed themselves and only cockroaches survive.

These plays are marked by a certain distortion of the reality that characterises dreams and hallucinations. Yet, such distorted visions are closer to possible experiences, and a brilliant caricature of the impotence of the old liberal standpoint in dealing with today's problems of criminalisation of politics, corruption of society, rise of neo-fascist forces and the threat of the looming nuclear war. At times, it seems as if Sircar is parodying his own vein of romantic self-pity and poetical soliloquies that fitted so comfortably the structure of his plays of the 1950s and 1960s, but which were found to be curiously out of place in the more complex years of the 1970-'90 period.

As mentioned earlier in the context of his staging *Spartacus*, an interesting stylistic development in these plays of the Third Theatre was the stress on the movements of the human body on the stage. In his plays of the earlier phase also, Sircar attached a lot of importance to the attitudes, gestures and movements of the body of the performer. But the emphasis on such bodily movements was usually prompted by the desire to use the slapstick to make a commentary on the absurdity of a situation, whether social or political. Thus, in *Ebong Indrajit*, in certain situations, the characters physically act in a way that makes us feel that their bodies are machines (as in Chaplin's *Modern Times*)—where the playwright seeks to highlight the mechanical routine lifestyle of these characters.

But, in the Third Theatre plays, Sircar uses the body in a different way. Explaining the playwright's conception of body movements in the Third Theatre, he says on one occasion: '...the basic tool of the trade of the art of theatre is the human body.' He then goes on to ask: 'All the paraphernalia of the conventional city theatre – sets, props, spotlights, costume, make-up – are they really essential? ...in other words, will theatre cease to be theatre if any or all of them are absent?' He adds after this: 'Without the human body, without the active presence of the human being, theatre will not exist.' A step forward from this view is the attempt to replace the conventional theatrical props and sets with human beings who represent them by their body movements. Separation of time and space on the stage are represented not by naturalistic devices like intervals or changing sets and props, but by the physical postures and gestures of the performers which symbolise the flow of action from one time to another, from one space to another. 'As sets and props are suggested rather than shown, so are events and actions suggested by signs rather than actual actions—like a series of abstract movements and gestures, like a burst of body energy and sound energy.'

Once again – as in Sircar's earlier plays like *Ebong Indrajit* – in these plays of the Third Theatre too, one can discover influences of contemporary western theories of alternative drama. His Angan Mancha is contemporaneous with the experiments made in different countries by theatre directors like Jerzy Grotowski, Richard Schechner and Augusto Boal, among others. They have also been trying to shake off the formal constraints of the conventional theatre and move towards the aesthetics of a theatre of the poor that could make it easily accessible to the downtrodden, use more open space, encourage active audience participation and make the performer an 'athlete of the emotions' (as described by Schechner).

But Badal Sircar, instead of copying these techniques from the western alternative theatre, has taken their underlying principles and fashioned his own Angan Mancha style. While remaining firmly embedded to the Indian socio-economic ground reality, and politically committed to the goal of a socialist transformation of our society, Sircar has been open-minded and eclectic enough to adopt and assimilate a variety of techniques from different sources—the alternative theatre of the West, the traditional rural folk cultural forms of Bengal, the recent experiments of political street theatre in different parts of India.

IV

> Theatre by itself will never change the world for the better, but let us allow theatre to stake a modest claim in the process of that change, and let us wish that the language of theatre continues to change everywhere accordingly.
>
> **Badal Sircar**

From the comedies of the 1950s to the Third Theatre (or Angan Mancha) of the latest phase, Badal Sircar's journey had been one of a restless inventor striving to bring about changes in the language of theatre. But there is a common thread that runs through all of them despite their changing thematic and stylistic differences. It is the concept of liberation in its various forms—whether it is the characters in his plays who want to free themselves from the yoke of conventions and authorities, or it is he himself who strives to free the form of his plays gradually, first from the traditional norms of the naturalistic theatre, and then altogether from the shackles of the proscenium.

Even in his earlier light-hearted comedies, his way of reinvigorating traditional romantic stories with innovative theatrical devices, acted as a liberating influence on the contemporary Bengali stage. The serious plays that followed were marked by a rebellion of the unshackled imagination against the conventions of thought and conduct. But the playwright, being bound by the theatrical obligations required in the presentation of a play in the urban middle-class environment, was still feeling uncomfortable with the form.

Sircar was soon to recognise that it was more than a problem of freeing the theatre from its conventional formal structure. In an environment of increasing commercialisation of the cultural scene, and rise of authoritarianism in the political sphere, Sircar was realising the need to trace the roots of the theatrical problems to the more fundamental issue of economic and political bondage of humankind in modern society. He had to move out from his limited framework of individual concerns of the middle-class intellectuals (*Ebong Indrajit*) to the wider arena of the concerns of the rural and urban poor. As he was to write sometime in the early 1970s: 'Man who was once free, created money for his own use. Thus, Frankenstein created a monster, that monster today has captured humankind and imprisoned it.... Money makes everyone work, everyone is a prisoner of money.' Coming to his own problem as a theatre-producer, Sircar then talks about how he and his colleagues in the profession have to cajole the monster of money all the time: 'We rent theatre halls. We buy costumes and props. We advertise in newspapers. We sell tickets. At every stage, we have to court this monster and use it. But do we use it? No, at every stage, the monster uses us. Our theatre is a prisoner in the hands of the monster.'

It is in the Third Theatre which he evolved later, that Badal Sircar claims to have freed himself from this monster. It is a world liberated from the expensive sets and props, as well as from the water-tight compartments of tragedy and comedy, poetry and prose, reality and illusion, proscenium and open-air, performers and audience. He could here bring together surrealistic fantasies, grotesque paraphernalia of fairy tale genies, and caricatures of mythological characters and modern political leaders, in order to make a serious comment on the contemporary situation.

He gives free rein here to his penchant for the comic. Satire adopts fantastic garb. Underneath the seeming gaiety, horrors of the pit are suddenly exposed. The comic in Badal Sircar has turned a full circle, but this time with a mission. It often appears first in the guise of fantasy, and then gradually shows its fangs which tear apart the ridiculous pretensions of politicians, the greed of the multinationals, the crimes of the war-mongers.

The Third Theatre also provides Sircar with a vehicle to break down another boundary—the barrier between the rural folk-cultural forms and the urban modern theatrical forms:

> ...the folk theatre, in spite of its vitality and popularity, preaches stagnant, back-dated and reactionary values; whereas the city theatre deals with advanced and progressive ideas for a sophisticated audience who would be stimulated mentally, but will not or cannot act upon them. In such a situation, a 'third theatre' or a theatre of synthesis appears to be the need of the day.

But by trying to assimilate elements of the folk culture and theatre (e.g. *panchali*, *jatra*, *kirtan*, etc.) in his plays, Sircar had to grapple with a perennial problem that had plagued Bengali theatre practitioners in the past. His predecessors (notable in the IPTA—Indian People's Theatre Association), had also tried to selectively adopt certain forms of traditional folk culture for political plays or musical narratives. *Lakshmichharar Panchali*, for instance, recalls the innovative experiments of the famous Bengali Communist composer and singer, the late Hemanga Biswas, who in 1948 came out with a song (called Mountbatten-Mangalkavya) lampooning the strategy of 'transfer of power' from the British rulers of the Indian Congress politicians, in a style that borrowed various forms from Bengali folk music. Similarly, still later, in the 1960s, a now forgotten Communist playwright and director, Biru Mukhopadhyay, wrote an anti-war play called *Rahumukto,* modelled on the traditional *jatra* form, which used to be enacted in the open air stage both in Calcutta and the villages. This was long before Utpal Dutt ventured into political experiments with *jatra*. But they had to ultimately face the question whether their experiments had lasting impact on their audience.

However, despite the success of the folk forms by these dramatists – as well as the temporary popularity of some of their plays in the countryside – one wonders whether the progressive messages that they sought to propagate prevailed over the obscurantist prejudices and superstitious beliefs of the rural people which still continue to dominate the countryside. Today the problem has been further aggravated in the rural areas. What Sircar describes as 'stagnant, back-dated and reactionary values' are not only being reinforced by the traditional rural media, but are being compounded by the crass consumerist messages blared by the commercial media (with video parlours thriving in interior villages). There is thus an unholy alliance between the feudal values preached by some of the traditional folk media, and the commercial self-interest propagated by the modern media. They pose a challenge to the practitioners of the Third Theatre who want to contribute to the process of change in the socio-economic situation which Badal Sircar envisaged when he started his Angan Mancha experiment in 1971.

To conclude, if we are to evaluate Badal Sircar's theatrical experiments over the last four decades, we shall have to estimate what he has added to the Indian dramatic scene, as well as how he has explained his purpose though these experiments. There is a need for honest wide-ranging inquiries that should go beyond the immediate popularity or relevance of his plays.

His plays have undoubtedly opened the doors of the theatre to the drama of ideas, and his innovative staging methods have brought the theatre to the poor. But at the same time, we have to recognise that he has been projecting ideas that we have heard before, and handling situations and feelings that are already familiar. Whether his plays of the 1960s, which were marked by a rather uneasy mixture of moral indignation and self-pity often expressed by the rhetoric of Existentialism, or his didactic plays of the Third Theatre with lively arguments on class conflicts usually ending with political harangue, there is nothing in them that we can call truly creative.

However, even though his plays might not have come up with any original ideas, his passionate commitment to the cause of social justice and his excellent skill in translating it into theatrical terms – helped by his penchant for witty dialogues – have remained undimmed all through the various stages of his experiments. But, there seems to be a certain lack of focus in his choice of issues and a dearth of conciseness in handling them. He wants to explain too many problems within the framework of a single play—the economic plight of the poor, the capitalist system which causes this plight, the political options before the exploited poor and the middle-class intellectuals who sympathise with them, the militarist nature of the world capitalist order, the danger of a nuclear war threatened by this order, etc., etc. While all these dimensions are surely relevant for a political analysis of the situation in India, Badal Sircar somehow fails to bind together these various strands into a pithy theatrical statement. As a result, these plays seem to exist in an amorphous zone—moving between the world of sentimental self-flagellation by the guilt-stricken middle-classes on the one hand, and that of political self-affirmation by the oppressed poor on the other. The dialogues therefore vary from gushing emotional outbursts to didactic political arguments. Badal Sircar's plays will thus remain a faithful, albeit imperfect and uneven at times, record of the conflicts and ideas of the troubled period of the last four decades, as well as an honest expression of his theatrical methods to explain them to a wider audience. It is his ability to inspire and influence a new generation of young practitioners in the alternative theatre movement in India that will be recognised as his major contribution to the development of India drama.

Published in Theatre India, *NSD journal, November 1999, Issue 2*
Courtesy: Natarang Pratishthan Archives

THIRD THEATRE METHODOLOGY

Sharad Nagar

Interview with **Badal Sircar** held in 1988

Sharad Nagar (SN): Let me first welcome you to Lucknow on behalf of the Sangeet Natak Akademi, You are here to conduct a workshop with the students of the Bhartendu Natya Akademi. How are you liking it here in Lucknow?

Badal Sircar (BS): I enjoy doing workshops outside. I can't do too many such workshops as my priority is with my theatre group Satabdi. Once in a while I come out to conduct workshops for about a week. I have gone to many states, many organisations—probably different kinds, and perhaps worked more with non-theatre people than those involved with theatre. Wherever I go the response is good and there is a definite kind of enjoyment.

SN: What kind of response have you got from the kids with whom you are working here?

BS: Very good, because they are young and very enthusiastic. Thanks to their institution, Bhartendu Natya Akademi, right from the beginning they are used to hard work. They know that theatre is serious business. I was really surprised. I asked them their working hours. They said they work from nine to six. Well, this is more than a factory's working hours. I said all right, I will also work from nine to six.

Right in the beginning I tell them that my workshop is related only to the theatre which I believe in and practise. I cannot teach all kinds of theatre. I have to tell them which is the kind of theatre I believe in and practise, so I keep aside some time for these discussions. By doing this we don't waste time during the workshops. So, this workshop is from 9:00 am to 4:30 pm and the discussion is from 5:00 pm to 6:00 pm after a short break. This is our routine for the duration of this entire eight-day workshop.

SN: What are the areas you have covered in these eight days? For instance what do you intend to show in tomorrow's demonstration?

BS: A workshop is such a thing that it is difficult to describe. I will try. Probably I should explain what I want to do? What is the purpose of a workshop? What do I want to achieve?

This is a theatre workshop but different from the conventional training in theatre schools. Here the fundamental point is the human being—the individual human being and not the theatre man. Start with him.

The theatre man comes afterwards. That's why I have done many workshops with non-theatre people. They will probably never do theatre but this will be of use to them also because the human being is the fundamental factor. In the world we live, this competitive society, a society based on inequality, we learn from childhood how to hide our real selves, how to suppress our true self, how not to express it. We need a mask, an armour, so that we can show ourselves to be superior—because it is a competitive society. First our parents tell us what to do and what not to do, then our teachers in school and then we teach ourselves to use these masks. This continuous suppression creates psychological blocks that are difficult to break. We develop inhibitions. We are always afraid of getting ridiculed by others, to be made a laughing stock by others. Thus even when we feel like dancing in the streets with joy, we will not do so. When I am bereaved I am afraid to shed tears because tears are a sign of weakness. To suppress the true nature and true feeling is the order of society, order of the day, but theatre is just the opposite: it is all about expression.

So in this seven-day workshop, the task is to go against what you have learnt through your entire life. That is definitely not an easy task! But it is important to remove those blocks—for theatre as well as for human beings. The human being is the prime concern here, not theatre skill; theatre skill comes later. Since the process of trying to remove psychological blocks is a sensitive matter, it is not possible for any observers to be present. The participants will need to open up, they will have to melt their inner selves and become vulnerable. They must feel safe.

SN: So how do you achieve this task?

BS: Through games. These are games which appear to be children's games—children's games which adults find difficult to play. They initially find them ridiculous. But it helps if no observers are present because then everyone present is part of this ridiculous act and no one can be laughed at. So we are all equally unsafe. Equally unsafe really means equally safe. We need that atmosphere and therefore this condition.

I know I am considered eccentric and unduly strict because I do not allow observers, but actually it is not eccentricity. It is respecting people's privacy and making them feel comfortable. This is important. The participants appreciate this rule.

After this there are many other games and exercises related to team-work, because theatre is teamwork. Teamwork in theatre means there should be mutual trust in the team. Mutual love should also be there. So, through the games we have to gradually create a condition where the participants come close to one another. And that's another thing. Through games, while they are learning things which they can use in theatre, this thing is happening as a by-product—coming closer and closer, holding each other's hands. Because for me theatre is human action. Theatre means we are trying to reach out and touch others, communicate with others, get close to others. That should be done amongst theatre people first, to have that kind of rapport, that kind of relationship amongst themselves.

So we have several games through which the participants can come closer. Accepting this, gradually we go nearer, nearer to the theatre. Like movement in space, creating sound, movement, rhythm, learning rhythm, setting sound and movement in rhythm, changing them by exploring sound and movement.

Strangely, in our civilised life we hardly use our body, we are hardly aware of it. So there are exercises that help them become aware of their own body, the hidden potential of the body. We use all extremities—the arms, the legs. We civilised urban people have practically become spineless because we hardly use the spinal cord. We don't know that we have a spine, we have forgotten that. So there are exercises for the spine, simple exercises, based on yoga. I don't know yoga but simple exercises are done. If I do not have time to teach, I demonstrate the exercises for them to be aware of the need of these exercises.

Then, an important part is to help creativity. Frankly, I believe every human being has the faculty of imagination, faculty of creation, even if he or she is not aware of it himself or herself. Quite a few of us don't have confidence. They think they can't write, they can't create. They believe they are dull and good for nothing, mostly because other people have told them so from their childhood. That is the important part of the workshop. Find out what creative faculty you have, what imaginative powers you have, give scope through the games again, give scope and prove to yourself that you have it. So actually in many ways it is multifaceted. But everywhere I try not to lose touch with…that human being. So I have done workshops with totally unsophisticated – not only unsophisticated, but illiterate – peasants and women of villages. I had some experience doing workshops with people who, thanks to our society, have been told right from the beginning that they are not even full human beings, let alone having any special faculty. Often at the end of seven days, or even two days of the workshop, I have found their whole personality to have changed because they had never had such an opportunity of proving themselves before. They seemed more confident because something had opened up in them.

There is another thing, which is that in most workshops participants are meeting each other for the first time so there are a lot of inhibitions. Here (at BNA) the case is different. Here the participants are the students of the same institution, they knew each other so that dimension was absent from this. I was conducting one workshop in Calcutta, where age wise the youngest participant was a girl of 14, and the oldest was my cousin sister who was 59 years old at that time. So 14 to 59 was the age difference. Classwise, for example, my sister was the headmistress of a school, there were M.A., M.Sc, or M.A. students. There was a…(young English couple). (They) came to India not as tourists, but like many others who have come to understand the Third World. They joined my workshop. There were two Roman Catholic fathers, three Roman Catholic nuns, sisters, and there were people from Kidderpore – that's the dock area – (hailing from) *bustees*, slums. A women's organisation had sent them.

Among the slum dwellers was a woman who was a sweeper. She was married, had two children and her husband had left her. It's a very common story. She was struggling hard with two children. As a participant, imagine her reaction to her colleagues in that workshop! She had never seen a 'memsahab' or a 'sahab' so closely. Europeans! She had probably seen them from a distance driving past in a car, and now to work together in a workshop with all these big and literate people!

Naturally she was absolutely 'blocked' the first day. But by the fifth day I saw, she couldn't care less who the others were, and was absolutely confident. The way she was behaving she felt equal to anybody present there. During the break I found her singing or dancing or talking to everybody on equal terms. I know she will never do theatre, she never did theatre, but what happened to her was a lifetime experience. That's why I said the human factor is the important thing. The theatre worker should also have that experience, this confidence, this real confidence. The confidence – 'I can act on the stage and people will applaud, people will praise me' – a different kind of confidence. I am talking of the real confidence as a creator, as an imaginative, creative, human being. In a way these things are much more important in my workshop than giving some superficial theatre skills. Although theatre skills are important, and hopefully they are getting some theatre skills also, but this is not the fundamental aim in my workshop.

SN: This was about helping them at a psychological plane, but when you talk about physical or body theatre, or use of the spine, is that also a part of your workshop process?

BS: See, I myself never use this term 'physical theatre.' I have seen other people using it. I am beginning to be annoyed by that term. It is a very misleading term. What is physical theatre? All the theatres are physical theatre. Is there any theatre without the body? All we know is, and you will agree with me, that if the performer is aware of his or her body, aware of the potentiality of his or her body and can use his or her body to enrich the language of theatre, then theatre becomes stronger. There is nothing called physical acting as such. It is just enriching the language through the powers we already have in our physique. Physical acting cannot be a separate term. The voice is also a part of the body and an important part of theatre. Theatre is expressed through the human body, but it is not acrobatics or circus or gymnastics, because in theatre the mind is no less important, rather it is more important than the body. Theatre is a mind-body combination. So you see the total human being involved.

SN: So according to you theatre involves the whole personality of the performer?

BS: To my mind there can be two distinct kinds of acting. If I am allowed to describe it this way. One is acting by enactment and the other is acting by a state of being. I will explain. Acting by enactment seems to me a redundant thing. What is the difference between enactment and acting? Nothing. But still I use this term. We can learn certain skills through our training. How to stand on the stage, how to stand the way the role demands. How to move about. How to project my voice. How to give facial expression or body expression. All these techniques we can learn by theatre practice or some others means. We can learn to act in such a way that I can communicate the theme, the mood, the emotion of the play. I can communicate it intensely. I can move my audience by my acting. At the same time I can remain uninvolved in the content of the play as a performer. The content of the play may not mean any thing personally to me. There have been great actors who may be moving their audience to tears, but while acting thinking of the after-theatre appointment or dinner. It is possible. By technique it is possible.

Now in our theatre, the starting point is content. Which means that our primary thing is what we have to say. What we feel an urge to say [*sic*]. Acting by enactment is not possible by us. We have to use our own feelings, own reactions to the theme. So it has to be a different way of acting. That is what I mean by acting by state of being. State of being means what? We always have some state of being. Our day-to-day life is one state of being. We have to go to the office, we have to worry about the promotion. We have to solve family problems in day-to-day state of being. Then we use the mask, our cover. When we go and listen to a good classical music programme or Ravi Shanker's sitar, maybe the operative term usually would be—I got moved. What does it mean? It means I could go from my day-to-day state of being to another state of being. That is exactly what I mean when I say I am moved. Good art moves me; (it) means good art takes me to another state of being. The principal medium of every art form is emotion and not intellect. This applies to all art forms including theatre. Now if the performer really genuinely thinks about a particular theme and if he gets a particular kind of training, where by his own feeling his feelings can be translated into outward theatrical expression, then that would be acting by state of being. So in a way our workshop is the process of learning to act by state of being, not acting by technique or acting by enactment. Maybe I am not being very clear, but I cannot be clearer because one has to go through the process to really understand.

SN: You said that you go from one state of being to another when you listen to music. How does this journey take place in the context of theatre? I mean, suppose you have to tell your actor to make this journey from one mental state to another, how will you instruct him?

BS: I don't have to do it that way. If the actors go through the process, their own feelings, reactions to the themes, will always come into play. They can't help it. Therefore I have seen *Basi Khabar* after the first performance. I did not have any role in the play. I directed the play. When I went backstage I found every single performer weeping profusely. That could not have happened if they acted by enactment. Actually they were moved by themselves when they were saying the lines. Our rehearsal process is a real workshop process through which we at least aim to come to a position whereby each performer begins to believe that such and such playwright, Badal Sircar or any other person, has not written this line. This line has been written by me, this is my line. I am speaking my line and it therefore has my feelings. Through the workshop process we try to come to that position. Therefore, if someone comes and congratulates our performers for their acting, I have seen real surprise on their face, probably because they feel that they had not acted. Though they did act yet they did not act. Of course they had acted because the structure of the play, structure of the direction, choreography, everything was in a format, but the question about acting is quite foreign that way. It is another kind of acting. The term acting, as applied normally, is foreign to the members of our group.

SN: Badal-da, your journey in theatre has been long and has gone through several turning points. As you said, you have finally bid farewell to proscenium theatre because through your Free Theatre you are able to communicate with your audience more finely and expressively. Till the middle of (the) 1970s, when you decided to switch to Free Theatre, you were doing proscenium theatre and were being recognised for your work. The experience that you are now getting with Free Theatre, did you ever get while watching or doing proscenium theatre? [*sic*] I am referring to productions of your own plays.

BS: I don't know whether I have understood your question properly. All I can say is that I will not exchange the experience I get now, for the experience I had on the proscenium stage. I never regretted my step. Rather as days go by I become more and more confirmed that this is what I wanted to do and want to do. This certainly is a better choice so far as I am concerned.

Q: What is the language you use in this kind of play? City language or the language of the people you want to reach out to? For instance, when you go to North Bengal or 24 Paraganas, where a different dialect is spoken, do you change the language of performance?

BS: Not at all, we cannot do that. No, we cannot do (that).

In our plays we do not have characters, we just have prototypes and we represent them as performers like in *Bhoma* and *Basi Khabar*. We say interrelated lines but not necessarily by having a dialogue amongst ourselves. As performers we are projecting practically everything directly to the audience. Therefore we use the Bengali we speak. There is no question of having any dialect or following any dialect. If there were specific characters in the play, maybe we would have allowed it. When he did Taranshankar's *Nagini Kanya*, we did not dramatise the novel, just presented the novel theatrically. That means we chose narrative lines as well as dialogues and projected both together, keeping the novel intact as far as possible. There we had to devise a dialect because we did not even know that particular dialect of Birbhum. So we added a certain distorted pronunciation to the Bengali we speak (normally), which sounded like a rural dialect but it was (actually) not (so). We tried to keep a kind of integrity in this too. For example we changed all the '*o*'s to '*au*'s. We tried to be strict about that to give it a certain integrity. It sounds rural. Tarashankar himself has written the way we are speaking the words so we tried to capture that in pronunciation. That was necessary. Well, anybody well-versed with that dialect will naturally condemn us—'what dialect have you taken?' (they would say). But my intention was to give an impression of a Bengali that is not our Bengali but that of a rural area.

SN: You have distorted Girish Chandra Ghosh's play *Abu Hossain*. You have based all the songs on film tunes. What was the reason for this decision?

BS: I have given the reason in the prologue.

SN: You wanted the distortion?

BS: You want to know its history? *Abu Hossain* is a play by Girish Ghosh, which I enjoyed when I was a child. I have been listening to it on the radio and reading it. Later on I found *Abu Hossain* remains surprisingly modern. There is no song. Songs are very old. Its courtship scenes were also old, I mean (scripted) in the old style. Otherwise the humorous part is surprisingly modern. There is no need to change it. It's fun to perform them. At the time when I did *Abu Hossain*, I had not arrived at this serious theatre—one which attempts to change society. I did theatre for fun. Our group was a small group. So far as singing these things was concerned, (it was) very ill-equipped to perform a Geeti Natya, which means a musical comedy, or musical farce. That's what he (Girish Ghosh) called it. Yet I wanted to keep that spirit. So I added... a few things to...the prologue as you know. In the prologue, Badal Sircar the director is protesting—

'Our Satabdi possibly cannot do this. We have not got so many people.'

'Use the same people over and over again!'

'We have not got the singers. Use playback just as it is done in cinemas.'

'We cannot afford those costumes.'

'Don't use costume. Do it in modern costume.'

'We cannot use sets.'

'Then don't use sets. Depend on the imagination of the people.'

'And so many songs? Those songs can't be sung in modern days.'

'Then (re)write the songs.'

'And what about the melodies, what about the tunes? I can't create them?'

Harun al Rashid answers, 'Then steal'.

'Where from?'

'Films. Steal from popular films.'

This is the apology I have given in the prologue. The play starts after this.

I must admit that after listening to the film songs, giving words to the songs was great fun.

SN: Now Badal-da, I want to ask you a personal question. You have gone through many stages—from town planner to initiating this movement of (the) Third theatre. What after this?

BS: After this—death. Yes, I have travelled a long way. I feel the way is not yet over because I am not dead. So in the next stage what development, what changes will be there, I cannot say that. I cannot predict that. Any thing may happen. Maybe that I leave the theatre.

SN: One question always bothers me. There are people who have been inspired by you and are doing your kind of theatre, or those doing street theatre – like Gursharan Singh – you mentioned his name, who is doing very exciting work. He is picking (up) very topical and relevant issues, many people come to his plays, understand what he is saying. Many others in Bihar, Punjab, Uttar Pradesh, Delhi are doing street theatre. But most of that street theatre is more of political sloganeering and not total theatre as you visualised it. Just taking up an issue and mouthing some slogans does not make theatre in my view. The situation of taking the audience from one state of being to another—where is the scope of that in these plays?

BS: I have some definite opinion, rather experience, about this. Those who are directly in political parties or attached to political parties and they use theatre to propagate their party line, or their revolutionary thoughts, quite often take up theatre just for name's sake, as a vehicle only. They take the basic theatrical structures. They put the characters and the dialogues and they think that theatre is created because the message is good. It is revolutionary. It is progressive. If that were so, there is no need to see theatre, there is no need of creating theatre. Yes, it becomes mere sloganeering. Even today while I was discussing with the participants, I talked about this. If we have chosen theatre then it must be art first and foremost. Through art if you can say what you have to say, what you want to say, what you want to propagate, then it is actually propagated. Sloganeering is neither art nor propaganda. It defeats its own purpose. There are a lot of such groups in Bengal whose intentions are very good, but the end result is actually defeating their own purpose, their own intentions, because they are not serious about the art form, theatre, or are not patient enough to learn the art form.

As far as propaganda is concerned, I think every single play is propaganda. Every art form propagates. If you write poetry, you are trying to propagate your feelings, your reactions to the life force, to other things. That is propagating. Art means propagating. So there is nothing wrong with the term propaganda. Even if I say the moon is beautiful, the earth is beautiful, everything is beautiful—that is propagating the status quo. If everything is beautiful we need not change anything. Those who say this are also propagating but they want to call it pure art. I do not think anything like pure art exists. Art is always related to life. Therefore you are propagating something or the other, either retrogressive or progressive; either status quo or change. But if you use an art form, it must be art first and foremost.

I was giving this example to the participants today from a very unlikely source. Alfred Hitchcock. I read a line written or said by Alfred Hitchcock. He said, 'My problem is that a person coming to see my film has to look at a white rectangle for ninety minutes and his eyes must be glued to this rectangle. If he removes his eyes even for a moment, that means I have failed partly.' That is my problem too. I need to hold the attention of the audience every single moment of the play. If I can do that then what I want to propagate is propagated. If I bore them, if they look away, if they start smoking, if they move away, then I am propagating nothing. I am neither creating theatre nor am I propagating anything. This is a question that can't be solved easily because social workers and political workers are impatient. It will remain.

When we want to learn dancing or painting or playing a musical instrument, we accept from the very beginning that before one can perform in front of friends, six hours a day practice will be needed for five years. We accept this. But it is not so in the field of theatre. If I don't have stage fright, if I don't stammer, if I have a loud voice then I am an actor. If I have acted in five plays then I am a director. Theatre workers never think theatre is an art form. We never compare it with Bharatnatyam or classical music. So theatre becomes weak. You need the same amount of practice for theatre.

This too poses a problem. Theatre, particularly our theatre, is in a way the theatre of emergency. We cannot afford to wait for five years. We will have to go on doing theatre.

There is only one answer, do theatre. Whatever praise you get from your friends, family and even outsiders, don't believe them. Because you have not worked as hard as a sitar player, whatever they might say, you could not have been good. Go on taking training. In the next production try to make it better. Even if there is praise, you know it cannot be true. A close friend of mine told me once very truthfully, 'Badal, you do not write good plays. It is just that others write even worse plays.' I think it is true. This happens in theatre because it has become the standard of theatre. There is no good theatre. So whatever is done, even (if) amateurish, is considered good. That's why theatre workers also very quickly acquire a kind of complacence.

I have always tried to learn. Two or three years back, in 1984, I attended one of the workshops of Kanhailal who had himself attended my workshop in 1972. I did that because I thought I have got something to learn. I knew he has got a lot which I do not know, he can teach me. I asked my group members too to join his workshop, and two others did.

Even now after so many years in theatre, I cannot honestly say that I put as much labour in theatre, or have got as much training in theatre as somebody learning Odissi dance has. So I cannot call myself a theatre artist yet.

SN: Lately you have done many shows of *Bhoma*. You did two other significant plays—*Michhil* and *Spartacus*. Have you done any of these plays in villages?

BS: Yes, lots of times. Actually maximum number of shows of Satabdi have been of *Michhil,* 177. Half of these (were) outdoors, not in our Angan Mancha. Either in Curzon Park or in a village, or in an open lawn. Even before coming to Lucknow, we had a two-day trip when we did two shows of *Michhil*. If we could have kept *Spartacus* alive till now, probably we would have done three hundred shows, because it worked equally well in both cities and villages. Unfortunately, the cast is very big and we could not maintain it. We revived it four times by replacement, then we gave up. The group became smaller and smaller and so we could not continue. We did 90 shows of *Spartacus* and then we had to stop. Of *Bhoma* we have done 99 shows. It was stopped for three or four years but we revived it again. However it could not complete a century. After 99, it stopped. It will complete a century this season.

SN: How many shows of *Gandi* have you done?

BS: I do not remember exactly but we have done about 80 shows. *Gandi* is also a comparatively large cast show. It was first a Satabdi production. When the group split we revived it as a joint production. Joint production means we already had some colleague groups—people believing in the same philosophy, who have come so close that they themselves demand joint productions. That means maybe I direct, rehearsals are in my group, most of the members are Satabdi members, and two or three members who are very hard working, they give time to their own group and they give extra time to rehearsals in this joint production. This works very well. Sometimes three groups join together to do one production. We do productions with large casts that way. So *Sagina Mahato* is a joint production of course. For *Sagina Mahato* we have done 75 to 80 shows in the proscenium.

Q: I am interested in communication. You said that out of an urge you reach a content. My first question is whose urge? Yours or that of your group members?

BS: The urge is mine and the urge is of our group members, who are like-minded people. In our group only like-minded people gather and we have to decide and agree on the theme we can take up. That's why it has to be like-minded. There may be differences of opinions in the details. But some basic agreement about the theme of the play must be there.

SN: Does that mean that before arriving at the content you have group discussions?

BS: It is not actually that way. Say, for example, I write a play. I will read the play to the group. If they also feel the urge to project that play, only then we take it up. Our members – we call them members not artists – have equal rights. If even one member feels that such and such play should not be done by Satabdi now, and if the other members, wanting to do it cannot convince that person, he has his way. The minority of one wins finally unless we can convince him. We never say if you do not agree you do not take any role. The role is not important. He is a member of Satabdi and if Satabdi is not in unison or if that member objects to a certain line in the play, a passage of the play, and others cannot convince him, we have to change that passage. This has happened.

Q: Badal-da, before you come to the point I have mentioned about communication, can you cite some example of how the urge for certain content came from a fellow member of your group and not from you.

BS: One play has been done by Satabdi which has been adapted from a short story by another member of our group and directed by her.

Q: But it is not frequently done? Basically you are the initiator?

BS: Not frequently done because there is the question of talent, of self-confidence also. But that play is totally hers because I was not even allowed in the rehearsals. When the play was almost prepared, I was invited one day to see the rehearsal and give my comments. I gave my comments; my suggestions were very few, because they had done a very good job. Then again I was out. Afterwards I saw only the final rehearsal and show. It was totally somebody else's. Now the same person has written five plays, original plays, not adaptations. I think all the group members have accepted the five plays as worth doing by Satabdi. These plays have come from a woman. Each of the five plays is from a woman's point of view—about women's problems. This had been a gap in our work because while in some of my plays there are references and scenes, but they are not basically about women. That way that's a great possibility opening (up) before us.

Directionwise I adapted a play on Apartheid and South Africa which I thought we cannot do here in India. It is too foreign. But the group members insisted that they will do it, against my good judgment. At that time I did not want to direct. I wanted some free time. I said, I do not want to direct it and another member of our group directed it. There also, in the beginning I was present in some rehearsals, then I was asked not to be present and again I started attending later on. Here or there maybe I made some little comments or suggestion, but nothing major. So that is also entirely his work – direction-wise – and surely he had acquired the confidence. It was a very challenging play. In between there was talk that I made a mistake in not doing this play, I should have directed the play. That person should have directed something a bit simpler because this presented many complexities. But I was adamant and he had the confidence. He did it and I think he made a very good job of it. *Basi Khabar* is another example of a group creation. Although I have directed it no doubt, but the play was prepared with all the material the group members collected, all the divisions group persons made, and on the basis of that I sort of acted as an editor.

SN: Pardon me, but because it is very vital for me to understand. So I repeat it in different ways. Do your group members have to relate their internal urges to the content devised and finalised by you? Then what happens to their own urge arising out of their social reality and context?

BS: You mean if those urges are different from mine.

SN: Maybe. They could be different.

BS: There are always common urges, and also differences in urges. So far what has happened is that the urges somehow tallied. That is why they agreed. When there is difference in urges, for example my wife's play—she has written it because her urge is different. I do not have the some urge. That's why it is a very significant factor. It is a different field. That play got a wonderful response particularly from the women members of the group. They thought it is a very personal thing for them which I could never do before. So this is an example. You should understand that these members…have a lot of sincerity and urge to work hard, but not necessarily a lot of talent. They want to do but may not be able to do. It could also be a kind of block. But I am proud to say and I am glad to see that this block is gradually disappearing. Take our colleague group. There is no Badal Sircar over there. There is nobody who can write a play. They have to make their own play. They take some short stories, take their themes. That short story might be a Bengali short story or by Premchand or by Krishen Chandar. They make a play from that. Play by play I find they are improving. Maybe my presence in Satabdi prevented that confidence and talent from growing for some time. But for quite a few years now I have been trying to keep out. I was adamant.

It even created a crisis during that play on Apartheid. Most of the Satabdi members were insisting that if it is to be done by Satabdi you must direct it. I said 'Look, I told you beforehand that I am not going to direct the next play,' I was adamant. 'If you think that this play is too difficult, then keep it away.' Somebody had to direct something else and something else was not readily available. So they had to take the challenge and do it. That is the only way I can get them to take the initiative.

SN: Badal-da, now tell me how do you achieve communication with the audience?

BS: To me it is a very simple thing. What I feel about a particular theme or what I have come to know, I have become conscious of it, I am trying to share with my audience. That is communication to me. I want them to feel the same way (as) I am feeling or I want them to have the same knowledge as I have got, the same awareness which I have got and put in the play. To me that is communication. If that can be done.

Q: To what extent?

BS: How can I measure the extent. It is very different because sometimes the extent even the audience themselves cannot measure. And how much of communication can we have outside the theatre with the audience? They go after seeing the play.

Even the shows we do in villages, our conditions are such that everyone is working in different offices during the day. We go on Sundays. After performing a show in day light we have to immediately catch the train to return. Therefore there is no time to communicate, I mean after the performance. Therefore it is difficult to assess.

I can give you a few examples which prevent us from getting absolutely frustrated. That *Bhoma* experience. We were trying to provoke one fellow who belonged to the poorest community, digging a canal. We went there. He had seen *Bhoma* the previous day. He was being provoked: 'Have you understood? Have you liked it? What have you understood? There is no costume, no story.' He very coolly replied: 'It is not difficult for us poor people to understand. Maybe the rich people will not understand it.' He said this about *Bhoma.* So I think *Bhoma* was communicated to him.

I remember another old Muslim gentleman in a village. He shoved the children aside and sat right in the front row with the children behind him, around him. He did not care. He was the only person with a long grey beard, and throughout the play we saw him doing this this… this. We got a wonderful feed-back. That same night some people had to return. Some of us stayed on. We went to another village about two-three kilometres away. We would enter any house and start talking. Then we met someone on the road and we invited ourselves to his house. While roaming around we entered one house. Coincidentally, that old man was there.

I asked him: 'How did you like Bhoma?' He said: 'We all liked it very much.' I said: 'I do not know much about a village. Whatever I have learnt I have tried to put. Maybe I did not put many things correctly.' He said: 'No, whatever you have put in *Bhoma* is all correct.' Then, thinking of the radio scene and the dollar scene, I said that maybe some of the scenes of *Bhoma* were difficult to understand, a bit foreign. He said: 'Why? What is there?' He started explaining *Bhoma* to me. He forgot that I am the director or the playwright. So these are very positive responses you know. It is a question of communication.

SN: You have had a variety of experiences?

BS: There are some reactions we come to know some times, but much of it we do not get to know. But I remember one old sick person when we performed in Sutia village. He is a landless agricultural labourer and because of his illness does not get a job every day. Maybe that day he could have got work but he started walking with us. The next village was 10 kilometres away and it was (the) end of March—very hot, cutting through the fields, (with) no shade. He walked with us with a broken umbrella. He walked. He saw the play. He would have to go back alone because we were going now to the next village – our last point – from where we would take the train, a semi-urban, semi-rural kind of place. He started walking with us towards that point. I asked him: 'Why are you walking with us?' What he said was in Bengali: '*Naisha lege gele.* (I have got addicted) I could not leave you, I came with you.' When we reached there the lunch was prepared. Suddenly I found that the man was missing. He had felt shy so he had gone and was sitting at the railway station. We got him and made him eat. When our performance got over late at night, I asked how he would go home that night. He told me that he could not see too well so he would spend the night at the station and go back the next morning. You see, he took all these risks—the old sick man, to come with us. For what? I do not know. I think it was a great communication with that person.

SN: Thanks Badal-da for this wide-ranging conversation.

The interview was recorded in Lucknow where Badal Sircar was conducting a workshop at Bhartendu Natya Akademi
Courtesy: Natya Shodh Sansthan, Kolkata

THIRD THEATRE WORKSHOP

An Inside View

Visual artists **Suvobrata Roy Chowdhury** and **Sanchayan Ghosh** talk to **Keshav Kumar**

Keshav Kumar (KK): As fine arts students, how did you get to join a workshop with Badal Sircar?

Suvobrata Roy Chowdhury (SRC): In 1994, when we were students of fine arts at Santiniketan, Badal-da had come for a project as a visiting professor in the drama section of Sangeet Bhavan, Santiniketan. Initially the workshop had been planned for Sangeet Bhavan drama students. At that time we approached Badal Sircar through the Kala Bhavan Students' Association, to take a workshop with us, and it was opened to all the students of Visva Bharati. Students from most departments – Art, Science and Kala Bhavan – joined. We arranged some space and planned a series of workshops. The very first workshop with Badal Sircar became popular. The response was tremendous. Participants responded with great enthusiasm even when they were not fully aware of what was going on. Basically Badal-da's workshop used to be a closed affair. Only a limited number of people were admitted, and only they had access to the workshop On the very first day he laid down some basic rules which were strictly followed for the rest of the days. No late comers were allowed, if anybody was absent even for a day he/she was not allowed to rejoin the workshop, and you could not participate as an observer. He had given a reason for why he did not allow anyone to be an observer—because that stopped the spontaneous participation of the participants. He felt that first time participants in the workshop had a lot of inhibitions and it was not easy for them to open up. Moreover, when everybody was a participant, everybody shared an equal risk of failure, and was therefore equally responsible and could learn from each other's failure or achievement.

KK: Can you tell us about the general nature of his workshop?

Sanchayan Ghosh (SG): I still remember the first day of the workshop. We were all seated in rows, one group behind the other, and Badal-da said that his workshop was not a class so there would be no back benchers and front benchers, and he would make us sit in a circle and do an energy passing game to complete the circle. He explained the completeness of a circle and how everyone in it was equally positioned. Then he conducted the Dots & Space Movement game, where he asked us to imagine that we were all points on a white paper equally positioned from each other and the margin. Now, maintaining this position he asked us to move to the opposite end of the space. Therefore everyone had to move together. Gradually he introduced different activities—morning activities, getting to a bus, etc. It became like a situation of everyday life.

Similarly he would conduct Follow the Leader, Mirror and Trust exercises and other games. He always referred to these exercises as games with him as the referee. Like any other game, he added that these games also had rules and all of us needed to follow his rules, otherwise the fun of the game would be lost. We sat in a circle and everyone had to participate and take turns to do the exercise. He never asked anyone to start; participants themselves had to gather courage to get up and perform. Naturally, the more confident ones took the initiative in the beginning, but gradually others also started initiating the process.

SRC: The most amazing part about his workshop was that he never explained why he did certain exercises. Rarely did he explain the reasons and would, in fact, discourage questions about it. The simple logic behind it was that the exercise would lose its meaning because then we would not be able to concentrate on its process. Also, participants would not explore anymore; they would not look inside and try to find out why they were doing a particular exercise, and try to discover what it did to them. However, sometimes he did explain some exercises. One of the exercises he explained was where six or seven people were instructed to cover as much ground as possible in a given space, in slow motion and without losing contact with each other. They had to cover a distance of approximately 30 metres. He called it a leadership-building exercise with the instruction that one didn't have to lead or try to get ahead of the others. His explanation was that if you were pushing to be a leader, you would never be able to reach the other end as everybody else would also be trying to move forward and no one would be willing to just follow. Leadership has to be gentle and passive at times. So, we learnt what he meant by following his instructions and found such things useful even later in life. Since he is the only theatre person with whom I have ever done a workshop, I cannot compare his process with anyone else's, but I found his process very exciting. I believe he is documenting and writing about his workshop process at present to dispel the mystery around it.

His workshop process was very simple. He himself used to perform like any other participant, being totally involved in it. This was the best part about Badal-da's workshop. And he has a definite orientation—a political ideology which guides his process. Also, he discusses specific subjects like theatre as a medium, Third Theatre etc., to mention a few. During the workshop he used to talk about these topics but not very directly. Similarly, there was this process called Indifference, where participants were divided into two groups. One group was instructed to ignore whatever the other group was asking or presenting. Also, they were not told anything about the presentation. He used to take one group along with him and secretly instruct them to enact a mass murder. So, one side was passionately asking for help and the other side was supposed to ignore them completely.

SG: The Indifference Game that I participated in was more like this: one group was instructed to be in a very merry mood, singing a song and moving in a circle, and they were advised that whatever happened they should continue in this mood and keep moving in a circle. The other group, that were not informed about this condition would be informed individually about the death of farmers in famines, about the rape of Santhal women in the British period etc., and their job would be to individually disrupt the jovial mood of the other group. This would evolve into a very intense workshop process. Then there was this exercise called 'Grow' where he would narrate a story of a tree growing in a darkroom and everyone had to grow like a tree through their body, in whatever way they responded to the situation. So in this way he encouraged imagination and interpretation, in that we were interpreting his narrative through our bodies.

SRC: The workshop was generally divided into two parts. The first one was preliminary or basic and the other one was advanced. I participated in five basic and five advanced workshops organised by Badal Sircar. I loved the process and it was quite enlightening. In the basic process I was learning a lot about my body, possibilities of my body, voice, trust, dance, etc.,—largely the physical aspects and those that helped in confidence building and group functioning. The exercise Indifference, that I described earlier, was a part of the advanced workshop. In whatever he did he worked with intense conviction; he had a strong belief in his ideas and process. We were all in our twenties and his idealism attracted us and gave us not just creative energy but also the confidence of being able to change things around us. It also gave us a political orientation and awareness of world events from a particular perspective. This kind of workshop was really needed at that stage of our lives. And he was not only a nice person, but also a very provocative teacher who forced us to think and debate.

Then there was play-making, where you had to make a short play which was very challenging and satisfying. Play-making was a part of the advanced workshop. Then we entered the production process and decided to start a production. The production enthused us so much that we subsequently formed a group called Saanko (meaning a bridge).

KK: Before discussing the production process, we would like to know about the basic and advance workshops. What philosophy was reflected in these two levels of workshops?

SG: His basic workshops had more to do with exploring the possibility of the body and other sensory organs. It was also about developing a team spirit. He used to tell us not to think and plan our actions, just to be in the moment and express whatever came to our minds then and there. Like there was this sound and movement game where he would insist that we used only sound, no words. He would give us some topic and we had to individually explore it only with sound, and then he would advise us to try and repeat the sound according to our normal breathing, so that one could continue making the sound without any break. This helped us develop a sense of the relationship between sound, rhythm and breathing in ourselves.

But advanced workshops were more internal. As Suvo mentioned the Tree Game, there was also a Mind Game where he would ask everyone to choose a path inside the workshop space and then to remember that path. Then he would ask everyone, one by one, to start walking along the paths which they had chosen. So, as we were all walking on our individual paths slowly, we moved together in the space on our own path without disturbing each other. Then he would slowly say certain words and lines and ask us to explore them mentally while we were walking. For example, he would ask me to remember some close friend or someone very close to me and explore how well I knew that person. Slowly that exploration would become a personal questioning and then a self-transformation in which that person himself was the questioner as well as the answering individual, and soon I became that person. It was an extremely intense and self-reflective game which was very individual and internal.

SRC: His philosophy for Third Theatre was always with him and he shared it with us. He started with the proscenium; all his early works are proscenium plays. He was very clear about why he selected the Third Theatre. These discussions, his reasons really affected and influenced us.

Being a fine arts student my mind was trying to take in as much as it could from that workshop. He talked about form—what form, which medium would be more useful for which ideas, how art could reach out to the common man, what form would facilitate dialogue with the viewer. This was very exciting for me as an artist as it allowed me to think about my medium and what I could do with it.

He did not preach or dictate but shared his ideas as an artist. He would explain his choices but never said that they should be our choices too. He would never impose his ideas on us. In a certain way he was very democratic, but his intensity and sincerity made you believe in his ideas and made it easy for everyone to accept his leadership.

KK: How many people participated, rather how many were allowed to participate and what was the duration of the workshop.

SRC: Eight was the minimum requirement as a lot of exercises required group efforts. He did not take a workshop if there were less than eight participants. Some exercises were to be done in groups of three. In case of a shortage he participated himself and managed it easily. A maximum of 25 people were allowed to participate. If there was an exercise like Trust that could be intimidating—like falling from a table on your back where people were supposed to catch you. He would take the initiative himself, go first, climb the table, fall from it and get people to hold him. This made it easier for all of us to follow. He was in his seventies at that time. We were impressed with his physical ability and energy at that age. It was a very subtle energy—not only an obvious physical kind of energy, but a sustained energy. For us young people it was very inspiring. This experience was beyond theatre. At least a hundred people attended the workshop, not all of them performers or artists who wanted to perform. It was a self-enhancement workshop for most of us.

KK: Do you remember any exercises in the advanced workshop?

SRC: That was almost sixteen years back. Play-making was at the end of the workshop and was the final process. Before that he would give you little things. He would give body exercises. With your body you were supposed to create postures that depicted something. In this body sculpting exercise, when done in pairs, whatever you are choreographing with the other person's body should also say something. Like there was this instance; one participant was doing this exercise with two other persons—a male and a female. He made the female sit on the ground and stoop down and made the male stand in an upright tiger posture. It was quite interesting. This was not designed by Badal Sircar, it was one of the participants, but Badal Sircar's instructions triggered these ideas, pushed the participant to doing this, to actually think like this. He never gave the idea. We had to think of it ourselves. Participants explored new methods and most of the time the meaning was clear. But occasionally, when a large number of the participants were not able to figure out a particular meaning or interpretation, it was discussed later on. This was part of the advanced workshop where he made people think a lot. Like in play-making he would ask you to do anything—a scene from any film or short film for three to five minutes. Only ten minutes were given to think of an idea, collect the things, arrange whatever was required and explain the idea to others. Then another ten minutes were allotted for the performance. It all happened in 20 minutes. The whole group used to perform—you were the playwright, the director, the designer for that piece. There was hardly any design, as whatever props were required were done through the human body. This, in fact, was another part of the workshop where he would make props out of human bodies and would invite you to imagine different props with the human body.

The advanced workshops also had other exercises like the 'Attachment' exercise. Here he would give you a prop, like a chair, and would tell you to build a relationship with the chair for about half an hour. You were supposed to be physical, like hug the chair, use it as a guitar or any property and think that it was your chair. Then suddenly he would come and take it away, tell you that you would never see it again, and leave. Some people cried during this exercise as they got quite attached to the property they worked with. It was quite an intense exercise and gave life to inanimate objects in a strange way.

He had a story-telling capability also. If you have seen any of his later plays, they are all like monologues—stories told in a *kathokatha* style (audio-visual narrative form of West Bengal, usually narrating a story from the scriptures) making a small performance. *Bhoma* is actually a *kathokatha*, since it's just being narrated. He has a great narrating ability and is a very coherent speaker. He used to get emotionally involved. As you can see, these exercises were not only about theatre.

SG: There was also a sound and movement advanced workshop. Here he would first narrate a story to all of us, like in our case it was about the Santhal revolt. Then he would make us stand in two uneven rows that met at a point and move diagonally to the other point of the square and then again join our respective rows at the back. So each time the combination of the pair kept changing and you would have a new partner in a continuous process. The idea was that we would have to generate the story through sound and movement in sequence, but always moving as a pair that is individuals in the pair would not only have to make their own sound, but would also have to follow their partners in both rhythm as well as speed. Moreover, one had to keep track of how the whole narrative was developing and then add one's bit to it so that the story also progressed. Initially there were lots of problems in adjusting individual speed and movement, but slowly we got adjusted to the process and collectively developed the story only by attending and observing each other's sounds and movements. So, basically we performed the story without a single rehearsal. It was incredible—like magic! We all felt the whole story unfolding in front of us.

KK: In many of his productions one notices a definite sound choreography. Throw some light on how he arrived at this choreography. Was it a part of the basic or advanced workshop?

SRC: Voice exercises, the way you use your voice—all that started at the basic workshop. He would ask you to change your voice, take a rhythm then gradually change it, not necessarily with any meaning and without it being noticed. Gradually this would turn into a sound design that would get used in a production. The sound choreography that we created in the workshops became a part of the production that we did.

SG: Sound was an integral part of his workshop and would lead to the sound choreography of any production. Sound workshops had both primary and advanced level games. At the primary level, the first game he would conduct would be—Follow the Leader. The leader could do anything and make any sound which would have to be copied by the group moving in a line behind him. Now copy here does not mean that everyone was following the leader; he would always suggest that we follow our immediate partners who were right in front of us. So everyone had to take the responsibility of following their immediate partner in order to follow the original gesture. And this would become fun as what the main leader did never reached the last person in the same form. There was always some change. In the next sound workshop he would make any sound in rhythm so that it was in harmony with one's breathing. He would demonstrate once how one could follow one's breathing and generate sound which could then be continued as long as possible. I think this game is unique to Third Theatre, as it makes one aware of the process of repetition and coordination with the body. Repetition, in fact, is a basic tool of Third Theatre.

There is another unique game which is like a slightly advanced stage of sound transformation. This is about how to transform a sound like *aaaa* to *mimimimimi* without stopping or making an abrupt break from *aa* to *mi*. It is a fantastic game. Later Badal-da would ask us to add movement of the body in relation to the change in sound. This whole game is about how one leaves the sound *aa* organically and approaches the sound *mm*...and slowly add *iii*...to *mmm*...to reach *mimi*.... This game makes one understand the core of any syllable and how sound is generated from different parts of the mouth and the actions of our body and breathing. These games really help in developing and choreographing Third Theatre.

KK: When did the Text enter the process? Was it part of the basic or advanced workshop?

SG: The Text never entered the workshop process, not even in the production. The production we did was a textless production. It was just a choreographic structure. Sometimes if there was a text, he would come up with an interesting exercise. He would make a team of three and then read one line and make all of them say the same line in as many ways as possible. So in the process not only did we memorise the line but we also learnt from each other's improvisations the many different ways in which it could be said, and then finally selected the appropriate one to generate maximum meaning and intensity. So there was no enactment or illusion of making a dialogue. It was more about an adoption of the appropriate version.

KK: Did you discuss the 'Attachment Exercise' with him? Why was it done? How was it useful for theatre?

SRC: I think the previous process did help in theatre. Intrinsically you cannot remain a character all your life. You have to get detached sometime. Badal-da never explained most of his exercises, as I told you before. He asked us to think about them but told us not to ask questions about them, and I am sure that all 20 participants who were there during this exercise…(derived) different things from it. It was not that everybody was getting the same emotion or feeling the same way.

KK: Were these different perceptions a topic of discussion later on?

SRC: We used to discuss among ourselves. Badal-da used to participate in these discussions but talked very little about the workshop process.

KK: So what exactly was the topic of discussion among the participants after the workshop sessions?

SRC: We never discussed the reasons or purpose of the exercise or in what way we were developing during that process. Badal-da, at that point of time, and later on also, was very dedicated to his ideology and his understanding of the art form—that used to be our topic of discussion. Most of us were not from a theatrical background; only a few had that experience. The ones with theatrical experience wanted to stick to Badal-da's ideology of Third Theatre. The rest wanted to try proscenium theatre also. Some of us said we would do only Badal-da's plays while some wanted to try other people's plays as well. These were the discussions we used to have.

KK: The journey from basic to advance to production…how did a person prepare to make this journey?

SRC: While doing workshops the performance of the play became easy. During the production, we would constantly do some exercises selected from the basic and advanced workshops as a warm up. This kept the energy of the performance very high. When we prepared a play we did three-four shows and then took the play to the villages to perform in front of the village populace. During our stay there too, we did workshop exercises continuously. No one person would lead; we just decided that we would do it and we took turns.

SG: Some of the exercises in the advanced workshops were probably designed keeping the production of *Manushey Manushey* in mind, so they were content-based -

- Hunger was the theme of one workshop (one day), so four people stood at the four corners of the square space and were engaged in eating expensive foods and in the centre there was a group who had nothing and was trying to collect whatever the four people were throwing to the ground.
- Breaking the Trust: This was to make us realise that some are exploited (one day).
- Wall exercise: The job of the wall is to not let two people meet. This could be used to represent so many situations when one encounters walls all around.
- Torture situation: One person was tied to a chair with his eyes closed and then we would touch him with the finger at any

point on the body. This generated tremendous response from the tortured.

- Through these exercises Badal-da developed a sense of politics. He would deal with simple polarities like privileged-underprivileged, exploiter-exploited—which were an essential part of the training process. This brought a kind of ritual energy into play through collectively shared ideas.

SRC: Badal-da's working process had less to do with acting, and was more of a physical process to liberate you from your physical inhibitions. It did not necessarily give you confidence to perform or get into performance, but there was some kind of enhancement of the personality, especially at the age of 22. And we were also affected by the persona of Badal-da. He did not say that this workshop process was intended towards theatre nor that everyone who was participating in the workshop should end up doing theatre or productions. Also, he never explained any of the 'technical aspects' of his theatre process, like sound choreography. He would make people create the sound and would do the choreography himself. Participants had no inkling about how the choreography would come into use. He did the physical choreography through different exercises. He gave them as exercises and nobody would understand how he was building them, how he was creating them. This was one side of it. Actually most people did not come for his theatre workshop so that they could get into production or theatre. Badal-da in his basic and advanced workshop was more interested in generating a 'performing body' rather than an expressive actor or theatre worker or even theatre-maker. These workshops were directed more towards working together or participating, understanding the body, understanding balance, the texture of voice. In Badal-da's theatre nobody can not think, everybody thinks and you have to think. And everybody tried and was able to generate new ideas.

Badal-da believed that everybody could sing and everybody could dance. For many people these are hindrances. Many people at that age, particularly those who belonged to urban educational backgrounds, were very self-conscious. It was very self-exploratory at a basic level.

The advanced stage had more theatre in it, like play-making, and play-making was a high theatrical point of the whole workshop.

SG: He would make you perform little things. For example, he would divide you into two tribal groups and a situation was given—two tribal groups living in two lands divided by a river without knowledge of the other's existence. The story was about how they come to know each other through surprise, fear, anger and war and finally start living together. Now this narrative was told to all members of the two groups, but no roles were assigned. And it was strictly mentioned that no words could be used. Members were allowed to communicate only through sound and gestures. So during the whole process the first step was to develop the members of the tribe, their individual roles in society, their everyday activities and so on, and all this had to be developed by understanding and respecting each other's gestures. And then, as a team, we had to pursue the narrative so that it became communicable to the observer, in this case Badal-da himself, who would watch from outside. He would give you a situation and would make you perform it not like you would perform for an audience, but as though you are performing purely for yourself. You were not bothered about how you were being looked at, what other people would think of you. You were not performing for others, you were simply participating. Since nobody was left out and no one was the audience, one could be free and try out different things.

KK: As visual artists, was there a moment where you felt that this process was not for you or that you got stuck at some point?

SRC: Never did that happen. In fact we used to love new exercises. I did ten workshops and no new workshop was a photocopy of the previous one. He used to break the pattern by bringing in new exercises. He had a plethora of exercises up his sleeve. The entire process did not change but few things were transformed. We had a curiosity towards his new exercises. He would say that he hadn't done a particular exercise for the past few years, so let's just do it.

There was a guy named Aditya Sen who was with me and who attended ten workshops of Badal-da as we were also the organisers. Seeing the increasing number of participants we requested him for more workshops. A few things became part of our routine. Since we had to participate, we participated. Some things, like voice exercises, were never ending. Every time we did them, we got something new out of it. Because it was improvisatory we were investing a lot of hard work into these exercises. We were always eager about new exercises.

KK: Did you ever feel that Badal-da created a structure?

SRC: Structure used to be there. From beginning till the end, he knew what he was going to do during a workshop. He knew precisely how he were would start, how he would carry on and where he would end. The dropout rate was very low and people who wanted to drop out did it on the very first day.

KK: How long were the sessions of the workshop?

SRC: Eight hours. Our first workshop had 22 participants. If five minutes were given to each participant then you can understand the long hours of the workshop. Actually, I think 22 was a large number for him. He would have been comfortable with around 14 or 16 participants.

KK: Was it individual work?

SRC: Yes, All participants used to sit in a group. He would begin with Individual Mirror exercises and then later move on to Group Mirror exercises. One person from each side was supposed to stand up. Badal-da never used to decide who would stand up. Participants had to take the initiative on their own. Even in the group, he used to say 'Stop' but never used the word 'Start'. If one participant was done with his part, the other had to start voluntarily. In the Group Mirror, the one who used to start first was followed by the rest of the group. Everybody had to participate. Those with higher heartbeats participated in the end but participated.

KK: Production Process…

SRC: After ten workshops some of us were interested to go into production. So we formed this group 'Saanko'. Initially there were 10 or 12 people, and we selected the play *Manushey Manushey*, which is a non-verbal play. This meant that there would no dialogues between the characters. It was completely based on sound choreography, physical choreography and interpretation. We created the text on our own. There was a chorus and a character who was supposed to be the operator. He sometimes became a religious leader, sometimes a political leader. He used to give commands and the chorus was supposed to obey the commands—which were like going through rituals and all that. So, it was all very non-verbal. We used sound and choreography to communicate. At one point in the play he gives a command but the chorus refuses to follow his (leader's) command by saying 'No' and they start rebelling. So we had to write that text using common advertisements as there was no text written for him. It depended on who was taking that role and what he wanted to say in that situation. They were statements like '*Dhundhte Reh Jaoge*', 'No', '*Beedi Peena Mana Hai*', and the statement at the end was 'No'. It was a very well-structured play. I was with the group for a year during which we performed at different places. Even after I left, others continued to do the play. Many members of the group joined other Badal Sircar groups and did his plays. One of them went to America and formed a 'Third Theatre Group' where he did Badal-da's plays.

But through the theatrical process he was a total dictator. He would never explain his processes. Like in a sound design he would never say why he designed a particular sound. He would ask you to perform accordingly. So, as a result, we ended up giving bad performances. Like there was this performance in Durgapur where we failed to perform, which means that we failed to generate the reaction we used to draw from the audience. Later on, on self analysis we found that the first sound that was given was too high, so no one could pick up the energy level and sustain that. But he had not told us anything about scale and what we should be careful about. He just wanted us to be spontaneous. But I feel that this is where Badal-da failed to create a dedicated Badal Sircar theatre. Because today we can ask who will take the position of Badal Sircar? Who will create new plays of the third form, using the tools he uses? Because he would never explain the tools, he would never explain that there was a sound design.

KK: He used to design the sound himself?

SRC: Yes, sound design was his forte. You know, he would tell you what was to be expressed and would give general directions, like produce any sound along with the movement, sound that would go with your physical energy.

KK: Has he ever restricted you to certain things?

SRC: Never.

KK: Did he pick up a good thing and ask you to develop it further during the production process?

SRC: The theatre process was quite different from the workshop. Theatre belonged to him. He was doing theatre, we were the bodies. Basically we were bodies he was using. This is what I was trying to say: that he couldn't generate a thinking mind within us. Perhaps if some of us worked with him for fifteen-twenty years, he would have given us something more. Maybe then we would have reached a deeper understanding of theatre. Like there was this person Deepankar, who started writing plays after a very long involvement with Badal-da. His plays were performed. He believed in him at that level. He never thought his performance would be low.

I would like to add that I am saying all this on the basis of one play/production, which is nothing in theatre.

SG: I think it is very important to do workshops on Third Theatre before joining any Third Theatre production. Generally in proscenium or other kinds of theatre the workshop is a separate system of exercise where the actor develops his sense of speech, sense of rhythm, sense of body and mind coordination and then the actor improvises alone with the support of his co-actors and the director. But in the Third Theatre developed by Badal-da, structure is the core of the theatrical form. How to move in Third Theatre when the audience is sitting all around you, how to throw a dialogue or a sound so that it reaches everyone sitting all around, how to repeat a gesture so that it reaches all the four sides of the space—all this is basic in Third Theatre. There is no space for improvisation in that. The structure has to be followed to make the action visible and audible to the public. So Badal-da used certain strategies of repetition of action, repetition of sound, repetition of dialogue; and all these methods evolved out of workshop situations. He was not trying to develop individualistic, performance-based theatre, but collective theatre action and that's how his plays have been scripted and that's how his form has evolved. So I do not agree to Badal-da's dictator kind of position. I believe that if you believe in the philosophy of Third Theatre you participate in it while accepting its philosophy and it is generated through the workshop where there is always a referee to conduct the games. And this position of the referee gets extended to a directorial position when there is more concrete action, based on particular themes. But then again, these themes are reworked in a workshop situation, so what you are basically performing is the energy and the memory of the emotion generated in the workshop.

I think Badal-da's workshops are his politics and the productions are extended imageries of his workshops. Like for our *Manushey Manushey* production, most of the actions evolved out of workshops. It is the memory of the emotions generated in the workshop that helped us to generate the same kind of emotions. It was not emulation of the memory but a reliving of the memories. But in this process of recollection I have found that once we have repeated our performance several times there is a certain mechanical element that emerges which internally disturbs our motivation and our expression. I think Badal-da's productions require a different kind of orientation towards skill, and that is how, even in the repetition of the action in repeated performances, one can regain one's original state of emotion. I have seen such skills in performers from Satabdi, the group developed by Badal-da. I have seen how in their repeat shows of the same production that sense of energy and timing is present in most performances. I wonder if it is the political motivation or a certain sense of commune which generates this unique skill of performing the same thing over and over again with the same intensity when there is very little space for individual excellence.

KK: The proscenium theatre laid a lot of stress on characterisation, while in Third Theatre it lost its existence. Why?

SRC: I think that after a certain period of time Badal-da understood that he was not going to get professional actors or trained actors. His work demanded reaching out to a large number of people—to the masses. So he moulded himself and his theatre in a way where he did not require expressions from the actor. The same with the props and sets, which have an expense and tantrums of their own. I feel that he had a similar thinking for the actors. I don't mean that he had a reservation for skilled acting – he used to appreciate good acting and allowed good actors to come forward – but he did not depend on them. So that was not the main thing in his performance. His performances were group activities. Through them he would create an environment through sound, through the body, through choreography. Sometimes the actor would talk to the audience to receive energy.

KK: As a part of thinking process, did he suggest any specific reading or observation?

SRC: As I mentioned earlier, he had a philosophical standpoint that was based on general topics like nuclear holocaust, poverty, population. His political ideology was not based on frivolous issues or on a particular political issue. He would never talk about the Hindu–Muslim communal issue or stuff like that. He would say that there is so much space and food that no one should die of hunger. In effect he was talking of the human situation in the world. It was not limited to the country—nor was he targeting the Indian Congress or Left parties. I think he had already transcended all that as a person.

KK: When we did theatre in Haryana our work was very close to the Third Theatre approach. But in our process reading and getting to know views of others was a very significant part and that is what helped us grow. Any such engagement during Badal-da's workshops or production process?

SRC: See, Badal-da's workshops were for everybody. Many times he conducted workshop with absolutely illiterate people. So his module was based on that, it was very basic. He would not always get MA students or graduate students who were trying to do theatre. Sometimes he would go to Tamil Nadu's remote regions to conduct workshops or to villages where people could not read. So there was no point in asking such people to read something that he had read. I think that was one of the reasons that he did not ask the participants to read. He would generally try to draw issues from people's every day experiences and would encourage them to think on their own and would not try to influence them politically. He would never try to tell you to read history or anthropology. Some reading sessions did take place outside the production, outside the workshop process, where he used to read his own plays and all of us listened. He read them very well.

SG: Badal-da had a very unique way of creating interaction if there was any issue or certain discussion to be done within the group. He would conduct the 'Follow the Leader' workshop but with a little shift. In this game everyone would have to keep walking and give his/her opinion, but the only rule of the game was that when one person was talking others would have to repeat what he was saying softly. So when one finished with one's comment he would have to say 'change' and everybody would stop and freeze until someone else from the group started talking. Anyone from the group could start. If more than one person started talking, the one whom the majority was following would automatically become the leader until he/she said 'change'. This whole process would continue until everyone had a chance to speak. This game, I thought, was a unique process of generating views, talking about one's personal opinion, about anything interesting. I have never seen anyone asking anybody why he /she said *that* in the game. It was liberating on the one hand and hypnotic on the other.

KK: Is not Badal Sircar's theatre totally urban in that the actors are urban, the sensibility is urban and the nature of 'physicalisation' is also urban? How does this gel with Badal-da's concept of Third Theatre?

SRC: I will tell you about our experience. There is a village near Santiniketan where we went to perform with the whole crew. We were the babus, the city babus going and performing there where they have local (theatre) traditions like *jaatra*, and local performances. So we did the performance and were not rejected. People were trying to interface. I don't know if you have seen or read *Manushey Manushey*, and how you would have interpreted it, but it is basically a very symbolic take, a statement on history. And this the people there understood and were influenced by. They remarked '*Yeh to itihas dikha raha hai*.'

(He is showing history)—there was a good response. We were also really happy to perform there, because after Badal Sircar's performances people are awed for a brief period of time. They are affected because it is so direct, so close. You are bound to get affected by the whole thing. One can't believe that this is actually happening, this kind of performance, this kind of change of atmosphere. Performing in an open space, he can easily convert it into a railway station or a stadium just with sound and visuals and actions—no need for a train or a time board! So that kind of transformation was a very new experience for the audience. We performed at many places in and around 50 kilometre of

Santiniketan. We got good responses from all the places, including that dismal performance I was talking about where the intonation was not right. Although even there the audience did not complain, we were the ones to realise that we have failed.

KK: In Angan Mancha and Muktakash does the nature of response from the audience change?

SRC: No. The actors' reactions were almost the same. But responses from the audience might get altered. For instance, we did close performances at Natyagrah which is a huge hall in Santiniketan with a stage but no formal seating arrangement. Badal-da particularly avoided the stage. Both the performers and the audience were in the hall arranged in a particular design that he called an arena. He earmarked a square area divided by a backdrop. The audience sat in this square space and the actors performed in the same space very close to the audience. Whenever they were not performing the performers were separated from the audience by this backdrop.

Now, usually when we performed at Natyagrah the audience was bigger but there was no external sound so it was not difficult to reach out. But on a street or in a factory compound there were a lot of other factors that you had to consider and you could not get the same response from the audience in all the performances. In Durgapur we gave two performances. One was in a residential area and one in the Officers Club. In the Officers Club we had just finished setting up the arena, when suddenly, we were shocked to see that officers had started putting chairs. We were clueless about how to stop them from putting chairs because they were officers. This was a completely new experience for us. We realised that they were not going to sit on the ground, so we accepted that arrangement since we were performing for them and it would not help to upset them. Other than this kind of cosmetic change there is hardly any change for the performer.

KK: What is the comparative scope of interaction at Muktakash and Angan Mancha—the relationship with the audience?

SRC: The audience which is coming to watch a performance in a closed space has a different level of attentiveness, mental status and analytical power. On the other hand, in open performances you are entering the lives of the potential audience and becoming a part of it. You are performing on an open ground and a person casually passing the road gets fascinated and stops to observe what is going on and gets involved – that makes the difference. In one the audience is coming to you and in the other you are going to them and entering their space. According to me, Muktakash has more scope of interacting with the audience because there we are equal. In Angan Mancha the audience is captive but in Muktakash they have the freedom to leave when they want. In the end when they would come and meet us they would come to us as normal people and not as performers.

KK: Did you perceive Third Theatre as Street Theatre? What was Badal-da's view of Street Theatre?

SG: Badal-da used to talk a lot about Street Theatre, Safdar Hashmi and Prabir Guha etc., and he had objections to some very small cosmetic things. Like Safdar Hashmi's group used to carry a mat and put it wherever they performed. Badal Sircar had strict reservations for the use of the mat. He felt that it defines a class difference because the moment you put the mat and perform on that, you become a 'babu' as you are not on the same ground with the audience anymore. I personally do not find this criticism valid. He says that this is when it becomes middle class theatre—detached from the audience, where you are thinking about your protection first and then about the performance.

KK: What do you think has been the impact of Badal Sircar's theatre on the theatre in Bengal? And also on your work, considering that you do not practise theatre?

SG: I think (it is my personal opinion) that many of the new directors in Bengal have adopted some of the chorographical strategies of Third

Theatre inside the proscenium. Like Suman Mukherjee's *Teesta Parer Brittanto* had elements of Third Theatre as a choreographical tool. Or seeing *Prachya* by Koushik Sen, Manish Mitra's *Shesh Rupkatha* and so on, one notices that they have been subconsciously influenced by Badal-da's work in that they have brought that energy and spatial philosophy onto the proscenium.

As far as impact on me is concerned, I joined Badal-da's workshop in Kala Bhavan in 1995, when I was in the final year of my bachelor's course in the department of painting. It was one of those transition points in my own practice as a painter when I was not satisfied with what I was doing as a two-dimensional activity. Badal-da's workshop was a great encounter in the sense that it opened up my understanding of visual experience in the domain of three dimensional space, and more than that, the domain of real space and interactivity. More than the theatre production of Badal-da, I was inspired by his workshop process and how he could transform that process into a creative energy. It immediately influenced my painting practice and I started exploring the possibility of extending painting as a space into the physical space of the viewer.

I became interested in transforming the ritualistic energy that is generated in different games of the workshop as a performative space together with physical space of visual images. In this respect I have felt that although Badal-da always talked about taking theatrical space as close as possible to the physical space of the viewer, he never addressed the variations in the different spatial reality of different places. The play has remained the same and also its spatial reality, as Third Theatre is always done in a specific format of a rectangle with a black backdrop positioned a little behind one side of the rectangle. Maybe this was created so that the production could be repeated over and over again in different places in the same way. I personally feel it is a limitation of Third Theatre that it does not allow improvisation in terms of changing space and situations.

I always felt that Badal-da's workshop situations could be transformed into performance situations if we did not repeat them. And this is where I was inspired to try out the workshop method as a performance art method, by transforming it into a site-specific installation performance, which addressed the context of the site both materially and physically. I left my studio practice and started collaborating with my theatre friends. Here, I would conceptualise the performance, conduct workshops and then provide a performance sequence to the performers who would follow the sequence through their individual improvisation with respect to the installation and the site. These were one-time, unrehearsed actions generated in different sites, like in front of theatre auditoriums, in front of a statue of Vidyasagar, inside a godown of a school or even in parking spaces in a group of buildings.

But I think Badal-da's workshops became a major inspiration when I decided to move on from site-specific installation performance to community-specific art activity. I was trying to move away from the interventionist mode of art activity towards a more participatory and interactive art activity. I think Badal-da's notion of an integrated performance space and his workshop with 'no observers but all participants' became a major inspiration to explore art activity in a situation where the border between the observer and the performer was blurred and overlapping. So presently, for the last ten years, I have been exploring methods of participating in community situations, and community here means not only a specific tribe or people, but also people with similar user relationships to space. So any space can generate a community situation for a temporary moment of time. In this respect I have tried to work with different groups of people from different communities or have generated a space to invite people to participate in it, like a tea *adda* with different people from different strata of life living near the Brahmaputra in Guwahati; or working with a group of weavers in Bodoland, or a group of immigrants from Pakistan in Bristol, UK. In all these situations I have tried to transform the Third Theatre games into games for exploring inter-community relationships, exploring memory spaces and also sometimes for generating a common working situation to develop a space of collective working. Presently I am conducting workshop-based art activity with people living on the border of the North-

East and South-East of India. This is a still ongoing collaborative project with Anshuman Das Gupta. In all these situations I have applied the games of Badal-da and combined them with different visual exercises to generate interactive spaces between people from different communities. I have tried to reshape/transform them from being theatre games into methods of exploring cultural difference, generating personal narratives, generating memory space and collectively seeing how a certain space of belonging and a relationship could be generated through an interdisciplinary art activity.

LEGACY

AN OPEN LETTER TO BADAL SIRCAR

Mahesh Elkunchwar

My dear Badal-da,

I am so happy and feel so privileged to be a part of this event today when theatre friends of my generation and the succeeding ones are here to express their gratitude to you—something I have been wanting to do on my own for many years but could not, simply because it would have embarrassed you, and I stood too much in awe of you to articulate my feelings. I remember the day when I first met you in Kolkata in 1976. You were already a legend then and I was a starry-eyed novice who was taking his first tentative steps in the domain of theatre that was illuminated by you, Tendulkar, Rakesh and Karnad. I came to you with a lot of apprehension and awe. I was tongue-tied and you, as is your wont, did not say much. I came back humbled, with an impression of having met a person who was modest to a fault and whose quietness spoke volumes. You do not speak much but, not surprisingly, your work speaks, and it is, unlike many other writers' writings, intricately linked with your persona. I do not know if one can understand and appreciate your work if one does not know your convictions and concerns. The latter are shot through all your work-body and remain a sustaining force, giving your creativity that extra energy which we all writers aspire to have in our work. I belong to a generation that had already begun to lose its faith in any ideology and perhaps did not even have enough stamina to hold on to some. That is why what struck us most in you was your ability to confront the ever-degrading reality, look it in the eye without losing your faith in humanity. When I think of those times, I remember how shrill we were in telling the whole world how no illusions have been left for us, no ideology. You had accepted it and yet had not given up hope and trust and courage. Yes, I think courage is one virtue, which has been the theme song of your life and your theatre.

It has been said that existentialism has coloured your work of the 1960s to a great extent, thereby robbing it of its originality. I do not really agree with this thesis. Slapping labels onto writers is the job of critics and all the power to them. They do their job and let us do ours. But I think it does grave injustice to you, because your sympathies were much wider and you simply could not have had the almost nihilistic trait implicit in most of the existential creative work of that time. You loved people and humanity and your faith in them was too deep to let the acid of nihilism corrode you. In its place you had courage. And that is the glory of your work. I do not like the tendency of people who divide a writer's career into phases and find suitable and convenient labels for each of them, cataloguing them. A writer's oeuvre should be seen and treated as a long unbroken journey...with unexpected twists and turns in its course; its unpredictable changes inviting curiosity rather than dismay, its evolution over a period covering a life-time of wonder, the broadening of its vision and the quiet depth it acquires in the whole process, respect.

In all your work, without exception, you have mostly talked about fundamental human situations filled with paradoxes: 'The unfair battle between the individual rebel and the exploitative social fabric as well as an inhospitable universe, the devastating divide between freedom and intellectual integrity, alienation and the quest for love.' And you have talked about these issues not in relation to big mythical heroes, but ordinary men in the street. For the first time, the anti-hero found his voice in Indian theatre through you. It was a small voice but no writer of deep sympathies could ignore its excruciating intensity. You broke many theatre conventions and while doing that, stretched the conventions of realism till they gasped, turned realism upside down, used many formalistic innovations. You used dramatic monologues in verse with tremendous confidence just when poetry and verse in theatre were considered passé. In fact, all you were doing was reviving the Bengali theatre tradition of such monologues, but with a different purpose and a different technique that brought it close to every day speech. This sudden shift from prose dialogue to verse reflected the shift in mood and feeling of the character. Your skills as a playwright are abundant and you have the ability to use many clichés with superb confidence, lending them many sub-textual meanings. I am sure you must have had a glorious time re-inventing new ways of articulation. The destination was not important. The journey was. The joy was in journeying. I remember a line from *Evam Indrajit*. 'Remember—it's not the pilgrimage, but the road to the pilgrimage which is our destiny.'

It has been an unending road and with courage in your heart, you are happy to trudge along it. When I speak of courage, I am not speaking only of the courage, which is an integral part of your world-view that is reflected in your work. I am speaking of another kind of courage as well, different from the first, the courage of the artist. You have used certain moulds and used them to achieve great artistic success, and then broken them with equanimity. This is not something many artists would risk. We become prisoners of our success and begin to repeat ourselves, afraid of venturing into new, unknown territories. You did it almost with a relish. Your changing awareness of life and expectations from it and understanding of theatre propelled you in this direction. That is obvious. But you took the risk, totally unmindful of the dangers fraught within this act. This leaves me speechless. What was the driving force that made you disown gems like *Evam Indrajit, Saari Raat* and *Baki Itihas*? You did it, knowing full well that your detractors would have a field day with this coming from you. But you had no time for these petty considerations and you were already busy with your 'Third Theatre,' your Angan Manch. I have seen with my own eyes the conditions you were working in and have never seen you even once complaining about them. You were working with untrained actors, you had no money, no rehearsal and performance space, no patronage and you wanted a new audience. This is in stark contrast to the kind of grumbling we hear from today's theatre workers. Your concern for the invisible ordinary man forced you to take on all these challenges, knowing full well that it might not yield expected results. I am tempted to quote you:

'Can we afford to put the spectators at a distance? At a different level? In darkness? (And the word darkness here is resonant with multiple meanings.) Have they not come to meet with us? Are they not an integral part of the theatre event? ...Why not be in the same space with the spectators to make it a three dimensional reality as theatre really is?'

Your Third Theatre was a product of the tumultuous times of the late 1960s and early 1970s when the Naxalite movement was lambasting the establishment by raising a number of fundamentally important political and social questions. You were and always are in the midst of people, with your fingers on their pulse, sharing their angst. It was an inner compulsion. Still is. You had to be with them and among them. The very phrase Angan Manch reflects your need for an immediate and urgent rapport with the common man. And it took you out of the proscenium into the open, from the urban milieu to the rural, from the city theatre sophisticate to the uninitiated village man. You even sacrificed Art in the process. You said that content is more important and form comes later. So ignited were you with the idea that theatre is irrelevant if it does not convey a political and social message, that you threw artistic conventions to the wind, much to the coy annoyance of the city aesthete. It mattered very little to you. You had found your audience and I think, you were amply rewarded when a villager remarked wryly that they understood these plays perfectly well. It is perhaps the city rich who do not.

We admire you for all this and more Badal-da. We admire you for your courage of convictions and commitment, for your ability to be low profile while doing such seminal work, your courage to break old moulds and create new ones. I do not measure your success in material terms although it too is of immense proportions. I measure your success in terms of the failures you have risked while pursuing single-mindedly a decided ideological goal and bringing about a fusion of it with your art. Such failures are magnificent achievements and give courage and hope to people who want to walk the path you have walked. You have created a soil where the coming generations will find it easy to strike their roots. Thank you so much for all this. We are blessed indeed to have a predecessor like you. Thank you.

This letter was read out when Badal Sircar was felicitated in Pune in August 2004

Published in Theatre India, *October 2004, NSD Journal*

BADAL SIRCAR AND HINDI THEATRE

Ashok Bhowmik

The cultural practices of any region or state are influenced by the local socio-political conditions and events. Just as the local social and political conditions leave an impact on the cultural and literary activity of the region, the nature, environment and geographical characteristics also leave their mark on such practices. The wide difference between the folk arts of Punjab and Manipur is probably being governed by the natural environments of these regions. Similarly the nature of performative expressions in martial races is very different from that of agricultural workers or fishermen. There is a distinctly different flavour in the arts of people who are regular victims of natural disasters. Their expressions are dominated by prayers and rituals to placate such destructive natural forces.

We would therefore easily identify the artistic expressions of such regions.

When we talk of Indian literature or Indian theatre, keeping in mind the relationship between the region and their culture, the issue is not limited to linguistic variations. The people living in different regions are very different given their different environment, experiences and cultural expressions, that words like 'Indian Culture' remain just empty, meaningless expressions even after six decades of Independence.

In spite of these diversities inevitably built into the cultural expression of the country, the 1970s decade saw in the theatre activity of different regions, a potential or the possibility of the idea of Indian theatre. In this historic unification of Indian theatre, Badal Sircar and his theatre played the most significant role. The fact that Badal Sircar's plays were written in Bangla soon became inconsequential for the theatre workers of the country, as what the struggles and problems he was writing about were not unknown to the people across the country—whether it be Kerala, or Maharashtra, Gujarat or Chhattisgarh. That is the reason why almost overnight plays like *Juloos, Bhoma, Spartacus, Ghera,* and *Basi Khabar* were performed very effectively in almost all parts of the country thereby breaking away from their identity as Bengali plays and acquiring the status of Indian plays.

Badal Sircar and the Cultural Heritage of Bengal

Badal Sircar's philosophy and theatre is a continuation of that cultural heritage of Bengal which has not only been witness to a host of political and social upheavals but has been giving them expression in its literature, music and drama.

This eastern region spread along the eastern coast of the country, has, due to several large rivers and other geographical reasons, been, from time immemorial, a victim of regular storms, floods, epidemics and other natural disasters. Probably due to this it gave rise to aggressive religious and fatalistic tendencies on the one hand, and a clear strain of protest against superstition, Brahminism, fatalism, hollow rituals and hypocrisy on the other. Both sides exploited culture to strengthen themselves. Literature, music and theatre gave expression to both these contradictory strands. While some Bangla literature depicted Kali, Krishna, Chaitanya, Durga and other gods and goddesses with great devotion and imagination, there was also parallel and significant literature that was very progressive and in direct opposition to the devotional expression. While most of Bengali rural and urban theatre was limited to the depiction of gods and goddesses and heroic tales of kings and queens, there was also a glorious and an almost 200-year-old history of plays dealing with the concerns of the common masses, their exploitation and struggles.

After the take-over by the East India Company, there is a long history of protest literature in Bengal against the exploitation of the common masses by the British rulers. On the one hand were strong protest plays like *Neel Darpan* by Dinabandhu Mitra, which exposed the atrocities of the indigo plantation owners against the farmers, and which acted as catalysts in creating widespread protests both among the intellectuals and the common man. On the other hand were plays by playwrights like Ramnarayan Tarkratna and Michael Madhusudan Dutt, which were critical of the social ills within the Indian society like caste discrimination and polygamy etc. But all these theatrical initiatives received a big jolt with the imposition of censorship through the promulgation of the 'Theatre Performances Control Act'. Subsequently, for several decades, the theatre of Bengal remained confined to historical and mythological extravaganzas meant only for entertainment.

The next move towards protest in the arts came via the Anti Fascists Writers and Artists Association (AFWAA) in 1942; however no theatre workers were included in this formation. Soon after this on 25 May 1943, Indian Peoples Theatre association (IPTA) was formed. This was a significant milestone in the development of Indian Theatre because for the first time theatre people became part of the movement against Fascism and Imperialism.

With the staging of the historic production of *Navanna* written by Bijon Bhattacharya, the theatre of protest marked a come back. As IPTA developed discussions continued, within the organisation, on the basic principles of theatre to be adopted. These included discussion on (1) how to get out of the proscenium – inspired by the European theatre model – and reach out to the common people; (2) how to structure the theatre performances that would express the contemporary reality emerging from the worldwide movements against Fascism and Imperialism. But IPTA could not totally get out of the proscenium. Sombhu Mitra opposed taking theatre to rural areas without proper infrastructure as that would compromise quality.

In any case, in no other region of the country, do we see the development of people's art or such a culture of protest as we do in Bengal.

Badal Sircar and the Leftist Art Movement

The generation after *Neel Darpan* not only understood the power of theatre but also used it effectively in fiction, poetry and fine art. They could also afford to be confident of this role of art at specific junctures of history because when the social conditions give birth to peoples' artists they also create readers, audience and spectators for these artists. This is particularly important for theatre because for a successful presentation of political plays it is not enough for just the playwright to be progressive but a group with a clear political understanding and orientation, and the right kind of spectators.

Badal Sircar has repeatedly emphasised these elements as necessary for political theatre. His Third Theatre, in its form, is not just an alternative to the urban proscenium theatre or the rural folk theatre, but is a meaningful political theatre. Badal Sircar through his work, also managed to break the stranglehold of the urban intellectuals on the progressive theatre stream. There is no doubt that a large section of the Indian intellectuals was highly influenced by the Russian Revolution. This section of the intellectuals and artists gave shape, in due course, to Left oriented organisations like Progressive Writers Association, Anti Fascists Writers and Artists Association (AFWAA), IPTA etc. IPTA carried on the longest as an active cultural organisation. But this cultural organisation that ran on the policy direction of the Communist Party (undivided) soon became like a puppet in the hands of the party with its constantly changing policies depending on the international political situation. Thus at some point, due to the decision to oppose Germany, it was compelled to form the AFWAA, at another, it rallied the masses to fight for independence and soon after had to reverse its stand and said that such an independence is fake. By the time of the Emergency (1975-77) it thought it better to keep altogether silent. In our parliamentary democracy both the major Left parties seemed to be positioned against the oppressed common man and in support of the ruling party.

What needs to be looked at here is that due to these changing stands and policies, not only have these parties been losing their political support but have also blunted the impact of the people's art movements. As we already know that just before Independence, the politics within the Communist Party had intensified resulting in its break-up after Independence. These changing equations and situations completely confused the artists associated with the leftist cultural organisations.

The progressive and people's artists were thus divided repeatedly and led to oppose each other. In this process their commitment towards 'creat(ing) an ideal tomorrow' lost strength and significance while the uniqueness of 'people's art' gradually disappeared. Looking at the problems and the resulting confusion within the Left parties and in the forum of artists associated with them, one is constantly reminded of Badal Sircar's statement—'I am a Marxist but I do not have faith in the Left parties.' By this statement he is speaking for thousands of committed artists who believe that their task is to create for the benefit of the common people, not to follow the dictat and be manipulated like puppets in support of changing policies and alignments of the party.

Bengal has had a long tradition of theatre gurus. Some of the names from that tradition are Dinabandhu Mitra, Michael Madhusudan Dutt, Girishchandra Ghosh, Shishir Bhaduri, Bijon Bhattacharya, Sombhu Mitra, Utpal Dutt etc. The tradition continues till today but it has never included the name of Badal Sircar till date. This may be because he was not limited by the notion of Bengali identity. For his Third Theatre the boundaries like Bengali Theatre or Hindi Theatre were redundant.

For the first time, Badal Sircar tried to search for a new language for political theatre where a direct dialogue with the spectator could be possible. He made his Third Theatre flexible and inexpensive so that one would be able to transport it easily from one place to another without much expenditure. Through this effort he succeeded in bringing theatre out of the clutches of the urban theatre workers and intellectuals and accessible to theatre workers in small towns and villages. He also tried to rid the performers of conventional adjectives like 'talented', 'famous' and 'actor'. In his Third Theatre there is no place for things like name, fame, career (and money, which is indispensably linked with these).

Badal Sircar's 'Free Theatre' is an intimate theatre which tries to minimise the distance between the performer and the spectator. His

Third Theatre broke the prevailing norm that if a spectator does not have money then he cannot enjoy theatre. Badal Sircar believed that Free Theatre is possible both in principle and practice as it can be run on the financial support received voluntarily from the spectators. Therefore it does not need anything like an entry fee. This is a very significant move, not just because more than half the population of the country cannot afford theatre tickets but also because theatre is essentially a 'human act' where the performers and spectators should be able to meet on common ground without any discrimination and forge a human bond. Keeping a fee changes the equation to that between a product and a consumer, which takes us away from a human bond. It is most important for any political theatre to reduce the distance between the actors and the spectators so that the flow of ideas passes seamlessly to the spectators and they are forced to confront them and think about them. This responsibility of political theatre is what places it apart from theatre for entertainment.

This flexible and inexpensive Third Theatre of Badal Sircar made theatre possible not just for Indians but also for artists in neighbouring Bangladesh, Nepal and Pakistan where there were almost no resources and infrastructure for theatre and also no training in theatre. At the centre of Badal Sircar's Third Theatre is the comment of the play, not the actor.

Badal Sircar and Hindi Theatre

The credit for introducing Badal Sircar to the Hindi world goes to Nemichandra Jain, Pratibha Agrawal and Yama Saraf, who translated several of his plays and made them accessible to the Hindi theatre workers. In the 1970s and '80s, in the entire Hindi-speaking region, both in big and small cities, wherever a proscenium theatre was available, Badal Sircar's plays remained the most performed plays compared to the plays of Dharmvir Bharti, Mohan Rakesh, Shankar Shesh, Vijay Tendulkar, Girish Karnad and Mani Madhukar, among others. The prime reason for this was not only the novelty of his themes but the fact that Badal Sircar's plays could be staged without too much attention to sets, lights, sound etc—elements that accompany most proscenium performances. Additionally, Badal Sircar's comedies and satires, due to his entertaining but sharp and witty dialogues, reduced the possibility of a production failing. During this phase of Hindi theatre, while comedies and farces like *Badi Buaji (Baro Pishima), Solution X, Ballabhpur Ki Roopkatha (Ballabhpurer Roopkatha)* were staged very extensively, his more serious plays like *Pagla Ghoda, Evam Indrajit* and *Baki Itihas* were also constantly being staged.

During this very period Badal Sircar was travelling regularly to various cities outside Calcutta for workshops related to his Third Theatre. Along with big cities like Ahmedabad and Delhi he also visited small cities like Pilani and Azamgarh. Azamgarh was a small town like any other small town of the Hindi region, where the local theatre was being encouraged and enriched by people coming to this town from other cities for various jobs. In this phase Hindi theatre in small towns and townships received encouragement from the audience also because the local intelligentsia was interested in serious entertainment but had virtually no options. Most towns had very few cinema halls and those too were ill equipped. And television had not yet reached these areas. In such circumstances, despite absence of resources and infrastructure, proscenium halls were somehow constructed, lights and sound equipment rented from the cities and plays continued to be staged. Through such efforts, the 1970s saw the beginning of the golden period of Hindi theatre.

In the Hindi-speaking region, the initial years of this decade saw the rise of students, workers and labour organisations backed by the Left. Along with the 'activisation' of Students' Unions in colleges and universities, railways, banks and government and non government employees' unions, one witnessed increased activity in the cultural field as well. Several theatre groups with close ties to the Left parties were constantly doing theatre. Apart from IPTA, in cities like Agra, Lucknow, Kanpur, Meerut, Bareilly, Patna, Jabalpur, Bhopal, Indore etc., cultural activities accelerated in general.

Around 1970, with the Naxalite movement of 1967 as the backdrop and the formation of the Communist Party of India (Marxist Leninist) or CPI(ML) as an independent political party, there was a renewed interest in the left movement among the young intellectuals and cultural activists of Uttar Pradesh. These Left-oriented intellectuals started staging new political plays as a parallel stream to the existing urban amateur plays. For innumerable people in the small towns of the Hindi belt, street plays did not remain an unfamiliar entity. In 1974 Badal Sircar wrote *Juloos,* entirely as a Third Theatre play. Badal Sircar's *Spartacus* (written in 1972, staged in 1973) was based on a novel that was situated in Rome. In spite of this, *Spartacus* ran successfully within Bengal for several years. But *Juloos* written in 1974 was available in Hindi almost at the same time as its Bengali production, and by 1975 had been produced in almost all the towns of the Hindi region. During the Emergency this play was produced by small amateur groups without any resources, at street corners and squares in accordance with the Third Theatre, to express their protest against the establishment. As a result large number of people in the small towns and villages of this region became familiar with the name 'Badal Sircar' and his play *Juloos.*

Based on this play, several original plays were written and staged at street corners during this period.

Around 1980 the leftist students' organisations started becoming active in colleges and universities, which gave a new momentum to the cultural activities in the Hindi region. Study circles, poetry recitation, poster poetry, street plays became the order of the day. Delhi too had several active theatre groups and many of them were regularly staging street plays.

In this phase Badal Sircar visited Delhi quite frequently to conduct Third Theatre workshops which gave a new direction to the theatre activity of this region. Badal Sircar's coming to Azamgarh in 1980 was historic from several points of view. In the Hindi region, this was Badal Sircar's first workshop on Third Theatre, and that too in a small town like Azamgarh. This introduced his Third Theatre to other theatre workers in small towns of this region. After his workshop, this small group of Azamgarh, which had practically no resources, presented many of the Third Theatre plays in several small towns of UP and other states. In that sense it played a pivotal role in popularising the Third Theatre in this entire region. After this successful workshop, a progressive student organisation of Allahabad University invited Badal Sircar in 1980 to conduct a workshop in Allahabad. The theatre group of this student organisation was more politically aware and had a clear focus. This group then presented several street plays in innumerable villages and towns of Bihar and Uttar Pradesh. For this group the priority was not to present only Badal Sircar's plays. But since they fully understood the principles of the Third Theatre, they, along with the staging of plays, paid equal attention to the 'follow up'. These performances gave an opportunity to political activists to establish a dialogue with the audiences. Badal Sircar had said in an interview:

> It is not true to say that the Third Theatre has been propagated in the country only through our workshops and performances. Instead it has spread due to the regular activity of the local groups and their follow up. Theatre workers identified the problems and issues of a community through thorough discussions with the community and its workers and prepared plays based on these issues. That the workshops and training of Third Theatre proved extremely useful for production of these plays is however accepted by all concerned.
>
> When I had done the Third Theatre workshop in Tamil Nadu, I had not imagined that it will be so successful. Tamil Nadu organisations did significant work through theatre. People were brought together on the Dalit issue. That was quite a struggle. The task was to organise the people, particularly the Dalits. Those areas of Tamil Nadu had hardly been exposed to any movement. This was the first time that some political awareness was created among the people of these areas. They now understand their issues and priorities and are doing theatre around those; also politics. Third Theatre has thus firmed its roots in Tamil Nadu. It may not be incorrect to say that people-oriented, progressive thought has reached here through theatre.

The depth with which the Great Famine of 1943 impacted on the literature, theatre and the arts of Bengal, was partly due to the changing political reality of the twentieth century and partly due to the new vision and critical understanding of this changing socio-political reality. It is this which allowed for the beginning and development of political theatre as a pan-Indian movement. Badal Sircar has found a connection with this movement through the experience of plays from *Neel Darpan* to *Navanna*. Badal Sircar's theatre seems primarily about local issues and problems, but he also opens up the larger national and international concerns related to these local issues. Badal Sircar's political commitment is better understood through his statement in an interview, where he talked about the incidents and dialogues of plays like *Bhoma*, *Juloos* and *Basi Khabar* etc.

'If dialogues of such plays are not altered with the changing times, then the performance will be totally mechanical. Theatre groups need to modify the dialogues according to their political understanding and vision at the time, only then will such theatre be meaningful as political theatre.'

Very few playwrights in the world are likely to make such a statement about their plays.

BADAL SIRCAR AND MARATHI THEATRE

An Interview with Amol Palekar

The interview was conducted by **Vidyanidhi Vanarase** in Pune, 2011

Vidyanidhi Vanarase (VV): What led you to select the plays of Badal Sircar (BS)?

Amol Palekar (AP): I did not know anything about Badal Sircar. Satyadev Dubey (SD) introduced me to BS. In fact, SD had asked me to accompany BS when he had come to Mumbai, after which he was to come to Pune. Rajabhau Natu had invited him to Pune and I was the boy scout who brought him there. We were together here for about two days, and in that period I was completely mesmerised. Just around that time I happened to see Shyamanand Jalan's *Evam Indrajit* and it was a mind blowing experience. In fact, one of my biggest regrets has been my inability to stage *Evam Indrajit*. The play has and continues to influence me and my generation. It is that one single play, I think, that has had a major impact on our entire generation. The impact of Shyamanand's production was so vivid that even today it has stayed with me. And then, followed by that, I was a part of Dubey's production of *Evam Indrajit*. I was managing the lights, sound and the general technical side. So having (the opportunity to see)…two absolute major productions of that play and two totally different interpretations of that same play at my formative stage, was, I think, one of the biggest boons to my growth. Therefore the fact that I could never do that play is a matter of regret.

But from there onwards my association with Badal-da continues to date. Whenever I go to Kolkata I make it a point to go and meet him, spend an hour or two, have *chai, sondesh* and enjoy his company. So it has been a very long association and I must say that I am really privileged to have been able to come so close to one of the living legends of Indian theatre.

VV: At the initial stage what actually triggered your decision to take up a Badal Sircar play for production.

AP: In fact, the whole thing is very interesting. When I saw *Evam. Indrajit* I was talking very excitedly to Satyadev Dubey about the play. He said that there was a very different play by Badal Sircar, and why don't I do that? And that was *Ballabhpur*. In my young fiery enthusiasm I said, 'But I don't know whether the play is really good or not.' Then Dubey just scolded me. He said, 'Listen, Badal Sircar is a great playwright. Even the worst of his plays would be outstanding. So you as a young boy don't sit on judgment. Just read that play and think of doing it.' So that's how I came across *Ballabhpur*. Then I translated it into Marathi and with that play the Marathi wing of Theatre Unit was started by Satyadev Dubey. So that was the first play of Badal-da that I did. Then immediately after that I came across *Pagla Ghoda* and then we did that as well. We did it in Hindi and Marathi simultaneously. That is how the whole journey started.

VV: Which of Badal-da's plays is your favourite? The one that attracted you most?

AP: Without doubt, *Evam Indrajit* is the play which attracts me, fascinates me even today. Hopefully I will be able to do it now sometime. But apart from that I did two more plays of Badal-da... one was *Juloos* and the other was *Pagla Ghoda*. It was very interesting. I did *Juloos* during the Emergency as my little protest against the Emergency, and then I revisited that play recently in 2005, taking all the young, absolutely fresh students from Pune, about twenty of them. None of them had ever acted earlier. This was done as a part of the Badal Sircar festival that I had organised here. The complete retrospective of Badal-da—where Badal-da himself was present and I think all those young boys and girls...they were simply floored that Badal-da was there for the first performance. And then Amrish Puri and Naseeruddin Shah were there, and to perform in front of such an august audience was a great experience for them. As I revisited *Juloos* I also revisited *Pagla Ghoda*. Quite a few times in fact. As I mentioned, I did it in Hindi and Marathi both. Then after a gap of a decade or so, I did it in Marathi again and then three years back or two years back I did it in Bengali. And to my pleasant surprise, the play still remains fresh and it offers so many things to explore. I could try and find out layers between man-woman relationships in that play. Particularly when I did it in Bengali I was really surprised that on the one hand it is a dated play but it has such depth at the thematic level. Dated, yes, because when you talk of Scotch whisky... Scotch whisky was absolutely rare in 1960s and '70s and it was not available to the common man. Today it is not so. Nor can you see those kinds of social structures...you can't see a doctor and his compounder, the compounder system is already non-existent today. So it does seem to be dated. But if you look slightly beyond that, if you look deeper, then the man-woman relationship that Badal-da talks about, the four different stratas of our society—the lower class, the middle class, the upper middle class and higher class etc. etc., then the kind of new insights that one could get were so fresh that it was really very exciting for me to find all those layers and try and do that all over again as recently in 2007 or 2008. I stand open to correction on exact dates, but it was really exciting to see what was reaffirmed while doing *Pagla Ghoda* all over again. *Pagla Ghoda* can be done only as a very exciting theatrical experience and that is its charm. I mean you can't make a film on *Pagla Ghoda;* you can't probably write a short story or novel on that. It is an experience to be cherished only as theatre, which was to me a very nice revelation and that validity of its theatricality was something which was really fascinating.

VV: You mentioned *Juloos.* When you read the play, it demands a different kind of performance space. In Maharashtra or in Marathi theatre that kind of experimentation was almost negligible till that point.

AP: Not really. I mean, I had done a play called *Gochi* by one of the foremost Marathi poets, Sadanand Rege, way back in the 1970s. That was one of the first attempts to bring theatre out of the proscenium arch. In fact, *Gochi* was not performed even once in regular theatre. We have performed it anywhere and everywhere, like in canteens, in somebody's garage, on a terrace, while exploring new spaces that way in a true sense. I had started long back. So doing *Juloos* was not different in that sense, but it was important in more ways than one. As I said it was my small little protest against the Emergency, and therefore we also did it as a part of the state drama competition, which was a very vibrant scenario in Maharashtra at that time. So to be able to make a protest against the government on a government platform with government funding gave us a different kind of a kick. We did that at Ravindra Natya Mandir. Later I was told that quite a few political leaders like Mrinal Gore and others who had gone underground by then, had come to see that play, and that was another very significant experience. But again, *Juloos* – though we opened it also on a proscenium stage – continued to (be staged)…anywhere and everywhere. I remember having done that performance in the Jaslok Hospital foyer. Its performance in Mood Indigo in IIT Pawai was one of the most talked about experiences not only for IIT but also for the theatre world. So we went on. *Juloos* had more than 200 performances at that time. I must mention that I had done that play for a group called Bohurupee which was led by Dr Hemachandra Adhikari, who by profession was a scientist with leftist leanings. The group invited me to do this play for them and that's how it happened.

VV: How did Marathi theatre people react? What was their response to this play as such, and what kind of influence did it have on Marathi theatre?

AP: See, I can very clearly see two kinds of trends. At a broader level one can say people were really charmed and mesmerised by Badal Sircar, particularly, this later phase of Badal-da, which he started calling Third Theatre, when he came out of the proscenium completely and now he doesn't even bother to perform anywhere in Kolkata. He performs only in villages. Now that kind of a thing, at one level was very fascinating and charming for the theatre world. At the same time the theatre world itself was not ready or was quite reluctant to come out of the set pattern of proscenium theatre etc. I will give you the best example of that. My group Aniket and I invited Badal-da with his troupe to Mumbai and we had organised a Badal Sircar festival. This was way back in the 1980s or beginning of the '90s. We just could not afford it because there was no financial help from any other group; everybody came to help us organise this but the financial burden was completely taken on by Aniket and we felt very proud about that. We had a week-long festival in Chhabildas based on all the Badal-da plays. At the end of the festival the very typical reaction that came was, 'all the plays look almost similar. I wish there was a bit of variety'. So, you know, if we are looking for a variety entertainment show, then you are naturally not going to be satisfied or happy, but if you are able to see a journey of a creative mind, you would appreciate it. You know, I have always felt that a retrospective of either a writer or director or any creative mind, is almost impossible in theatre for obvious reasons. But when we are able to see a journey of a painter, say of Van Gogh, we say, 'Here is the blue period and then from this point onwards...oh it changed....' And then to be able to have a look at a complete body of work, if not complete—a sizeable amount of work, it gives you a different insight, a different kind of pleasure. The same thing can be done with writing, with fiction, with stories. You can do it in films. Only in theatre it is not possible. So when you are able to see a complete journey and a body of work, something like what I organised in Pune, then you can see that oh! Badal Sircar started with very simple, loveable comedies like *Ballabhpur Ki Roopkatha* or *Badi Buaji*...and then went on to write *Evam Indrajit* or *Saari Raat*, and others. You can see the growth of the playwright, the theatre person, exploring all the possibilities of the theatrical idiom in different ways. And then you can see how he slowly comes out of the proscenium theatre and starts exploring much beyond that. As you rightly said, if you see the script of *Juloos*, you can't call it a play. It is just a skeleton and I had lots of discussions with Badal-da on that. He, in fact, wanted the theatre groups to explore and fill in all those spaces instead of preparing very tightly written scripts. His approach was-'Here is a skeleton and now you go and explore while trying to keep the same structure in mind and keeping the content intact. Go ahead.' In fact, it was very enriching for me when I did it recently in Pune. After that we sat down with Badal-da and though it was in Marathi, he could follow it well and said:

> Amol, what I loved in this new interpretation is that the idiom itself has changed. Whether we like it not, whether we realise or not, television and consumerism play such a major part in our life. All the time using those advertisements on television or those jingles and that kind of expression made it so very relevant and so very contemporary and yet it was my play. I felt very nice.

Then I shared with him how I had done a workshop with these boys and girls before we actually started the play and I wanted to discover their idiom, elicit the response of the youth as to understand how they react, how they think, what the influences on their lives are, and what is their lingo etc. And it was by using all those things that this particular production of *Juloos* was evolved. So it was extremely relevant, extremely contemporary and yet it was Badal-da's *Juloos*.

VV: When you mention this play and the way it is written, would you say that there is a different theatre aesthetics in Badal-da's plays as compared to let's say the Marathi theatre? Is there a difference also in their understanding of aesthetics as such?

AP: Well, I am quite harsh and critical about aesthetics in Marathi theatre, because I genuinely think that Marathi theatre got badly stuck in one kind of theatre language and it has not come out of the drawing room where all the issues can be discussed only in the drawing room of a middle class household. It does not come out of that, barring a few exceptions of course. So, therefore, Marathi theatre in that sense—as a majority choice—did not take any influence from Badal-da. The point that I wanted to make earlier, you know, when I organised the Badal-da festival earlier in the 1980s or '90s in Chhabildas, that was also the time when I started realising that the Chhabildas movement had also started to wane. There were many other reasons of course, one can't say that it was a failure only of the artists or the creative people, but we cannot shrug off our responsibility either. To specify further, at Chhabildas we had this great opportunity of exploring different spaces and different theatrical idioms, but that did not happen. We slowly but surely, converted Chhabildas into another proscenium arch, which is to say that the divide between the performer and the audience continued. You may not have the actual curtain, but that division was there and that is one of the things which even now disturbs me hell of a lot. I feel that Marathi playwrights, particularly, didn't take up that challenge and didn't come up with different explorations which could have taken Marathi theatre in a different direction. I am not saying good, bad or whatever, but definitely a distinctly different direction was possible through the Chhabildas movement. But instead of taking that path we chose the easier and safer path of converting Chabildas into a small, poor man's proscenium theatre. As it happens today in Sudarshan in Pune. And I ask a disturbing question—why are we not exploring different spaces and working towards a different language of theatrical expression. The audience which came to Chhabildas or comes to Sudarshan, in fact, wants to have that experience today. We are failing to do that as theatre artists and that disturbs me.

VV: As you mentioned that Hemu kaka and you were doing *Juloos* as a protest, do you subscribe to the political beliefs of Badal-da?

AP: Yes, of course I do endorse that and I have always been a strong believer in anti-establishment protests of our times—whichever establishment it may be. That's again one of the reasons I was never near any political party, because I don't want to be patronised by any political party and lose the freedom of protesting against that. So in that sense I am very much with Badal-da. His crusade, as he is taking it today, is something which is extremely difficult for theatre people to understand and follow. That also I realise. Ultimately the 'recognition' comes from the established proscenium arch theatre. Be it theatre practitioners, be it the critics, be it people who matter—you want to be recognised by them. If you want to be recognised by them, this journey is out of bounds. It is very interesting to know how we came to do the Badal Sircar retrospective in 2005. I heard that Badal-da had met with a serious accident. I desperately called up a few friends in Kolkata, but what saddened me was that nobody knew. Badal-da is a major theatre personality and if he met with an accident everybody ought to know. And then I realised that he is not part of the theatre scene in Kolkata, so he is forgotten; nobody knows him and he also is perfectly happy being away from that scene. I finally managed to locate him and I rushed there and that's when we realised that as theatre practitioners we must pay our respects, our homage to this living legend and say that, 'You have given us so much pleasure – not merely pleasure but you have enriched our lives – and we bow down to you all over again.' That was the starting point of this theatre festival. Then I went on to do same thing with Vijay Tendulkar, Ratan Thiyyam and then the Sangeet tradition of Marathi and Karnataka theatre and all that. But it was very special to be able to bow down to a living legend in theatre and for the Pune audiences, the younger generation particularly, to know who Badal Sircar is, what is his ideology, what is the specificity of his theatrical expression, which is so different from the theatre that one knows. And again, I must say that I am really happy to note how the Badal Sircar retrospective in 2005 percolated to the state drama competition. There were seven Badal Sircar plays in that competition which were performed in different parts of the state. They were done by the groups of younger people, the younger generation. They awakened all over again to the fact that here was a very exciting playwright, still very relevant and let's do his plays. I felt very happy that I was able to reintroduce Badal Sircar to the younger generation after all.

VV: Now about the plays you did apart from Badal Sircar's. What kind of influence did this whole experience have, when you did *Rashomon,* for example?

AP: One of the major influences that Badal-da has had on me is of trying to go as deep as possible, trying to go between the lines. Badal-da had given me a way of doing that. I remember very clearly, after *Ballabhpur* when I decided to do *Pagla Ghoda,* I was in Kolkata. I called and told him that I want to do *Pagla Ghoda* and he said 'Great! Go ahead and do it.' I said, 'But I want to discuss that with you' and he said, 'Discuss what? Whatever I had to write I put it down on paper. Now it is entirely up to you—whatever you want to do with that play, you go ahead and do it.' I was quite taken aback because I had seen big egos of small people who were playwrights. They were very insistent that not even a comma in their text should be changed, altered etc., which I respect, of course, but this kind of a complete 'blank cheque' to a new director was totally unexpected. I said 'But I need your okay for the ideas that I have in my mind, so I want to discuss with you. You have to tell me if I am correct.' He said, 'Amol please, there is nothing to discuss. Whatever ideas you have, go ahead and do the play.' In fact, he said, and these were his words,

> Please go ahead and murder my play. You have full freedom to do that. In return, I only retain the right to criticise you publicly and say that you have murdered my play. That is all. But please go ahead and do that. Whatever I have to say I have already put it there; now beyond this don't get stuck by my visualisation, my interpretation, and what I have in mind. If my play can offer you some scope for a different interpretation, some different ways of doing that, I would only be too happy.

That has really been a major inspiration in whatever I did. Not only theatre but also in films. That was a major influence. It really took me in. I could approach, try and find many layers, explore many different ways of looking at my subject or script. I also realised that it is only when a play or the content is full of many possibilities, that it is called a great play. If you don't have interpretations, if it can be done only in one possible way I don't get excited by such plays; I would not call it a great play or a classic. But I would call many of Badal-da's plays great plays as they would offer you so many possibilities, so many ways to explore your own self. If you want to extend yourself, if you want to explore whatever you do not know, struggle to discover how best you can express a particular idea, Badal Sircar is the playwright for you.

VV: You were a part of the two decades of 1960s and '70s when the entire idea of Indian theatre was emerging. How would you respond to Badal-da's contribution to that entire idea of making of Indian theatre?

AP: It is like a wager, if I may use the word, as it is difficult to define (analyse) what is 'Indian'. Today, our existence, the Maharashtrian existence, is distinctly different from the Bengali existence. Why think of other states? In our own state you can see so many different cultures, so many different flavours of the language, so many different flavours in cuisines. That, I think, is our strength. There is something when I say wager, there is something which goes far beyond all these and binds us together, that, I believe, is the Indianness. I mean, that is why a Hindi film song does go and become popular even in south India. So in that sense the influences on each other's works and each other are more evident. I don't have to elaborate on that. But there is one more thing which I would like to mention—that in that period this kind of a multi-state, multi-cultural and multi-lingual dialogue was very much on and I must say I was privileged to be part of that. When a new play by Badal Sircar came up in Bengal, they would inform us immediately that he had written a new play, and ask if we would like to do it or have it. And communication wasn't all that easy as it is today. It is just a click away today and yet we were keen to share it with each other and even beyond that. I think it was one of the most enriching and fulfilling experiences that a playwright of Girish Karnad's caliber, who is himself one of the major playwrights in Indian theatre history, would go out of his way and translate a Badal Sircar play, and then Vijay Tendulkar would translate Mohan Rakesh's play. So this kind of openness and give-and-take did enrich Marathi theatre. I mean, Mohan Rakesh's *Aadhe Adhure* being translated by Vijay Tendullkar, an excellent translation! So it was an enriching experience at many different levels and I think that was one part of this phenomenon—the Indian theatre experiences. It was happening at that time all around us and at a smaller level, as I mentioned, all the theatre groups were passionately involved. We would have our fights after the production was over. We would sit down and criticise each other and even fight, but for the production all the groups would come together and help, because there was a kind of a camaraderie. All of us were trying to work towards the same goal. This was very evident in Mumbai. I am sorry to say it wasn't there in Pune. It is not there even today in Pune. This kind of camaraderie, this kind of interaction, this kind of exchange was not restricted only to theatre—people from literature, visual arts, plastic arts, all would come together, try and find something, some common platform for the exchange of ideas and that really enriched our generation and I think that is why that era was so vibrant.

VV: Today in the morning I was talking to my mother (Shyamala Vanarase) and she remembers watching Badal-babu's FTII workshop demonstration and attending your workshop in the 1970s. She had then written a short play *Pratidnya* which was then performed at various places by various theatre groups. She said that it was the result of the impact of his kind of work that she had as an individual or as a theatre person or as someone who was interested in theatre. I believe there are many more such people. So could you…

AP: I hope there are many more such people, I don't know. Two things I did very consciously—one thing was that in my entire theatre career I did only Indian plays. I did not do any western play, barring the sole exception of *Rashomon,* which I was fascinated with for a different reason. Usually the journey is from theatre to cinema but here it was the other way round—from cinema to theatre. So there were different challenges but that is a different thing. So barring that one exception I never ever did any play that was not an Indian play. That was a very conscious choice for me. Secondly, another thing I consciously did, and that was due to Dubey's influence on me, was that I tried to take theatre outside—not only outside the proscenium arch but also out of Mumbai. Why I said due to Dubey's influence is because Dubey started doing it and I grew up in that tradition. Whenever we would open even a Hindi play in Mumbai, Dubey would say, 'Let's go to Pune and perform.' Why a Hindi play in Pune? What was the audience? There was no audience. But he said, 'No. The same Marathi play lovers would come. Let them be exposed to Hindi theatre and what is good in Hindi theatre.' That's how plays like *Pagla Ghoda* and *Aadhe Adhure* were opened by us first in Mumbai and immediately after that in Pune. I took that a little further and we did plays like *Gochi* where we were exploring spaces that were unheard of. In fact, that terminology had not even entered our dictionaries. Beyond proscenium arch—terrace theatre, luncheon theatre, intimate theatre, street theatre...these terminologies did not exist at that time or we were not aware of them, but we were trying in our own way to explore all those spaces and different ways to reach out to the people. I felt that while we are doing this let's also try and reach out to different people. So let's not restrict our performances to Mumbai and Pune. Let's go to Nashik or Kolhapur, Nagpur, Aurangabad. At least in Maharashtra itself we started doing that. In fact, since you mentioned theatre workshop, I remember conducting a theatre workshop for the first time in Kolhapur. I did that and I could see new ideas and new kind of enthusiasm enter the Kolhapur scenario and youngsters in Kolhapur. That's how we even went to the extent of performing a Marathi play in Ahmedabad, and Bangalore—because somewhere we had this intrinsic faith that the language of theatre overwrites everything else. Unless, of course, it is a very verbose play, which is solely dependent on language or words. We were sure that they will be able to respond to us and they did. So it was on different levels that I made an attempt to reach out with new ideas and I am very happy that your mother remembers that fondly.

VV: There are two more things. Briefly, how would you sum up Badal-da's contribution to Marathi theatre? And how do you look at it today?

I see that you initially had done a lot of work and then it started percolating as you mentioned. Suddenly when you see a group from Ambejogai doing Badal-da's play, how do you feel about it?

AP: See it is very simple. When you talk of Marathi theatre and particularly the journey of experimental theatre, whether you like it or not, or whether you intend to or not, the name Badal Sircar would obviously be there—invariably. Though he is not a Marathi playwright, though he has written in some foreign language, he is part and parcel of that entire growth, the entire journey of experimentation in drama that happened in Maharashtra. Badal Sircar's is an inevitable name and all the top practitioners of theatre of that time wanted to do a Badal Sircar play in Marathi. Be it Arvind-Sulabha Deshpande…I think Vijaya Bai also did Badal-da's play; P.L. Deshpande wanted to translate one of Badal-da's plays into Marathi…so all this exchange and interaction was going on in Marathi. So I don't have to elaborate on the influence of Badal Sircar—in what ways and how many ways. You simply cannot omit Badal Sircar's name when you talk of the complete journey and exploration that experimental Marathi theatre did in that period.

I think I am very privileged to have had such a wonderful professional and personal relationship with Badal-da. In fact, when we did his retrospective here in 2005, I think it was also very important to see how Badal-da was a part of the Marathi theatre scene and culture…. He was emotionally moved, thoroughly moved to see such a retrospective in which anybody and everybody in theatre was present to perform, not only to applaud but to perform. From every corner of the country they came together. At the end of the day, at the end of the retrospective, Badal-da said and he meant every single word of it: 'The kind of love, affection and respect you Maharashtrians, particularly from Pune, have given me, I haven't got that kind of a thing even in Kolkata or in my own state.' And he had tears in his eyes. The gratitude is mutual.

AN ENCOUNTER WITH BADAL SIRCAR

Heisnam Kanhailal

The meeting with Badal Sircar and the consequent practice under him for a short span of time were truly an encounter. It is not that I learned his system and followed it fully, as that would mean abandoning my own practice, nor can I say that the roots of my work are based in his method. So, how the encounter took place and the areas that had an impact on me, are the main features of this essay.

My last meeting with Badal Sircar, after a gap of eight years, was in 1981 at Kolkata, where I conducted a workshop sponsored by Seagull for three weeks. His sudden presence as one of the participants surprised me, and made me feel psychologically inhibited. While fighting my own inhibitions I understood that he was there because he had chosen to remain a learner throughout his life—a positive attitude towards learning in the practice of art making. This confirms what others have said—'a true artist is the child who never wants to grow'. In the later phase of my practice this has remained with me and enabled me to perceive the true nature of an artist. In my view, the spirit of a true artist is formed by a harmonious integration of two basic elements of his soul, the cognitive and the normative. The cognitive element has to do with sensing, perceiving, understanding and so on, that transforms itself into fiction, whilst the normative guides it in making moral sense of life of humility and sincerity. It is interesting to find a similar articulation in France's Jacques Copeau and America's Joshep Chaikin who phrased it as 'monstrous sincerity' and 'urgent sincerity' respectively.

Since this encounter there has been a long gap of thirty years and hence no dialogue with him. Very recently, Kirti Jain asked me, on behalf of Natarang Pratisthan, to write a piece on Badal Sircar for this book, particularly on my contact with him during my early formative years and the impact he had on me. I immediately accepted this offer as it provided me with an opportunity to do something that is already overdue in my case, as I honestly respect him as the true rebel in Indian theatre.

A few questions came up before me to find out what this something could be. Of them the main one was whether I should speak of him in a way that glorifies his life of rebellion or whether I should submit a critique on his vision and practice? In my answer, I reject the above and follow the principle of 'what are the things not to be done'. Perhaps then, I may come to what is expected generally by the readers. Now, therefore I will look back afresh, and critically, at my contact with Badal Sircar and assess the impact he has had on the formation of my own practice. This piece is therefore narratively and analytically approached.

Context

1969 and 1970—these two years in the last century were a time of intense psychological loneliness and isolation for me. This was because of my personal failure in proving myself as a theatre maker, as also the uncertainty regarding the direction I wanted to continue in.

The theatre mainstream at that time was occupied by Alkazi's academically and intellectually defined model of production style based on the European conventions of urban theatre. As playwrights, Badal Sircar and Mohan Rakesh took centre stage for their intellectually empowered new plays dealing with urban middle class life. In my own region too, this wind of change arrived alongside the western movements of absurd theatre and existential theatre. I felt completely lost in this storm. Simply put, I failed to cope with the then legitimate theatre. I felt like a stray dog.

Thanks to my instinctive urge, for a year in 1971, I wandered bewildered, into the ethnic jungle of impulses, peeping through the wild sources of my wild native soil, to get some clues for a possible direction. The word 'wild' here is not used in its modern pejorative sense, meaning out of control, but in its original sense, that means to live a natural life—elemental, pristine, vital. And consequently, this turned out to be my wild teacher, wild mentor, wild mother that gives birth to the lightening sources of creativity, and supports the inner and outer lives of the 'doers' who risk such a cultural expedition in the wild space of theatre.

Why I was shadowing *Nognthang Leima* (*The Lightning Lady*) of my Meitei creation myth in her home of dark woods, was to explore an original alternative for an instructive and subtle awareness in reacting to the dominant tensions of the time, in my local context.

The search resulted in *Tamnalai* (*The Haunting Spirit*), my first experimental public production in January 1972. It succeeded in creating shattering ways of seeing and doing theatre, dominantly physical rather than psychological, and without heavy sets, costume, make up and background music. It broke the grounds of legitimate theatre by making the body speak. It vindicated itself by removing acting tricks and embodying the bitter social experiences in the body in a manner that it had a haunting effect. I wrote the text of this production as a theatre script (like a filmscript) rather than a formal play. Images were transformed into theatrical (non-dramatic) fluid actions, rhythmic and sensuous, with logical development. Non-dramatic patterned speech (charged by music) and a choreographic design of the roles became the process of acting in order to focus on soul-expression and soul-satiation on the part of the actor. The sole intention was to create a 'haunting effect' in the audience.

In the later phase of my practice, I developed this sense of a haunting effect into a well propounded aesthetics. The efficacy of art is justified by the inner dialogue between the actor and spectator at the sensory and spiritual levels. This energetically charged dialogue creates 'alertness', or disturbs the body of the spectator while striking at the core of the spirit of human resilience. On the other hand, it is an inner process aimed at creating a haunting effect by informing and provoking the individual soul of the spectator and in him, creating a perception of a meaning that lies between experience and reflection.

Sabitri's presence operated the transformation of this aesthetic sense into action and justified its efficacy in *Tamnalai* whilst she privileges herself over the character. Since then she has been practising this as a conscious process towards the ideal of a total actor.

In the later phase of our practice we were able to formulate whatever we had artistically accomplished into a conscious process. But, we could not articulate the process of communication at the time of creation. This is because whatever has been accomplished artistically has been done through natural instinct and intuition compounded by tradition and spontaneity. That is why Ayn Rand, the objectivist philosopher and novelist, comments: 'They (artists) do not know: we know.'

The then Manipuri audiences and particularly Badal Sircar's positive reaction reinforced my decision to continue my experimental practice. *Tamnalai* created a closer contact between Badal Sircar and me. In September 1972, Badal-da (since then I began to address him 'Da'), commented, just after seeing the performance, that he had seen many plays in the country and abroad, and had found Sabitri to be the best actor. In the beginning he found the play melodramatic but as the process continued it became tense and moving. He found the choreographic characterisation particularly theatrically profound.

Contact

I spent a very brief span of time in contact with Badal-da, beginning from February of the next year. I spent this month at Kolkata, learning psychophysical exercises from him. He told me that he had learnt these exercises from Richard Schechner in America under the Nehru Fellowship Project that had been awarded to him. This project became the basis of the foundational formation of his notional 'Third Theatre' that rejects the proscenium theatre in favour of an intimate one, which he named Angan Manch, a space where urban and rural theatre get synthesised.

I came back to Imphal with a basic practical knowledge of the above mentioned exercises. The State Akademi agreed to my proposal of a workshop under Badal-da, which was organised at Imphal for three weeks in April 1973. Here I was given the opportunity of being assistant director to Badal-da. Below is a brief summation of that workshop experience.

At the very outset a 'circle' was introduced which underlined the absence of hierarchy in the group with the director too letting go of his privileged position and becoming a member like other members of the group. He was just an artistic leader who initiated things. Any activity that happened had to continue in circulation within the circumference of the circle; and actions and reactions were spontaneously at work. We also drank tea in the circle. Badal-da managed to remain out of the frame of a political leader who conducts indoctrination, and also from that of the institutional classroom teacher. He did not allow the participants to call him 'Sir' and all of us addressed him only as 'Badal-da'.

No guests were allowed in the circle. Exceptions were made only in special cases and even then, only on the condition that the guest would observe the entire session. The circle became a discipline that led towards the ideological formation of theatre as social action which was Badal-da's vital concern.

In this circle, Badal-da carried out exercises in an initiatory process of acting. These self-contained exercises were concentrated on body rolls, head rolls, serpentine movements, body bending, vocal resonation and so on. Exercises for strength, flexibility and endurance are for normal awareness. What was specific was for the actor to create a conscious process based on how the blood flows, how muscles move and energy is restored, in order to prevent his/her body from fighting with itself during acting. The main focus was on the spine, which plays a vital function in loosening muscles and restoring spent energy.

- Technically, these self-contained exercises transform automatic behaviour into a conscious process so that the body becomes supple and malleable.

- Ideologically, it is a psycho-physical process of de-urbanisation that removes urban sophistication and brings one closer to the rural nature of body behaviour.
- Artistically, suppleness and de-urbanisation interrelate to acting.

The concerns of the spine and de-urbanisation are not new in the context of the actor-training in the West. The 'method acting' trend right from Stanislavski through Poland's Staniweski in the last century addressed these concerns effectively in the course of its objective scientific research aimed at understanding human nature. I will return to this issue further in detail in the later part of this essay.

In group exercises games were introduced. To remove social inhibition two actors were called upon to stand facing each other and asked to play the mirroring game without following logical imitation. This was a psychological process through which the actor discovered his own social persona (from within his private persona) in the context of a social interaction.

As the workshop progressed, Trust Games followed In these one actor jumped down from a high level while trusting that his partners would catch him and not let him fall. In another situation, the eyes of an actor were blind-folded and he was asked to move freely in a space where others had put big obstacles. He had to move freely with confidence that partners would make sure that he did not bump into them. As in acrobatic exercise, here too, there are elements both of danger and safety within this situation. For some, the initial and unfamiliar experience and the possibility of falling and clashing can create a nervousness which needs to be overcome through the bond of trust.

These games make one aware of the qualities of trust and mutuality, thereby establishing a sense of confidence and cooperation within a social unit that is born from a theatre culture that concerns itself with theatre sociology. It further ideologically contributed towards Badal-da's belief in social action.

I did not find any specific acting sessions. However, there were play-making sessions. These allowed the actors to explore themselves through a series of situations and actions where they were asked to react spontaneously (not act) outside the frame of naturalistic acting. They were asked to trust the body to execute the role given as well as substitute for the props and sets demanded by the situation.

Now let me come to performance. *Spartacus* was taken up for production. Badal-da had written this play particularly for his Angan Manch. Breaking away from his past style he explored the idea through a simplified narrative in a verbal and physical dramaturgy. He treated the verbal as the original text. To me it seems that he preferred a performed text to a performance text as such. He created *Spartacus* as a more focused reflection on the historical meaning of oppression and resistance from his social stand point. He intended that the performed text addressed itself to an audience that was located in a social space where the urban and rural could meet. What he expected from the actor was the preparation required to address this kind of audience. His political considerations seemed to be stronger than his aesthetic considerations. His intention was no more than educating the audience through philosophy and a method of practice that was different from that of Bertolt Brecht. While the latter gave equal emphasis to both philosophy and acting and considered acting to be the carrier of his philosophy, in the case of Badal-da acting appears less attended. On the other hand he declares publicly that he is an amateur and his theatre also belongs to this category.

I have a reservation as to how art could be simplified in an arithmetical sense. Badal-da believes in simplification. Perhaps this might be the ideological reason for making it simple—perceptibly simple without sacrificing the efficacy of art.

He appears in the guise of a taskmaster who manages both training and production in a new process unfamiliar to all the actors, in a very short period of three weeks. The success can be partly attributed to the instinctive response of the actors who being close to rural nature, still had physical and mental flexibility, so their senses were truly at work. Performing in a mandap (*Spartacus* was performed in the Kali Mai *mandap* of Imphal), surrounded by the audience, is a traditional and familiar experience in Manipur. So the spatial and cultural conditions demanded of this kind of performance were not causing much of a performative perplexity to the actor. The actors could simply experience a new possibility of coming out of the proscenium frame fortified by dry rules and rituals. For Badal-da, his Angan Manch could vehemently defy the class consciousness and illusionism inherited by the proscenium, and locate his challenge in a social space where there was no class discrimination. He saw his Third Theatre as that which allowed communication to flow to the expected audience intimately and directly.

Impact on my Practice

The contact with Badal-da at this point of his practice excited me and made me aware of the need for discipline which is significant in all diverse contexts of theatre. I had some sense of it in the kind of institutional practice that Alkazi emphasised on to maximise professional impact. But Badal-da reached it differently as he was in individualised practice which is worked out under a certain personal philosophy. The reason for my excitement was that I had now got some clues about how to form a sense of discipline in the context of my own individual socio-cultural experiences. The principles he applied could not be followed as they were, as he had worked them out for his own specific context. I believe that the aesthetics born out of an individual's personal context decides his own methodology.

I received his practice as my wordless experience, and began to articulate it later in the process of forming my own practice systematically. How the evolution of these personal systems took place can be traced back through processes of mutual cross-fertilisation. Finding similar interests, rejecting previous ideas, assimilating new ideas, re-interpreting for new elements and so on, have given me the space to clarify a new trajectory. We have no reason to deny a universal phenomenon, but we should keep ourselves open to searching for our own direction. I join Joseph Chaikin when he says that 'inspiration and urgent sincerity have affected me and many others…still, we are on different journeys.'

I am deeply rooted in my socio-ethnic tradition and am a progeny of it. My practice tends to be the localised theatre of identity, difference and nationalism, although I make it strategic rather than obviously political. In this context, the principles of rights and equality proposed by Badal-da for the social unit of the 'circle' are integrated with my notion of the traditional values of duty and obligation/ performance that serve social life from family to community and then to nation. It aims to see how democratic principles and traditional values co-exist as a single vital process in serving a human unit that can invent a new traditional value of theatre making. I also look further into the traditional value of practice—*shraddha, sadhana* and *abhyasa*, and how these can be re-interpreted in the making of a new tradition.

Now the circle lives within and without as it spreads out ecologically to all spheres of the environment of theatre making. When it is located in my context it becomes the spine of learning that begins with understanding how to learn in reciprocity. An elder asks someone 'to do' something, while the junior says 'yes'. Through this process we understand the meaning of 'learning reciprocally', in a way that ensures humility and sincerity as a way of life of the practitioner. Sabitri still continues to tell her juniors, 'I am not worthy to be a master. Don't address me as a master. I still continue to be a "doer."'

Urbanisation in Manipur is a very recent social experience. Our childhood has been spent in rural and natural environments. Apart from the traditionally conditioned manners and behaviour in human relationships, we still work on the basis of natural responses in opposition to the urban way of life that is 'sport like—aseptic and banal'. All the exercises and games introduced by Badal-da are very familiar to us as we have played them joyfully in contact with the earth and natural environment as part of our daily routines during our childhood. What is mainly derived from him is the system that re-organises and re-defines the exercises objectively in order to discipline the actor.

After continuing these exercises for a couple of years the process became lifeless because of mechanical repetition. The confrontation with this mechanicalness on the one hand, and aesthetic demands on the other, compelled me to look into my own tradition. Our actors began to learn Thangta (Manipuri martial art), ritual performances, traditional story telling, speech patterns of specific castes, old vibrant songs of Meitei and Naga tribes and so on. This learning took about eight years. On the basis of the exercises introduced by Badal-da we continued to explore and evolve intricate extra-body techniques for an instinctive and subtle form of awareness. We also continue to look into the materials and sources of other cultural traditions/forms like *kalari*, *chhau*, *terukuttu*, *yakshagan*, *vipasana* meditation, *taichi*, and *shamanic* tradition of Malaysia, Javanese and Balinese traditions of performance art, etc.

The empirical nature of theatre demands we employ a trial and error method that enables us to create a process for practical objective impact, and also helps elicit the essence of traditional values. It should cognitively transform materials/sources into abstraction for subtler expression. By now we have learnt how the cognitive function transforms itself into fiction in the artistic process of theatre making.

The impact of my contact with Badal-da has thus been the inspiration that led me to decide on my own road and embark on my own different journey. Thanks to Badal-da for picking me up from the wilderness.

Conclusion

Badal-da has been continuing to perform regular public shows from the day he launched his Third Theatre. He maintains this schedule strictly. This is also an unavoidable part of his discipline and commitment towards a social movement. He succeeded undoubtedly in this respect. In my case, I do not count this as part of my practice as I need to give due attention to my research in theatre, which lays emphasis on training and workshops in relation to theatre making. And our attitude towards practice is shaped by the sense of professional responsibility though we can't be professionals in the true sense due to our Indian reality. Indian art and culture 'occupies a space which falls between two spaces—the place left by the withdrawal of the state and the place the corporate agency refuses to enter.' It is indeed remarkable that despite this vacuum we are able to work with a certain degree of artistic and social responsibility.

Badal-da, it seems to me, gives less attention to the artistic process than to his regular public shows, as a way of ensuring that the movement for social action should not stop. There are also other reasons for his stand of remaining an 'amateur' throughout. He never takes any financial support from anyone. He never looks towards media or established public relation departments for anything. For all this he has his own strategic explanations which no one can question. All these help him ensure that his theatre remains in the form of exercise.

I do not see any other individual or group in Manipur or for that matter in the entire north-east of India, which has been able to continue its work under his influence. Recently I came across a group named Chorus, based at Silchar, Assam. It is led by Biswajit Das. Badal-da conducted workshops with them twice in 1986 and 1993. The group was active in the 1980s and '90s, and worked with enthusiasm in the villages, particularly for the labourers in the tea garden. Now, it is very difficult to find enthusiasts from the younger generation of the entire region, who can be motivated and oriented towards this kind of practice, as it needs immense commitment, challenge, rigour and risk. They are more interested in techniques that get them overnight fame and money and help them go to Delhi and other big cities.

I respect him immensely as one of few rebels Indian theatre has produced so far. I conclude this essay with the following quote from my own essay, 'Ritual Theatre' (Theatre of Transition)[1]:

> What we have learnt from our past heretics (Stanislavski and Meyerhold, Craig, Copeau, Artaud, Brecht, Grotowski, and Badal Sircar and Habib Tanvir in India) is to be in transition which invents personal values of our own theatre. Transition is itself a culture. In the universal perspective, every culture must have three aspects: material production by means of particular techniques, biological reproduction making possible the transmission of experience from generation to generation, and the production of meanings.
>
> Meanings are essential for a culture. In the absence of it there is no culture.

1. *Published in issue No. 10, 2004 of* Theatre India *of NSD, New Delhi and in* Theatre in Theory: *1900–2000, Blackwell Press, USA, December 2007*

TRACING BADAL SIRCAR'S LEGACY IN SOUTH INDIA

Pralayan

The name 'Badal Sircar' has been familiar to me since my college days, during the late 1970s.

We started our group Chennai Kalai Kuzhu in Chennai in 1984. Since its inception a major emphasis of our activity has been on open-air political theatre. You can call it 'Third Theatre' or 'Street Theatre,' or even 'Open-air Political Theatre.' But our activities are totally identified with this genre of theatre.

We do not do only open-air and street performances, but are also at ease with proscenium spaces. We have done several proscenium productions through our group.

In the late 1980s and early '90s, whenever and wherever we performed our plays, after the performance someone from the audience would come to me and ask questions like: 'Have you worked with Badal Sircar?' or 'Have you got your orientation from Badal Sircar?' I faced this quite often. Actually, it was a difficult question for me to answer. Because I know about Badal Sircar and his Third Theatre, but I have never attended any of his workshops so far.

I've attended theatre workshops conducted by Prof. S.Ramanujam, Prof. S.P. Srinivasan, S.V. Sahasranamam, disciples of Jose Chiramul from Kerala and Prasanna, Raghunandan, Basavalingaiah from Karnataka, Ingeborg-Mayer from Grotowski's Polish Theatre Laboratory. I also attended a one-month workshop conducted by M.K. Raina in Delhi in 1991, under the aegis of SAHMAT. Habib Tanvir and several other stalwarts of Indian theatre took sessions in that workshop. That was my orientation in theatre up to the year 1992.

Badal Sircar came to Tamil Nadu and conducted workshops once in 1980 then in 1992 and 1994.

I met him in 1992 when he was doing a workshop in Chennai. Theatre practitioners of Chennai were invited to a face-to-face discussion with Badal Sircar by the organisers of the workshop. The entire discussion was around the Sangeet Natak Akademi's 'Theatre of the Roots' Project. The day before that meet Badal Sircar had seen one of the Tamil productions selected for the 'Young Director's Award' of that project. It was a well-made production done in the traditional koothu style of Tamil Nadu. Badal Sircar dismissed that production branding it as an 'export production'. After that meet I invited him to see our performance.

We performed three of our plays—*Mahanagar* (Metropolis), *James Fund* or *James Bond* and *Uram* (The Fertiliser). The performances were held at a slum which is situated in the heart of Chennai, near Loyola College. After the performance he expressed his appreciation of it and talked to our group.

He said to us, 'Your performance has a sense of rhythm, physicalisation, choreography, music and imagery that actually makes it dynamic. Nice, keep it up!'

So far this has been my only direct encounter with Badal Sircar.

But while trying to understand or decode the questions of getting our orientation from Badal Sircar, in a deeper sense, I realised that those who asked me those questions found some legacy of Badal Sircar in our performances. It is quite natural. After all Badal Sircar is the person who conceptualised the idea of theatre in the open-air and non-conventional performing spaces. He developed a new idiom and a language for that kind of theatre. He travelled all over the country and disseminated his idea of theatre everywhere. It reached innumerable theatre practitioners, directly or indirectly.

Safdar Hashmi also started doing theatre in the open-air and non-conventional performing spaces around the same time. But he did not travel that much or spread his ideas of theatre. Only after Safdar's brutal murder did his ideas on street theatre spread all over the country.

Here I'm not trying to compare Safdar Hashmi's theatre with that of Badal Sircar. What I want to do is to try to trace Badal Sircar's legacy and see how it directly or indirectly had an impact in the contemporary theatre scenario in the southern part of India, particularly in Tamil Nadu.

In Tamil Nadu, before our Chennai Kalai Kuzhu, this kind of open-air political theatre practice was noticed in 1977-78 in Mu.Ramaswamy's Nija Nataka Iyakkam in Madurai, Aswaghosh alias Rajendra Cholan's Chenjudar Kalaikuzhu in Neyveli, K.S. Rajendran Veethi Nataka Iyakkam or Veethi, Agni Puthran, K.V. Ramaswamy, Veerachamy and many others in Chennai, at a time when all these groups were taking theatre to the streets, parks, beaches and other non-conventional performing spaces.

The theatre activists of these groups participated in the state level theatre workshop which was hosted by Gandhigram Rural University, Dindugal District, on its premises and conducted by Prof. S. Ramanujam and Prof. S.P. Srinivasan from June 20-26, 1977. Actually this workshop gave an impetus to a new kind of theatre activity and added momentum to theatrical activity in Tamil Nadu. But preference for non-conventional performing spaces and taking theatre to the streets was influenced by Badal Sircar and his thoughts.

One of the participants of the June 1977 workshop and the founder of the Nija Nataka Iyakkam, Mu. Ramaswamy, recalls Badal Sircar's influence on his theatre in his book titled *Tamil Theatre, Yesterday-Today-Tomorrow* (*Tamil Natakam, Netru indru Nalai;* Mu. Ramaswamy, Rudra Pathippagam, August 1998). In that book he says: 'Not only my theatre activity, but most of the theatre groups of that time were influenced by Badal Sircar and his thoughts.' Some of Badal Sircar's early plays like *Ebong Indrajit* and *Baki Itihas* were translated into Tamil in the mid-1970s. Theatre practitioners of that time were familiar with the Tamil version of *Ebong Indrajit.*

When Badal Sircar came to Tamil Nadu in 1980 and conducted a ten-day workshop in September at Cholamandal artists' village, 28 people participated in that workshop. Among the participants K.S. Rajendran, Mu. Ramaswamy, K.A. Gunasekaran, Gnani, Veerachamy, Veli. Rangarajan, Amshankumar are still doing theatre or something which is associated with theatre. One of the participants who was also a playwright, K.V. Ramaswamy, has passed away.

Writer and critic, Venkat Swaminathan, recalled this workshop: 'He (Badal Sircar) gave orientation to the actors not just to perform the roles given to them but oriented them to be in that role. His thrust to the actors was not performing but being.'

One of the participants, Amshankumar, later turned into a filmmaker. He made several feature and documentary films. One of his documentary films was on Badal Sircar and his Third Theatre. In a conversation with me, Amshankumar recalls Badal Sircar's first workshop at Chennai in the year 1980. He says: 'People like me attended that workshop to know the Badal Sircar of *Ebong Indrajit*. There we came to know that Badal Sircar had rejected those plays and his earlier notions of theatre. It really shocked and surprised us.'

But people like Mu. Ramaswamy did not feel this way, nor was he confused. When he started his group, Nija Nataka Iyakkam, which literally means 'Real Theatre Movement' in Tamil, in 1978, he was aware of Badal Sircar and his concept of Third Theatre, and also considered his 1980 workshop in Chennai as an important and a new beginning in Tamil contemporary theatre practice, much like the workshop conducted by Prof. Ramanujam in 1977. His productions like *Velai*, *Kabadi Match*, *Niyayangkal*, are open-air oriented productions which were very influenced by the concept of Third Theatre.

When Nija Nataka Iyakkam plans to perform a play somewhere, the actors of the group carry a small cardboard hung on their necks, with the name of the play, venue, date and time of the performance written on it. They travel with this cardboard in city buses and on the streets, to announce the play and attract audiences for their performances. These things were reported in the little magazines of the time. As an under-graduate student, I came to know about the performances and such methods of publicity only through such little magazines.

Personally I came to know about this kind of theatre in 1978, at a state level conference of Tamil Nadu Progressive Writers' Association held at Coimbatore. A theatre group, Samudaya, had come there from the Kolar district of Karnataka and performed a play called *Oh! Chaasnala* in that conference. That play tried to depict the accident where several coal mine workers of Bihar drowned to death in the water that seeped into the mine. It was totally a mimetic play. No dialogues were used. At the end of the play a girl appeared like a television news presenter and announced the death of several workers by drowning. Words were used only in this last scene.

The play was very well received by the audience in that conference. After this performance the Samudaya Kolar district unit performers went to Chennai and performed *Oh!Chaasnala* there.

I've not seen this play, but people who had seen it described it to me. Many people only heard about it from those who attended the Coimbatore Conference but got inspired enough to start theatre activity in their city. Actually this performance gave inspiration to start several new groups in Tamil Nadu, such as Veethi in Chennai and Nija Nataka Iyakkam in Madurai. Later I came to know that the play had been produced by Samudaya in the workshop done with Badal Sircar. He had conducted a two-week workshop with Samudaya in 1977-78, which initiated Samudaya into the Third Theatre.

Krishnaswamy's *Belchi* and *May Day* and Laskhmi Chandrashekhar and M.C. Anand's play *Struggle,* were the outcome of this workshop with Badal Sircar. Samudaya was started in 1975 as an amateur theatre group in Bangalore to make a meaningful intervention in Kannada theatre by Prasanna, an NSD graduate of the early 1970s. It went on to become a socio-cultural movement in Karnataka. In his book *Staging a Change,* Narendar Pani mentioned:

> Samudaya's first play was *Hutava Badidare* [*Hitting a Snake's Mound*].This play was adapted by K.V. Narayan from a play by Samsa—*Vigada Vikrama Raya*. The feudal nature of the original

> play was completely altered to a progressive message by changing its focus. The protagonists were no longer members of the royal family but two palace guards. Backed by some magnificent folk music by B.V. Karanth, *Hutava Badidare* is still performed in Karnataka. Prasanna's direction of this play was interesting in itself. Though each scene had a good deal of Brechtian influence, the overall format was that of Company theatre.

I am mentioning these things to reveal the fact that actually Samudaya was the pioneer of the travelling street theatre activity or open-air political theatre activity in southern India. When they started Samudaya, theatre was not being done in open- air or street corners. The initial productions were proscenium bound and in the company theatre format. Not only that, the next productions done by Prasanna were also in the same format. His short plays like *Pataa Ondhu* [Lesson-1] was an adaptation of Ionesco's *Lesson* and *Pataa Yeradu* was a dramatisation of a long poem by the Dalit activist-poet, Siddalinghaiah. Even though these two productions tried to experiment with or expand the proscenium spaces, they still needed an auditorium or some conventional performing space for performance.

Only after having a workshop with Badal Sircar did Samudaya start doing street theatre or open-air political theatre. One Amit Sircar, (a scientist working in Viswesrayya Institute in Bangalore, was active in the Bengali Association of Bangalore and also associated with Samudaya activities as a designer for their posters and other printing work), suggested that Samudaya invite Badal Sircar for a workshop. Prasanna, who was familiar with Badal Sircar and his work, made this workshop happen. The Bengali Association of Bangalore and Samudaya jointly organised and invited Badal Sircar and his troupe, Satabdi, to Bangalore in early 1978. Satabdi performed *Procession (Michhil)* and two other plays in Bangalore. Then Badal Sircar conducted a two-week long workshop with Samudaya members. Janardan, Lakshmi Chandrasekhar, M.G. Venkatesh, Gundanna, Krishnaswamy, Surendra (the present General Secretary of Samudaya), M.C. Anand, Navarasan and several others participated in that workshop.

One of the participants and former secretary of Samudaya, Gundanna, recalls and shares his experiences of Badal Sircar's workshop in a conversation with me:

> Actually Badal Sircar's workshop pushed the boundaries of our theatre activities. We did not have many auditoria in our state at that time. Our activities had been limited to urban centres that had an auditorium, though we had devised a makeshift and mobile stage to travel, and did perform some of our proscenium productions even in villages. But such shows were limited. In this workshop we learnt to work in open-air and arena spaces. After this workshop several productions were made and several groups were formed all over the state. We became a state-level organization then.

In that workshop two productions were prepared—*Oh! Chasnala!* and another done by Prasanna titled *Bathre Sangappa Kole Vivakarna*' (About Bathre Sangappa's murder) which was a dramatic introspection of an activist's murder.

Narendar Pani wrote about this workshop in his book:

> Of course. The greatest use of this technique, i.e. Third Theatre, was in Samudaya's participation in the Chickmagalur Lok Sabha bi-election. Four Samudaya troupes from Mangalore and Bangalore put up over two hundred and fifty shows which were seen by seven lakh people. The whole experience has enriched Samudaya especially in the art of getting across to the village people.

After the workshop Samudaya members produced several plays for arena spaces. Amongst them the most significant one was Krishnaswamy's *Belchi*. In Narendar Pani's words, '*Belchi* was one of the most striking plays Samudaya has done so far.'

The play *Belchi* deals with the gruesome massacre of Dalit agricultural workers by landlords in a remote Bihar village. New actors were recruited for this play which was done as a workshop production. Samudaya travelled extensively with this play and performed it in many places, including Chennai, in 1979.

In 1978, on reading about Samudaya's travelling theatrical ventures in open-air and arena spaces, a poet and playwright, Karivallur Murali, of the Kannur District of Kerala, started doing open-air performances and took them to nearby villages. He named this theatrical expedition *kala jatha*, which means travelling art or travelling theatre. (Karivallur Murali himself shared this fact with me.)

Later the idea of *kala jatha* was taken up in a big way and popularised by the Kerala Sastra Sahitya Parishat (KSSP), a peoples' science movement of Kerala in the early 1980s.

Meanwhile, in 1980 Badal Sircar conducted a workshop at Trivandrum for two weeks. Samudaya's Prasanna also accompanied him in that workshop. Actually Prasanna was the strongest advocate of Badal Sircar's Third Theatre in those days. In 1979 a three-day theatre festival was held at Thanjavur, in Tamil Nadu, organised by the Tamil Nadu Progressive Writers' Association. More than 20 theatre groups participated in that festival.

I was a student then. With my fellow student friends, who were from my native town of Tiruvannamalai, we performed two short plays, *Parimuthal* (Seizure) and *Vattathirku Veliye* (Beyond the Circle), in that festival. We did not have any proper orientation to do these kind of plays then, just some idea from what one had heard about the play *Oh! Chasnala!*

I saw some of the well-developed open air performances in that festival. Particularly Parambai Selvan's *Niraakarippukal* (Negligence), and Aswaghosh's *Visaaranaikal* (Enquiries). There were also some important plays that had experimented with proscenium spaces like Melur Kalyanasundaram's *Kalangkalin Nizalil* (In the Shadow of Times, a loose adaptation of a Bengali play) and Jeyanthan's *Ninaikkappadum* (Has to be Thought), which were performed by Madurai People's Theatre.

Samudaya's Prasanna gave a lecture during that festival, sharing his experience of Badal Sircar's workshop and telling us how it changed and led Samudaya's activities to new frontiers. It was a very provocative speech. In a sense he was actually explaining Badal Sircar's Third Theatre concept. Somebody got agitated, some felt it was polemical, but most people, like me, got excited by his speech. In fact, throughout the three-day festival I spent most of my time with Prasanna, engaging in a discussion and dialogue with him. It was very enlightening.

After the Trivandrum workshop most of the participants started doing Third Theatre. Among them the most important was the eminent theatre personality of Kerala, late Jose Chiramul. Jose Chiramul, a graduate of Trichur School of Drama, Calicut University, was the first person in Kerala to take up Badal Sircar's Third Theatre plays *Procession*, *Spartacus* and *Bhoma* for productions, in the early 1980s. He was also responsible for the KSSP's *kala jatha* plays. Most of the plays performed by KSSP in their *kala jatha*s (theatre caravans) were designed and directed by Jose Chiramul.

Oru Chothyam [One Question], a short musical play written by Karivallur Murali and inspired by Bertolt Brecht's poem, is a typical example of the development of the Third Theatre. In this short play actors used their bodies in a novel way. They created the Taj Mahal, debris of the war, and so many other visual images – all through the actors in an empty space.

We too did that play in Tamil through our group, Chennai Kalai Kuzhu.

When KSSP wanted to do a *kala jatha* in Tamil Nadu in association with Tamil Nadu Science Forum, they invited Chennai Kalai Kuzhu for that mission. Eight actors from our group, including myself, and eight actors from KSSP, collaborated and had a workshop for two weeks in Kanyakumari District. For them I translated all the KSSP plays into Tamil. The design, images, choreography, movements and music of the original were retained, only the language changed. We then travelled all over Tamil Nadu for a month and performed in almost 140 centres and got a tremendous response everywhere. We learnt a lot from these experiences. Actually this one month of the performance tour gave us a great insight into the potential and challenges of performing in open-air spaces.

Among the KSSP plays, *Resist Oh! Friends* [*Ethirkkanum Koottare*] and *Come Along Everybody* [*Kuravar Kali*], written by the late Thangappan Pillai, were the best examples of the fusion of First and Second theatre as categorised by Badal Sircar. Traditional dance forms of the fisher folk called *kolkali*, and dance forms of the hill tribes called *kuravarisai* or *kuravarkali*, were taken and transformed into modern theatre performance with contemporary relevance.

In the year 1987 KSSP spearheaded an initiative called Bharat Jan Vigyan Jatha, known as BJVJ, with the help of Department of Science and Technology under the Ministry of Culture, Government of India. Five theatre groups travelled all over the country and performed all the KSSP plays in all the Indian languages. I too was part of that two month long BJVJ. While KSSP performances were inspired by the Third Theatre, they never tried to create or do productions like Badal Sircar's *Bhoma* or *Spartacus,* which provide an experience of viewing 'Total Theatre'. There has been some criticism of KSSP *jatha*s. Though the KSSP *jatha*s popularised the Third Theatre concept and took it to another realm, it reduced its methodology to just disseminate messages, converting it into a 'media strategy'.

Apart from engaging himself in producing the plays for KSSP *jatha*s, Jose Chiramul formed his theatre group Roots at Trichur in 1983. He took his group to the villages and performed most of the plays of Badal Sircar. In 1988 theatre activist and scholar, Eugene von Erven from Utrecht University, also accompanied the group to a village where *Bhoma* was being performed.

He writes:

> On Sunday, 17 April 1988, I travelled with Roots to a tiny fishing village near Ernakulam. When the play started at seven, there were easily a couple of thousand spectators seated in the round. Jose Chiramul introduced the play by explaining that the people would get to see a new kind of theatre without make-up, without microphones and without the elevated make-shift stage normally used for theatre performances. He also told them that the play would lack a continuous

> storyline and that it was inspired by the real life story of a simple Bengali lumberjack named *Bhoma*. The spectators then watched silently and with intense concentration during the one hour performance that followed.
>
> (*The Playful Revolution: Theatre and Liberation in Asia* by Eugene von Erven, Indiana University Press, 1992, p. 131)

Similarly, a great deal of vibrant theatre activity happened in Tamil Nadu after the 1980 workshop with Badal Sircar. One of the participants, Aswaghosh alias Rajendra Cholan, worked with Tirupur hosiery workers and produced a play called *Vattangal* [literally meanings 'circles'] and performed it in many places. The play deals with the problems of unemployment, price rise, corruption, exploitation by moneylenders of agricultural workers, and so on. It does not have a linear or continuous storyline. It was designed as a collage. A folk dance form is used for the chorus which links the different episodes and interprets them with a distinct perspective. It is a well-made play with the audiences seated around.

Makkal Kalai Ilakkiya Kazakam (People's Art and Literary Association), a Marxist-Leninist outfit, also started doing theatre in the open after this workshop. One of the participants, Veerachamy, was behind this effort. They translated Samudaya's *Belchi* into Tamil and travelled with it throughout the state.

This hectic statewide theatre activity attracted severe repressive measures from the Tamil Nadu Police, who filed more than 44 criminal cases against theatre groups from different parts of the state. One classic example of this was booking Chandralekha—the internationally renowned choreographer and danseuse, and her associates, on charges of 'sedition'. Chandralekha had done a poster display and a poetry reading at Chennai Marina beach to represent her solidarity with democratic values. And this, according to the police, was an act of sedition!

This kind of continued state repression totally paralysed open-air theatre activities of that time in Tamil Nadu. Some left theatre, others shifted and turned towards mainstream theatre. It is only around 1984, also the year of Chennai Kalai Kuzhu's inception that politically oriented open-air theatre activities came to life again. One can safely assume that Badal Sircar's workshop in Karnataka in 1978, kickstarted this kind of theatre movement which later spread to Kerala and Tamil Nadu like a 'chain reaction'.

But Badal Sircar's workshops should be understood in the context of those times. That was the post-Emergency period. Memories of authoritarianism and its bloody repressions were fresh in the minds of people. People's consciousness was alive with the values of democracy. This situation definitely provided a fertile breeding ground for any democratic cultural activities and expressions. Badal Sircar's Third Theatre was absorbed and accepted at that time as one among those expressions.

In 1989, a three-day festival was held at Tiruchirappalli to honour Badal Sircar. It was named 'The Badal Sircar Festival'. Six plays of Badal Sircar were performed. The most important one was *Spartacus*, produced by Mu. Ramswamy, for the audience seated in the round. A seminar was also organised during this festival. The problem was that there was no clarity regarding the historicity of Badal Sircar. No one was trying to understand the reasons of transition and development from the Badal Sircar of *Ebong Indrajit* to the Badal Sircar of the Third Theatre. Idolising Badal Sircar was the only dominant trend in that festival, and it disallowed a better understanding of the phenomemon that Badal Sircar was.

Theatre activist, A. Mangai, recalls that festival and seminar in an article:

> The politics projected by Badal Sircar's texts were not discussed and were not taken to another level. One section of the actors who were listening to these discussions got irritated and enacted a procession outside the dais by lifting one person on their shoulders and shouting slogans, 'Long live Badal Sircar! Long live, long live'. This spontaneous reaction of some participants was the outcome of criticism on idolising Badal Sircar. But Tamil theatre practitioners had not taken this incident into a proper discussion.

(A. Mangai, Thamizhil Naveena Natakam [*Modern Theatre in Tamil*] a collection of articles by different authors, published by International Institute of Tamil Studies,1996, p. 157)

In 1992 and 1994 Badal Sircar again conducted workshops in Tamil Nadu in Chennai and Madurai respectively. Sister Claire and Father Britto, who had participated in these workshops, started conducting Third Theatre workshops all over Tamil Nadu. Theatre activist A.Mangai who participated in both these workshops compared these with the first workshop that had happened in the year 1980: 'Except myself and Mu.Ramaswamy, most of the participants of this workshop were Christian missionaries who were working for some reformist development agenda. But this was not the case in the 1980s. Actually this type of theatre needs not just actors, but actors who are committed to political activism.'

Nowadays Badal Sircar's workshops happen only with those into political activism. I don't want to be judgemental and don't want to dismiss anyone's right to perform or do theatre in open-air spaces. But criticism prevails on this legacy.

As a playwright, director and an ideologue of Third Theatre, whether one agrees with him or not, Badal Sircar has definitely put his signature on the Indian theatre scene through his contribution. He legitimised open-air and non-conventional theatrical spaces through his continuous and dynamic interventions in these spaces and pushed the boundaries of Indian theatre in the process.

PLAY:
Spartacus (Hindi)
PLAYWRIGHT:
Dramatisation in Bangla by Badal Sircar of Howard Fast's novel, Translation: Rati Bartholomew and Virendra Saxena
DIRECTOR:
Anil Ranjan Bhowmik
GROUP:
Samanantar, Azamgarh, UP
(Nemichandra Jain Collection, Natarang Pratishthan Archives)

PLAY:
Juloos (Hindi) (1978)
PLAYWRIGHT:
Badal Sircar, Translation: Yama Shroff
DIRECTOR:
Susheel Kumar Singh
GROUP:
Rangshivir, Pratapgarh
(Nemichandra Jain Collection, Natarang Pratishthan Archives)

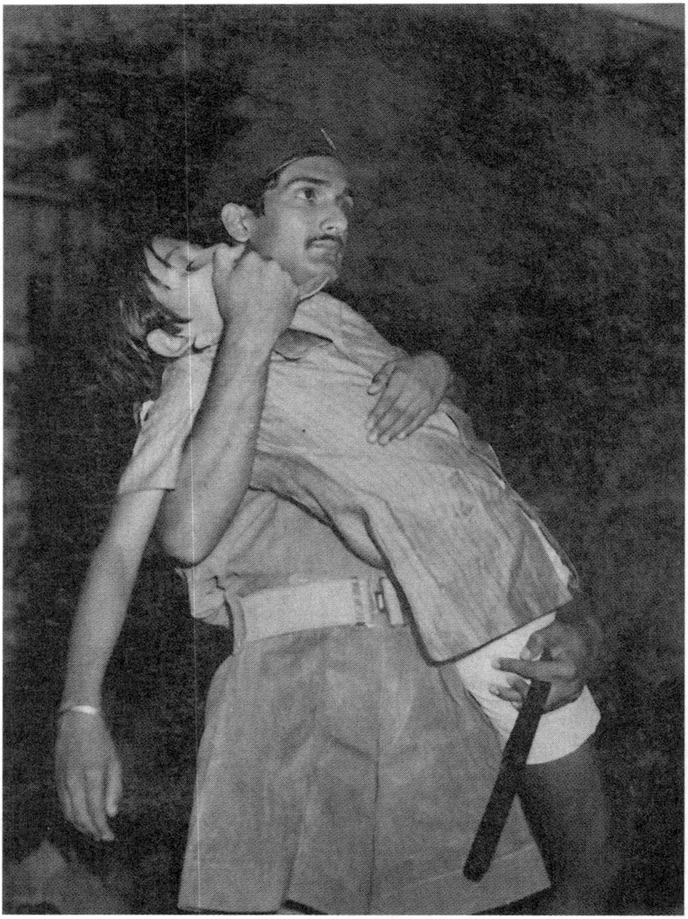

ACTOR:
Bhaskar and Paritosh Shukla (Police and Munna)

PLAY:
Juloos (Hindi) (1978)

PLAYWRIGHT:
Badal Sircar, Translation: Yama Shroff

DIRECTOR:
Satish Anand

GROUP:
Kala Sangam, Patna

(Nemichandra Jain Collection, Natarang Pratishthan Archives)

Actor:
L to R - Standing - Ratan Kandekar (Spartacus), Veeru Vasvani, Sumer Lalbhai, Dashrath Raman Lal, Kumari Bhairavi Ghasi, Raj Vasvani, Ramesh Khanvani, Shyam Sathnani. On floor (all slaves)

Play:
Aadi Vidrohi Spartacus (Hindi) (1980-81)

Playwright:
Dramatisation in Bangla by Badal Sircar of Howard Fast's novel, Translation: Rati Bartholomew and Virendra Saxena

Director:
Prem Prakash

Group:
Sindhi Drama Workshop, Ahmedabad, Gujarat

(Nemichandra Jain Collection, Natarang Pratishthan Archives)

Above and left:

Actor:
Badal Sircar (Above, standing right) with group

Workshop:
Short term theatre workshop (1981)

Director:
Badal Sircar

Group:
Samanantar, Azamgarh, UP

(Nemichandra Jain Collection, Natarang Pratishthan Archives)

PLAY:
Spartacus (Hindi)

PLAYWRIGHT:
Dramatised in Bangla by Badal Sircar from Howard Fast's novel, Translation: Rati Bartholomew and Virendra Saxena

DIRECTOR:
Anil Ranjan Bhowmik

GROUP:
Samanantar, Azamgarh

(Nemichandra Jain Collection, Natarang Pratishthan Archives)

ACTORS:
Ajay Gupta, Akshaya Yadav, Subhash Singh, Jagdish Sharma, Rajesh Deshpande and others

PLAY:
Bhoma (Hindi) (1985)

PLAYWRIGHT:
Badal Sircar, Translation: Collectively by Sudhir-Sudhanshu Mishra, Meera Mishra, Sushmita Mukherjee, Ein Lal, Beena Pal, Manohar Khushlani, Anamika Haksar, and Meenu Moolchandani

DIRECTOR:
Bhaskar Shivalkar

GROUP:
Rangdhara, Hyderabad

(Nemichandra Jain Collection, Natarang Pratishthan Archives)

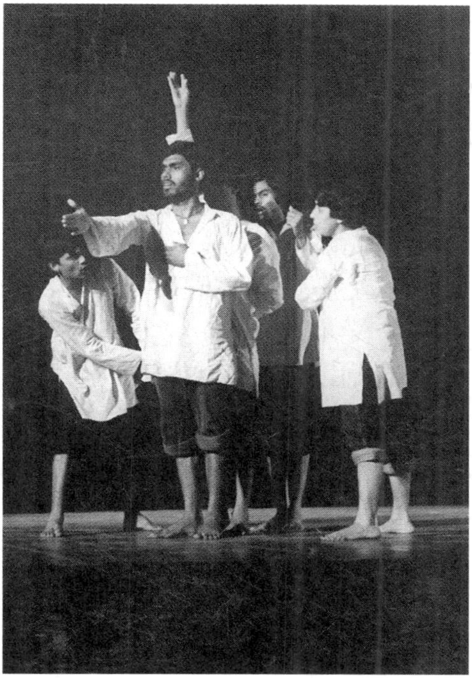

PLAY:
Bhoma (Hindi) (1982)

PLAYWRIGHT:
Badal Sircar,
Translation:
Ashok Bhowmik

DIRECTOR:
Anil Ranjan Bhowmik

GROUP:
Samanantar, Azamgarh

(Nemichandra Jain Collection, Natarang Pratishthan Archives)

PLAY:
Juloos (Hindi) (1988)

PLAYWRIGHT:
Badal Sircar,
Translation:
Yama Shroff

DIRECTOR:
Kavirattan Sharma

GROUP:
Jammu-Kashmir Academy of Art, Culture and Language, Jammu

(Nemichandra Jain Collection, Natarang Pratishthan Archives)

ACTOR:
Shailesh Shrivastav (Abu Hasan)

PLAY:
Abu Hasan (Hindi) (in Nautanki form) (1993)

PLAYWRIGHT:
Girishchandra Ghosh's novel dramatised in Bangla by Badal Sircar, Translation: Pratibha Agrawal

DIRECTOR:
Urmil Kumar Thapliyal

GROUP:
Manjushri Natya Manch, Gorakhpur

(Natarang Pratishthan Archives)

PLAY:
Aadi Vidrohi Spartacus (Hindi) (1995)

PLAYWRIGHT:
Dramatised in Bangla by Badal Sircar from Howard Fast's novel, Translation: Rati Bartholomew and Virendra Saxena

DIRECTOR:
Vibhas Upadhyay

GROUP:
IPTA, Ambikapur, MP

(Natarang Pratishthan Archives)

Above and left:

Play:
Baki Itihas (Hindi) (1995)

Playwright:
Badal Sircar, Translation: Nemichandra Jain

Director:
Robin Das

Group:
National School of Drama Final Year Students

(National School of Dama)

Actor:
National School of Drama Second Year Students

Play:
Basi Khabar (Hindi)

Playwright:
Badal Sircar, Translation: Yama Shroff

Director:
Badal Sircar

Group:
National School of Drama

(National School of Drama)

Play:
Ebong Indrajit (Bangla)

Playwright:
Badal Sircar

Director:
Santanu Das

Group:
Kalyani Kala Mandala, W.B.

(National School of Drama).

ABOVE AND LEFT:

PLAY:
Ebong Indrajit (Bangla) (2001)

PLAYWRIGHT:
Badal Sircar

DIRECTOR:
Santanu Das

GROUP:
Kalyani Kalamandal, Kolkata

(National School of Drama)

Actor:
Rajesh Babbar as (Husband) Sumit Kumar (Old man)

Play:
Saari Raat (2003)

Playwright:
Badal Sircar, Translation: Pratibha Agrawal

Director:
Suresh Bharadwaj

Group:
Aakar Kala Sangam theatre group, Delhi

(National School of Drama)

Actor:
Ishwar (Bhupati) and Sanjeev Johri (Haldar)

Play:
Ballabhpur Ki Roopkatha (Hindi) (2004)

Playwright:
Badal Sircar, Translation: Pratibha Agrawal

Director:
Rajinder Nath

Group:
Abhiyan, Delhi

(Natarang Pratishthan Archives)

Play:
Saari Raat (Hindi) (2003)
Playwright:
Badal Sircar, Translation: Pratibha Agrawal
Director:
Suresh Bharadwaj
Group:
Aakar Kala Sangam, Delhi
(National School of Drama)

Play:
Spartacus (Hindi) (2007)
Playwright:
Dramatised by Badal Sircar from Howard Fast's novel, Translation: Anis Aazmi and Rati Bartholomew
Director:
Lokendra Trivedi
Group:
Shri Ram Centre 2nd Year students
(Natarang Pratishthan Archives)

ACTOR:
Aseem Hattangady (Indrajit) and others
PLAY:
Evam Indrajit (Hindi) (2008)
PLAYWRIGHT:
Badal Sircar, Translation: Pratibha Agrawal
DIRECTOR:
Jaydev Hattangadi
GROUP:
Kalashray, Mumbai
(National School of Drama)

PLAY:
Aadi Vidrohi (Hindi)
PLAYWRIGHT:
Dramatised in Bangla by Badal Sircar from Howard Fast's novel, Translation: Rati Bartholomew and Virendra Saxena
DIRECTOR:
Anil Ranjan Bhowmik
GROUP:
Samanantar, Allahabad
(Natarang Pratishthan Archives)

Actor:
Badal Sircar

Play:
Michhil (Bangla) (2000)

Playwright:
Badal Sircar

Director:
Badal Sircar

Group:
Satabdi

(National School of Drama)

ACTOR:
Badal Sircar

PLAY:
Michhil (Bangla) (2000)

PLAYWRIGHT:
Badal Sircar

DIRECTOR:
Badal Sircar

GROUP:
Satabdi, Kolkata

(National School of Drama)

ACTOR:
Badal Sircar

PLAY:
Michhil (Bangla) (2000)

PLAYWRIGHT:
Badal Sircar

DIRECTOR:
Badal Sircar

GROUP:
Satabdi, Kolkata.

(National School of Drama)

L TO R:
Smt. Induja Awasthi, Smt. Rekha Jain, Shri Nemichandra Jain, Shri Suresh Awasthi , Smt. Tripti Mitra, Shri Badal Sircar and Smt. Badal Sircar (1982)

At Academy of Fine Arts Theatre, Kolkata

(Nemichandra Jain Collection, Natarang Pratishthan Archives)

ABOVE AND LEFT:
Badal Sircar's portraits
(Satabdi, Natarang Pratishthan Archives)

BADAL SIRCAR

Playwright, Theorist and Teacher of Theatre

A. Mangai

> Theatre is desire, bodily struggle, personal defence. Theatre, if it tells the truth, proffers a quest for oneself, oneself in others and others in oneself. It proffers the humanisation of human kind. This cannot be done without struggle.
>
> Today, theatre is a martial art.
>
> **—(Boal, Augusto, 2001, 314)**

If we mark Piscator's 'Political Theatre' and Brecht's 'Epic Theatre' as questioning the very foundations of Aristotelian aesthetics, we enter the realm of democratising theatre and move towards people's theatre. Boal however has expanded people's theatre to become participatory theatre through his theatre of the oppressed. He talks about the creation of spect-actors. Today, we learn about 'Playback Theatre', where one's stories are played back to the audience in order to arrive at crucial decisions and clarity. PETA has evolved a genre called Informance (Information and Performance) in its process of addressing violence against women (Barrameda, Teresita V., 2000). These disjointed events in history point to one fact for sure—that theatre can play a role in social change. Though seemingly sloganistic, one must think back on repressions unleashed on theatre down the history to know that those in power never took theatre lightly. Jan Cohen-Cruz defines street performance as 'Radical acts that question or re-envision ingrained social arrangements of power' (1998 1). Diana Taylor says in her opening remarks in *Negotiating Performance* (1994) that any 'conscious move out of "cultural spaces" in the strictest sense of the word...posits that society as a whole is culture—the site in which symbols and identity are forged, negotiated and contested' (12). If we read the former as referring to the intent and content of street theatre, the latter adds the performative context and ideology ingrained in the choice that one makes. Therefore theatre, especially theatre in non-traditional performance spaces, questions structures of power; it makes any available and chosen space its stage; and its ideological import is of primary significance. That perhaps explains why we in India still have the Dramatic License Act passed by the Britishers (1876). It is this background that makes Badal Sircar's work special and unique. As someone who practised a kind of theatre in which text and performance cannot be separately analysed, his texts and performative texts are studied here as a continuum. As a theatre worker based in Tamil Nadu and working in Tamil, my readings are also contextualised in the specific context of Tamil Nadu, where Badal-da had a major role to play.

The second major phase of political activity through theatre in India, after the heyday of IPTA, flourished during the Emergency period. The mid 1970s and early '80s saw the growth of many theatre groups which mobilised people against repressive practices of the State. Samudaya of Karnataka deserves special mention here. Prasanna, an NSD graduate took to the streets as part of Samudaya. Their *Belchi* remains a classic street theatre performance till date. The 1980s also saw the reach and power of Jana Natya Manch led by Safdar Hashmi in Delhi. The brutal murder of Hashmi during a performance of *Halla Bol* spearheaded a revival of interest in Street Theatre in 1989 (Erven, 1992, 140-156). The mid-1980s was the era of literacy campaigns. Kerala Sashtriya Sahitya Parishad was the vanguard of cultural *jatha*s spreading the need for literacy in India. Andhra Pradesh saw the rise of Gaddar, a people's artist who voiced through his performative songs the demands of the peasants and workers. In fact, his style had a great impact on Telugu films.

It is important to juxtapose in this context the Third Theatre launched by Badal Sircar. Disclaiming his theatre's affinity to the First Theatre, namely traditional theatres of India and the Second Theatre, the colonial proscenium theatre, Sircar proclaimed the need for a Third Theatre. He was working on a theatre which is live, mobile and free. Though his theatre has political critique, it is skeptical about organised struggles of any kind. Drawing his inspiration from Grotowski's Poor Theatre and Schechner's Performance Group's improvisatory practices, Sircar reacted against Calcutta's commercial theatre practices. While his theatre is highly physical, performed in the open and dealing with political issues, it is far from collective mobilisation and action. His influence on actor's training, image building and dramatising the abstract are beyond question a major contribution in almost all parts of India.

This paper deals with how the ideological skepticism – sometimes read as openness/complex understanding – is evident in Badal-da's texts and more so in performances. However the passion with which the actors participate in both the workshops and performances richly compensate the doubtful directions found in the texts. At least in the case of Tamil Nadu, most groups that evolved out of Badal-da's workshops chose to do what we would call Street Theatre rather than any of his texts or anything close to them. I would like to discuss them as evidence of the disjuncture in the workshop process and production process of Badal Sircar's school of training.

Ella Datta's introduction to *Three Plays* by Badal Sircar (2009; first edition 1983) refers to three strands in Sircar's life that 'intertwine to lend a striking texture to his work and introduce a new value to Indian theatre: his professional career as an urban planner plus his training as a civil engineer; his inner life as a playwright; and his outward expression in his role as a theatre director and actor'. As early as in 1981 he said, 'What can I write? I am no writer of essays. I am a theatre man. I wrote some plays because I am a man of the theatre, not because I am a writer.' (Letter to *The Drama Review,* November 1981). His graph as a theatre practitioner and writer went through at least three distinct phases: he started with light-hearted comedies (*Ballabhpurer Roopkatha* being the best known, and is still popular); then went on to express the angst and rootlessness of the urban middle class in his classic plays; and eventually, in his post-proscenium phase, he became more consciously anti-establishment.

In order to capture his world view he employed cut-and-paste methods. He revelled in montages and collages, both verbal and physical. He made a fine art of the short, punchy vignette. He freely jumped from idea to idea, concern to concern. He pooh-poohed the over-hyped virtues of structure, form and technical virtuosity. But anyone who is able to capture the cadence of his prose will be able to grasp the musicality of his plays. They are almost carefully notated. In *Procession* (*Michhil*), the whole play rests on the idea of endless processions, none of them right ones: 'Michhil, Michhil, Michhils for food and clothes, Michhils for salvation, Michhils for the revolution, military Michhils, Michils for refugees, Michhils for flood relief, mourning Michhils, protest Michhils, festive Michhils, star-studded Michhils' (18). This roll call of *michhil*s is one of the fast moving energetic sections of the performance. When you are part of an audience, it is difficult to take in the list in detail. But when one sits with the text in hand, and finds '*michhil*s for revolution' followed by 'military *michhil*s', or when protest *michhil*s are closely followed by 'festive *michhil*s, star-studded *michhil*s', the text becomes an endlessly relativist argument about the uselessness of all processions. Samik Bandyopadhyay in his translator's afterword to *Three Plays* says, 'The irony implicit in the choice of slogans as abstractions is in the suggestion of historical trends and tendencies degenerating almost immediately into dehumanised, vacuous verbiage—dead words' (167). Though Badal-da's texts are rich in its resonance to historical moments that shaped our era, what really strikes one is the irony of it all and not the passionate moment and its traces. Added to it are the formal aspects of bringing in familiar kirtans, bhajans and Christian liturgy. The distinction between a workers' march and these religious or other political festivities are not marked either bodily or textually.

It is in the same breath, different philosophies are also mentioned. As someone who was a cardholding member of the Communist Party and a believer in communist ideology, he does bring in discussions on that. In *Procession*, the religious master tries to indoctrinate in people the thought that Communism is 'the greatest enemy of the civilisation.' *Beyond the Land of Hattamala* (*Hattomalar Oparey*) is a dramatic articulation of 'to each according to need' in a fantasy mode. Still no attempt is made to distinguish communism from lets say Fascism, which finds a place in *Ebong Indrajit*, one of his plays from the early phase (1963). His hope in changing the system gets caught in the mindless blabbering of Amals, Vimals and Kamals.

'Plutocracy – monarchy – democracy.
Imperialism, Fascism, Marxism.
Economics, Politics, Sociology…
Uncle, niece, mother-in-law.' (1989; first published 1974, 53).

But Badal-da is not a pessimist. He wants the 'procession of dreams. A song of dreams. … The people in the procession are holding hands. …The audience is invited to join. The procession continues'. The question that remains unanswered is, how this procession is different from the rest. Nor is the mobilisation of audience as people participating in the procession articulated. Also, a procession of dreams is certainly a luxury for those whose minimum demands are crushed. Badal Sircar said, 'I live in a fragmented world, a chaotic world full of contradictions; is it not absurd even to seek coherence in such an absurd world?' While this explains the structure of his plays, it does not answer his ideological position.

It is this aspect of Badal Sircar that Safdar Hashmi criticised vehemently:

> As far as the content is concerned, it is anarchic from the word go. It is cynicism embodied. I know many people who consider themselves revolutionaries like this, … who stand on the rooftop and shout at the top of their voices that everyone is a bastard and everyone is corrupt. It is the easiest option to take because it doesn't commit you to anything. …It is the worst kind of cynicism. In one breath he goes from Marx to Engels to Lenin, to Hitler, to Boris Becker. You equate everything (1989, 145).

Even if we overrule Hashmi's comment as hardcore party-based view, one does sense the unease Badal has with organised struggles. *Spartacus*, the most inspiring and challenging of Badal-da's plays captures that sense of justice that 'springs' up when in total helplessness. Since there is nothing to lose, the struggle continues. Every slave is a Spartacus! Ironically the plays that include all human beings as possible victims are the plays on nuclear energy. The spontaneity and passion for justice these plays evoke are unmistakable. But an organised struggle or mobilisation of people are seen as suspect.

The rigour found in the Satabdi group during their recent tour in Tamil Nadu (1-2, December 2011), revealed the commitment and involvement of the group to whatever Badal-da stood for. The lack of similar perfection and passion in groups that follow Badal-da's methodology in Tamil Nadu struck one as surprising while watching Satabdi's shows. But almost all those groups and people keeping the momentum going for these many years are part of the struggles in the region—be it dalits, women, tribals or Tamil identity! It is this dichotomy between sense of justice and actual struggle for the same (which can be tiresome and brutal), that gets articulated in the way groups and persons trained by Badal Sircar in Tamil Nadu choose to function.

II

Satabdi's Tamil Nadu tour – 2011

The Department of English, Stella Maris College, Chennai conducted a two-day National Seminar titled *Badal Sircar: Changing Theatrescapes* on 1 and 2 December 2011. The seminar sought to celebrate and remember the contribution of Badal Sircar to contemporary Indian theatre. An inter-collegiate competition in Third Theatre saw two prize-winning groups performing excerpts from *Bhoma*, one in English and the other in Tamil. The group that performed in Tamil used Gnani's adaptation of *Bhoma* as *Muniyan*. This was followed by Moonram Arangu performing *Spartacus* directed by M. Ramaswamy, who had been part of a Badal Sircar workshop in 1993 at Madurai. The second day had Prasanna's keynote address followed by Satabdi's performance of *Michhil.* When almost the whole hall joined hands together, clearly there was a momentum. The young students for whom watching a performance with no gimmicks and frills was a novel experience, this was an eye opener. And as Prasanna had said in his opening remarks, Badal-da's emphasis on the use of 'body' as a major mode of articulation to counter the mechanisation process of our globalised world was driven home in a practical manner.

Satabdi was in Chennai for a whole week. They performed at different venues. The synopses of some of the plays which were not available in English are given in detail. They reveal the sources of Badal-da's play texts and the range of variety in their narrative pattern. Most plays had the same ideological fervour to dream of a better world—a world where there is equality and justice. The style of performance was also similar to the one found in *Michhil* in many ways, with minor changes in terms of a few visualisations, the establishment of the protagonist's view point and the handling of props in some cases.

They began with the performance of two shows in Vedanthangal. They did *Hattomalar Oparey* and *Picnic.* Buddar Kalai Kuzhu led by Manimaran organised this show and they also performed a play in Tamil. *Charuibhati (Picnic)*, is an adaptation of Fernando Arrabal's *Picnic on the Battlefield.* It was composed and first produced in 1994. *Picnic*, a black comedy, makes a mockery of the idealism surrounding war presenting it as a game that children play. A young man finding himself alone at his post on the battlefield knits muffler to avoid boredom when his parents arrive to spend the day with him picnicking. The occasion soon becomes a hilarious exhibition of all wars, both past and present. The Father glorifies wars he fought in his youth as more exciting when swords and horses were in use. The Mother, likewise, remembers the spectacular wars she witnessed from the balcony, betting on the probable winner. The idea of war as a game continues even after an enemy soldier is held captive. Discussions with him reveal how identical both the soldiers are as regards their cowardice and boredom. Furthermore, the circumstances that dragged them to the battlefield and the jingoistic speeches made by their respective generals appear similar. The stretcher-bearers, disappointed at finding no one dead or wounded, exhibit the common tendency playing the part assigned to them by the war mongers. The callous attitude, therefore, continues regarding the killing of human beings. However, refusing to fight is quite easy as it is to quit playing any game. A united effort of the people forced to fight among themselves for a few profiteers can effectively stop wars. But the death of all the characters at the end points out that the game of war still remains unchecked.

Progressive Writers and Artsists Association, Pondicherry arranged for a show in Pondy, where Satabdi did *Hattomalar Oparey* and *Bhool Rasta*. Reminiscent of the folk tradition, *Bhool Rasta* (*Wrong Route)* is a story-telling play. An actor narrates the adventure of a young prince born and brought up amidst luxury who sets off to a distant land in search of a rare fruit needed to cure his queen-mother. He is accompanied by officers and a whole regiment of soldiers on horseback. On the way they are fed by the masses, following the convention that the poor must serve the privileged few. Things, however, take a new turn when the prince loses his way in the dense forest and is forced to survive on his own. Having limited recourse to food and rest, he comes across a young uncivilised wood-cutter and is surprised by his discourteous attitude in treating a royal master. The forest-dweller is not even aware of the existence of kings as he lives in a land of equality, in harmony with nature. The prince enjoys his friendship and continues to stay in the forest till he himself becomes a wood-cutter. Taking the wrong route to the forest-dweller's hut, he not only forgets about the mission that he set out for but also the way back to the palace. Relinquishing his masterly nature he begins to treat human beings in an altogether different way. But had he found the way back home, the narrator informs, the prince surely would have regained his previous attitude. The play ends posing a question: was the route to the wood-cutter's hut that made the prince a poor man's friend really wrong?

At Asian College of Journalism, the group performed *Nadite (Come to the River)*, an adaptation of Edward Bond's *We Come to the*

River, which was originally composed in 1980 and revised in 1992. It was first produced in 2002. *Come to the River* depicts the plight of the masses bearing the burden of war in the reign of a tyrannical emperor. The enemy is defeated but it is only after the soldiers fighting for the tyrant have suffered heavy losses. The loyal General seeks to maintain order and discipline in the victorious army (even by issuing order to execute the deserters). Things, however, change once he encounters the looters. Having lost their near and dear ones the women are forced to survive looting the dead and wounded soldiers. A baby in a mad widow's arms makes the General see the reality he has helped to perpetuate, the merciless killing of the people in the name of war. His thoughts being subversive, the General soon finds himself confined in an asylum waiting to go blind owing to a previous injury. In the mean time, the oppressive regime continues to do away with the detractors. But the voice of the people ultimately finds expression in a rebellion which draws inspiration from the General. Therefore, in an attempt to demoralise the rebels, the emperor sends assassins to the asylum who drive a knife into the eyes of the General. However, the General, having lost eyesight, sees an altogether new world where all the dead victims return to life. The play ends with a song that restores faith in the revolutionary strength of the masses, symbolised by a baby who, though vulnerable, is the potential source of power that can change the world in a radically different way.

At Spaces, they did *Michhil* and *Ore Bihongo*. This was organised by Casual Dramatics, which works closely with Bengal Association in Chennai. *Ore Bihanga* (*O Bird*), was composed in 1994 and first produced in 2009. *O Bird* exploits excerpts from songs, dialogues and poems by Tagore to drive home its message. The entire action takes place in Pagal-dada's (Crazy Brother) room that is used for rehearsals. However, Pagal-dada's real objective seems not to be performing plays. The people who frequent the room come from the lower strata of the society, daily labourers and rickshaw-pullers. The newest entrant, Rajlaxmi, is brought by Moksada, a charwoman who has learnt songs and dialogues while working at Pagal-dada's house. Coming in contact with Pagal-dada has inspired Moksada to see life in a new light.

She has learnt not only to remain unaffected by her overburdened existence but also to stand up against the injustices meted out to her. Likewise Rajlaxmi, in the course of the play, is transformed from an ordinary charwoman to an altogether different human being. Helped by Pagal-dada and Moksada she gets a new lease of life, beginning to think beyond the drudgery of her menial condition. It is to make the commoners live an untiring life that Pagal-dada strives for. He believes that the prior condition to do anything worthwhile is to remain alive. The whole idea to continue dreaming and not to be bogged down by the unpleasant circumstances is expressed through a poem by Tagore with the refrain: 'And yet O bird, O bird of mine/ Do not blind, do not close your wings just now'. This was performed by three actors—one male and two females. The performance was moving in the way, it brought the transformation of the human being right in front of our eyes. This was also one show that foregrounded the presence and expressions of women in a non-stereotypical way.

Badal Sircar had said that, 'None of the Satabdi members are paid anything. They work in banks, schools, offices, factories: they assemble in evenings exhausted by loveless work and sardine-packed public transport.' Therefore the group spends a long time in rehearsal process. It was moving to find the seriousness with which the group rehearsed each day in Chennai. One could find the discipline that has gone into such a practice. As someone who has attended two of his workshops in the early 1990s, I had been thoroughly convinced by his training of internalising the context even if the text was a single slogan. We have also seen *Sada Kalo* (based on Woza Albert) performed by Sadak group consisting of three members—Dipankar (who is no more), Taposh and Kalyan right from 1993. In one of my conversations with Badal-da about the 'presence' of women as actors, characters and trainers in his scheme of things, he politely laughed and said those are aspects to be carried forward. But if we look at *Procession* or *Nadite*, the woman is a prototype of a woman suffering and therefore resilient; a survivor. There is no focus on the female subjectivity in any of Badal Sircar's plays. But meeting Santa Dutta and Krishna Ghosh along with a few other younger women in the team helped me understand that they were taking crucial decisions within the group. They were not frills attached to the group. And they have earned their place.

III

Influence of Badal Sircar in Tamil Nadu

For the past one year, any meeting on Badal-da wondered about his influence in Tamil Nadu. I would like to record the ways in which Badal Sircar shaped the course of Tamil theatre. In his interview with Subhendu Sarkar (2010), Badal Sircar refers to the workshops he conducted in Tamil Nadu when asked about 'the strong presence of your kind of theatre in Tamil Nadu' thus:

> Oxfam arranged a workshop in Madurai in which participants were from three states—Karnataka, Andhra Pradesh and Tamil Nadu. They were all engaged in social development activities. There were Roman Catholic Brothers, Fathers and Sisters. Everyone participated freely. Later Sister Clare and Father Britto continued working among various social groups using their workshop experience. Roman Catholics have a good network in Tamil Nadu. Later I conducted advanced workshops there.

This workshop he is referring to took place in 1984 for eight days as recalled by S. Clare.

But this workshop was not the first one Badal-da held in Tamil Nadu. Following the workshop he did in Karnataka and Samudaya taking it up in full scale plays like *Belchi* and *Oh! Chasnella Brothers!* were very popular.

Veedhi Nataka Iyakkam (Street Theatre Movement) of Chennai is perhaps the first to hold a serious discussion on street theatre. They organised a seminar on street theatre under the banner of the literary organisation Parivarthana. The invitation of this seminar (1979) has this to say:

> Theatre has been performed not only in auditoriums, but also in the streets. Street theatre has been functioning effectively in many parts of India. Tamils familiar with Therukoothu may not find this novel; but our perspectives on art have been so destroyed by films and sabha dramas, that we may look at the introduction of street theatre with wonder. If street theatre has to be artistically enriched and powerful enough to affect our lives, theatre persons should come forward to take this form seriously. Veedhi movement is already engaged in this effort. In order to strengthen such efforts further, this literary forum is conducting a seminar on street theatre.

(Quoted in Arasu, V., 2001, 50) (All translations from Tamil sources to English are mine unless stated otherwise).

It is this group that invited Badal Sircar for the first time to Chennai to conduct a ten-day workshop at the Artists Village in 1980. K.V. Ramaswami, S. Swaminathan, V. Rajendran and Gnani were active in this group. Swaminathan tells us how the group evolved its plays:

> Most plays of Veedhi did not have any one individual director. On a holiday, we will assemble in a place, discuss the important issues and choose one of them. Together we will give it a shape, rehearse scene by scene, decide our dialogues, and characters. The same evening, at the beach, the group would gather a crowd of about 300 people with the help of a percussion instrument and perform the play rehearsed in the morning for about 45 minutes.

(*Manudam*, October 1980, quoted in ibid. 51). I can personally recall the performance of a short play with the use of mime called *Velai* performed by this group. I remember the interaction the audience had after the show at the Natesan Park, T. Nagar. Veerasami, who was closely working with Muthuswami in the formation of Koothu-P-Pattarai was also part of Pallavaram Makkal Marumalarcchi Manram. Their performance of *Belchi* was a major inspiration to many street theatre groups.

It was around the same time that Pareeksha was formed. Gnani Sankaran had attended both the Badal Sircar workshop and the Gandhigram workshop conducted by Bansi Kaul (1979). Proclaiming itself as an urban theatre group Pareeksha aimed to 'expose the hypocrisies of the middle class about life and drama and by so doing hopes to uproot the hypocrisies and social chains' (Brochure 1978 quoted in Arasu, V. 2001, 47). Pareeksha staged the plays of Indra Parthasarathi, Na. Muthuswami, K.V. Ramaswami, Jayanthan, Prabhanjan, Tendulkar and Badal Sircar. The credit for doing most of the plays of Badal Sircar in Tamil goes to this group. G. Rajaram translated the plays from Bengali almost as soon as they were available in the original. But it must be borne in mind that though the group took up Badal-da's texts, they did not follow the theatrical aspects of Badal-da. The physicalisation of the scenes found in Badal-da's productions was not followed in Pareeksha's productions. There were also other ideological issues. For instance, the play *Procession* ended with the song 'We shall overcome' in Pareeksha's production. One should also remember that most of Pareeksha's plays were performed in auditoriums and not in the open, except on few occasions. The group's productions left much to be desired in terms of theatrical perfection and intensity of performance. However the political overtures of the texts and the process of work in Pareeksha made the group an activist group.

Mu. Ramaswami formed his Nija Nataka Iyakkam in Madurai at about the same period. The group performed mainly street plays in and around Madurai. Ramaswami's allegiance to left ideology led him to choose plays with political intent whether performed in the street or proscenium. His adaptation of *Antigone* as *Durkira Avalam* in the wake of custodial killings of comrades in Naxalbari movement created a new vista of thought in Tamil theatre. He also performed *Spartacus* of Sircar in the open and one can confidently say that it was the most successful production of Badal Sircar's play in Tamil. His recent production of *Periyar*, though performed in the auditorium broke the boundaries of proscenium in its narrative style and performative aspects.

Parambai Selvan of Paramakudi, Asvaghosh of Neyveli and Jayanthan were others who were active in theatre with political insight in the 1980s. Not enough documentation of their work has been undertaken. Some of their texts are published. Mid-1980s also saw the interaction of Tamil Nadu artists with KSSP and Gaddar. Therefore the Oxfam workshop held by Badal Sircar was part of the momentum of Street Theatre in Tamil Nadu. The earlier workshop conducted by him at Artists Village was organised by many who were broadly from the left groups, while the Oxfam one was predominantly attended by Christian groups/persons involved in social activism. It is through these contacts all the future interactions with Badal-da continued in the state. In 1989, a festival of Badal Sircar's plays was held in Trichy from 22-24 September. Six plays of Badal Sircar were performed by various groups in that festival. That festival witnessed heated debates about the form and ideology of Badal Sircar.

Sr. Clare had been the heart and soul of this sustained interest in theatre among various Christian groups and other NGOs. What follows is the data given by her over telephone on 8 June 2012 for this paper. After the '84 workshop, she was instrumental along with Fr. Britto and many others to organise the following workshops:

In 1992, Culture and Communication, Loyola College, Chennai organised a week long workshop at AICUF house. In 1993, a five-day long internal workshop was held in IDEAS, Madurai. This was followed by the performances of *Sada Kalo* by Sadak group in and around Tirunelveli organised by the Manonmaniam Sundaranar University where I was working at that time. Sadak group, especially Dipankar became part of the workshops held in Tamil Nadu after this workshop. In 1995, a play-making workshop was organised for four days in Karur. The Sadak group was part of this workshop. They also visited many places in Tamil Nadu where the members of Puvi Arangam, an umbrella organisation of people who formed different groups in their respective places after the earlier workshops, were active. They also performed *Sada Kalo* in different places like Karur, Trichy, Thiruvananthapuram – Kerala, Nagercoil (organised by *Kaalachuvadu* magazine), Dindugal, Chennai and Bangalore (organised by Samudaya).

An Advanced Workhsop was held in Madurai for five days by Badal-da and Dipankar. That year Badal-da also conducted a drawing workshop for children in Palli Agaram, Chengalpet for Social Action Movement. In 1998, Sadak conducted a play-making workshop for members of Puvi Arangam. The four zones of the group brought their own respective plays and Badal-da and his team helped them polish two of them. The plays dealt with themes such as land rights, globalisation, child labour, women and feminisation of poverty. In 2000, two-day advanced workshops were held in Bangalore and Andhra Pradesh. A face to face was also organised in Bangalore, Chennai and Thanjavur. In Thanjavur, Badal-da saw the performance of a play called *Samban*, dealing with dalit empowerment and gave his feedback.

Sr. Clare refers to the focus on dalit, women, tribals, Sri Lankan repatriots and environmental groups with which she had interacted over these years. She speaks movingly of at least 16 people she met in the World Social Forum, Mumbai who have trained under her. As early as in 1998, Amar Sevalaya consisting of physically challenged actors performed an anti-nuclear play on wheel chairs and crutches. Most groups have taken up issues that are relevant to their current struggles, like the fisher folk in the Tamil Nadu, Kerala coastal belt. She had also been close to women's groups right from the 1980s and always emphasised the role of role play and short improvisations to trigger discussions. If Tamil Nadu has small theatre groups in almost every district the credit goes to literacy campaign spearheaded by Arivoli Iyakkam and the efforts of many NGOs and Christian groups.

Sr. Clare however admits that they have never performed any of Badal-da's plays in full length, even though they have attempted to visualise a few scenes of *Beyond the Topsy–turvey Land.* Except a few core members, many did not have access to the plays of Badal Sircar. The members who attended the workshops were from different walks of life. In her own words, 'rather than Third or Street theatre, it is Free theatre for me'.

Except Sakthi group in Dindugal, led by Sr. Chandra, which specialises in *tappattam* by young dalit, school drop-out women, the other groups have not managed to survive. Recently I had an opportunity to watch Murasu group from Nagercoil that has been sustaining itself for over a decade now. They did a play on Vaikunta

Sami, a social reformer of the early nineteenth century in Travancore region. The style of performance however was in the rhetorical style of regular street theatre. This group lives as a commune and gives and takes training regularly. Their cultural work is part of their social work as well.

Santhappan whose involvement in theatre began with Nija Nataka Iyakkam was a participant in at least three of Badal Sircar's workshops mentioned above. He also worked with Palkalai Arangam's production of *Ekalaivan*. He was part of the group that produced *Bhoma* in Tamil and participated in the Badal Sircar festival organised in Trichy in 1989. Around the same he was also active in organising student groups to get involved in anti-nuclear campaigns in and around Tirunelveli and Kanyakumari districts regarding the setting up of Kudankulam plant. This is a crucial venture as it is these campaigns, especially within the Christian communities of this area that has resulted in the major campaign of this era in Tamil Nadu. He refers to how in Tirunelveli, working closely with Fr. Gnanaprakasam who led the DCLM – Dalit Christian Liberation Movement, many plays were evolved on dalit issues. K.A. Gunasekaran, who had participated in the first workshop in Artists' Village was part of this process. Some of the plays considered to have spearheaded dalit theatre in the state were produced here under the aegis of Thannane Kalai Kuzhu. *Pali Adukal* (Scapegoats) (1993) is a play based on an inscriptional evidence of a dalit man ordained to be sacrificed initially, and the wife of that dalit was considered a suitable alternative to the decree. *Ari Kuri* (1995) and *Thee* (Fire) (1996) were some of the other plays evolved by Gunasekaran. Jeeva who was part of this process has been involved with feminist issues as well and worked closely with Voicing Silence in *Pacha Mannu* and a few other plays dealing with atrocities against dalits.

Almost all the groups mentioned above have a very strong folk dances repertoire like most Tamil theatre groups, especially in *tappu* and other lesser known non-narrative forms. These dances have become the mainstay of Tamil theatre training and performance in the past two decades. These dances are included in the syllabus of state government instituted colleges of music and fine arts. Street plays play a relatively minor role in their scheme of things. But in the workshops, many improvisations and role-plays are held. Workshops and the outcome of the workshops in most of these groups are a good mixture of regular street theatre format that has come to be standardised in the state and a call for social and political action. Most of the performances are performed as part of NGOs or sometimes with cultural groups of the two electoral communist parties. Very rarely does one come across cultural activism of a kind that pushes the debate on the issue into complex understanding of the same. The power of theatre which Badal-da so forcefully underlined is rarely felt in these shows, except the heartwarming participation of artists who manage to practice art amidst great difficulties and those who do not have the luxury of pursuing it further. Nor do these texts reveal the wide reading that Badal-da exuded. Most often one encounters an anti-intellectual position that's frighteningly essentialist. In short that power of reading against the grain that theatre offers, the sustenance of aesthetic conviction which provides energy and fillip to social movements and the complexity of presenting the issues that can balance a sense of apprehension with dream of hope are tragically absent in most of these efforts. Since the groups are not part of the theatre circuit in general, it is difficult to keep track. And in its own way, there is an exclusivity that's practised which does not allow for critical engagement.

As early as in 1992, Eugene Van Erven has said, 'Just as in the Philippines, progressive Catholic priests in India are using the theatre of liberation as instrument for evangelisation and politicisation. Most of these Indian priests were first exposed to Paulo Friere and liberation theology during their studies. Unlike the Philippines, however, the Indian clerical theatre of liberation activists rarely have connections with the organised left' (135). It is this rift between street theatre and third theatre practice (for want of other nomenclature) that made Hashmi comment, 'But ever since he (Badal Sircar) has started "Third Theatre" he has done no end of mischief to the people's theatre movement in this country' (1989, 145). He does not however hesitate to acknowledge the charisma of Badal-da as a person.

> Badal Sircar has made some contribution in developing some kind of exercises for the body that are good for technique. But as with tradition it is important to establish a critical relation with what it offers you. As far as I know, no one who has come under Badal Sircar's influence has been able to establish a critical relation with his work. They are too overwhelmed by the man.
>
> (ibid. 146)

Though not for the same reasons, I can sense the critique of Hashmi and Erven true in the case of both Badal Sircar and his school of theatre as practised in Tamil Nadu. That does not undermine his hold over my own practice of theatre. The dichotomy between democratising the practice of theatre through Third/Free Theatre and the moral high ground with which all other practices are dubbed as bourgeoisie does not make sense to me. I fail to understand how the director has the right to design the audience as in the case of Badal Sircar's Procession, given in the Seagull volume and discussed at length by Rustom Bharucha in his book Rehearsals of Revolution. Assuming the intimacy of the audience as a given is equally troublesome for me. I have raised my doubts to Parnab Mukherjee who replied saying that the artist has to trust his/her instincts. As someone who had watched a student of mine who ran to puke in the rest room, during one of his shows in Chennai, I am troubled at that dependence on instinct. Nor was I convinced of the few representative audience being seated near the Satabdi screen on the fourth side of the audience circle, as practised by his Mukta Mancha shows. Some of our students who were made to sit at that vantage point raised doubts about how do they watch the play while sitting there and why should they be privy to what the actors are doing back stage, if they are supposed to be doing it behind the curtain. The questions may sound naïve, but are basic.

Badal Sircar was a playwright who changed the course of Indian theatre and his texts have a narrative that's unique, one needs to engage with it critically. As texts, I find it difficult to negotiate the quick succession of thoughts that are made out to be checklists in them. Since there is a conscious effort to move away from characterisation, the prototypes need to have a depth and intensity without falling into the trap of stereotyped clichés. As a theorist of theatre, his criticism of the First and Second theatres while valid, have also been bent around with amazing virtuosity and finesse by many playwrights and directors. The political use of this theatre for mobilisation and social action has been part of Indian theatre from IPTA days. Even in those times, many political theatres were allowed and treated on par. It is as a teacher of theatre, a person who introduced workshop process for actors' training and theatre production that I find Badal-da inimitable. His workshops are indeed spaces for rehearsing revolution, however ephemeral they are! And it is that fervour that we have to carry forward as his legacy.

Endnotes

Works cited

Arasu, V., *Octopusum Karikkozhihalum*, Chennai: Elavalagan Pathippagam, 2001.

Barrameda, Teresita V., *Breaking Silence*, Philippines: PETA and UNIFEM, 2000.

Cohen- Cruz, Jan., (Ed.), *Radical Street Performance*, London: Routledge, 1998.

Erven, Eugene Van., *The Playful Revolution: Theatre and Liberation in Asia*, Bloomington and Indianapolis: Indiana University Press, 1992.

Sircar, Badal., *Piragoru Indrajit* (*Evam Indrajit* in Tamil. Tr: Rajaram), Annam, 1978.

Sircar, Badal., Meethi Sarithiram (*Bakhi Ithihass* in Tamil. Tr: R. Bhanumathi), C-rea, 1992.

Sircar, Badal., *Beyond the Land of Hattamala* and *Scandal in Fairyland* (Tr: Suchanda Sarkar), Seagull, 1992.

Sircar, Badal., *Three Plays* (Translated by Samik Bandyopadhyay, Badal Sircar and Kalyani Ghosh), Seagull, 2009.

Sircar, Badal., *Two Plays: Indian History made Easy and Life of Bagala* (Translation and introduction Subhendu Sarkar), OUP, 2010.

Taylor, Diana and Juan Vilujas (Eds), *Negotiating Performance, Durham, NC and London*: Duke

University Press, 1994.

SAHMAT, *The Right to Perform: Selected Writings of Safdar Hashmi*, Delhi. 1989.

Three Modern Indian Plays, OUP, 1989.

THEATRE OF THE STREETS

Eugene van Erven

Excerpts from an interview with **Safdar Hashmi**

Eugene van Erven (EVE): The name of Badal Sircar and Third Theatre pops up everywhere in India with people who do popular theatre. I have strong reservations about his work, both aesthetically and ideologically. How do you feel about it?

Safdar Hashmi (SH): I don't know how many reservations you have, but I have many reservations. I have all the reservations one can have about Badal Sircar. Although in Pakistan I was sharing a room with him for seven days. We related to each other very well as human beings. First of all, he has made a significant contribution to Bengali theatre by writing four or five major plays. But ever since he has started the Third Theatre, he has done no end of mischief to the people's theatre in the country.

No matter what he says, through his practice and his innumerable workshops and through the multiplied effects of his students and groups he has worked with, for a large number of cultural workers he has very effectively pushed into the background the question of content and foregrounded form as if that is all there is to theatre. It is more important for adherents of Badal Sircar to do theatre in a certain way rather than to do theatre for a particular cause. They have made a kind of merit out of doing theatre only with one's body as sole resource. It is a mere display of technique. It is a spectacle, nothing more. People watch spellbound—'Ah, wonderful! They have made a canon with their bodies!' That is all that happens. As far as the content is concerned, it is anarchic from the word go. It is cynicism embodied. I know many people who consider themselves revolutionaries like this, Eugene, who stand on the rooftop and shout at the top of their voices that everyone is a bastard and everyone is corrupt. It is the easiest position to take because it doesn't commit you to anything.

There is a play of his called *Juloos* (*Procession*). It went like a wave all over the country. As you know, it also went to Pakistan. I talked to all those people and asked them how it related to their experiences. They were not able to answer. It is the worst kind of cynicism. In one breath he goes from Marx to Engels to Freud to Lenin to Hitler to Boris Becker. You equate everything. He does it constantly. There is anarchy in his thought. I think it is calculated. It is reflected in his style also. It is so fragmented. While it goes on you think there is lots of energy but once it is over it leaves you only confused.

Badal Sircar has created a cult. He always tries to glorify his own sacrifices, which I find tasteless. I think he does it for a purpose. He always talks about his poverty, how he walks everywhere, drinks tea without sugar. He builds a personal myth around himself. Bengal is a state looked up to by all the democratic forces in the country. Badal Sircar works in Bengal with forces opposed to the Left Front government. He is working with church organisations in remote areas of Bengal and Bihar. He openly mitigates against the CPI(M). I would never associate with him. The bourgeois press gives him a lot of publicity and makes it sound as if he had caused this revolution in theatre and as if street theatre in India were his invention. It is quite untrue. As far as our troupe is concerned, we had never seen any of his work or even heard from him when we started our street theatre. It was born purely out of a necessity. For many other groups it was the same.

Badal Sircar has made some contribution in developing some kind of exercises for the body that are good for technique. But as with tradition, it is important to establish a critical relation with what it offers you. As far as I know, no one who has come under Badal Sircar's influence has been able to establish a critical relation with his work. They are too overwhelmed by the man. I have even expressed these opinions to his face during the workshop we held in Pakistan.

EVE: How did he respond to it?

SH: (laughs) He became the smiling Buddha.

EVE: Are people like Utpal Dutt more important for the overall democratic movement, you think? He rarely goes to the streets nowadays, doesn't he? And how about his work in the awful Bombay feature films?

SH: After Independence Utpal Dutt was the first person to do street theatre at the time of the second general elections. He goes into the villages and performs there. And his plays are performed everywhere. His contribution to the cultural movement has been vast. But I think, Eugene, that Utpal Dutt's realism-charged theatre has had its day. Long, epic speeches are made and the emotions of the people are manipulated. But at the same time he wrote a powerful play on a tragic chapter in the history of the Independence movement.

During a peaceful demonstration in Amritsar in 1919, the British opened fire, killing 3,000 unarmed people on the spot. They just surrounded them from all sides. Utpal Dutt has written a play on that in the *jatra* style. It is a lot heightened. I have always wanted to do that play for the simple reason that I had always wanted to go to the people and tell them what had happened in Amritsar and there is no other powerful play on that subject. It gives them a lot to think about, you see, although it manipulates them also. I am temperamentally opposed to any kind of theatre, cinema, or art that manipulates the consciousness of the people or which gives them an experience by proxy. It is like taking someone by his collar and shaking him until he accepts your viewpoint. In that sense I am more of a Brechtian. I'd rather appeal to the people with reasonable arguments and make them reflect about what's going on. But having said that, I think that Utpal Dutt's contribution to the people's theatre movement in India is far, far greater than Badal Sircar's, whose influence has only been negative. I'm very clear about that.

Taken from 'The People Gave Us So Much Energy' in Theatre of the Streets
Jana Natya Manch, 2007

A CURTAIN CALL FOR POLITICAL THEATRE

(Badal Sircar 1925-2011)

Sadanand Menon

Badal Sircar was no politician; neither was he a teacher. However when he set out on the second phase of his theatre-making in 1972, with his group Satabdi in Calcutta, he was to inaugurate the most historic artistic programme in contemporary India of educating and conscientising theatre audiences on the travesty – nay absurdity – of their contemporary post-colonial deprivation.

A significant section of his audiences were urban middle or working classes. But he also made unforgettable interventions with the rural poor, like in the Sundarbans and in the Santhal villages. His was a theatre that relentlessly and self-consciously chose to operate as a Paulo Freirean kind of 'pedagogy for the oppressed'. Sircar had internalised a dictum that to wash one's hands off the conflict between the powerful and the powerless meant not neutrality but a tacit siding with the powerful.

Outraged by the idea of 'selling' plays to audiences, Sircar and his group evolved the notion of a 'Free Theatre'. He was among the initiators of the Curzon Park open-air theatre expression from 1974, subsequent to massive protests after a young spectator, Prabir Datta, was killed in a brutal lathi-charge there. The collective protest by theatre practitioners of Calcutta drew over 3,000 people crowding the park every Saturday to witness half-a-dozen groups enact volatile plays in an intensely charged atmosphere. The only time that activity was suspended was during the 19 months of the Emergency.

Badal Sircar's 50-odd productions, cumulatively performed over a thousand times by his own group, and multiplied many more times by other theatre groups in other linguistic regions of India—setting up a sort of relay transmission from the 1970s through to the 1990s. Almost all dealt with the continuing asphyxiation caused by 'colonial violence' in a free nation. Frantz Fanon, in his *The Wretched of the Earth* had described most artists and professors as '*disorientateurs*' (obfuscators) who continually propagated 'respect for the established order', thereby separating and insulating the exploiters from the exploited. Fanon had proposed that a true artist, rather than colluding with this order, could only contest it – turning theatre, for example, into a site for resistance. This was a strategy most consistently explored in post-colonial Indian theatre by Badal Sircar.

In an insightful chapter on Sircar's work in his 1983 book on Bengali political theatre *Rehearsals of Revolution*, Rustom Bharucha makes a lucid point: 'His theatre does not pretend to be militant.... It is content with disturbing the consciousness of its spectators.... Sircar focuses on the callousness of the middle class and their capacity to watch the suffering of people without doing anything about it.' In fact, a recurring chant in one of Sircar's most performed plays *Bhoma*, is: '*Akhon manusher rakta thanda/Thanda, Thanda, Thanda*' (Today human blood has turned cold/Cold, Cold, Cold).

Sircar's search was never for something as abstract as coherence. He was to say, 'I live in a fragmented world, a chaotic world full of contradictions; is it not absurd even to seek coherence in such an absurd world?' Instead, he made a virtue of disjointedness. For his themes he adapted liberally from available and already published material. He took random passages from his own extensive notebook entries (*Book of Feelings*). He employed cut-and-paste methods. He reveled in montages and collages, both verbal and physical. He made a fine art of the short, punchy vignette. He freely jumped from idea to idea, concern to concern. He pooh-poohed the over-hyped virtues of structure and form and technical virtuosity. He dismissed the importance of sets, props, costumes, lights. To an extent, he even questioned the need for learning any acting or performing technique. He had no need for continuing with that mainstay of naturalistic theatre—the creation of the illusion of reality. He jettisoned the English language as alienating. He militated against the artificial divide between the actor and the audience, a fire-wall that was intrinsic to the proscenium stage. He genuinely regarded money as irrelevant and profit as vulgar. His basic concern, till the end, remained exploring the untapped energy of the individual and collective body to create a transformative experience for both, the performer and the spectator—an idea he elaborated in his slim 1978 volume *The Third Theatre*.

But one resource Sircar did not abandon was his own training and early career as a town planner. He remained acutely aware of dimensions, planes, elevations, entrances, exits and movement flows. Space was his forte and he was comfortable with planning the spatial algorithms of human agony. Sitting alone one day in1974, in the small hall (capacity of 60 to 75) above the Academy of Fine Arts, Calcutta, which had become his group's main performance and work space and thinking of the *mise-en-scene* for his newly written play *Michhil* (*Procession*), he casually began rearranging the benches meant for the audience in a manner that would distribute the spectators and set the players right amidst them. He suddenly realised he was, in fact, choreographing the audience. Henceforth, his audience would have no other choice but to be in the thick of the action, to 'participate'. There could be no neutral voyeurism or disavowal.

Earlier too, in his plays like *Sagina Mahato* (1971) and *Spartacus* (1972), Sircar had begun exploring the unconventional use of space, entirely rejecting the proscenium idea of the 'invisible audience' that sits in the dark at one side of the auditorium, merely consuming the play. Many of these ideas crystallised after a Nehru Fellowship enabled him, in 1972, to travel to the United States and spend time observing the training and performance methodologies of the East Coast avant garde groups like the Performance Group of Richard Schechner and Joan Littlewood, the Living Theatre of Julian Beck and Judith Malina and La Mama of Antony Serchio. He was also taken aback, when he saw in Poland, the intensity of Jerzy Grotowski's actors in *Apocalypsis cum Figuris*.

From the derivative existentialism of his early scripts like *Ebong Indrajit* and *Baagh* (Tiger), Sircar took a more affirmative direction in 1966-67 in his 'anti-nuclear' trilogy *Baki Itihas* (*Remaining History*), *Tringsha Shatabdi* (*Thirtieth Century*) and *Shesh Nei* (No End). To date, these remain the only critique in Indian theatre of the country's demented nuclear pursuits. Sharadindu and Sumanta, the protagonists of these plays, are simply unable to accept the violence and bestiality of twentieth century's potential for mass destruction and exhort their audiences to reflect on how much they themselves might be implicated in the perpetration of crimes against humanity like the atom bomb and what their own complicity might be in calamities like Hiroshima.

Learning from the experiences of Schechner's Environmental Theatre and Grotowski's Poor Theatre, Sircar created the idea of the intimate Angan Mancha (Courtyard Theatre) in 1972 and, typically, created plays that would have an open-ended, dialogic character rather than something dogmatic or deterministic. Many of the plays were constructed in the format of *tarja*, a Bengali folk form of debate between two poets with opposite points of view. *Prastab, Gondi, Basi Khabar, Pagla Ghoda, Solution X, Hattomalar Oparey, Ekti Hatyar Natyakatha, Khatmat Kring, Churna Prithvi, Sukhapathya Bharater Itihas, Bhanga Manush*—all tested out the strategy of creating internal resistance to the propositions within a play. This resistance corresponds to the initial scepticism within audiences, who are then won over through a judicious marshalling of arguments from the opposite flank.

Sircar explained this to me in an interview published twenty-five years ago:

> We set out to expose commonly held myths. Quite often, therefore, our plays acquire a documentary nature. But we have to make it theatre, for it is the art form we have chosen. For example, it is said that India's agricultural produce has doubled since Independence. It is true. But if you stop there, it gives the

> impression we have developed economically, become wealthier. But there's another figure: that the number of landless agricultural labourers has also doubled during the last decade. That means poverty has also increased. You have to couple these two bits of information to arrive at the reality. That is what we do. We put both facts together and let audiences decide what is true.

However, as Sircar elaborated in the Sri Ram Memorial Lecture in Delhi, in 1993, all this is done with 'an unforgiving anger towards those who cause poverty and hunger as well as to those who remain indifferent to them'. To achieve this, of course, each performer needs to be aware of the subject and be 'immersed in the content' even as he abandons the route of conventional 'enactment' and strives to attain a 'state of being' during the play.

Eventually, it was ironic that after almost five decades of exploring at the frontiers of critical theatre work, Sircar (aged 86) chose his final curtain-call for May 13, the day the Bengal electorate decided on a new experiment in the theatre of politics. The Left Front government conceded power after thirty-four years. The victors called it a 'new Independence Day'. No Badal Sircar script, saturated with the angst and agony of his times, could have captured the cacophonic confusion of the moment, laden with inverted symbols of 'liberation' and replete with degenerate slogans with pretentions to 'peoples' power'.

Badal-babu would have winced in his civilised sort of way at this evacuation of meaning from language. He would have been aghast at this ironic 'revenge of the spectators' in real life. The legendary Brazilian theatre activist Augusto Boal, during the staging of his plays of the Theatre of the Oppressed constantly warned against such 'false' or 'magical' solutions masquerading as 'real' solutions. But Badal-da knew 'the play's the thing' where strategic exits are important and eased himself gently into the night.

Of course, it is tantalising to reflect now on how much the humiliated Left Front in Bengal might have benefited if only they had watched and listened and paid attention to half the things on rural poverty, deprivation and the brutalisation of the poor in the state that Sircar had dealt with in his plays through the 1970s and '80s. Being more alert and receptive to an artist's voice might, perhaps, have never brought them to this pass. Instead, they conveniently dismissed him as a 'middle class messiah'. They ranted and raved against him, called him names, briefly restrained him from performing outdoors and dubbed him an agent of the decadent American avant garde. In their typically bureaucratic manner, the Left party shut its eyes and ears to the signposts of concerns this sensitive playwright was laying out for them.

What they refused to acknowledge was that Sircar and his Satabdi group represented the cleanest example within modern Indian theatre of a group relentlessly questioning its own politics and, in the process, persuading its audiences also into intense self-reflexivity. What the flag-wavers of the organised Left failed to see was that while they themselves picked up issues that concerned a narrow bandwidth in India called the 'proletariat', Sircar was speaking about a much more capacious bandwidth called the 'poor'.

A card-holding member of the undivided Communist Party from 1943 to 1951, he left the party when he found it 'making too many compromises'. As he told Nilanjan Datta in an interview last year (*Current E-paper*): 'I did not join the party under the influence of some dada. I came to the party from a feeling that this world has to be changed. Even after leaving the party, I feel I'm still doing its work—the work of changing the world. That is not finished and I'm still doing it through theatre. I am still a Marxist, though outside the party.'

The radical post-colonial theatre activity of the 1940s-50s epitomised in the directly political intentions of IPTA (Indian Peoples Theatre Association) was to suddenly run dry in the 1960s, to be replaced by the more existentialist preoccupations of the newly emergent urbanistas like Mohan Rakesh, Vijay Tendulkar, Girish Karnad and Sircar himself. Preoccupations turned inward and psycho-social rather than outward and political. It was as if the idea of resistance had bypassed modern Indian theatre, as if it was to serve no more as the voice and expression of the oppressed. No wonder a more powerful theatrical impulse – disguised as a mass movement called Naxalism – overran the moment, proclaiming its own catharsis of violence to counter the brutalities of rampaging state violence. Overnight, Indian theatre had lost its agency.

It is to Badal Sircar's credit that a decade down the line, he could bridge the chasm and recapture this strand of political engagement in theatre. He built upon this in an even more significant way by embarking on a tireless schedule of short workshops across the country whose main purpose was the removal of psychological blocks and inhibitions in the participants. For Sircar, that was the primary goal. He had a series of elaborate trust exercises and improvisations to achieve this. He also provoked the participants to try writing short ten-minute plays as an exercise towards sharpening their ideas. In 30 years he would have easily conducted over 300 long and short workshops and catalysed the work of a large roll-call of prominent theatre personalities—from Heisnam Kanhailal in Manipur to Prasanna in Karnataka; from Probir Guha in Bengal to Madeeha Gauhar in Pakistan.

The first time I met Badal-da was in 1970 when, still an undergrad, I dropped in on the late choreographer Chandralekha's lovely home in Madras. He was there smoking a beedi even as he elaborated his idea of a physical theatre. What I remember is the mercilessly teasing Chandra subjected him to, about his ignorance of Indian performance traditions and training disciplines. Chandra was on strong ground here and one could see Badal-da wilting under her taunts. After some time she asked me to drop him to his hotel on my scooter. Immediately Badal-da went 'No, no, no' and recoiled in protest. Later I learnt he was sitting on a scooter for the first time. Forty years later, last year, I happened to be on the jury of the International Theatre Festival of Kerala (ITFoK) which selected Badal-da for the first Ammanur Puraskaram (2010) for lifetime contribution to theatre. There was a hefty purse with it too. I called Badal-da to congratulate him and also to convey that there was provision for an escort to travel along with him for receiving the award. Promptly, from the other end came the exclamation 'No, no, no.' I laughed and reminded him of the same protest I had heard 40 years ago and said, 'Now don't tell me you are travelling on a plane for the first time.' He chuckled and agreed to bring an escort.

Much of Badal-da's personality was formed by his Protestant Christian background and its work ethic. Spartan in his personal life, he was frugal and forever on a guilt trip about spending money. His only indulgence was the smoke which he enjoyed. On two occasions during workshops in Chennai, one at the Kalakshetra dance school and the other at the IIT, Madras, I had to drive down on my scooter every two hours to bring him out of those sprawling and strict campuses so that he could have a relaxing puff outside the gate, before being deposited back in the workshop.

His other little known passion was, of course, Esperanto language of which he was a pioneer in India and an important figure in the international Esperanto community. He acknowledged the 'guruship' of the Polish physician L.L. Zamenhof, who had created this International Auxiliary Language in 1887. It was particularly significant to Badal-da that it afforded the possibility of breaking the barriers of language. He told me once that he responded to the meaning of Esperanto—to live in hope. One of his treatises *Theaterer Bhasha* (The Language of Theatre) is also available in Esperanto as *Thiye Tarera Bhasha* (1990).

My last meeting with Badal-da was three months ago, last February, when I called on him at his second floor room in the little 'red building' on Peary Row, off Beadon Road in Manicktala. We were meeting after almost a decade and he leapt from his chair for the customary embrace. He had been busy scribbling the final segment of his predictably self-deprecatorily titled autobiography *Purano Kasundi* (Stale Mustard Pickle). The cramped room had a cot in the middle, two Godrej steel almirahs cleverly de-commoditised by being pasted over with a profusion of multi-colour paper cuttings from illustrated magazines and his table and chair overlooking the window.

After some quick reminiscences of Chandralekha and Dashrath Patel and expressing his condolences over their passing away, he said:

> I have two important things to tell you. One is that I'm feeling twenty-five years younger. I have never felt better. The second is that I've recently come into some money through some awards which have substantial monetary value (for one of which you too are responsible). I am feeling rich. Now, I have no intention of saving this money. I plan to spend it well. So I have decided to go on a world tour for six months and once again meet up with all those friends I made around the world. I have no worry because my Esperanto community will look after my boarding and lodging in various cities.

He then proceeded to rattle off a breathless itinerary of cities and people he intended to visit spanning Europe, England, North and South America, Japan, Korea, Laos, Thailand, Myanmar and then back to Kolkata. I said rather amusedly, 'But Badal-da, there's a big black hole in your tour plan – you have missed out on Chennai.' He chuckled and said, 'Yes, of course. Long time since I had that lovely filter coffee you make.'

However, like many of his plans, all this will remain unfulfilled. The big dream he had was part of his unique *Third Theatre* manifesto:

> The ultimate answer…is not for a city group to prepare plays for and about the working people. The working people – factory workers, peasants, the landless labourers will have to make and perform their own plays… This process, of course, can become widespread only when the socio-economic emancipation of the working class has also spread widely. When that happens, the Third Theatre will no longer have a specific function and will merge with a reformed First Theatre.

That awaits the lifetime's work of another Badal Sircar.

This article was published in Economic and Political Weekly *Vol. XLVI no.22, on 28 May 2011, as a homage to Badal Sircar after his demise*

APPENDIX-I

List of Plays by Badal Sircar

1. Solution X, (1956, Maithan), First performance 1961 by Chakra, Kolkata.
2. Baro Pisima (1959, London)/Badi Buaji, First perf. 1960 by Chakra, Kolkata
3. Shanibar/Shonibar (1959, London)
4. Ram Shyam Jadu (1961, Paris) First performance 1962, Chakra, kolkata
5. Samabritta (1961)
6. Ebong Indrajit, (1963),/Evam Indrajit/And Indrajit First performance 1965, Souvanik, Kolkata
7. Sara Rattir, (1963, Paris)/Saari Raat), First performance 1969, Satabdi, Kolkata
8. Ballabhpurer Rupkatha, (1963, Paris)/Ballabhpur Ki Roopkatha/Ek Tha Raja, First performance 1968 in Hindi, Anamika, Kolkata
9. Kobi Kahini, 1964 (Paris)/Kavi Kahani, First performance 1964, Chakra, Kolkata
10. Bichitranushthan (1963, Paris), First performance 1968, Satabdi, kolkata
11. Baagh, (1965, Nigeria)
12. Baki Itihas (1966, Nigeria)/That Other History, First performance1967, Bohurupee, Kolkata
13. Jadi Aar Ek Baar, (1966, Nigeria) /Yadi Ek Baar Phir, First performance 1976, Bohurupee, Kolkata
14. Tringsha Shatabadi, (1966, Nigeria)/Teesvin Shatabdi/Hiroshima, First performance 1969, Bohurupee, Kolkata
15. Pare Kono Din, (1966)/Phir Kisi Din
16. Pralaap (Nigeria 1966), First performance 1969, Satabdi, Kolkata
17. Pagla Ghoda, (1967, Nigeria), First performance 1967, Bohurupee, Kolkata
18. Bibar, (1967)
19. Circus, (1968), First performance 1969, Satabdi, kolkata
20. Shesh Nei, (1970)/Ant Nahin/There is No End, First performance 1970, Satabdi, Kolkata
21. Sagina Mahato, (1970), First performance 1971, Satabdi, Kolkata
22. Abu Hossain, (1971), First performance 1972, Satabdi, Kolkata
23. Spartacus, (1972), First performance 1973, Satabdi, Kolkata
24. Suitcase, (1972), First performance 1972, Satabdi, Kolkata

25. Beej, (1973), First performance 1973, Satabdi, Kolkata
26. Prastab (1973), First performance 1974, Satabdi, Agartala
27. Michhil, (1974)/Juloos/Procession, First performance 1974, Satabdi, Kolkata
28. Bhanumati Ka Khel, (1974), First performance 1974, Satabdi, Kolkata
29. Lakshmichharar Paanchali, (1974), First performance 1974, Satabdi, Kolkata
29. Natyakarer Sandhane Tinti Charitra, (1974)/Natakkar Ki Khoj Mein Teen Charitra
30. Rupakathar Kelenkari (1974)/Scandal in Fairyland, First performance 1975, Satabdi, Kolkata
31. Bhoma, (1975), First performance 1975, Satabdi, Kolkata
32. Sukhapathya Bharat-er Itihas, (1976)/Indian History Made Easy, First performance 1976, Satabdi, Kolkata
33. Hattomalar O Parey, (1977) Hattamala Ke Us Paar/Beyond The Land Of Hattamala, First performance 1977, Satabdi, Kolkata
34. Manikanchan, (1977), First performance 1977, Satabdi, Kolkata
35. Gandi (1977)/Ghera, First performance 1978, Satabdi, Kolkata
36. Captain Hurrah (1977), First performance 1977, Satabdi, Kolkata
37. Padma Nadir Majhi (1978), First performance 1990, Satabdi, Kolkata
38. Basi Khabor (1978)/Basi Khabar/Stale News, First performance 1979, Satabdi, Kolkata
39. Memorandum (1979)
40. Ekti Hatyar Natya Kahini (1979) First performance 1980, Satabdi, Ritam, Cave, Kolkata
41. Nadite (1980), First performance 2002, Satabdi, Sealdah
42. Nagini Kanya (1981), First performance 1982, Satabdi, Kolkata
43. Manushey Manushey (1981) First performance 1981, Satabdi, Kolkata
44. Androcles o Singha (1982) First performance 1991, Satabdi, Kolkata
45. Dwairatha (1982) First performance 2001, Satabdi, Sealdah
46. Udyog Parba (1982)
47. Khat Mat Kring (1983), First performance 1983, Satabdi, Kolkata
48. Sniri (1984), First performance 1985, Satabdi, Kolkata
49. Shanabarir Katho Katha (1985), First performance 1985, Satabdi, Kolkata
50. Sada Kalo (1986), First performance 1987, Satabdi and Pathasena, Kolkata
51. Janmabhumi Aaj (1986), First performance 1986, Satabdi, W.B
52. Churna Prithibi (1987), First performance 1988, Pathasena and Satabdi, Kolkata
53. Bhul Rasta (1988), First performance 1989, Satabdi, Kolkata

54. Bioscope (1989), First performance 1989, Satabdi, Kolkata
55. Dampatya (1988)
56. Ka Cha Ta Ta Pa (1993), First performance 1995, Satak, Kolkata
57. Chaduibhati (1994), First performance 1994, Satabdi, Kolkata
58. Bagala Charit Manas (1997)/Life Of Bagala, First performance 1998, Ayena, Kolkata
59. O re Bihanga (1994), First performance 2009, Satabdi, Kolkata
60. Andhakare (1999)
61. Aeschylus-er Natak (2002)
62. Parashuram (2003)

The list has been compiled with the help of following sources:
List provided by Badal Sircar to the Editor
Natarang Pratishthan Archives
Natya Shodh Sansthan Archives
Badal Sircar, Vyakti Aur Rangmanch by Ashok Bhowmik
Badal Sircar, Two Plays; Ed. by Subhendu Sarkar

APPENDIX-II

Satabdi's Invited Shows

(All the plays are written and directed by Badal Sircar)

Sl.	Year	Date	Place of Performance	Name of the Play	Remarks / Notes
1	1968	14/05	Lilua (Howrah) W.B	Kobi Kahini	
2	1968	19/06	Marquis Square (At-Banga Sanskriti Sammelan, Kolkata), W.B	Kobi Kahini	
3	1968	24/06	Burnpur, W.B	Kobi Kahini	
4	1968	08/07	Howrah, W.B	Kobi Kahini	
5	1969	In March	Delhi, India	Kobi Kahini	
6	1970	06/02	Lilua, W.B	Pralap	
7	1970	01/03	Durgapur, W.B	Sara Rattir	
8	1970	19/03	Santiniketan, W.B	Pralap	
9	1970	12/04	Patna, Bihar	Ballabhurer Roopkatha	
10	1971	10/02	Asansol, W.B	Ballabhpurer Roopkatha	
11	1971	07/03	Birlapur, W.B	Ballabhpurer Roopkatha	
12	1971	05/05	Kolkata(?), W.B	Ballabhpurer Rupkatha	
13	1971	09/05	Dhanbad, Bihar	Ballabhpurer Roopkatha	
14	1971	12/09	Durgapur, W.B	Ballabhpurer Roopkatha	
15	1971	23/10	Kolkata-Padmapukur, W.B	Ballabhpurer Rupkatha	
16	1971	27/10	Lilua, W.B	Ballabhpurer Roopkatha	
17	1971	31/10	Kolkata-Rabindra Sadan, W.B	Sagina Mahato	
18	1971	12/04	Sitarampur, W.B	Sagina Mahato	
19	1971	08/12	Hyderabad-Rabindra Bharti, A.P	Ballabhpurer Roopkatha	
20	1971	09/12	Hyderabad-Rabindra Bharti, A.P	Sagina Mahato	
21	1971	10/12	Hyderabad-Rabindra Bharti, A.P	Shesh Nei	
22	1972	06/01	Howrah, W.B	Sagina Mahato	
23	1972	08/01	Basirhat, W.B	Sagina Mahato	
24	1972	31/01	Kolkata-Rabindra Sadan, W.B	Sagina Mahato	
25	1972	12/02	Singur, W.B	Sagina Mahato	
26	1972	19/02	Bhilai, M.P	Sagina Mahato	
27	1972	20/02	Bhilai, M.P	Ballabhpurer Rupkatha	
28	1972	22/02	Chirimiri, M.P	Sagina Mahato	This play had double shows, at 3 P.M & 6 P.M.
29	1972	23/02	Chirimiri, M.P	Ballabhpurer Roopkatha	This play had double shows, at 3 P.M & 6 P.M.
30	1972	27/04	Kolkata(?), W.B	Abu Hossain	

31	1972	20/05	Durgapur, W.B	Abu Hossain	
32	1972	09/06	Kolkata-Kalamandir, W.B	Abu Hossain	
33	1972	10/06	Kolkata-Kalamandir, W.B	Abu Hossain	
34	1972	11/06	Kolkata-Kalamandir, W.B	Abu Hossain	
35	1972	12/06	Kolkata-Kalamandir, W.B	Abu Hossain	
36	1972	13/06	Kolkata-Kalamandir, W.B	Abu Hossain	
37	1972	22/07	Kolkata-Academy of Fine Arts, W.B	Ballabhpurer Roopkatha	
38	1972	27/09	Kolkata-Academy of Fine Arts, W.B	Abu Hossain	
39	1972	29/09	Kolkata-Kalamandir, W.B	Abu Hossain	
40	1972	26/10	Imphal, Manipur	Ballabhpurer Roopkatha	
41	1972	28/10	Imphal, Manipur	Shesh Nei	
42	1972	30/10	Imphal, Manipur	Ebong Indrajit	
43	1972	23/11	Delhi, India	Sagina Mahato	
44	1972	24/11	Delhi, India	Sagina Mahato	
45	1972	25/11	Delhi, India	Abu Hossain	
46	1972	26/11	Delhi, India	Abu Hossain	
47	1973	17/03	Kolkata-Curzon Park, W.B	Spartacus	
48	1973	31/03	Kolkata-Curzon Park, W.B	Spartacus	
49	1973	19/04	Kolkata-Shyam Square, W.B	Sagina Mahato	performed on stage
50	1973	02/06	Kolkata-Ranjit Stadium, W.B	Spartacus	
51	1973	10/11	Kolkata-Curzon Park, W.B	Spartacus	
52	1973	01/12	Kolkata-Curzon Park, W.B	Spartacus	
53	1973	22/12	Kolkata-Academy Angan Mancha, W.B	Spartacus	
54	1974	19/01	Kolkata-Curzon Park, W.B	Spartacus	Invited by Silhouette
55	1974	26/01	Kolkata-Lake Town, W.B	Spartacus	
56	1974	28/01	Kolkata-Medical College, W.B	Spartacus	
57	1974	09/02	Kolkata- Hare School, W.B	Spartacus	
58	1974	23/02	Kolkata- Kashipur Basti, W.B	Spartacus	
59	1974	02/03	Kolkata- Howrah Basti, W.B	Spartacus	
60	1974	13/04	Ramchandrapur, W.B	Michhil	This show had to be shifted midway from outdoors to a room due to rains. Since very few audience members could fit in it was performed again the next day in the bazaar where many people saw it.
61	1974	14/04	Ramchandrapur Bazar, W.B	Michhil	
62	1974	In April	Agartala, Tripura	Prastab	

63	1974	01/05	Bata Nagar (Near Kolkata), W.B	Swadheen Bharat	
64	1974	13/07	Kolkata-Bagbazar Reading Library, W.B	Michhil	
65	1974	18/07	Kolkata-La Martinaire School, W.B	Michhil	
66	1974	24/07	Kolkata-Curzon Park, W.B	Michhil	Together with another group to protest against the murder of Pradip Dutta. The Other Group performed their own play.
67	1974	31/08	Kolkata-Curzon Park, W.B	Michhil	
68	1974	14/09	Kolkata-Scottish Church School, W.B	Michhil	
69	1974	07/11	Kolkata-Indian Statistical Institute's Boy's Hostel, W.B	Michhil	
70	1974	08/11	Kolkata-Indian Statistical Institute's Boy's Hostel, W.B	Tringsha Satabdi	
71	1974	10/11	Kolkata-Paris Hall (St. John's Cathedral's Hall), W.B	Michhil	
72	1974	17/11	Elachigram, W.B	Tringsha Satabdi	
73	1974	23/11	Kolkata-Kashipur Basti, W.B	Michhil	
74	1974	24/11	Kolkata-Sabjibagan Basti, W.B	Tringsha Satabdi	
75	1974	04/12	Kolkata-Indian Institute of Management, W.B	Michhil	
76	1975	01/01	Kolkata-Dharmasala, W.B	Michhil	
77	1975	31/01	Kolkata-Cathedral Mission School, W.B	Michhil	
78	1975	01/02	Kolkata-Panchkori Radha Rani School, W.B	Michhil	
79	1975	05/02	Kolkata-Indian Statistical Institute, W.B	Spartacus	
80	1975	13/02	Choto Simulia, W.B	Laksmichharar Panchali, Michhil	
81	1975	18/02	Rangabelia, W.B	Michhil, Rupkathar Kelenkari	
82	1975	19/02	Rangabelia, W.B	Spartacus, Laksmichharar Panchali	
83	1975	20/02	Rangabelia, W.B	Prastab	
84	1975	23/02	Kolkata-Sri Shiksha Yatan School, W.B	Michhil	
85	1975	23/03	Kolkata-Presidency College, W.B	Michhil	
86	1975	05/04	Kolkata-National Medical College, W.B	Spartacus	

87	1975	12/04	Chandrakona (Medinipore), W.B	Spartacus	
88	1975	13/04	Dumdum, W.B	Laksmichharar Panchali	
89	1975	25/05	Chandar Nagar, W.B	Spartacus	
90	1975	27/05	Kolkata-Subodh Mullik Square, W.B	Spartacus	
91	1975	31/05	Meralgram, W.B	Spartacus, Michhil	
92	1975	01/06	Meralgram, W.B	Laksmichharar Panchali, Tringsha Shatabdi	
93	1975	03/06	Kolkata-General Post Office, W.B	Spartacus	
94	1975	10/06	Kolkata-Scottish Church School, W.B	Tringsha Shatabdi	
95	1975	02/07	Kolkata-Sanskrita College, W.B	Michhil	
96	1975	13/07	Singjola, W.B	Prastab	
97	1975	07/09	Bardhaman (Burdwan), W.B	Laksmichharar Panchali, Spartacus	
98	1975	17/09	Kolkata-In a Karkhana (In a Factory), W.B	Michhil	
99	1975	22/09	Tatanagar, Bihar (Now in Jharkhand)	Michhil, Spartacus	
100	1975	28/09	Kolkata-Paris Hall, W.B	Spartacus	
101	1975	04/11	Kolkata-Shyam Bazar, W.B	Michhil	
102	1975	08/11	Bohirgachhi (Near Bangladesh Border), W.B	Spartacus, Laksmichharar Panchali, Rupkathar Kelenkari	
103	1975	22/11	Singjole, W.B	Shesh Nei, Michhil	
104	1975	23/11	Singjole, W.B	Spartacus, Laksmichharar Panchali, Rupkathar Kelenkari	
105	1975	02/12	Kolkata-N.R.S. Medical College, W.B	Spartacus	
106	1976	25/01	Kolkata-Ballygunge, W.B	Spartacus	
107	1976	01/02	Kolkata-Presidency College, W.B	Tringsha Shatabdi	
108	1976	05/02	Kolkata-N.R.S. Medical Hostel, W.B	Michhil	
109	1976	14/02	Kolkata-National Medical College, W.B	Michhil	
110	1976	22/02	Bnoichi, W.B	Spartacus, Laksmichharar Panchali	
111	1976	29/02	Kolkata-Beleghata, W.B	Michhil,Spartacus	
112	1976	13/03	Kolkata (?), W.B	Spartacus	

113	1976	21/03	Rangabelia, W.B	Bhoma, Laksmichharar Panchali (?)	
114	1976	22/03	Manmatha Nagar (Sundarban), W.B	Bhoma, Laksmichharar Panchali	
115	1976	10/04	Kolkata-Calcutta University Economics Department, W.B	Bhoma	
116	1976	16/04	Durgapur, W.B	Spartacus, Rupkathar Kelenkari	
117	1976	25/04	Dingjole, W.B	Bhoma, Laksmichharar Panchali	
118	1976	23/05	Arambagh, W.B	Bhoma, Michhil	
119	1976	12/06	Gaighata, W.B	Bhoma	
120	1976	04/07	Kolkata (?), W.B	Spartacus	
121	1976	11/07	Kolkata-Grand Hotel, W.B	Michhil	In the U.S.E.F.I Conference
122	1976	14/07	Kolkata-Northern Park, W.B	Tringsha Shatabdi	
123	1976	15/07	Kolkata-Northern Park, W.B	Bhoma	
124	1976	18/10	Bally, W.B	Michhil	
125	1976	14/11	Tribeni, W.B	Bhoma	
126	1976	04/12	Kolkata-N.R.S. Medical College, W.B	Bhoma	
127	1976	19/12	Kolkata-Presidency College Physics Department, W.B	Sukhopatthya Bharater Itihas	
128	1977	04/01	Kolkata-Theosophical Society Hall (Sindari Association Invited), W.B	Michhil	
129	1977	09/01	Duttapulia, W.B	Bhoma, Laksmichharar Panchali	
130	1977	24/01	Simulpur, W.B	Sukhopatthya Bharater Itihas, Laksmichharar Panchali	
131	1977	29/01	Kolkata-Science College, W.B	Sukhopatthya Bharater Itihas	
132	1977	06/02	Delhi, India	Bhoma	
133	1977	07/02	Delhi, India	Sukhopatthya Bharater Itihas	
134	1977	20/02	Rangabelia, W.B	Sukhopatthya Bharater Itihas	
135	1977	13/03	Santiniketan, W.B	Bhoma	
136	1977	27/03	Singjole, W.B	Bhoma	
137	1977	03/04	Kolkata-Presidency College, W.B	Bhoma	
138	1977	21/04	Kolkata-National Medical College, W.B	Bhoma	
139	1977	08/05	Kolkata-Ballygunge Science College, W.B	Sukhopatthya Bharater Itihas	

140	1977	17/07	Kolkata-Jaipuria College,	Sukhopatthya Bharater Itihas	
141	1977	06/08	Kolkata-Ballygunge Science College W.B	Bhoma	
142	1977	03/09	Kolkata-Bagbazar Reading Library, W.B	Bhoma	
143	1977	11/09	Kolkata-Ashoknagar, W.B	Sukhopatthya Bharater Itihas, Hattomalar Oparey	
144	1977	09/10	Kolkata-Archaeology (?), W.B	Sukhopatthya Bharater Itihas	
145	1977	26/11	Kolkata-Science College(Rajabazar), W.B	Bhoma	
146	1977	29/11	Kolkata-Mercantile Bank, W.B	Bhoma	
147	1977	11/12	Singole, W.B	Monikanchan, Hattomalar Oparey	
148	1977	18/12	Kolkata-Presidency College, W.B	Captain Hurrah	
149	1977	24/12	Kolkata-Indian Statistical Institute, W.B	Bhoma	
150	1978	08/01	Durgapur, W.B	Sukhopatthya Bharater Itihas, Hattomalar Oparey	
151	1978	22/01	Kolkata-Pragnyanananda Bhavan (Moulbi Yuba Kendra), W.B	Monikanchan, Hattomalar Oparey	
152	1978	23/01	Madhyamgram, W.B	Hattomalar Oparey	
153	1978	05/02	Nutanhat, W.B	Bhoma	
154	1978	26/02	Santiniketan, W.B	Sukhopatthya Bharater Itihas, Hattomalar Oparey	
155	1978	12/03	Simulpur, W.B	Monikanchan, Hattomalar Oparey	
156	1978	26/03	Barasat, W.B	Monikanchan, Hattomalar Oparey	
157	1978	14/05	Chittoranjan Colony, W.B	Michhil	
158	1978	22/05	Mysore, Bangalore	Bhoma	
159	1978	23/05	Mysore, Bangalore	Gondi	
160	1978	24/05	Mysore, Bangalore	Michhil	
161	1978	25/05	Mysore, Bangalore	Hattomalar Oparey	
162	1978	11/06	Kolkata-Talapank, W.B	Bhanumati ka Khel	
163	1978	24/09	Kolkata-Andhra Hall, W.B	Michhil	
164	1978	18/11	Kolkata-Science College (Rajabazar), W.B	Hattomalar Oparey	
165	1978	28/11	Kolkata-Theosophical Society, W.B	Gondi	
166	1979	03/01	Kolkata-Northern Park Scout Hall, W.B	Sukhopatthya Bharater Itihas	

167	1979	27/01	Kapastekri Gram (Santosh Pargana), W.B	Michhil	
168	1979	28/01	Hnaspukuria (Santosh Pargana), W.B	Michhil, Hattomalar Oparey	
169	1979	12/02	Kolkata-National Medical College, W.B	Rupkathar Kelenkari, Hattomalar Oparey	
170	1979	17/03	Kolkata-N.R.S. Medical College, W.B	Rupkathar Kelenkari, Hattomalar Oparey	
171	1979	18/03	Jhangram, W.B	Michhil	
172	1979	19/03	Jhangram, W.B	Rupkathar Kelenkari, Hattomalar Oparey	
173	1979	26/03	Durgapur, W.B	Michhil	
174	1979	07/04	Y.M.C.A. Hall, Calcutta, W.B	Hattomalar Oparey	
175	1979	06/05	Durgapur, W.B	Michhil	
176	1979	18/08	Kolkata-Nizam Palace, W.B	Rupkathar Kelenkari, Hattomalar Oparey	
177	1979	19/08	Kolkata-Rabindra Bharati University, W.B	Gondi	
178	1979	09/09	Kolkata-St. Xavier's Collegiate School, W.B	Gondi	
179	1979	16/09	Ranchi, Bihar	Gondi	
180	1979	15/10	Bombay-Chhabildas Hall, Maharashtra	Gondi, Bhoma	2 Shows of both plays-6pm & 8:30pm
181	1979	16/10	Bombay-Chhabildas Hall, Maharashtra	Basi-Khabar	
182	1979	17/10	Bombay-Chhabildas Hall, Maharashtra	Gondi, Bhoma	
183	1979	18/10	Bombay-Chhabildas Hall, Maharashtra	Sukhopatthya Bharater Itihas (6pm), Rupkathar Kelenkari (8:30pm), Hattomalar Oparey (8:30pm)	
184	1979	28/10	Dumdum, W.B	Hattomalar Oparey	
185	1979	11/11	Ranaghat, W.B	Bhoma	
186	1979	13/11	Kolkata(?), W.B	Michhil	
187	1979	08/12	Baruipur, W.B	Bhoma	
188	1979	18/12	Kotkata-Tollygunje Basti, W.B	Hattomalar Oparey	
189	1980	20/01	Duttapulia, W.B	Michhil, Hattomalar Oparey	
190	1980	22/01	Kolkata-All India Radio, W.B	Bhoma	
191	1980	27/01	Bally, W.B	Rupkathar Kelenkari, Hattomalar Oparey	
192	1980	10/02	Bohirgachhi, W.B	Michhil, Hattomalar Oparey	
193	1980	17/02	Krishnanagar, W.B	Michhil	
194	1980	22/02	Howrah Basti, W.B	Michhil	

195	1980	23/02	Rangabelia, W.B	Gondi	
196	1980	25/02	Basanti, W.B	Bhoma	
197	1980	08/03	Agarpara, W.B	Michhil	
198	1980	09/03	Dumdum, W.B	Michhil	
199	1980	11/03	Ramrajatala, W.B	Michhil	
200	1980	23/03	Kadamtala (Howrah), W.B	Michhil	
201	1980	20/04	Kanchrapara, W.B	Michhil	
202	1981	04/01	Duttapulia, W.B	Gondi	
203	1981	22/02	Bela Nagar, W.B	Michhil	
204	1981	15/03	Bally, W.B	Gondi	
205	1981	22/03	Knachrapara, W.B	Gondi	
206	1981	24/03	Birati, W.B	Gondi	
207	1981	05/04	Krishnanager, W.B	Basi Khabar	
208	1981	12/04	Kolkata-Jagat Mukherjee Park, W.B	Michhil	
209	1981	20/04	Kolkata-National Medical College, W.B	Gondi	
210	1981	10/05	Beleghata, W.B	Michhil	
211	1981	06/09	Santiniketan, W.B	Sagina Mahato	
212	1981	18/10	Chandan Nagar, W.B	Hattomalar Oparey	
213	1981	24/10	Kolkata-Grindlays Bank, W.B	Sagina Mahato	
214	1981	20/12	Bnatra Library, W.B	Sagina Mahato	
215	1981	27/12	Uttarpara, W.B	Michhil	
216	1982	03/01	Baruipur, W.B	Sagina Mahato	
217	1982	24/01	Baruipur, W.B	Michhil	
218	1982	14/02	Duttapulia, W.B	Sagina Mahato	
219	1982	28/02	Kharagpur IIT, W.B	Sagina Mahato	
220	1982	07/03	Hindmotor, W.B	Hattomalar Oparey	
221	1982	13/03	Amrar Gan (Mankar), W.B	Michhil, Hattomalar Oparey	
222	1982	25/03	Kolkata-La Martiniere Girls School, W.B	Gondi	Organised by Seagull
223	1982	27/03	Kolkata-La Martiniere Girls School, W.B	Sagina Mahato	
224	1982	31/03	Kolkata-La Martiniere Girls School, W.B	Hattomalar Oparey	
225	1982	03/04	Kalyani University, W.B	Hattomalar Oparey	
226	1982	17/04	Kolkata-St. Xaviers Collegiate School, W.B	Michhil	
227	1982	22/09	Garia, W.B	Michhil	
228	1982	28/09	Krishnanagar, W.B	Gondi	
229	1982	23/10	Kolkata-Gangulibagan, W.B	Michhil	
230	1982	09/11	Digboy, Assam	Gondi	

231	1982	10/11	Digboy, Assam	Michhil, Hattomalar Oparey	
232	1982	11/11	Tinsukia, Assam	Michhil, Gondi	
233	1982	12/11	Tinsukia, Assam	Hattomalar Oparey	
234	1983	08/01	Madhyamgram,W.B	Michhil	
235	1983	16/01	Suri, W.B	Gondi	
236	1983	23/01	Kolkata-Video Recording, W.B	Manushey Manushey	
237	1983	26/01	Kolkata-Video Recording, W.B	Hattomalar Oparey	
238	1983	20/01	Baruipur, W.B	Sagina Mahato	
239	1983	23/02	Kolkata-St. Anthony School, W.B	Hattomalar Oparey	
240	1983	06/02	Bally, W.B	Sukhopatthya Bharater Itihas	
241	1983	09/3	Kolkata-St. Xavier's Hostel, W.B	Michhil	
242	1983	03/03	Baruipur, W.B	Gondi	
243	1983	22/05	Allahabad, Uttar Pradesh	Basi Khabar	
244	1983	23/05	Lucknow, Uttar Pradesh	Basi Khabar	
245	1983	24/05	Lucknow, Uttar Pradesh	Bhoma	
246	1983	26/05	Azamgad (Azamgar), Uttar Pradesh	Basi Khabar	
247	1983	27/05	Azamgad (Azamgar), Uttar Pradesh	Manushey Manushey	
248	1983	13/07	Kolkata-Sindhu Bhawan (Sindhu Vaban), W.B	Bhoma	
249	1983	04/09	Durgapur, W.B	Sagina Mahato	
250	1983	30/10	Kolkata-Baranpur, W.B	Michhil	
251	1983	05/11	Kolkata-Saltlake, W.B	Michhil	
252	1983	30/11	Kolkata-Basanti Devi College, W.B	Michhil	
253	1983	18/12	Mython (Mithon), W.B	Khat Mat Kring	
254	1983	22/12	Kolkata-Bank Of India, W.B	Khat Mat Kring	
255	1984	07/01	Madhyamgram, W.B	Gondi	
256	1984	08/01	Baruipur, W.B	Sukhopatthya Bharater Itihas	
257	1984	15/01	Nanakuri, W.B	Michhil	
258	1984	22/01	Krishnanagar, W.B	Bhoma	
259	1984	25/01	Kalighat, W.B	Hattomalar Oparey	
260	1984	26/01	Hridaypur, W.B	Hattomalar Oparey	
261	1984	11/02	Shewraphuli, W.B	Hattomalar Oparey	
262	1984	03/03	Kolkata(?), W.B	Hattomalar Oparey	
263	1984	18/03	Jairambati, W.B	Lakshmichharar Panchali, Bhoma	
264	1984	25/03	Dankuri, W.B	Hattomalar Oparey	

265	1984	02/04	Kolkata-Government Art College, W.B	Bhoma	
266	1984	08/04	Santiniketan, W.B	Khat Mat Kring	
267	1984	05/05	Kolkata-Jodhpur Park, W.B	Hattomalar Oparey	
268	1984	13/05	Krishnanagar, W.B	Khat Mat Kring	
269	1984	21/10	Kolkata-Bara Nagar, W.B	Bhoma	
270	1984	18/11	Haringhata, W.B	Bhoma	
271	1984	27/12	Kolkata(?), W.B	Manushey Manushey	
272	1985	06/01	Madhyamgram, W.B	Khat Mat Kring	
273	1985	22/01	Kolkata(?), W.B	Manushey Manushey	
274	1985	03/02	Madhyamgram, W.B	Khat Mat Kring	
275	1985	19/02	Bhopal, Madhya Pradesh		Invitation from Rangamandal
276	1985	20/02	Bhopal, Madhya Pradesh	Manushey Manushey	Invitation from Rangamandal
277	1985	21/02	Bhopal, Madhya Pradesh	Bhoma	Invitation from Rangamandal
278	1985	22/02	Bhopal, Madhya Pradesh	Basi Khabar	Invitation from Rangamandal
279	1985	10/03	Burnpur, W.B	Basi Khabar	
280	1985	13/03	Jadavpur University, W.B	Basi Khabar	
281	1985	08/04	Bardhaman (Burdwan), W.B	Lakshmichharar, Panchali, Hattomalar Oparey	
282	1985	12/05	Dhaharkandha, W.B	Lakshmichharar Panchali	
283	1985	29/05	Kolkata-Bank of India, W.B	Sagina Mahato	
284	1985	05/12	Basanti Devi College, W.B	Khat Mat Kring	
285	1985	25/12	Kanchrapara, W.B	Shanabarir Kathokatha	
286	1985	29/12	Vadutala (Midnapur), W.B	Shanabarir Kathokatha, Lakshmichharar Panchali	
287	1986	04/01	Kolkata-Presidency College, W.B	Khat Mat Kring	
288	1986	26/01	Haridaypur, W.B	Lakshmichharar Panchali	
289	1986	09/02	Krishnanagar, W.B	Sagina Mahato	
290	1986	19/02	Kolkata-Gouribari, W.B	Hattomalar Oparey	From 28/3 to 30/3–Gram Parikrama
291	1986	03/05	Kolkata-Sarojnalini School, W.B	Lakshmichharar Panchali, Hattomalar Oparey	
292	1986	15/08	Horinghata, W.B	Michhil	
293	1986	14/09	Borhall, W.B	Michhil, Hattomalar Oparey	
294	1986	09/11	Maldah, W.B	Michhil, Hattomalar Oparey	21-22/11-Gram Parikrama
295	1986	30/11	Jangipara, W.B	Michhil, Hattomalar Oparey	

296	1986	07/12	Raigunj, W.B	Michhil, Hattomalar Oparey	
297	1986	14/12	Subhasgram, W.B	Michhil	
298	1986	25/12	Halisahar, W.B	Janmabhumi Aaj	
299	1986	27/12	Kolkata-Sindhu Bhawan, W.B	Hattomalar Oparey	
300	1986	28/12	Baranagar, W.B	Hattomalar Oparey, Lakshmichharar Panchali	
301	1987	11/01	Banipur(Hawra), W.B	Michhil	
302	1987	17/01	Madhyamgram, W.B	Janmabhumi Aaj	
303	1987	18/01	Krishna Nagar, W.B	Janmabhumi Aaj	
304	1987	25/01	Kancharapara, W.B	Janmabhumi Aaj	
305	1987	01/02	Hridaypur, W.B	Gondi	
306	1987	08/02	Andharia, W.B	Lakshmichharar Panchali, Hattomalar Oparey	
307	1987	15/02	Purulia, W.B	Michhil	
308	1987	22/02	Baripur-Rasmath, W.B	Gondi	
309	1987	01/03	Duttapulia, W.B	Gondi	
310	1987	30/05	Kolkata(?), W.B	Janmabhumi Aaj	
311	1987	05/07	Bosirhat, W.B	Janmabhumi Aaj	
312	1987	08/09	Tinsukhia, Assam	Lakshmichharar Panchali, Sniri (Snidi)	
313	1987	09/09	Tinsukhia, Assam	Shanabarir Kathokatha, Janmabhumi Aaj	
314	1987	10/09	Dibrugarh, Assam	Sniri, Janmabhumi Aaj	13&15/11-Gram Parikrama
315	1987	29/11	Akra-Kanchantala, W.B	Lakshmichharar Panchali, Hattomalar Oparey	
316	1987	13/12	Bally, W.B	Janmabhumi Aaj	
317	1987	20/12	Andharia-Baruipur, W.B	Michhil	
318	1988	17/01	Haridaypur, W.B	Sada Kalo	
319	1988	26/01	Krishnanagar, W.B	Sada Kalo	
320	1988	07/02	Banipur-Howrah, W.B	Hattomalar Oparey	
321	1988	24/03	Knachrapara, W.B	Hattomalar Oparey	
322	1988	27/03	Duttapulia, W.B	Sada Kalo	
323	1988	05/06	Sarsuna, W.B	Bhoma	29/10-30/10-Gram Parikarama
324	1988	In July	Kolkata-Tathyakendra (Kolkata Information Centre), W.B	Sada Kalo	19/11-20/11-Gram Parikarama
325	1988	13/11	Jaynagar, W.B	Hattomalar Oparey	
326	1988	04/12	Haridaypur, W.B	Michhil	
327	1989	22/01	Haridaypur, W.B	Bioscope	
328	1989	27/01	Kolkata-Presidency College, W.B	Michhil	

329	1989	29/01	Krishnanagar, W.B	Bioscope	
330	1989	05/02	Knachrapara, W.B	Bioscope	
331	1989	19/02	Banipur-Hobra, W.B	Bioscope	
332	1989	27/02	Knachrapara, W.B	Michhil	05/03-06/03-Gram Parikarama
333	1989	09/03	Kolkata-Tangra, W.B	Lakshmichharar Panchali, Bhul Rasta	
334	1989	24/03	Agarpata, W.B	Bhul Rasta	
335	1989	28/03	Kolkata-Tala, W.B	Michhil	
336	1989	02/04	Kolkata-Gurudas College, W.B	Bhoma	
337	1989	21/04	Kolkata-Khudiram Bose Road, W.B	Michhil	
338	1989	23/04	Bahirgoda, W.B	Bioscope, Bhul Rasta	
339	1989	11/06	Nabadweep, W.B	Sagina Mahato	
340	1989	08/07	Kolkata-Muralidhar Girl's College, W.B	Gondi, Bhul Rasta	
341	1989	26/07	Kolkata-Hongkong Bank, W.B	Bioscope	
342	1989	10/09	Kolkata-Baranagar, W.B	Bhul Rasta	
343	1989	06/10	Kolkata-Salt Lake, W.B	Bhul Rasta, Bioscope	
344	1989	02/11	Rajballavpur, W.B	Bioscope, Hattomalar Oparey	
345	1989	28/11	Delhi Trade Fair, Delhi	Gondi	
346	1989	29/11	Delhi Trade Fair, Delhi	Sada Kalo	
347	1990	20/01	Kolkata-Arts Acre, W.B	Bioscope	
348	1990	28/01	Krishnanagar, W.B	Bhul Rasta	
349	1990	04/02	Banipur-Hawra, W.B	Janmabhumi Aaj	
350	1990	11/02	Rahra-Ramkrishna Mission College, W.B	Hattomalar Oparey	
351	1990	12/02	Holisahar, W.B	Hattomalar Oparey	
352	1990	20/02	Khardah, W.B	Bioscope	
353	1990	25/02	Duttapulia, W.B	Bioscope	Had to be stopped halfway due to rains
354	1990	04/03	Hridaypur, W.B	Bhul Rasta	
355	1990	08/03	Kolkata-Sursuna, W.B	Michhil	
356	1990	15/03	Kolkata-Indian Stastistical Institute, W.B	Michhil	
357	1990	18/03	Kolkata-Amtala, W.B	Hattomalar Oparey	
358	1990	08/04	Duttapulia, W.B	Bioscope	
359	1990	27/04	Kolkata-Ashoknagar, W.B	Sada Kalo	
360	1990	01/05	Kolkata-Sarsuna, W.B	Sagina Mahato	
361	1990	02/05	Kolkata-Sarsuna, W.B	Bioscope	
362	1990	27/05	Kolkata-Shyambazar, W.B	Lakshmichharar Panchali, Hattomalar Oparey	

363	1990	17/06	Naihati, W.B	Sagina Mahato	
364	1990	20/09	Purnia, Bihar	Bioscope, Hattomalar Oparey	
365	1990	20/12	Kolkata (?), W.B	Michhil	
366	1990	23/12	Shewraphuli, W.B	Dakhal	
367	1990	30/12	Rabindra Bharti University, W.B	Michhil	
368	1991	10/02	Banipur-Hawra, W.B	Khat Mat Kring	
369	1991	15/02	Kolkata-Sarsuna, W.B	Khat Mat Kring	
370	1991	29/03	Holisahar, W.B	Sagina Mahato	
371	1991	30/03	Bardhaman (Burdwan), W.B	Sagina Mahato	
372	1991	06/04	Purba Khejurberia, W.B	Dakhal	
373	1991	06/04	Hingalgunj Block, W.B	Hattomalar Oparey	
374	1991	14/04	Katoa, W.B	Sagina Mahato	
375	1991	04/05	Kolkata-(In a Bank), W.B	Michhil	
376	1991	20/06	Kolkata-Birla Museum, W.B	Hattomalar Oparey	
377	1991	03/11	Gultia, W.B	Michhil, Androcles O Singho	
378	1992	01/02	Madhyamgram, W.B	Androcles O Singho	
379	1992	14/02	Kolkata-Hajra Park, W.B	Hattomalar Oparey	
380	1992	16/02	Asansol, W.B	Hattomalar Oparey, Michhil	
381	1992	21/02	Kolkata-Student's Hall, W.B	Hattomalar Oparey	
382	1992	01/03	Howrah, W.B	Hattomalar Oparey	
383	1992	06/03	Khardah, W.B	Michhil	
384	1992	02/05	Kolkata-Sarsuna, W.B	Androcles O Singho	
385	1992	08/08	Kolkata-Hong Kong Bank, W.B	Tringsha Satabdi	
386	1992	25/08	Kolkata-Baranagar, W.B	Tringsha Shatabdi	
387	1992	29/08	Kolkata-Hindi High School, W.B	Hattomalar Oparey	
388	1992	10/09	Kolkata-Srirampur, W.B	Hattomalar Oparey	
389	1992	12/09	Kolkata-In School, W.B	Hattomalar Oparey	
390	1993	27/01	Belur, W.B	Khat Mat Kring	
391	1993	14/02	Banipur-Hawra, W.B	Bhul Rasta, Lakshmichharar Panchali	
392	1993	07/03	Bagnihati, W.B	Lakshmichharar Panchali	
393	1993	23/03	Bhubaneswar, Orissa	Hattomalar Oparey	
394	1993	24/03	Bhubaneswar, Orissa	Michhil	
395	1993	28/03	Katoa, W.B	Sada Kalo	
396	1993	31/03	Kolkata-Jadavpur University, W.B	Sada Kalo	
397	1993	02/05	Kolkata-Sarsuna, W.B	Hattomalar Oparey	
398	1993	09/05	Kolkata-Manevila Gardens, W.B	Michhil	

399	1993	26/07	Baguihati, W.B	Sada Kalo	
400	1993	27/07	Kolkata-Jadavpur	Sada Kalo	University, W.B
401	1993	22/08	Bally, W.B	Sada Kalo	
402	1993	12/09	Kolkata-Sarsuna, W.B	Nagini Kanya	
403	1993	18/09	Kolkata-Hong Kong Bank, W.B	Sada Kalo	
404	1993	02/10	Kolkata-St Lawrence High School, W.B	Sada Kalo	
405	1993	03/11	Kolkata-Bagnihati, W.B	Hattomalar Oparey	
406	1993	09/12	Kolkata-Shyambazar, W.B	Hattomalar Oparey	
407	1993	20/12	Kolkata-St. Xaviers College, W.B	Sada Kalo	
408	1993	26/12	Bally, W.B	Hattomalar Oparey	
409	1994	16/01	Bally, W.B	Hattomalar Oparey	
410	1994	06/02	Krishnanagar, W.B	Sada Kalo	
411	1994	09/02	Kolkata-Don Bosco School, W.B	Hattomalar Oparey	
412	1994	12/02	Banipur-Howrah, W.B	Sada Kalo	
413	1994	13/02	Asansol, W.B	Sada Kalo	
414	1994	14/02	Asansol, W.B	Sada Kalo	
415	1994	19/02	Dnaihat, W.B	Hattomalar Oparey	
416	1994	22/02	Kolkata-Sarala Memorial School, W.B	Sada Kalo	
417	1994	27/02	Krishnanagar, W.B	Nagini Kanya	
418	1994	05/03	Bhadreswar, W.B	Nagini Kanya	
419	1994	05/03	Bhadreswar, W.B	Sagina Mahato	
420	1994	08/03	Kolkata-Medical College, W.B	Sada Kalo	
421	1994	19/03	Kolkata-Jadavpur University, W.B	Hattomalar Oparey	
422	1994	20/03	Santiniketan, W.B	Hattomalar Oparey	
423	1994	20/03	Santiniketan, W.B	Nagini Kanya	
424	1994	21/03	Santiniketan, W.B	Sada Kalo	
425	1994	30/03	Sreerampur, W.B	Hattomalar Oparey	
426	1994	07/05	Bally, W.B	Michhil	
427	1994	29/05	Phuleswar, W.B	Sada Kalo	
428	1994	04/06	Kanovia, W.B	Michhil	
429	1994	05/06	Kolkata-Ballygunje, W.B	Sada Kalo	
430	1994	11/06	Bally, W.B	Michhil	
431	1994	16/06	Kolkata-Grindlay's Bank, W.B	Nagini Kanya	
432	1994	03/07	Santiniketan, W.B	Michhil	
433	1994	04/07	Santiniketan, W.B	Bhul Rasta	
434	1994	14/08	Kolkata-Baranagar, W.B	Hattomalar Oparey	
435	1994	29/08	Barasat, W.B	Michhil	

436	1994	18/11	Kolkata-Shyambazar, W.B	Charuibhati	
437	1994	19/11	Kolkata-Presidency College, W.B	Sada Kalo	
438	1994	05/12	Bhowanipore, W.B	Hattomalar Oparey	CESC invitation
439	1994	05/12	Kolkata, W.B	Hattomalar Oparey	CESC invitation, another location in kolkata
440	1995	05/02	Trichi, Tamilnadu	Sada Kalo	
441	1995	06/02	Trivandrum, Kerala	Sada Kalo	
442	1995	08/02	Nagarkod, Tamilnadu	Sada Kalo	
443	1995	09/02	Domdogadi, Tamilnadu	Sada Kalo	
444	1995	13/02	Madras, Tamilnadu	Sada Kalo	
445	1995	14/02	Bangalore, Mysore	Sada Kalo	
446	1995	05/03	Khardah, W.B	Hattomalar Oparey	
447	1995	03/05	Kolkata-Sarsuna, W.B	Charuibhati	
448	1995	04/06	Uttarpara, W.B	Hattomalar Oparey	
449	1995	24/06	Shyamnazar, W.B	Ka Cha Ta Ta Pa	
450	1995	22/07	Madhyamgram, W.B	Charuibhati	
451	1995	27/08	Hyderabad, Andhra Pradesh	Sada Kalo	
452	1995	28/08	Hyderabad, Andhra Pradesh	Charuibhati,Michhil	
453	1995	29/08	Hyderabad, Andhra Pradesh	Michhil	
454	1995	16/09	Kolaghat, W.B	Hattomalar Oparey	
455	1996	24/01	Kolaghat, W.B	Lakshmichharar Panchali, Bhul Rasta	
456	1996	28/01	Kolkata-Sarsuna, W.B	Lakshmichharar Panchali, Bhul Rasta	
457	1996	08/02	Kolkata-Sarala Memorial School, W.B	Nagini Kanya	
458	1996	10/02	Kolkata- Lake town, W.B	Ka Cha Ta Ta Pa	
459	1996	16/02	Kanchrapara, W.B	Ka Cha Ta Ta Pa	
460	1996	12/10	Kolkata-Rajballavpara, W.B	Manushey Manushey	
461	1996	18/10	Kolkata-Dumdum, W.B	Michhil	
462	1996	07/11	Kolkata-Presidency College, W.B	Manushey Manushey	
463	1996	18/12	Kolkata-Presidency College, W.B	Sada Kalo	
464	1996	21/12	Baruipur, W.B	Sada Kalo	
465	1996	27/12	Kolkata-Sarsuna, W.B	Sada Kalo	
466	1996	28/12	Kolkata-Sarsuna, W.B	Ka Cha Ta Ta Pa	
467	1997	25/01	Dakshin Barasat, W.B	Manushey Manushey	
468	1997	01/02	Sanitiniketan, W.B	Sada Kalo	
469	1997	08/02	Kolkata-Salt Lake, W.B	Manushey Manushey	
470	1997	09/02	Kolaghat, W.B	Sada Kalo	
471	1997	11/02	Palpara, W.B	Ka Cha Ta Ta Pa	

472	1997	12/02	B.E. College, Dhibpur, W.B	Michhil, Hattomalar Oparey	
473	1997	22/02	Kanchrapara, W.B	Khat Mat Kring	
474	1997	13/03	Chandan Nagar, W.B	Khat Mat Kring	
475	1997	16/03	Panchla, W.B	Manushey Manushey	
476	1997	11/04	Belgharia, W.B	Khat Mat Kring	
477	1997	18/07	Calcutta University Asutosh Hall, W.B	Michhil	
478	1997	25/10	Suhrabordi Park-Dhaka, Bangladesh	Hattomalar Oparey	
479	1997	26/10	Suhrabordi Park-Dhaka, Bangladesh	Charuibhati, Hattomalar Oparey, Ka Cha Ta Ta Pa	
480	1997	27/10	Suhrabordi Park-Dhaka, Bangladesh	Bhoma	
481	1997	28/10	Suhrabordi Park-Dhaka, Bangladesh	Bhul Rasta	
482	1997	30/10	Jashahan, W.B	Hattomalar Oparey	
483	1997	18/11	Kolkata-Hatibagan, W.B	Charuibhati	
484	1997	23/11	Kolkata(?), W.B	Sada Kalo	
485	1997	30/11	Kolkata(?), W.B	Michhil	
486	1997	28/12	Kolkata-Lake Town, W.B	Hattomalar Oparey	
487	1998	31/01	Kolaghat, W.B	Michhil	
488	1998	04/02	Baharampur, W.B	Michhil	
489	1998	06/02	Kolkata-Sarsuna, W.B	Hattomalar Oparey	
490	1998	07/02	Kolkata-Sarsuna, W.B	Bhoma	
491	1998	14/02	Kanchrapara, W.B	Hattomalar Oparey, Ka Cha Ta Ta Pa	
492	1998	11/07	Kolkata-All India Radio (Recording), W.B	Bhul Rasta	
493	1998	09/08	Jangipara, W.B	Bhoma	
494	1999	26/01	Kolkata-Salt Lake, W.B	Hattomalar Oparey	
495	1999	01/02	Baharampur, W.B	Hattomalar Oparey, Ka Cha Ta Ta Pa	
496	1999	08/02	Kolkata-Science College, W.B	Janmabhumi Aaj	
497	1999	27/02	Kanchrapara, W.B	Michhil	
498	1999	28/02	Kanchrapara, W.B	Androcles O Singha	
499	1999	20/03	Shijberia, W.B	Hattomalar Oparey	
500	1999	08/08	Kanchrapara, W.B	Charuibhati	
501	1999	11/09	Kolkata-Bhartiya Bhasa Parishad, W.B	Sada Kalo	
502	1999	18/09	Kolkata-Bhartiya Bhasa Parishad, W.B	Janmabhumi Aaj	
503	1999	05/12	Kolkata-Sarsuna, W.B	Manushey Manushey	
504	2000	01/01	Kolkata-Bagbazar,W.B	Ka Cha Ta Ta Pa	

505	2000	07/03	National School of Drama, Delhi	Manushey Manushey, Michhil	
506	2000	08/03	National School of Drama, Delhi	Manushey Manushey, Michhil	
507	2000	08/04	Kolkata-Loretto School, W.B	Hattomalar Oparey	
508	2000	01/05	Kolkata-Santoshpur (Jadavpur), W.B	Michhil	
509	2000	12/11	Chnuchura, W.B	Michhil	
510	2000	18/11	Barasat, W.B	Michhil	250th Show
511	2000	In Dec.	Kolkata-Sarsuna, W.B	Ekti Hatyar Natyakatha	
512	2001	13/01	Shovabazar, W.B	Ka Cha Ta Ta Pa	
513	2001	In Jan, Feb	Bhubaneshwar, Orissa	Manushey Manushey	
514	2001	24/02	Kolkata-Loretto School, W.B	Bhul Rasta	
515	2001	11/03	Kolkata-Dumdum, W.B	Janmabhumi Aaj	
516	2001	08/04	Bally, W.B	Janmabhumi Aaj	
517	2001	26/08	Bally library, W.B	Janmabhumi Aaj	
518	2001	24/11	Nandan Chattar, Natyamela 2003-Kolkata, W.B	Janmabhumi Aaj	
519	2001	15/12	Sarsuna, Ayna-Kolkata, W.B	Captain Hurrah	
520	2001	16/12	Ramrajatala, Howrah, Mandal, W.B	Captain Hurrah	
521	2001	29/12	Duttapukur, 24 parganas, North, W.B	Michhil	
522	2002	05/01	Dankuni Bolmela, Dankuri, W.B	Janmabhumi Aaj	
523	2002	06/01	Belur-Shakti Sangha, W.B	Janmabhumi Aaj	
524	2002	24/02	YMCA, Maniktala, Bivaban, Kolkata, W.B	Captain Hurrah	
525	2002	09/03	Salt Lake Stadium, Durbar Mahila Samiti, Kolkata W.B	Hattomalar Oparey	
526	2002	14/12	Sarsuna, Ayna-Kolkata, W.B	Nadite	
527	2002	21/12	Baranagar-Kolkata, W.B	Janmabhumi Aaj	
528	2003	10/08	Lake gardens-Kolkata, W.B	Hattomalar Oparey	
529	2003	20/09	Kishalay Shishu Bidyalay, Siliguri, W.B	Hattomalar Oparey, Nadite	
530	2003	21/09	Kishalay Shishu Bidyalay, Siliguri, W.B	Charuibhati, Janmabhumi Aaj	
531	2003	15/11	Kandi, Murshidabad, W.B	Nadite	
532	2003	16/11	Kandi, Murshidabad, W.B	Hattomalar Oparey	
533	2003	29/11	Ganguly Bagan-Kolkata, W.B	Hattomalar Oparey	
534	2003	30/11	Nandan Chattar, Natyamela 2003-Kolkata, W.B	Nadite	
535	2003	20/12	Sarsuna, Ayna-Kolkata, W.B	Charuibhati	

536	2003	25/12	Uttarpara Jayakrishna Library, Samthat, W.B	Nadite	
537	2004	10/01	Panchpota, Garia-Kolkata, W.B	Charuibhati	
538	2004	01/03	Rabindra Kanan, Durbar Mahila Samiti-Kolkata, W.B	Amra Manush Boti	
539	2004	18/03	Jadavpur University-Kolkata, W.B	Hattomalar Oparey	
540	2004	04/09	Moldar Gate, Budge-Budge Road, Chhatrasangha, W.B	Hattomalar Oparey	
541	2004	26/11	Gaganindra Pradarshanshala, Natyamela, 2004-Kolkata, W.B	Amra Manush Boti	
542	2004	17/12	Bharat Petroleum Recreation Club, Hong Kong Bank, Howrah	Nadite	
543	2005	08/01	Bibekananda Patthaghar, Jadavpur, Kolkata, W.B	Nadite	
544	2005	30/01	Kalna College, Hadkama, Kalna, W.B	Janmabhumi Aaj	
545	2005	20/02	Baruipur, W.B	Nadite	
546	2005	27/03	YMCA, Maniktala, Bivaban, Kolkata, W.B	Janmabhumi Aaj	
547	2005	21/05	Baguihati Narayantala-Mobamela, W.B	Janmabhumi Aaj	
548	2005	25/09	Rani Bhabani School, Shyambazar, Kolkata, W.B	Nadite	
549	2006	07/01	Bibekananda Patthaghar, Jadavpur-Kolkata, W.B	Janmabhumi Aaj	
550	2006	15/01	Belgharia, W.B	Nadite	
551	2006	17/01	Barasat College, W,B	Khat Mat Kring	
552	2006	22/01	Jhangram, Prayas, W,B	Nadite	
553	2006	05/02	B.K.E.College, Banhooghly, W.B	Janmabhumi Aaj	
554	2006	16/02	Swabhumi-Kolkata, W.B	Nadite	
555	2006	21/05	Sarberia Shramajibi Hospital, W.B	Hattomalar Oparey	
556	2006	27/05	Baguihati Narayantala-Mobamela, W.B	Hattomalar Oparey	
557	2006	10/06	Medical College-Kolkata, W.B	Hattomalar Oparey	
558	2006	11/06	Sodpur High School, Manab, W.B	Hattomalar Oparey	
559	2006	09/07	Rabindra Sadan Chetana, W.B	Hattomalar Oparey	
560	2006	14/11	Dakshini Kolkata, Sebashrani, W.B	Hattomalar Oparey	
561	2006	24/11	Jhargram, Prayas, W.B	Dwairath	
562	2006	25/11	Jhargram, Prayas, W.B	Khat Mat Kring	

563	2007	07/01	Bibekananda Patthagar, Jadavpur-Kolkata, W.B	Khat Mat Kring	
564	2007	20/01	Baharampur, Breehi, W.B	Khat Mat Kring	
565	2007	04/02	Baharampur, Jagyagni, W.B	Janmabhumi Aaj	
566	2007	22/02	Jadavpur University-Kolkata, W.B	Dwairath	
567	2007	27/02	Rabindra Kanan, Durbar Mohila Samiti-Kolkata, W.B	Hattomalar Oparey	
568	2007	14/03	Medical College-Kolkata, W.B	Dwairath	
569	2007	19/05	Sarsuna, Rabitirtha, Kolkata, W.B	Hattomalar Oparey	
570	2007	03/06	YMCA, Maniktala, Bivaban-Kolkata, W.B	Dwairath	
571	2007	25/08	Student's Hall, Chhatra Sanhati-Kolkata, W.B	Janmabhumi Aaj	
572	2007	10/10	Jayenpur, Sanlap, W.B	Hattomalar Oparey	
573	2007	23/12	Sarsuna, Ayna-Kolkata, W.B	Pralap	
574	2008	12/01	Jaykrishna Library, Uttarpara Silpi Sansad, W.B	Nadite	
575	2008	24/01	Belur Shramajibi Hospital (Belur E.S.I Hospital), W.B	Hattomalar Oparey	
576	2008	11/02	Salt Lake, Cluster X-Kolkata, W.B	Pralap	
577	2008	01/03	Banshberia, Nabakur, W.B	Pralap	
578	2008	03/03	Alliance Francaise, Kalighat rotary Club-Kolkata, W.B	Pralap	
579	2008	09/04	Bharatiya Sanskriti Parishad-Kolkata, W.B	Pralap	
580	2008	12/04	Khardah, Kharij, W.B	Hattomalar Oparey	
581	2008	20/04	Mondirtala, Howrah, Behag, W.B	Hattomalar Oparey	
582	2008	17/05	Baguihati Narayantala Molamela, W.B	Pralap	
583	2008	27/06	Mohabodhi Society, Kolkata, W.B	Khat Mat Kring	
1	1986	28/03	Dargah Near Charghat, W.B	Shana Barir Kathokatha	First Time
2	1986	28/03	Malladanga-Kolkata, W.B	Lakshmichharar Panchali	
3	1986	28/03	Charghat, W.B	Shishuder Raksha Karo	
4	1986	29/03	Dakshin Kachdaha, W.B	Lakshmichharar Panchali	
5	1986	29/03	Sutia, W.B	Shishuder Raksha Karo	
6	1986	30/03	Ramchandrapur, W.B	Shishuder Raksha Karo	
7	1986	30/03	Tunakurghar, W.B	Lakshmichharar Panchali, Shishuder Raksha Karo	
1	1987	13/11	Dakshinbari, W.B	Hattomalar Oparey	2nd Time
2	1987	13/11	Jabdapota, W.B	Michhil	

3	1987	14/11	Telihati, W.B	Hattomalar Oparey	
4	1987	14/11	Baghata, W.B	Lakshmichharar Panchali	
5	1987	14/11	Punba Gobindapur, W.B	Hattomalar Oparey	
6	1987	15/11	Borehall, W.B	Janmabhumi Aaj	
7	1987	15/11	Borehall, W.B	Lakshmichharar Panchali	
1	1988	29/10	Birahee, W.B	Hattomalar Oparey	3rd Time
2	1988	29/10	Narayanpur, W.B	Sada Kalo	
3	1988	30/10	Nalkure, W.B	Michhil	
4	1988	30/10	Uttar Rajapur Battala, W.B	Hattomalar Oparey	
1	1988	19/11	Jabdapota, W.B	Sagina Mahato	4th Time
2	1988	19/11	Rudrapur, W.B	Sada Kalo	
3	1988	20/11	Wadipur, W.B	Michhil	
4	1988	20/11	Deulpur, W.B	Michhil	
1	1993	05/08	'Karur', Tamilnadu (16 miles interior from the Railway station)	Sada Kalo	5th Time
2	1993	12/08	Madurai, Tamilnadu	Sada Kalo	
3	1993	13/08	Palayamkottai, Tamilnadu	Sada Kalo	
4	1993	15/08	Chennai, Tamilnadu	Sada Kalo	

Note:

This list of invited shows of Satabdi, all written and directed by Badal Sircar, has been collected and compiled for Natarang Pratishthan by Tripti (Rani) Mitra in 2008 from Badal Sircar's personal collection and from Satabdi's records. This gives an idea of the number of shows that were being done by Badal Sircar and Satabdi right till 2008, and the meticulousness with which he personally kept records of each performance.

Names of cities and towns that could not be cross checked have been mentioned as in the records. The editor does not take responsibility for the veracity of these names or their spellings.

APPENDIX-III

Sircar's Plays Staged by Other Groups

Sl.	Name of Play	Director	Group	Language	Year
1.	Abu Hossain 1971	Vimal Lath	Anamika, Kolkata	Hindi	1973
		Urmil Kr Thapalyal	Darpan, Lucknow	Hindi	1975
		Ravi Vasvani	Daryaganj Club, Delhi	Hindi	1976
		Suraj Sharma	Shoonya, Delhi	Hindi	1982
		Chandra Mohan	Kala Manch, Dehradoon	Hindi	1985
		Urmil Kr Thapaliyal	BNA, Lucknow	Hindi	1994
		Urmil Kr Thapaliyal	Manjushri, Gorakhpur	Hindi	–
		Sanjay Kr Sonu	My Theatre, Patna	Hindi	–
			Prekshak, Bhopal	Hindi	
2.	Baki Itihas 1966	Rajinder Nath	Abhiyan, Delhi	Hindi	1968
		–	Chaturang, Kolkata	Bengali	1968
		Gopinath Mukherji	Bohurupee, Kolkata	Bengali	1969
		S. Rajdeep	Pragati, Varanasi	Hindi	1970
		Prabhat Mandal	–	Hindi	1971
		Satyavrat Rout	Artist Association, Allahabad	Hindi	1971
		Vimal Awasthi	Hastakshar, Raipur	Hindi	1971
		Mahendra Singh	Hindi Natya Sangh	Hindi	1972
		Kishan Kumar	Yavanika, Kolkata	Hindi	1972
		Bansi Kaul	IIT, Kanpur	Hindi	1973
			Nagarik Natya Sampradaya, Dhaka		1973
		Shiv Kumar Jhunjhunwala	Anamika, Kolkata	Hindi	1975
		Purushottam Agrawal	Rangshilp, Gwalior	Hindi	1977
		Rita Khanna	Mumbai University, Mumbai	Hindi	1977
		Dinesh Thakur	Indian National Theatre, Mumbai	Hindi	1977
		Raju Sharma	St. Stephens College, Delhi	Hindi	1980
		Sanakhya Ebotombi	NSD, Delhi	Hindi	1981
		Bansi Kaul	Darpan, Lucknow	Hindi	1981
		Shekhar Vaishnavi	Shri Ram College of Com. Delhi	Hindi	1982
		Raj Bisaria	BNA, Lucknow	Hindi	1984
		Devdeep	Sanket, Alwar	Hindi	1986
		Satish Anand	Kala Sangam, Patna	Hindi	1986
		Amita Udgata	NSD, Delhi	Hindi	1988
		Robin Das	NSD, Delhi	Hindi	1995
		Uday	Paridhi, Bhagalpur	Hindi	1996

		Shivmurat Singh	Madhyam, Gazipur	Hindi	1997
		Bipul Pachouri	IPTA, JNU	Hindi	2009
		Sombhu Mitra	Bohurupee, Kolkata	Bengali	–
		Madhukar Pandit	Amateur Drama Club, Baroda	Hindi	–
		Kamla Shankar	Prayog, Sagar	Hindi	–
		Neel Kamal	Natya Parishad, Varanasi	Hindi	–
		Purushattam Aggrawal	Rangshilp, Gwalior	Hindi	–
		–	Artists Combine, Gwalior	Hindi	–
		Dhirendra Kumar	Hillol Sangam, Ujjain	Hindi	–
		Laxman Verma	Lacrees, Lucknow	Hindi	–
		Shail Choyal	Seva Mandir, Udaipur	Hindi	–
		S.G. Sahgal	Bhagat Singh College, Delhi	Hindi	–
3.	Ballabhpurer Roopkatha/ Ek Tha Raja 1963	Krishan Kumar	Anamika, Kolkata	Hindi	1969
		Dinanath	Agredoot, Delhi	Hindi	1971
			Rabindra Bharti, Hyderabad		1971
		Balraj Pandit	Kala Mandir, Gwalior	Hindi	1976
		Ashok Bhatia	Triveni, Udaipur	Hindi	1977
		Ravi Vasvani	St. Stephens College, Delhi	Hindi	1978
		Robin Das	Hum, Delhi	Hindi	1978
		Neelkamal Chatterjee	Natya Parishad, Varanasi	Hindi	1978
		Jaydev Hattangadi	SRC, Delhi	Hindi	1981
		–	Antarang, Patna	Hindi	1982
		Mudra Rakshas	Lucknow	Hindi	1983
		Sahay Parikh	Rajasthan Culture Society, Jaipur	Hindi	1983
		Satish Anand	BNA, Lucknow	Hindi	1993
		Ravi Vasvani	Ekjut, Mumbai	Hindi	2000
		Prakash Bhatia	Yatrik, Delhi	Hindi	2001
		Anurag Mishra	American Cultural Center, Delhi	Hindi	2003
		Rajinder Nath	Abhiyan, Delhi	Hindi	2004
		Avinash Chandra	Sanskar Bharti	Hindi	2009
		Afsar Hussain	Rangayan, Bikaner	Hindi	–
		A.H. Theodore	Ayaam, Kanpur	Hindi	–
		Jyoti Swaroop	Ujjain	Hindi	–
		Archana Gidwani	Dramatech, Delhi	Hindi	–
		Balai Chowdhery	Natukera, Assam		
		Mukesh Sharma	Samantar, Bhopal	Hindi	–
4.	Basi Khobor/ Basi Khabar 1978		Chhabildas Hall, Mumbai		1979
		Badal Sircar	NSD, Delhi	Hindi	1981
			Allahabad		1983
		Anil Ranjan Bhowmik	Samanantar, Azamgarh		1983
5.	Beej 1973	Badal Sircar	Anamika, Kolkata	Hindi	1973

6.	Bhoma 1975	Subrato Roy	–	Hindi	1981
		A.R. Bhowmik	Samanantar, Azamgarh	Hindi	1982
		Bhaskar Shevalkar	Rangdhara, Hyderabad	Hindi	1985
		Balwant Thakur	Natrang, Jammu	Hindi	1989
		Tanvir Akhtar	IPTA, Patna	Hindi	2000
		Gyandev Singh	Mafiya, Chandigarh	Hindi	2001
		Ranveer	Navshakti, Goa	Hindi	–
		Satish Mehta	Indore	Hindi	–
		Shashi Sharma	Shri Ram Kala Kendra, Kota	Hindi	–
		Afsar Hussain	Ayaam, Bikaner	Hindi	–
7.	Boro Pishima Badi Buaji 1959	Shivkumar Joshi	Anamika, Kolkata	Bengali	1974
		Deep Sharma	Darpan, Lucknow	Hindi	1978
		Ashok Rahi	Shri Nagri Natak Mandali, Varanasi	Hindi	1981
		Vimal Lath	Anamika, Kolkata	Hindi	1991
		Virendra Saxena	St. Stephens College, Delhi	Hindi	–
		Surendra Adhikari	Sanket, Lucknow	Hindi	–
		Uttar Chachra/ T.K. Agrawal	Kala Manch, Dehradun	Hindi	–
8.	Ebong Indrajit/ Evam Indrajit 1963	Satyadev Dubey	Theatre Unit, Mumbai	Hindi	1963
		Govind Ganguli	Souvanik, Kolkata	Bengali	1965
		Mohan Maharishi	Yatrik, Delhi	Hindi	1967
		Shyamanand Jalan	Anamika, Kolkata	Hindi	1968
		Basu Bhattacharya	Sangam, Mumbai		1969
		S.B. Joshi	–	Marathi	1971
		Anil Pateria	Agragami, Delhi	Hindi	1971
		Dilip Ghosh	Chaturang, Muzzafarpur	Hindi	1972
		S. Vasudev	Abhisarika, Jaipur	Hindi	1973
		Vimal Mukherjee	Darpan, Lucknow	Hindi	1974
		Girish Karnad	IIT, Bombay	English	1975
		M.K. Raina	Rangshivir, Raipur	Hindi	1976
		Atulvir Arora	Abhinet, Chandigarh	Hindi	1976
		Balraj Pandit	Darpan, Kanpur, Bareilly and Sitapur	Hindi	1978
		B.V. Karanth	NSD, Delhi	Hindi	1979
		M.K. Raina	Prayog, Delhi	Hindi	1985
		K. Penneswaran	Tamil Cultural Association	Tamil	1989
		Girish Karnad	Madras Players	–	1992
		Md. Farookh	Delhi	Hindi	1995
		Pratap Roy	Antarang	Hindi	2000
		–	Anya, Kolkata	Bengali	2000
		Shantanu Das	Kalyani Kalamandal, Kolkata	Bengali	2001

		Sudhir Mahajan	Samooh, Jammu	Hindi	2001
		Pranav Mukherji	Indraprashtha College, Delhi.	Hindi	2001
		Mushtak Kak	SRC, Delhi	Hindi	2003
			Patna	Hindi	2003
		Rohini Hattangadi	Kalashray, Mumbai	–	2008
		B.V. Karanth	–	Kannad	–
		Balraj Pandit	BNA Lucknow	Hindi	–
		Ajit Ganguly	Bihar Art Theatre, Patna	Bengali	–
		R. Singh	Tarana, Nainital	Hindi	–
		Shyamanand Jalan	Padatik, Kolkata	Hindi	–
		A. Choudhary	Natyarang, Aurangabad	Hindi	
		B.V. Karanth	Darpan, Lucknow	Hindi	–
		Prabhat Ganguly	Little Ballet Troupe, Bhopal	Hindi	–
		Mohan Maharishi	Dishantar, Delhi	Hindi	–
9.	Gondi/Ghera 1977	Anil Ranjan Bhowmik	Samanantar, Azamgarh		
		Sadhan Chakravorti	Sayudh, Jalpaiguri	Bengali	1997
		–	Shabdkar, Kolkata	Bengali	–
		Madhuri Subodh	Lady Shriram College, Delhi	Hindi	–
10.	Hattomalar Opare/	Abhishek Goswami	Goonj, Jaipur	Hindi	2000
	Hattmala Ke Us Paar 1977	–	Shabdkar, Kolkata	Bengali	–
11.	Jodi Aar Ek Bar/Yadi Ek	Shivkumar Jhunjhunwala	Sarjana, Kolkata	Bengali	1976
	Baar Phir Se 1966	Tripti Mitra	Bohrupee, Kolkata	Bengali	–
12.	Kobi Kahini/ Kavi Kahani 1964	Dinanath	Agredoot, Delhi	Hindi	1971
		–	Sangeet Kala Mandir, Kolkata	Bengali	1984
		Sabina Mehta Sood	SRC Repertory, Delhi	Hindi	1984
		Rajinder Nath	BNA, Lucknow	Hindi	1998
13.	Michhil/Juloos 1974	Bansi Kaul	Artists Combine, Gwalior	Hindi	1977
		Vageesh Kumar Singh	Rang Bharti, Bikaner	Hindi	1977
		M.K. Raina	Prayog, Delhi	Hindi	1978
		Sushil Kr Singh	Nehru Yuva Kendra, Pratapgarh	Hindi	1978
		Vijay Kapoor	Darpan, Sitapur	Hindi	1978
		Mohammad Ayub Siddiqui	Rangashram, Gorakhpur	Hindi	1978
		Rishi Ritwik	Rangmanch, Rohtak	Hindi	1978
		A.R. Bhowmik	Samanantar, Azamgarh	Hindi	1979
		Rana Vijay	Abhiyan, Rudrapur	Hindi	1980
		Girish Rastogi	Rupantar, Gorakhpur	Hindi	1980
		Yaduraj Singh	–	Hindi	1981

		Anjali Rai Mehta	Ruchika, Delhi	Hindi	1982
		Hafiz Khan, H.S. Walia	Sanskritik Kendra, Baitul	Hindi	1983
		K.K. Sinha	Natya, Saharanpur	Hindi	1983
		Satish Anand	Kala Sangam, Patna	Hindi	1988
		Sushil Kr Singh	Rangshivir, Pratapgarh	Hindi	–
		Kavi Rattan Sharma	Bahurang, Jammu	Hindi	–
		Lokendra N. Kaushik	Jagriti Kala Manch, Mathura	Hindi	–
		–	Shabdkar, Kolkata	Bengali	–
		Sham Ganguli	Agragami	Bengali	–
		Arjun Dev Charan	Eklavya, Jodhpur	Hindi	–
		Arun Pande	Abhirang, Dehradoon	Hindi	–
		Satish Mehta	Prayog, Indore	Hindi	–
		Jayant Deshmukh	Rachana, Raipur	–	–
		Amol Palekar	Mumbai	Marathi	
14.	Pagla Ghoda 1967	T.P. Jain	Abhiyan, Delhi	Hindi	1970
		Satyadev Dubey	Theatre Unit, Mumbai	Hindi	1971
		Sombhu Mitra	Bohurupee, Kolkata	Bengali	1971
		Shyamanand Jalan	Anamika, Kolkata	Hindi	1971
		Awadh Bihari	Anupama, Varanasi	Hindi	1972
		Mirza Masood	Avantika, Raipur	Hindi	1974
		P.K. Mitra	Peoples Theatre, Bhilai	Hindi	1975
		Shailendra Goyal	Ankur Arts, Delhi	Hindi	1976
		Sushil Choudhary	Rangika, Delhi	Hindi	1977
		Rajinder Nath	SRC Repertory, Delhi	Hindi	1980
		Shashi Bhushan Prashant	Nav Natyam, Azamgarh	Hindi	1982
		Dinesh Thakur	Ank, Mumbai	Hindi	1984
		Satyadev Dubey	NSD Repertory, Delhi	Hindi	1988
		Rajendra Sharma	Astha, Allahabad	Hindi	1993
		Bipin Kumar	Kshitij, Delhi	Hindi	1995
		Tapan Bannerjee	Vyaktikram, Kolkata	Bengali	1996
		Amol Palekar	Durgabari Association	English	2007
		Shyam Dixit	Upasana, Kanpur	Hindi	–
		Kamal Vashishtha	Natyayan, Gwalior	Hindi	–
		Nand Kishore, Jamil Ahmad	Rachna, Delhi	Hindi	–
		–	Yavanika, Kolkata	Bengali	–
		Sunil Nagar	Pushpanjali, Jaipur	Hindi	–
		Devan Joshi	Himachal SKP, Simla	Hindi	
15.	Ram Shyam Jadu 1961	Badal Sircar	Anamika, Kolkata	Hindi	1970
		Sushil Choudhary	Rangika, Delhi	Bengali	1977
		Suresh Azad	Sun Rise, Delhi	Hindi	1977
		Vijay Kapoor	Darpan, Sitapur	Hindi	1979

		Anjali Rai Mehta	Rupantar, Delhi	Hindi	1981
		Madan Mohan Shrivastava	Rupayan, Jamshedpur	Hindi	1985
		Ajay Manchanda	Geeta Arts, Delhi	Hindi	1985
		Dinesh Ahlawat	–	Hindi	1990
		Alok Aggrawal	Akriti, Lucknow	Hindi	1998
		Baharul Islam	Seagull Repertory, Gauhati		2002
		A. Bhushan	Satyashri, Chandigarh	Hindi	–
		Surendra Adhikari	Sanket, Lucknow	Hindi	–
		Ramesh Chouhan	Kala Ranjan, Ujjain	Hindi	–
16.	Sagina Mahato 1970	Shiv Kumar Jhunjhunwala	Sarjana, Kolkata	Hindi	1979
		J.N. Kaushal	Delhi Natya Sangh, Delhi	Hindi	1981
		Alok Chatterjee	Vivechana, Jabalpur	Hindi	
		Sourabh Shukla	Sakshikala Manch, Delhi	Hindi	1992
17.	Sara Rattir/	Rajinder Nath	Abhiyan, Delhi	Hindi	1970
	Saari Raat 1963	Shivkumar Jhunjhunwala	Anamika, Kolkata	Hindi	1974
		Atulvir Arora	Abhinet, Chandigarh	Hindi	1978
		Anil Khanna	Parichay, Delhi	Hindi	1979
		Vijay Dixit	Pratidhwani, Kanpur	Hindi	1980
		Varun Vora	Natya Nidhi, Mumbai	–	1982
		Vijay Soni	Theatre Ensemble, Delhi	Hindi	1987
		Mukteshwar Jha	IPTA, Kanpur	Hindi	1997
		Sachitanand Joshi	Rang Yatri, Bhopal	Hindi	2003
		Suresh Bharadwaj	Aakar Kala Sangam, Delhi	Hindi	2003
		Rahim Darediya	Yuva Thespo, Mumbai	Hindi	2007
		–	Nav Durga Kala Manch, Jammu	Hindi	2009
		Amrish Puri	Theatre Unit, Mumbai	Hindi	–
		Prabhat Ganguly	Rangashri LBT, Gwalior	Hindi	–
18.	Shesh Nei/	Ramgopal Bajaj	Dishantar, Delhi	Hindi	1973
	Ant Nahin	Harish Bhatia	Abhinet, Chandigarh	Hindi	1977
	1970	Robin Bhattacharya	Jajavar Gosthi	Hindi	1977
		Anjali Rai Mehta	Rupantar, Delhi	Hindi	1981
		Koushal Kumar	IPTA, Lucknow	Hindi	1983
		Anurag Chouhan	Ras, Delhi	Hindi	1998
		–	MCD DAV, Chandigarh	Hindi	2001
		Ramgopal Bajaj	NSD, Delhi	Hindi	2005
		Kirti Jain	Lady Sri Ram College, Delhi	Hindi	–
		–	Shabdkar, Kolkata	Bengali	–
		Devendra Raj Gupta	Parivartan, Bhopal	Hindi	–
19.	Spartacus 1972	–	Ayaan Theatre, Imphal	Manipuri	1973

		Nandkishore	Rachana, Delhi	Hindi	1976
		Vibhav Upadhyay	IPTA, Ambikapur	Hindi	1995
		Walter D'souza	–	–	1995
		Goutam Mazumdar	SRC, Delhi	Hindi	2001
		Lokendra Trivedi	SRC, Delhi	Hindi	2007
		A.R. Bhowmik	Samanantar, Azamgarh	Hindi	–
		–	Shabdkar, Kolkata	Bengali	–
		M.K.Raina	Prayog, Delhi	Hindi	
		Tanvir Akhtar	IPTA, Patna	Hindi	
		Prem Prakash	Sindhi Drama Workshop, Ahmedabad		
		Tripurari Sharma	Natya, Saharanpur	Hindi	
20.	Solution X 1956	Vijay Dixit	Pratidhwani, Kanpur	Hindi	1980
		Rajendra Verma	Triveni, Udaipur	Hindi	–
		Jitendra Mittal	Yayavar, Lucknow	Hindi	1982
		Satish Sharma	Cultural Society of Rajasthan	Hindi	2008
21.	Tringsha Shatabdi/ Teesvin Shatabdi/ Hiroshima 1966	Himanshu Chattopadhyaya	Bohurupee, Kolkata	Bengali	1969
		Ebrahim Alkazi	Dishantar, Delhi	Hindi	1969
		Rajinder Nath	Abhiyan, Delhi	Hindi	1998
		Sudhir Mahajan	Samooh, Jammu	Hindi	2001
		Sushil Kumar Singh	–	Hindi	2003
		Jugal Kishore	BNA, Lucknow	Hindi	–

Note:

This is not an exhaustive list but just an indicative list of performances of his plays in different cities by different groups. It is compiled from varied sources but the prime source being Natarang Pratishthan, more details are available of the groups located in the northern region. Also the list mentions only those of Badal Sircar's plays which were taken up by other groups as well. Most of his later plays were not performed by other groups.

Select Bibliography

BOOKS

Banfield, Chris and Brian Crow: 1996, 'Badal Sircar's Third Theatre of Kolkata.' In *An Introduction to Post-Colonial Theatre*. Cambridge University Press, Cambridge

Bannerjee, Arundhati: 1990, *Brecht: Adaptations in Modern Bengali Theatre: A Study in Reception*. Honolulu, Hawai

Bharucha, Rustom: 1983, *Rehearsals of Revolution—The Political Theatre of Bengal,* Seagull Books, Kolkata

1993 [1990] *Theatre and the World: Performance and the Politics of Culture*. Routledge, London

Bhowmik, Ashok (Hindi): 2009, *Badal Sircar Vyakti aur Rangmanch*. Antika Prakashan, Ghaziabad

Boal, Augusto: 1985, *Theater of the Oppressed*. Theatre Communications Group, New York

Chandrashekhar, Laxmi: 1999, *Plays, Players and Playwrights*. B.R. Publishing Corporation, New Delhi

Deshpande, Sudhanva (Ed): 2007, *Theatre of the Streets: The Jana Natya Experience*. Janam, New Delhi

Grotowski, Jerzy: 1969, *Towards a Poor Theatre*. Methuen & Co Ltd, London

Hashmi, Safdar: 1989, The Right to Perform—*Selected Writings of Safdar Hashmi,* Safdar Hashmi Memorial Trust, New Delhi

Jain, Nemichandra: 2003, *ASIDES Themes in Contemporary Indian Theatre*. National School of Drama, New Delhi

Jain, Nemichandra: 2007, *From the Wings: Notes on Indian Theatre*. National School of Drama, New Delhi

Lal, Ananda: 2003, 'Badal Sircar.' In *The Oxford Encyclopedia of Theatre and Performance, Volume 2*. Edited by Dennis Kennedy. Oxford University Press, Oxford

Nadkarni, Dnyaneshwar: 1999, *The Indian Theatre*, Shri Ram Memorial Lectures-X11, Shri Ram Centre for Performing Arts, New Delhi

Raha, Kironmoy: 1978, 'The "Other Theatre."' In *Bengali Theatre*. National Book Trust of India, New Delhi

Richmond, Farley P.: 1993, 'Characteristics of the Modern Theatre.' *Indian Theatre: Traditions of Performance, Volume 1*, edited by Farley P. Richmond, Darrius L. Swann, and Philip B. Zarrilli. Motilal Banarsidass Publishers Private Limited, New Delhi:

Saha, Kamal: *Kavi-Natakkar—Baul Badal Sircar*. Translated into Hindi by Ranjeet Saha

Schechner, Richard: 1973, *Environmental Theatre*. Hawthorn Books INC., New York

1983 *Performative Circumstances: From the Avant Garde to Ramlila*. Seagull Books, Kolkata

Sircar, Badal: 1993, *Voyages in the Theatre*, Shri Ram Memorial Lectures-1V. Shri Ram Centre for Performing Arts, New Delhi

Sircar, Badal (Hindi): 2009, *Pravasi ki Kalam Se* translated into Hindi by Pratibha Agrawal. Rashtriya Natya Vidyalaya, New Delhi

Sircar, Badal: 2009, *On Theatre: Selected Essays*. Seagull Books, Kolkata

JOURNALS

Agrawal, Pratibha: 1968, 'A Heavy Burden Calcutta'. *Enact*, New Delhi

1977, 'Rang Sansthan (Hindi)—Shri Ram Centre for Art and Culture', Natyavarta, Kolkata

1986, 'The Prithvi Anniversary Week: A Report'. *Oviton Qty*, Mumbai

Arambam, Lokendra: 1997, 'Working for Change: An Interview'. *Seagull Theatre Qty*, Kolkata

Awasthi, Satish: 1971, 'Baki Itihas': Raipur. *Enact*, New Delhi

Bandyopadhyay, Samik: 1972, 'Calcutta Seventy One-Seventy Two'. *Enact*, New Delhi

1996, 'Theatrescapes'. *Seagull Theatre Qty*, Kolkata

Bandyopadhyay, Samik: 1997, 'Theatrescapes'. *Seagull Theatre Qty*, (NP), Kolkata

Bannerjee, Paramita: 1996, 'Theatre Log: A Review'. *Seagull Theatre Qty,* Kolkata

Bannerjee, Sumanta: 1969, *Pagla Ghora: A Review*

1971, 'Playwright in Perspective: A Review'. *Enact*, New Delhi

Bhanoomathi, Anjali: 1968, 'Baki Itihas, Last Month in Delhi'. *Enact*, New Delhi

Bhattacharya, Satish: 1978, 'Translations and Adaptations to the Rescue'. *Enact*, New Delhi

Chander, Romesh: 1971, 'A Search for Identity'. *Sangeet Natak Akademi Qty*, New Delhi

Chandra, Romesh: 1969, 'Looking Up Old Fields'. *Enact*, New Delhi

Deshpande, Govind: 2002, 'Theatre of Modernity: A Celebration of Modernity?' *Theatre India, 5,* May: 8–14, National School of Drama, New Delhi

Deshpande, Sudhanva: 1997, 'The Inexhaustible Work of Criticism in Action Street Theatre of the Left'. *Seagull Theatre Qty*, Kolkata

Dubey, Satyadev: 1970, 'Satyadev's Interview'. *Enact*, New Delhi

1971, 'Sircar and Indian Theatre'. *Enact*, New Delhi

Salanas, Fernando and Octavio Gettino: 1969, 'Towards a Third Cinema', Tricontinental by OSPAAL

Ghosh, Avik: 1969, 'Interview of E. Alkazi'. *Enact*, New Delhi

1971, 'Interview of Badal Sircar'. *Enact*, New Delhi

Gopalie, S.: 1970, 'Sartre Sircar and Sabha'. *Enact,* New Delhi

Guha, Prabir: 1984, 'Interview of Prabir Guha: The Living Theatre'. *Enact*, New Delhi

Gunawardana, A.J.: 1971, 'Problems and Directions: Calcutta's New Theatre'. *TDR* 15, 3 (T50)

Gupta, Nibedita Karl: 1996, 'Theatre Log: Calcutta Theatre Round-Up'. *Seagull Theatre Qty*, Kolkata

Homji Minocher, Zarin N.: 1975, 'Evam Indrajit; A Review'. *Enact*, New Delhi

Jacob, Paul: 1975, 'Pagla Ghora: A Review'. *Enact*, New Delhi

Jagannathan, N.S.: 1969, 'Baki Itihas: Which History'. *Enact*, New Delhi

1973, 'Report on the Theatre Workshop', *Sangeet Natak Akademi Qty,* New Delhi

Jain, Nemichandra (Hindi): 1970, 'Dilli ka Rangmanch', Natarang Qty, New Delhi

Jain, T.P.: 1969, 'Baki Itihas, Realisation is All'. *Enact*, New Delhi

Katyal, Anjum: 1996, 'A Coming Together; An Affirmation A Sharing; A Report'. *Seagull Theatre Qty*, Kolkata

2000, Bangla Group Theatre: 'A Report on a Colloquium'. *Seagull Theatre Qty,* Kolkata

Kaushal, J.N.: 1972, 'Last Month in Delhi: Shatabdi Plays'. *Enact*, New Delhi

1984, 'Kolkata: Anamika's "Intimate Seminar"'. *Enact* 207–208, March–April, New Delhi

Kharbanda, Kulbhushan: 1971, 'Actors in Interview'. *Enact*, New Delhi

Lahiri, Indrajit: 1972, 'Sircar's "Sagina Mahato"; A Report'. *Enact*, New Delhi

Masud, Iqbal: 1976, 'The Savage God: A Review'. *Enact*, New Delhi

Menon, Meera and Anjali Mathur: 1985, 'People's Theatre'. *Oviton Qty*, Mumbai

Mitra, Sayoni: 2004, *Badal Sircar: Scripting a Movement*, TDR48, 3(T183) Fall 2004. New York University and The Massachusetts Institute of Technology

Naikar, Basavaraj: 1975, 'Annus Dramatis Gulbarga: A Review'. *Enact*, New Delhi

Nadkarni, Dnyaneshwar: 1976, 'Khanolkar and After'. *Enact*, New Delhi

Nigam, R.L.: 1968, 'Two Modern Indian Plays'. *Enact*, New Delhi

Paul, Rajinder: 1971, Editorials in Jan/Mar/Jun/Oct/Nov issues, *Enact*, New Delhi

1971, 'Interview of Girish Karnad'. *Enact*, New Delhi

Rana, K.: 1969, 'Bengali Plays: A Review'. *Enact*, New Delhi

Sastri, Indra: 1981, 'Sircar: A Report on Three Plays in Bangalore'. *Enact*, New Delhi

Schechner, Richard: 1972, 'On Badal Sircar and Tripti Mitra'. *Enact*, 61–62, New Delhi

Sondhi, Reeta: 1977, 'Last Month in Delhi: Bhoma'. *Enact*, New Delhi

Swarup, Shanti (Hindi): 1981, 'Azamgarh Mein Badal Sircar'. *Natarang Qty*, New Delhi

Taneja, Jaidev (Hindi): 2002, 'Badal Sircar ki Rangyatra aur Teesra Rangmanch'. *Chhayanat*, Sangeet Natak Akademi, Lucknow, UP

Tanvir, Habib: 1970, 'HB's Interview'. *Enact*, New Delhi

Thakurdas, Frank: 1969, 'Pagla Ghora: A Review'. *Enact*, New Delhi

Trowsdale, Jo: 1997, 'Sitting in Badal's Circle: Artist and Pedagogue—The Theatre of Badal Sircar, *Research in Drama Education Vol 2, Issue 1.* Taylor and Francis group

Uppal, Kamlesh: 1979, 'The Performer's Body'. *Enact*, New Delhi

Verma, Surendra: 1970, 'Last Month in Delhi: Hiroshima'. *Enact*, New Delhi

1996, 'Theatre Log: Groups and Organisations'. *Seagull Qty,* Kolkata

Note:

A comprehensive listing of material on Badal Sircar, in books, journals, newspapers, brochures and scripts is available in Natarang Pratishthan Archives, New Delhi.

Acknowledgements

I would like to express my heartfelt gratitude to

- H.Kanhailal, Pralayan, A. Mangai and Ashok Bhowmik, for writing original pieces for the book.
- Amol Palekar for finding time for an exhaustive interview and also allowing me to use a long, rare interview he had taken of Badal Sircar, which I have quoted extensively in the introduction.
- Samik Bannerjee, Sumanta Bannerjee, Mahesh Elkunchwar, Pratibha Agrawal, Sadanand Menon, Naveen Kishore for allowing me to use their pieces in the book or pieces from their publications and Samik also for helping me with correct names of plays.
- Suvobrata Roy Chowdhury and Sanchayan Ghosh, Kalyan Ghosh and other team members of Satabdi, Prasanna, Dr. Jamil Ahmad and Manvita Baradi for agreeing to talk to us about their encounter with Badal Sircar.
- The team of young theatre professionals consisting of Keshav Kumar, who helped in several interviews and locating research material from different archives; Vidyanidhi Vanarase who interviewed and transcribed the interview with Amol Palekar; Gargi Bharadwaj who translated the memoirs of Badal Sircar in English and Santanu Bose who helped with several references in Bengali and also translated some of the Bengali material for helping me choose for the book.
- Those who are no longer with us but whose pieces have been included in this book-Satyadev Dubey, Shyamanand Jalan, Sharad Nagar, Dnyaneshwar Nadkarni, Rajinder Paul, Amrish Puri and Vimal Lath.
- My profuse thanks to Pratibha Ji and Natya Shodh Sansthan, and Rashmi Vajpeyi and the team of Natarang Pratishthan from where major part of the material has been drawn, for facilitating my search.

- National school of Drama and Sangeet Natak Akademi, and Enact from whose journals I have included certain articles in this collection.
- UP Sangeet Natak Akademi for allowing the use of the symposium and the interview with Sharad Nagar and to Jugal Kishore for making it available to me.
- Tripti (Rani) Mitra who collected photos and compiled material from Badal Sircar's collection in Kolkata.
- Anuradha Kapur for her valuable suggestions on the entire compilation.
- My colleague Sonal Parmar for providing early editorial assistance with great diligence.
- Mohua Mitra of Niyogi Books for her painstaking effort in giving the book its final shape.
- Of course my husband Tanvir Ahmad and daughters Kuhu and Barkha for their help and putting up with my tension for these many years when I was not able to work on this book but was wanting to.
- Last but not the least Badal-da who gave his blessings to go ahead with the book and for generously providing visual and documentary material for use in the book.

Kirti Jain

INDEX

B

C

R

S

U

V

W

Y

Z